ROADS TO REGIONALISM

The International Political Economy of New Regionalisms Series

The International Political Economy of New Regionalisms series presents innovative analyses of a range of novel regional relations and institutions. Going beyond established, formal, interstate economic organizations, this essential series provides informed interdisciplinary and international research and debate about myriad heterogeneous intermediate level interactions.

Reflective of its cosmopolitan and creative orientation, this series is developed by an international editorial team of established and emerging scholars in both the South and North. It reinforces ongoing networks of analysts in both academia and think-tanks as well as international agencies concerned with micro-, meso- and macro-level regionalisms.

Editorial Board

Timothy M. Shaw, Visiting Professor, University of Massachusetts, Boston, USA
Isidro Morales, Instituto Tecnológico de Estudios Superiores de Monterrey (ITESM), Mexico
Maria Nzomo, University of Nairobi, Kenya
Nicola Phillips, University of Manchester, UK
Johan Saravanamuttu, Institute of Southeast Asian Studies, Singapore
Fredrik Söderbaum, School of Global Studies, University of Gothenburg, Sweden and UNU-CRIS, Belgium

Recent titles in the series (continued at the back of the book)

New Regionalism or No Regionalism?
Emerging Regionalism in the Black Sea Area
Edited by Ruxandra Ivan

Our North America
Social and Political Issues beyond NAFTA
Edited by Julián Castro-Rea

Community of Insecurity
SADC's Struggle for Peace and Security in Southern Africa
Laurie Nathan

Roads to Regionalism
Genesis, Design, and Effects of Regional Organizations

Edited by

TANJA A. BÖRZEL
LUKAS GOLTERMANN
MATHIS LOHAUS
KAI STRIEBINGER
Freie Universität Berlin, Germany

ASHGATE

© Tanja A. Börzel, Lukas Goltermann, Mathis Lohaus and Kai Striebinger 2012

All rights reserved. No part of this publication may be reproduced, stored in a retrieval system or transmitted in any form or by any means, electronic, mechanical, photocopying, recording or otherwise without the prior permission of the publisher.

Tanja A. Börzel, Lukas Goltermann, Mathis Lohaus and Kai Striebinger have asserted their right under the Copyright, Designs and Patents Act, 1988, to be identified as the editors of this work.

Published by
Ashgate Publishing Limited
Wey Court East
Union Road
Farnham
Surrey, GU9 7PT
England

Ashgate Publishing Company
Suite 420
101 Cherry Street
Burlington
VT 05401-4405
USA

www.ashgate.com

British Library Cataloguing in Publication Data
Roads to regionalism : genesis, design, and effects of regional organizations. --
  (The international political economy of new regionalisms series)
  1. Regionalism (International organization)
  2. International agencies. 3. Intergovernmental cooperation.
  I. Series II. Börzel, Tanja A., 1970-
  341.2'4-dc23

Library of Congress Cataloging-in-Publication Data
Roads to regionalism : genesis, design, and effects of regional organizations / [edited] by Tanja A. Börzel ... [et al.].
    p. cm. -- (The international political economy of new regionalisms series)
  Includes bibliographical references and index.
  ISBN 978-1-4094-3464-1 (hbk) -- ISBN 978-1-4094-3465-8 (ebook)
  1. Regionalism (International organization) 2. Regionalism (International organization)--Case studies. I. Börzel, Tanja A., 1970-

JZ5330.R63 2012
341.24--dc23
                                                                        2011036971

ISBN 9781409434641 (hbk)
ISBN 9781409434658 (ebk)

Printed and bound in Great Britain by the
MPG Books Group, UK.

Contents

List of Figures	*vii*
List of Tables	*ix*
List of Contributors	*xi*
Foreword by Anja Jetschke	*xiii*
Acknowledgments	*xv*
List of Abbreviations	*xvii*

PART 1: INTRODUCTION

1   Roads to Regionalism: Concepts, Issues, and Cases   3
     Lukas Goltermann, Mathis Lohaus, Alexander Spielau, and Kai Striebinger

PART 2: GENESIS AND GROWTH

2   Ephemeral Regionalism:
     The Proliferation of (Failed) Regional Integration
     Initiatives in Post-Soviet Eurasia   25
     Niklas Wirminghaus

3   Joining the Neighbors: The Accessions to ASEAN in the 1990s   45
     Niklas Aschhoff

4   MERCOSUR: Integration through Presidents and Paymasters   59
     Felix Hummel and Mathis Lohaus

PART 3: INSTITUTIONAL DESIGN

5   Explaining Differences in the Institutional Design
     of ASEAN and NAFTA   81
     Leon Kanthak

6	Why Did NAFTA and ASEAN Set Up Dispute Settlement Procedures? *Annika Korte*	101
7	Institutional Similarities Between Regional Organizations: An Analysis of ECOWAS and the Arab League *Constanze Koitzsch*	117

PART 4: MEMBER STATES' BEHAVIOR

8	Does Regime Type Matter? Regional Integration from the Nation States' Perspectives in ECOWAS *Veronika Kirschner and Sören Stapel*	141
9	State Capacity and Compliance in ASEAN *Lukas Goltermann*	159
10	When Pigs Fly: ECOWAS and the Protection of Constitutional Order in Events of Coups d'État *Kai Striebinger*	179

PART 5: EFFECTS ON MEMBER STATES

11	MERCOSUR's Contribution to Democratic Consolidation *Christian Pirzer*	199
12	ASEAN and Civil Society: An Incompatible Relationship? *Corinna Krome*	215
13	Monetary Integration Through the Backdoor: Does NAFTA Promote Monetary Policy Harmonization in North America? *Alexander Spielau*	235

PART 6: CONCLUSION

14	Do All Roads Lead to Regionalism? *Tanja A. Börzel*	255

Index — *269*

List of Figures

3.1	CLMV's share of trade with ASEAN in percent for 2009	52
6.1	Symmetric trade introversion index (NAFTA)	104
6.2	Number of cases filed under Chapter 19	106
6.3	Symmetric trade introversion index (ASEAN)	108
8.1	Ratification according to regime type	151
8.2	Ratification in democratic regimes	151
8.3	Ratification according to neopatrimonialism	153
8.4	Ratification in neopatrimonial states	153
11.1	Democratic support in MERCOSUR member states and MERCOSUR average (in % of the population), 1995–2009	207

List of Tables

1.1	Four aspects of regional integration	10
1.2	Overview about regional organizations since 1945 sorted by macro-region	12
1.3	Overview of the ROs covered in this book	14
2.1	Main regional integration projects in the post-Soviet space 1991–2009	28
4.1	Intra-regional trade share before the foundation of MERCOSUR	62
5.1	Selected trade statistics for ASEAN and NAFTA members	90
5.2	Main trading partners for ASEAN and NAFTA members	92
7.1	Institutional design of the Arab League and the Economic Community of West African States	120
7.2	Status of political rights (PR) in ECOWAS (1990–1992)	126
7.3	Status of political rights (PR) in the Arab League (2001–2003)	126
9.1	Overview of operationalization	166
9.2	Implementation of ASEAN Single Window	168
9.3	Implementation of ACD (ranked by date of implementation)	171
10.1	Measuring democratic identity	182
10.2	Successful coups, 1991–2008	185
10.3	From coup to ECOMOGII mandate	189
10.4	Level of legalization of democracy standards, 1991–2008	191
10.5	Case study results	193
11.1	Number of coups and coup attempts in MERCOSUR member states, 1946–2010	208
12.1	Development of civil society in ASEAN's documents	221
13.1	Operationalization of the research design	243
13.2	Outcomes by variable	248

List of Contributors

Niklas Aschhoff is a graduate of Freie Universität Berlin. He studied political science, public administration and European studies in Germany, the Netherlands and Lithuania.

Tanja A. Börzel is professor of political science and holds the chair of European Integration at the Freie Universität Berlin, Germany. She co-directs the Research College "The Transformative Power of Europe" with Thomas Risse and conducts several research projects on regionalism and governance in areas of limited statehood.

Lukas Goltermann studied international relations and politics in Sheffield, Berlin and Potsdam. He works as research assistant at the department of international politics at Humboldt-Universität zu Berlin. His research focuses on regionalism, development studies and energy policy.

Felix Hummel is a graduate of the Freie Universität Berlin, the Universität Bremen and the Universiteit van Amsterdam in political science. His current research is focused on European integration and European foreign policy.

Leon Kanthak is a graduate of the University of Kent in politics and international relations. He works as a junior research assistant at the Jean Monnet Centre of Excellence for European Integration in Berlin. His research is focused on European integration and political theory.

Veronika Kirschner is a graduate of the Freie Universität Berlin, the Université Libre de Bruxelles and the Universität Konstanz. She holds a Master's degree in political science. Her fields of interest are regional integration processes in Africa as well as development studies and international gender politics.

Constanze Koitzsch holds a Master's degree in international relations from the Freie Universität Berlin, the Humboldt-Universität zu Berlin as well as the Universität Potsdam. Her work is focused on processes of regional integration, (new) actors of governance and gender issues, particularly in the Middle East and North Africa region.

Annika Korte is a graduate of the Freie Universität Berlin and the Universität Münster. Her fields of interest include international relations, and regional integration, especially in North America and Southeast Asia.

Corinna Krome holds a Master's degree in international relations from the Freie Universität Berlin, the Humboldt-Universität zu Berlin and the Universität Potsdam. She works as project assistant for CERI, Sciences Po and has been a research assistant for the Collaborative Research Center "Governance in Areas of Limited Statehood" at Freie Universität.

Mathis Lohaus is a graduate of the Freie Universität Berlin in political science and works as research assistant at the Collaborative Research Center "Governance in Areas of Limited Statehood." Fields of interest are international relations and transnational governance.

Christian Pirzer is a graduate of the Freie Universität Berlin in political science and of the Universidad de Granada in social science. His fields of interest are comparative politics and development studies with a special focus on Latin American countries.

Alexander Spielau is a graduate of the Freie Universität Berlin in political science. He has worked as a research assistant at the Jean Monnet Centre of Excellence for European Integration and at the Center for Global Politics. His major fields of interest are international trade and economic relations as well as regional economic integration with particular interest in monetary integration schemes.

Sören Stapel studied political science at the Freie Universität Berlin and Université de Montréal, Canada. He currently works as a research assistant at the chair of European Integration at Freie Universität Berlin. His fields of interest cover topics such as diffusion of regionalism, regional integration in general and especially in Africa.

Kai Striebinger is a PhD candidate at the Berlin Graduate School for Transnational Studies. He has worked as research assistant at the Collaborative Research Center "Governance in Areas of Limited Statehood." His fields of interest are regional organizations, especially in Africa, and democratization processes.

Niklas Wirminghaus is a political journalist, who studied at the Freie Universität in Berlin and Duke University in Durham, NC. His academic work focuses on regional integration, political philosophy and democratic theory.

Foreword

This book emerged out of a research seminar conducted by Tanja Börzel and myself during the summer of 2009. The title of the research seminar was "Comparative Regionalism" and it attracted a number of outstanding young scholars. Our aim was to broaden our knowledge of regional organizations well beyond our own respective research fields, the European Union in the case of Tanja and the Association of Southeast Asian Nations in my case. For both regional organizations, an abundant literature already exists. But this is not the case for other, less well-known organizations such as the Economic Community of West African States (ECOWAS) and the many regional organizations that have emerged after the collapse of the Soviet Union. Our goal was to take a fresh look at regional organizations by individuals who had not worked on these organizations for several years and to engage them in an intense discussion about regional organizations (ROs) that is comparative from the outset.

Comparative Regionalism is one of the most lively research areas that have developed in the last decade. We live in an age of regionalization, but the way we study regions and the very definition of regionalism varies widely. Comparative Regionalism is also an area which is approached from various disciplines. Economists are interested primarily in the question whether regionalism and the various preferential trade agreements that contribute to regionalism provides a "stumbling block" or "building block" for the global liberalization of trade. Rather than being interested in the designs of regional institutions, they are interested in the effects on trade that they produce. Political scientists are interested in the ability of ROs to provide governance on a regional level, and—perhaps the longest established research field and now increasingly criticized—whether regional integration outside of Europe exhibits the same trajectories and pathways that we observe in Europe. Area specialists are interested in ROs as expressions of dynamics within the regions themselves and view them, among others, as institutions which also communicate specific regional identities. Critical geographers, finally, are interested in the question of what constitutes a region and how it is being established, but they are less interested in how these organizations are set up from an institutional perspective. Over the last five years or so, a number of important contributions have been made to this emerging field of research, and one of the most important advances is to develop new methodologies to systematically compare regions. However, this research focuses on the outcomes of regional organizations in terms of their performance, and less on other features, such as their institutional designs.

Roads to Regionalism fills a gap in this research. It is a much needed book in terms of the regional organizations that it covers and its focus on institutional design features as well as outcomes of regional cooperation. It assembles a collection of chapters on selected regional organizations and acquires its strength out of its strictly comparative perspective. The aim of the research seminar was to systematically compare regional organizations along a range of dimensions: what were the drivers of regionalism? What were the outcomes of regionalism in terms of regional integration? What were the internal effects of regional organizations on member states? And to what extent were the regional organizations able to shape their environment?

The book is as much an outcome of a unifying research question as it is of a congenial research environment. The research environment came from the project's embeddedness in a larger research context, provided by "The Transformative Power of Europe" Research College at the Freie Universität of Berlin. Since 2008, the Research College has organized conferences, workshops and has published a number of working papers. It also allowed us, along with interested graduate students, to feed in the ideas developed within the Research College to a research seminar dedicated to comparative regionalism. Even though the research seminar ended in the summer of 2010, participants continued working on this project. I am impressed by how this group of researchers gradually developed their own sense of identity and purpose and how they transformed our group discussions, presentations and manuscript into an independent book publication. It is a dynamic that certainly cannot be taken for granted and it pays great tribute to the leadership qualities of the editors. Congratulations to everyone on this important book!

Anja Jetschke
Chair of International Relations, University of Göttingen
Hamburg, May 2011

Acknowledgments

This volume is inspired by the research seminar "Comparative Regionalism," held at Freie Universität Berlin in 2009/2010. Tanja Börzel and Anja Jetschke cannot be praised enough for their hard work and dedication, not only in supervising the seminar but also in creating a group spirit that enabled us to proceed with the project. Their encouragement and advice as well as their scientific and personal inspiration made this publication possible. We are very grateful for all of it! Furthermore, we thank all contributors for their efforts, which in some cases go well beyond submitting a chapter: Alexander Spielau and Sören Stapel crucially supported and shaped this project. We are indebted to Jean Grugel, Timothy M. Shaw and Vera van Hüllen for their helpful comments on drafts and the overall concept of this book. For their generous support, we wish to thank the Collaborative Research Center SFB 700, the Kolleg-Forschergruppe "The Transformative Power of Europe" at Freie Universität Berlin, and the Alumni Association of the Master of International Relations of the Freie Universität Berlin, the Humboldt-Universität zu Berlin and the Universität Potsdam ("IB an der Spree"). Last but not least, we would like to thank everyone at Ashgate Publishing for their support.

Lukas Goltermann
Mathis Lohaus
Kai Striebinger
Berlin, November 2011

List of Abbreviations

ACD	ASEAN Cosmetics Directive
AEC	ASEAN Economic Community
AEM	ASEAN Economic Ministers Meeting
AFTA	ASEAN Free Trade Area
APEC	Asia-Pacific Economic Cooperation
APSC	ASEAN Political-Security Community
ASCC	ASEAN Socio-Cultural Community
ASEAN	Association of Southeast Asian Nations
ASEAN-6	Brunei Darussalam, Indonesia, Malaysia, Philippines, Singapore, Thailand
ASEAN-ISIS	ASEAN Institute for Strategic and International Studies
ASC	ASEAN Standing Committee
AU	African Union
C4	Committee of Four (Nigeria, Ghana, Guinea, Côte d'Ivoire)
CAEC	Central Asian Economic Community
CAEU	Central Asian Economic Union
CACO	Central Asian Cooperation Organizations
CEEC	Central and Eastern European Countries
CEPT	Common Effective Preferential Tariff
CES/SES	Common/Single Economic Space
CET	Common External Tariff
CIS	Commonwealth of Independent States
CLMV	Cambodia, Laos, Myanmar, Vietnam
CMC	Common Market Council
CME	Coordinated Market Economy
CMG	Common Market Group
CSO	Civil Society Organization
CST(O)	Collective Security Treaty (Organization)
CUFTA	Canada-US Free Trade Agreement
DSM	Dispute Settlement Mechanism
DSP	Dispute Settlement Procedure
EC	European Community
ECJ	European Court of Justice
ECOMOG	ECOWAS Cease-Fire Monitoring Group
ECOWAS	Economic Community of West African States
ECPF	ECOWAS Conflict Prevention Framework
EMS	European Monetary System
EMU	(European) Economic and Monetary Union

ERM	(European) Exchange Rate Mechanism
EU	European Union
EurAsEC	Eurasion Economic Community
FDI	Foreign Direct Investment
FHI	Freedom House Index
FOCEM	Fondo de Convergencia Estructuraldel MERCOSUR (Regional Convergence Fund)
FTA	Free Trade Agreement
FTAA	Free Trade Area of the Americas
GDP	Gross Domestic Product
GUAM	Organization for Democracy and Development
HME	Hierarchical Market Economy
IMF	International Monetary Fund
IR	International Relations
ITS	Intra-regional trade share
LAFTA	Latin American Free Trade Association
LAIA	Latin American Integration Association
LAS	League of Arab States
LME	Liberal Market Economy
MERCOSUR	Mercado Común del Sur (Southern Common Market)
MTC	MERCOSUR Trade Commission
NAFTA	North American Free Trade Agreement
NGO	Non-Governmental Organization
NSW	National Single Window
OAU	Organization of African Unity
OCA	Optimum Currency Area
PTA	Preferential Trade Agreement
RDII	Rational Design of International Institutions
RO	Regional Organization
SEOM	Senior Economic Officials Meeting
TAC	Treaty of Amity and Cooperation
UK	United Kingdom of Great Britain and Northern Ireland
UN	United Nations
US	United States of America
USD	US Dollar
VoC	Varieties of Capitalism
WTO	World Trade Organization

PART 1
Introduction

Chapter 1

Roads to Regionalism: Concepts, Issues, and Cases

Lukas Goltermann, Mathis Lohaus,
Alexander Spielau, and Kai Striebinger

Introduction

The influence of regional organizations can be felt in every corner of the world. Fascinating institutional developments have taken place in recent years that have given new momentum to regional integration projects, with a visible impact on the lives of millions of people. Landmark instances of regional engagement included military intervention in Sierra Leone as well as the empowerment of civil society in Southeast Asia. With more than 50 regional organizations already in existence, developments like these confront the observer with a new set of questions. For example, how can we explain the emergence of regional organizations? How can we study their institutions? How can we account for member states' behavior? And what is their impact on the domestic level?

In this volume, we have brought together a number of studies, which seek to address these and other related questions. We approach regional organizations as an outcome of regionalism, which we understand as forms of regional institution building, ranging from international cooperation to highly legalized integration. In order to grasp multiple dimensions of the complex nature of regionalism, we propose four distinct perspectives—or "roads"—to the study of regionalism. The four roads will broadly follow the four questions raised in the previous paragraph and structure the contributions to this volume. Accordingly, we introduce the reader to the phenomenon of regionalism in the first part of this book by dealing with reasons for setting up or joining regional organizations (ROs). Secondly, we aim to find out why institutions are designed in specific ways. The third perspective on regionalism looks at how domestic factors influence state behavior on the regional level. Lastly, the fourth approach seeks to determine and explain the impact of regional organizations on their member states.

Conceptualizing Regions, Regionalism, and Regional Organizations

Before we start to construct our roads to regionalism, it is necessary to lay the groundwork of the crucial concepts employed in this volume. Already the term "region" itself is a contested concept. A basic understanding is that regions are constituted by groupings of territorial units in geographical proximity, constituting a spatially bound and contiguous area (Hurrell 1995: 333–334, Sbragia 2008).

Yet, the study of regionalism inevitably touches upon the more contested elements of "regions." Indeed, apart from signifying a geographic space, the term is also charged with a political dimension. Therefore, to obtain political, social, and/or economic importance, a region must display a certain degree of mutual interdependence (Nye 1968).

While scholars from an economic background tend to reduce regions to integrated market places (Bhagwati 1993, Mansfield and Milner 1999), the contributions to this volume define regions as political ideas and administrative units as well. As such, we subscribe to the idea that regions are socially constructed, spatial ideas, which follow concepts of community and society. This includes shared aspects of cultural identity (for example, religion and language), which foster a common socio-cultural understanding of a region. As van Langenhove points out, regions stem from a two-fold process: "they are imagined and they are created in an institutional way" (2011: 1). Consequently, as readers will see throughout the book, different understandings of regions have influenced the institutional design of ROs as well as the degree of cooperation and integration among its member states.[1]

The studies in this volume share a conceptualization of regionalism as a state-led project based on intergovernmental negotiations and treaties (Breslin and Higgott 2000, Gamble and Payne 1996). In addition, most scholars "would agree that regionalism includes processes and structures of region-building in regard to closer relations on economic, political, security and socio-cultural level" (Börzel 2012). This clearly distinguishes regionalism from processes of regionalization, which describe an increase of intra-regional social and economic interaction of private actors.

The observable outcome of regionalism can take different forms, ranging from cooperation to integration. The latter means a transfer and pooling of sovereignty rights to a third body, usually a regional organization (Börzel 2012). In order to be classified as a regional organization, they need to have more than two member states in geographical proximity,[2] have exclusive membership and serve multiple purposes.[3]

---

1   Moreover, regions can be formed on three spatial levels: (1) on supra-national level by a group of neighboring states; (2) on sub-national level by territories forming an entity within an existing state; and (3) on cross-border level by sub-national territories (De Lombaerde et al. 2010: 736). This book will focus on regions above the national level and regional organizations composed of sovereign states.

2   However, even geographic proximity is relative when one considers the existence of ROs like APEC and the Arctic Council. Also, ROs can be built upon a common cultural background, like the League of Arab States.

3   Consequently, single-purpose arrangements like PTAs, military alliances (for instance NATO) or organizations such as OPEC are excluded.

Four Roads to Regionalism

In this volume we propose four guiding questions, which provide a coherent and comprehensive framework for the research on regionalism. In this we attempt to cover multiple dimensions of regionalism. While a number of scholarly contributions to the "New Regionalism" debate were published in recent years, they tend to provide detailed analyses of specific aspects of regionalism or a single regional organization (Cai 2010, Dieter 2007, Pevehouse 2005, Ribeiro Hoffmann and van der Vleuten 2007, Thomas 2008). In contrast, this volume covers multiple regional organizations in a comparative perspective. In the absence of a general theory on the development and effects of regional organizations, we combine numerous theoretical and analytical approaches to the study of regionalism in one overarching research framework. In this approach, we sympathize with the call by Warleigh-Lack and colleagues for a bridging of European Integration studies and the New Regionalism Approach (Warleigh-Lack and Rosamond 2010, Warleigh-Lack et al. 2011).

Genesis and Growth

First, we analyze the genesis and growth of regional organizations: when, how and why are they created, and what can be said about their developmental paths? Why do states choose to join or remain outside a regional organization? These are questions that have occupied the literature on regionalism for a long time. In particular, theories of European integration have influenced our understanding of the drivers of regional integration. Liberal intergovernmentalism and neofunctionalism offer different accounts of why states form, join or leave regional organizations.

For liberal intergovernmentalism, regional integration can be traced back to member states' preferences, which are in turn shaped by domestic actors. Following the logic of liberal IR theory, states are seen as transmission belts for societal interests and are the primary unit of analysis. Regional integration can then be understood as the result of bargaining processes between member states (Moravcsik 1991, 1993, 1998).

Neofunctionalism, in contrast, puts emphasis on the concept of spillovers, elites, and supra-national actors (Haas 1958, 1961, Lindberg 1963).[4] For neofunctionalists, regional integration is driven by functional spillovers in the context of interdependence: cooperation in one field induces pressure to integrate in another, for example, as a result of unintended consequences. Political spillover, on the other hand, occurs when domestic elites shift their attention to the level above the nation state, prompted by increasing transnational exchange or the belief that problems cannot be solved domestically. Additionally, supra-national actors are important for neofunctionalism as they become "agents of integration"

---

4 For a collection of recent contributions to neofunctionalism, see the 2005 special issue of the *Journal of European Public Policy* (Vol. 12, No. 2).

(Niemann 1998). We argue that these theories, although developed in the European context, can inspire the study of regionalism in general.

To account for the importance of functional pressures as well as governments' decision-making, it is useful to distinguish between demand and supply factors driving regionalism (Mattli 1999). The demand side follows the logic of economic gains, by assuming that economic integration is likely to require increasingly sophisticated safeguards, namely integrated governance. However, demand is necessary, but not sufficient for integration. On the supply side, Mattli argues that actors need to establish commitment institutions to minimize violations of cooperation rules, and that success depends on the existence of a paymaster country willing and able to bear distributional costs (Mattli 1999).

Our research agenda is not limited to theories of regional integration. Especially when we seek to understand why third states decide (not) to join a regional organization, it is fruitful to consider arguments from other parts of International Relations theory. Examples are neorealism—with its focus on security concerns that could stimulate regional cooperation or conflict—and neoliberal institutionalism, which highlights the importance of economic interdependence. To account for the enlargement of ROs, there is a range of rationalist arguments regarding the costs and benefits of accession to a RO (Schimmelfennig and Sedelmeier 2002).

Institutional Design

A second focal point of this volume is the institutional design of regional organizations. Given the striking similarities but also differences that can be observed between organizations, it is of great utility to explore different ways of characterizing and accounting for them. Contributions in this volume use three main concepts and explanatory approaches: the Rational Design of International Institutions (RDII), the legalization concept, and the diffusion concept aiming at a more process-oriented account for the institutional design of international organizations.

Originally developed by Koremenos, Snidal, and Lipson, the RDII can be employed to categorize and map international organizations while at the same time pointing out factors capable of explaining differences and similarities (Koremenos et al. 2001). Rooted in rational-choice theory, five dimensions of international institutions are identified: membership, scope, centralization, control, and flexibility (Koremenos et al. 2001: 768–773).[5] The independent variables accounting for the specific institutional design are distribution and enforcement problems, the number and asymmetries of actors, and uncertainties about behavior, the state of the world, and other actors' preferences (Koremenos et al. 2001: 773–780).

---

5 For a similar classification see Acharya and Johnston (2007). Criticizing the rational-choice bias of RDII, they put emphasis on the role of norms and legitimacy. Also, they consider ID as an independent variable potentially in the position to explain the nature of cooperation. See Duffield (2003) for another critique of RDII.

Abbott, Keohane, Moravcsik, Slaughter, and Snidel have added the concept of legalization to the study of international organizations (Abbott et al. 2000). Legalization, as the name indicates, focuses primarily on the analysis of legal documents creating formal institutions. It thereby allows for a more differentiated comparison of specific types of policy fields or of international organizations. The legalization concept measures three distinct characteristics of international organizations: *precision* "means that rules unambiguously define the conduct they require, authorize, or proscribe"; *obligation* describes the extent to which actors are legally bound by arrangements; and *delegation* addresses the degree of authority of independent third parties "to implement, interpret, and apply the rules; to resolve disputes; and (possibly) to make further rules" (Abbott et al. 2000: 401).[6]

Mapping differences and similarities is, however, only the first step of analysis. In a second step, the specific forms of institutional designs need to be explained. Although the three approaches and general IR as well as regional integration theory provide explanatory factors, the concept of diffusion is a fruitful framework that specifically addresses institutional design. Diffusion is defined as a process in which "the adoption of innovation by member(s) of a social system is communicated through certain channels and over time and triggers mechanisms that increase the probability of its adoption by other members who have not yet adopted it" (Levi-Faur 2005: 23). Sociological institutionalism has developed three analytical mechanisms to describe processes of institutional diffusion: through international coercion, emulation or mimicry (Campbell 2004, Di Maggio and Powell 1983, Henisz et al. 2005, Jepperson and Meyer 1991).

Member States' Behavior in ROs

Third, we examine how member states act within regional organizations and what explains their behavior. More precisely, this research question focuses on factors that determine the level of commitment to, and compliance with, regional initiatives. Compliance in this regard means that member states follow the rules set at the regional level, for example, by implementing decisions on time. Commitment goes beyond these duties, indicating a preference to deal with problems at the regional level. Thus, the concept of commitment is linked to voluntary decisions, whereas compliance is determined by member states' capabilities or willingness.

The level of regional commitment can be influenced by the structure of the domestic political system, for example, the regime type. Although there exists an extensive body of literature on democracy in Africa, Asia, and Latin America, relatively little research has been conducted on the effects that regime types might have on the international level. In particular, characteristics of national political

---

6   For a critique see Finnemore and Toope (2001), and a reply see Goldstein et al. (2001).

systems such as neopatrimonialism can impact on state behavior (Bach 2005, Mansfield et al. 2002, 2008, Rüland 2009).

With regard to compliance, the question as to why states sign agreements and make commitments that they do not fulfill is a subject of debate. One approach focuses primarily on enforcement: from this perspective compliance is best achieved by means of monitoring and sanctions, because defection is seen as a result of states' cost-benefit calculations. On the other hand, there is the managerial approach which puts more emphasis on domestic aspects: capabilities—rather than choices—have to be considered to explain the degree of compliance (Simmons 1998, 2002, Tallberg 2002).

Thus, both compliance and commitment at the regional level are connected to the domestic polity dimension. This is not to say, however, that those structural factors completely determine member states' behavior. Other sub-fields of IR studies should also be considered. On the one hand, from a neorealist perspective, security interests and power politics are expected to be strong factors shaping member states' decisions. Especially in the area of regional security policies, such as military interventions, we expect those arguments to yield a great deal of explanatory power. The constructivist strand of IR literature, on the other hand, emphasizes the role of regional identities and norms, in effect widening our analytical focus beyond the domestic level (Choi and Caporaso 2002, Van der Vleuten and Ribeiro Hoffmann 2010).

Effects on Member States

Fourth, we consider the effect of ROs on their member states: how can we study a regional organization's impact on the domestic level? Although the effects of international processes at the domestic level have already been conceptualized in the late 1970s (Gourevitch 1978), it is only recently that the "second image reversed" literature has been applied to regional organizations and their relationship to member states. This necessarily poses questions about the independent actor quality of international organizations. Not every RO has a high form of centralization or delegation. In fact, most ROs remain firmly in the hands of their member states. It is probably because of the European Union's supranational characteristics that questions about domestic impact, under the name of "Europeanization," have mainly been addressed with regard to the EU (for an overview see Axt et al. 2007, Featherstone and Radaelli 2003, Olsen 2002, Vink and Graziano 2007).

A comprehensive definition is provided by Radaelli who has described Europeanization as processes consisting of "a) construction, b) diffusion and c) institutionalization of formal and informal rules, procedures, policy paradigms, styles, 'ways of doing things', and shared beliefs and norms which are first defined and consolidated in the EU policy process and then incorporated in the logic of domestic (national and subnational) discourse, political structures and public policies" (Radaelli 2004: 4). Particularly useful for the analysis of the impact of a regional organization on the domestic level are the concepts developed in the so-called new institutionalism debate (Börzel and Risse 2003). Again, rational choice approaches compete with sociological-based approaches for explanatory power. The rational choice strand of new institutionalism is concerned with the ways in which "changes in the political opportunity structure lead to a domestic redistribution of power" (Börzel and Risse 2003: 58). In contrast, sociological institutionalism holds that the process of regional integration can involve cognitive changes, through the proliferation of regional norms, values, and ideas. Sociological institutionalism looks at the possibility that regional norms and collective understandings exert adaptational pressure, and impact on the behavior of political actors (March and Olsen 1989).

A Guide to Analyzing the Genesis, Design, and Effects of Regional Organizations

After having outlined the four questions and their respective theoretical umbrella, we bring together our comprehensive research agenda in Table 1.1. It is meant to provide an overview of this book's structure as well as a reference point for students of regionalism. We do not claim that the suggestions made here are an exhaustive account of the field of research. We rather want to propose an analytical guideline to structure research on the topic of regionalism. As indicated by the table, each of the research questions touches upon several aspects of regionalism.

Our thematic grouping allows us to study regional integration on both the independent and dependent variables. This flexibility also requires a high degree of theoretical pluralism. We want to leave the selection of the theoretical approach to the researcher. This openness is driven by the belief that attempts to unite different analytical approaches in one comprehensive framework are more valuable than academic turf battles.

Building on this research agenda, the chapters in this volume offer explanations for the complex processes of regionalism and seek to point out possibilities for further research. Clearly, Europe does not have to be the standard by which everything else is measured. Instances of regionalism such as ASEAN, ECOWAS, the League of Arab States, MERCOSUR, or NAFTA may all be unique in some way—but that does not preclude a comparative perspective (Warleigh-Lack and Rosamond 2010). Placing the individual case studies in the broader context of our thematic framework allows for an original view not only on the theories themselves, but also on the global state of regional integration.

Table 1.1 Four aspects of regional integration

	1. Genesis and Growth	2. Institutional Design	3. Member States' Behaviour	4. Effects on Member States
Research Questions	Why do sovereign states institutionalize cooperation on a regional level? Why do states join regional organizations?	How can we describe and explain the institutional design of ROs?	How do domestic factors shape state behavior at the regional level?	How does the pooling and transferring of sovereignty impact back on the domestic structures of the states involved?
Independent Variable(s)	State preferences / economic pressures / subnational actors / systemic changes	State preferences / other ROs	RO / member states / subnational actors	RO
Dependent Variable(s)	Regional cooperation	Institutional Design	Member states' behavior / Commitment / Compliance	Polity, policy, politics of member states
Central Actors	Governments / subnational, transnational actors	Governments	Governments / RO	RO / subnational norm entrepreneurs / veto players
Empirical focus	Supply and demand for regional cooperation	Institution building	Regime type, compliance issues, state capacity	Mechanisms of change, intended/unintended consequences
Theoretical/ Analytical Approaches	Neofunctionalism, Neoliberal Institutionalism, Mattli, Liberal Intergovern-mentalism, IR theory	RDII, Legalization concept, Diffusion, IR theory	Compliance Theory, regime type analysis, IR theory	Second image reversed, Europeanization literature
Actor quality of RO			increasing	

Source: Author.

Empirical Overview: A World of Regions

Regional organizations, as defined above, are a relatively new phenomenon. Mansfield and Milner's (1999) argument that there have been four waves of regionalism in modern history is based on instances of regional trade agreements; regionalism resulting in state-led integration schemes, however, did not become prominent until the post-World War II era. Since then, we can observe two waves of regional integration out of which a total of 56 regional organizations emerged (see Table 1.2).[7]

During the first period from 1945 to 1990, ROs focused on reconciliation, economic recovery, and security through regional stabilization. The most prominent projects of regional integration emerged in Europe as well as in the Middle East, Latin America, and Africa. Additionally, there was also a mushrooming of regional integration projects among the newly independent states in Africa, Asia, and the Caribbean in the 1960s and 1970s. The second period from 1990 onwards is characterized by regional integration projects in Eastern Europe and Central Asia, the construction of new schemes in North and South America (for instance NAFTA and MERCOSUR) as well as the renewal and reformation of old integration schemes (such as the EC which became the EU, and the Organization of African Unity which became the African Union).

---

[7] Compared to the 51 regional organizations, some 474 regional trade agreements have been negotiated up to now (World Trade Organization 2011a) of which 211 are currently in force (World Trade Organization 2011b). Yet, more than 50 percent of those are either bilateral or not in regional proximity (World Trade Organization 2011b).

Table 1.2 Overview about regional organizations since 1945 sorted by macro-region

	Africa	Middle East & Maghreb	Asia and the Pacific	Europe	The Americas and the Caribbean
1945 – 1990	Communauté Economique de l'Afrique de l'Ouest (CEAO)	League of Arab States (LAS)	Secretariat of the Pacific Community (SPC)	Council of Europe	Org. of American States (OAS)
	Council of the Entente	Council for Arab Econ. Unity (CAEU)	Assoc. of South East Asian Nations (ASEAN)	Nordic Council	Org. of American States (OAS)
	Org. of African Unity (OAU), since 2002: African Union (AU)	Council for Arab Econ. Unity (CAEU)	Assoc. of South East Asian Nations (ASEAN)	European Community (EC), since 1993: European Union (EU)	Org. of American States (OAS)
	Eastern African Community (EAC)	Gulf Cooperation Council (GCC)	South Pacific Forum	Benelux Economic Union	Org. of Central American States (OCAS)
	South African Customs Union (SACU)	Arab Cooperation Council (ACC)	South Asian Assoc. for Regional Cooperation (SAARC)	European Free Trade Assoc. (EFTA)	Latin American Free Trade Assoc. (LAFTA), since 1980: Latin American Integration Assoc. (ALADI)
	Mano River Union (MRU)	Arab Maghreb Union (AMU)	Asia-Pacific Economic Cooperation (APEC)	Org. for Security and Cooperation in Europe (OSCE)	Andean Pact
	Economic Community of the Great Lake Countries (CPEGL)				Caribbean Community (CARICOM)
	Economic Community of West African States (ECOWAS)				Amazonian Cooperation Treaty Org. (ACTO)
	Intergovernmental Authority on Drought and Development (IGADD), since 1996: Intergovernmental Authority on Development (IGAD)				Org. of East Caribbean States (OECS)

	South African Development Coordination Conference (SADCC), since 1992: South African Development Community (SADC)	Economic Cooperation Organization (ECO)			
	Economic Community of Central African States (ECCAS)				
1990 - Today	Africa Economic Community (AEC)	Melanesian Spearhead Group	Central Asian Cooperation Org. (CACO)	Council of the Baltic Sea States (CBSS)	Common Market of the South (MERCOSUR)
	Communauté Economique et Monétaire de l'Afrique Centrale (CEMAC)	Bay of Bengal Initiative for Multi-Sectoral Technical and Economic Cooperation (BIMSTEC)		European Economic Area (EEA)	North American Free Trade Assoc. (NAFTA)
	Community of Sahel-Saharan States (CEN-SAD)		Commonwealth of Independent States (CIS)		Assoc. of Caribbean States (ACS)
			Eurasian Economic Community (EurAsEC)		Bolivarian Alliance for the Peoples of Our America (ALBA)
			GUAM Org. for Democracy and Development (GUAM)		Union of South American Nations (UNASUR)
		Black Sea Economic Cooperation (BSEC)			Community of Latin American and Caribbean States (CELAC)
	Indian Ocean Rim Assoc. for Regional Cooperation (IOR-ARC)		Arctic Council		
			Stability Pact for South Eastern Europe, defunct now: Regional Cooperation Council (RCC)		

Source: Own table with data retrieved from Börzel (2012), UNU-CRIS (2010) and Jiménez (2010).

Regional Organizations Covered

The cases covered in this volume are considered to be the most important instances of regionalism beyond Europe (see Börzel 2012, Sbragia 2008).[8] Covering all macro-regions, we analyze the Association of South East Asian Nations (ASEAN), the Common Market of the South (MERCOSUR), the Economic Community of West African States (ECOWAS), the League of Arab States (LAS), and the North American Free Trade Agreement (NAFTA) (see Table 1.3). Furthermore, a broad and in-depth description of the post-Soviet realm is presented in Chapter 2.

Table 1.3 Overview of the ROs covered in this book

RO	Founding year	Member states
ASEAN	1967	Brunei, Cambodia, Indonesia, Laos, Malaysia, Myanmar, Philippines, Singapore, Thailand, Vietnam
ECOWAS	1975	Benin, Burkina Faso, Côte d'Ivoire, Cape Verde, Gambia, Ghana, Guinea, Guinea-Bissau, Liberia, Mali, Niger, Nigeria, Senegal, Sierra Leone, Togo
LAS	1945	Algeria, Bahrain, Comoros, Djibouti, Egypt, Iraq, Jordan, Kuwait, Lebanon, Libya, Mauritania, Morocco, Oman, State of Palestine, Qatar, Saudi Arabia, Somalia, Sudan, Syria, Tunisia, United Arab Emirates, Yemen
MERCOSUR	1991	Argentina, Brazil, Paraguay, Uruguay, Venezuela (prospective); Associated members: Bolivia, Chile, Colombia, Ecuador, Peru
NAFTA	1994	Canada, Mexico, United States of America

Source: own table.

Note: the post-Soviet realm is not included in this table as Wirminghaus does not analyze a particular RO but presents a descriptive overview of the multitude of integration schemes in the region. Venezuela has applied for membership in MERCOSUR, but has not yet been officially accepted.

---

8   It should be noted, however, that even our relatively inclusive framework leaves room for additions as well as different conceptualizations. Other scholars, for example, examine the role of non-state actors and informal regional developments, and take into account other instances of regionalism than the well-established, formally integrated regions (Shaw et al. 2011).

In conclusion, this volume explores four roads to regionalism and a variety of regional integration schemes in a comparative perspective. The framework developed in this introduction, with geographical inclusiveness and multi-dimensionality as its central strengths, constitutes both an addition to the debate as well as a link to further research. Our results can enter into a mutually stimulating dialogue with research on other regional organizations, less formalized regional arrangements including non-state actors, and other issue areas such as transnational crime, migration, or ecology (see Shaw et al. 2011).

Contributions to this Volume

Contributions to this volume provide a first indication on how the four roads can be explored. In Part 2 of the book, the authors look at the genesis and growth of regional organizations. Why does regional integration take place? Why are demand and supply factors changing over time and with what effects? What determines the failure and success of regional organizations? To address these questions, the second chapter by Niklas Wirminghaus provides a classification of different regional integration schemes in the post-Soviet space as well as a literature review on the reasons for successes and failures. As Wirminghaus points out, regional integration schemes can serve a huge variety of purposes and aims. To account for the emergence (and failure) of the many attempts at regionalism, he identifies factors that drive or hinder integration as well as a set of factors with ambiguous effects.

Niklas Aschhoff analyzes the accession of Cambodia, Laos, Myanmar, and Vietnam (CLMV) to ASEAN in the third chapter. Differentiating between general systemic conditions, organization-specific systemic conditions, and the positional characteristics of the candidate states, Aschhoff finds that a combination of economic and geopolitical factors incited CLMV to join ASEAN. The expectation to attract more foreign investment, to gain more international bargaining power, as well as the collapse of the Soviet Union as an important ally were key motivations for a pro-accession policy.

In Chapter 4, Felix Hummel and Mathis Lohaus consider regional integration in South America. To explain the genesis and development of MERCOSUR, the authors adopt an analytical framework developed by Walter Mattli. Analyzing supply and demand conditions, they find that leadership plays a central role in advancing MERCOSUR. The big players in the region and their presidents drive integration forward—while favoring a low level of institutionalization that allows them to maintain control of the process.

Part 3 then deals with the specific institutional design of regional organizations. In Chapter 5, Leon Kanthak explains differences in institutional design between ASEAN (lowly legalized, highly flexible) and NAFTA (highly legalized, inflexible), by combining the legalization concept and the rational design framework. Kanthak argues for differentiating between sources of political uncertainty. ASEAN is exposed to uncertainty from outside the region, and therefore chooses a highly flexible institutional structure. NAFTA member states, however, aim to constrain their biggest member, the United States. This uncertainty stemming from inside the region makes states agree upon a highly legalized structure. The trade-off between legalization and flexibility therefore depends on the type of uncertainty the member states are facing.

In Chapter 6, Annika Korte examines the reasons for the establishment of dispute settlement procedures (DSP) in NAFTA and ASEAN. More importantly, Korte asks why DSPs are used in some cases and not in others. Evaluating the idea that increased trade leads to increased conflicts and increased formalized dispute settlement, she finds that ASEAN member states—contrary to NAFTA—did not pursue a functional goal with the DSP but instead looked for more international legitimacy.

In Chapter 7, Constanze Koitzsch addresses the institutional designs of the LAS and ECOWAS. Comparing the institutional reforms planned (in the case of the LAS) and those already adopted (in the case of ECOWAS), she finds surprising similarities between the two organizations. While "traditional" functionalist and power-based explanations can account for the creation and timing of the specific institutional design and the reforms, they fail to explain the processes by which institutional similarities arise. Koitzsch advances, similarly to Korte (Chapter 6), the idea of a "global script" of diffusing international norms.

The general interaction between member states and the regional organization is at the core of Part 4. Veronika Kirschner and Sören Stapel consider regional integration in West Africa in Chapter 8. They scrutinize the effects of domestic regime characteristics on the progress of integration in ECOWAS. Measuring the commitment to regional integration via the time span from adoption to ratification, Kirschner and Stapel find that regime type seems to matter. Neither autocratic nor neopatrimonial regimes ratify as quickly and as comprehensively as their democratic counterparts.

In Chapter 9, Lukas Goltermann probes the reasons for non-compliance with regional commitments in ASEAN. Starting from the observation that compliance differs among member states, Goltermann looks at two competing explanations. The chapter finds that a lack of state capacity offers more explanatory power for variation in legal implementation than cost-benefit calculations. Goltermann thus concludes that it is not primarily the question whether or not member states are willing to comply, but instead whether they are able to comply.

In Chapter 10, Kai Striebinger looks at the decision-making process in ECOWAS and asks under what conditions the regional organization intervenes in order to protect the constitutional order in its member states. Finding that neither domestic nor international pressure is constitutive for such an action, he concludes that depending on the type of intervention a high democratic identity or a strong hegemonic interest are sufficient conditions for such an action.

In Part 5 we focus on questions relating to the effects of regional integration projects on the member states. This aspect of regionalism pays particular attention to the intended and unintended consequences of regionalism. In Chapter 11, Christian Pirzer scrutinizes MERCOSUR's impact on democratic consolidation in its member states. While improvements in the attitudinal dimension of democratic consolidation cannot be confirmed due the strong intervening effect of the economic crisis in 2001, a significant influence of MERCOSUR on the behavioral dimension of democratic consolidation is observable. Since the establishment of MERCOSUR's credible democratic commitments, the degree of anti-system behavior decreased significantly in its member states.

Looking at a different policy field, Corinna Krome analyzes the role ASEAN plays in increasing the role of civil society organizations (CSO) in its member states (Chapter 12). Refining the common picture of ASEAN as being a "weak" regional organization that neither progresses very far in regional integration nor influences its member states, she finds that ASEAN does indeed possess mechanisms through which it aims at empowering CSOs in its member states.

Alexander Spielau (Chapter 13) investigates the impact of NAFTA on monetary policies in the United States and in Mexico. He argues that regional economic integration has unintended consequences for monetary policy. In line with the argument of functional spillover, Spielau argues that even though NAFTA does not explicitly pursue a policy of monetary policy harmonization, trade integration and business cycle synchronization create the need for this harmonization.

In the final chapter, Tanja Börzel summarizes the results and links them to the wider debates between "new" and "old" regionalism. She makes the case for systematically exploring the four roads to regionalism across time and space in order to test mainstream theoretical approaches to regional integration and gain new empirical insights.

References

Abbott, K. W., Keohane, R. O., Moravcsik, A., Slaughter, A.-M. and Snidal, D. 2000. The Concept of Legalization. *International Organization*, 54(3), 401–419.

Acharya, A. and Johnston, A. I. 2007. Comparing Regional Institutions: An Introduction, in *Crafting Cooperation: Regional International Institutions in Comparative Perspective*, edited by A. Acharya and A. I. Johnston. Cambridge: Cambridge University Press, 1–31.

Axt, H.-J., Milososki, A. and Schwarz, O. 2007. Europäisierung – ein weites Feld. Literaturbericht und Forschungsfragen. *Politische Vierteljahresschrift*, 48(1), 136–149.

Bach, D. C. 2005. The Global Politics of Regionalism: Africa, in *Global Politics of Regionalism. Theory and Practice*, edited by M. Farell, B. Hettne and L. van Langenhove. London: Pluto Press, 171–186.

Bhagwati, J. 1993. Regionalism and Multilateralism: An Overview, in *New Dimensions in Regional Integration*, edited by J. de Melo and A. Panagariya. New York: Cambridge University Press, 22–51.

Börzel, T. A. 2012. Comparative Regionalism: European Integration and Beyond, in *Handbook on International Relations*, edited by W. Carlsnaes, T. Risse and B. A. Simmons. London: Sage.

Börzel, T. A. and Risse, T. 2003. Conceptualizing the Domestic Impact of Europe, in *The Politics of Europeanization*, edited by K. Featherstone and C. M. Radaelli. Oxford: Oxford University Press, 57–80.

Breslin, S. and Higgott, R. 2000. Studying Regions: Learning from the Old, Constructing the New. *New Political Economy*, 5(3), 333–352.

Cai, K. 2010. *The Politics of Economic Regionalism. Explaining Regional Economic Integration in East Asia*. Basingstoke: Palgrave Macmillan.

Campbell, J. L. 2004. *Institutional Change and Globalization*. Princeton: Princeton University Press.

Choi, Y. J. and Caporaso, J. A. 2002. Comparative Regional Integration, in *Handbook of International Relations*, edited by W. Carlsnaes, T. Risse and B. A. Simmons. London: Sage, 480–499.

De Lombaerde, P., Söderbaum, F., Van Langenhove, L. and Baert, F. 2010. The Problem of Comparison in Comparative Regionalism. *Review of International Studies*, 36(3), 731–753.

Di Maggio, P. J. and Powell, W. 1983. The Iron Cage Revisited: Institutional Isomorphism and Collective Rationality in Organizational Fields. *American Sociological Review*, 48, 147–160.

Dieter, H. (ed.). 2007. *The Evolution of Regionalism in Asia. Economic and Security Issues*. London: Routledge.

Duffield, J. S. 2003. The Limits of "Rational Design." *International Organization*, 57(2), 411–430.

Featherstone, K. and Radaelli, C. M. (eds). 2003. *The Politics of Europeanization*. Oxford: Oxford University Press.

Finnemore, M. and Toope, S. J. 2001. Alternatives to "Legalization": Richer Views of Law and Politics. *International Organization*, 55(3), 743–758.

Gamble, A. and Payne, A. 1996. Introduction: The Political Economy of Regionalism and World Order, in *Regionalism and World Order*, edited by A. Gamble and A. Payne. New York: St. Martin's Press, 1–20.

Goldstein, J. O., Kahler, M., Keohane, R. O. and Slaughter, A.-M. 2001. Response to Finnemore and Toope. *International Organization*, 55(3), 759–760.

Gourevitch, P. 1978. The Second Image Reversed: The International Sources of Domestic Politics. *International Organization*, 32(4), 881–912.

Haas, E. B. 1958. *The Uniting of Europe: Political, Social, and Economic Forces, 1950–1957*. Stanford: Stanford University Press.

Haas, E. B. 1961. International Integration: The European and the Universal Process. *International Organization*, 15(3), 366–392.

Henisz, W. J., Zelner, B. A. and Guillén, M. F. 2005. The Worldwide Diffusion of Market-oriented Infrastructure Reform, 1977–1999. *American Sociological Review*, 70(6), 871–897.

Hurrell, A. 1995. Explaining the Resurgence of Regionalism in World Politics. *Review of International Studies*, 21(4), 331–358.

Jepperson, R. L. and Meyer, J. W. 1991. The Public Order and the Construction of Formal Organization, in *The New Institutionalism in Organizational Analysis*, edited by W. Powell and P. J. Di Maggio. Chicago: University of Chicago Press, 204–231.

Jiménez, E. M. 2010. *The Contribution of the Regional UN Economic Commissions to Regional Integration Processes: The Case of ECLAC*. UNU-CRIS Working Papers, W-2010/8.

Koremenos, B., Lipson, C. and Snidal, D. 2001. The Rational Design of International Institutions. *International Organization*, 55(4), 761–799.

Levi-Faur, D. 2005. The Global Diffusion of Regulatory Capitalism. *Annals of the American Academy of Political and Social Science*, 598, 12–32.

Lindberg, L. 1963. *The Political Dynamics of European Integration*. Stanford: Stanford University Press.

Mansfield, E. D. and Milner, H. V. 1999. The New Wave of Regionalism. *International Organization*, 53(3), 589–627.

Mansfield, E. D., Milner, H. V. and Pevehouse, J. C. 2008. Democracy, Veto Players and the Depth of Regional Integration. *The World Economy*, 31(1), 67–96.

Mansfield, E. D., Milner, H. V. and Rosendorff, B. P. 2002. Why Democracies Cooperate More: Electoral Control and International Trade Agreements. *International Organization*, 56(3), 477–513.

March, J. and Olsen, J. P. 1989. *Institutions: The Organizational Basis of Politics*. New York: Free Press.

Mattli, W. 1999. *The Logic of Regional Integration. Europe and Beyond*. Cambridge: Cambridge University Press.

Moravcsik, A. 1991. Taking Preferences Seriously: A Liberal Theory of International Politics. *International Organization*, 51(4), 513–553.

Moravcsik, A. 1993. Preferences and Power in the European Community: A Liberal Intergovernmentalist Approach. *Journal of Common Market Studies*, 31(4), 473–524.

Moravcsik, A. 1998. *The Choice for Europe – Social Purpose & State Power from Messina to Maastricht*. London: UCL Press.

Niemann, A. 1998. The PHARE Programme and the Concept of Spillover: Neofunctionalism in the Making. *Journal of European Public Policy*, 5(3), 428–446.

Nye, J. S. 1968. Comparative Regional Integration: Concept and Measurement. *International Organization*, 22, 855–880.

Olsen, J. P. 2002. The Many Faces of Europeanization. *JCMS: Journal of Common Market Studies*, 40(5), 921–952.

Pevehouse, J. C. 2005. *Democracy from Above: Regional Organizations and Democratization*. Cambridge: Cambridge University Press.

Radaelli, C. M. 2004. The Politics of Europeanization. *European Integration online Papers (EIoP)* [Online], 8. Available at: http://eiop.or.at/eiop/pdf/2004-016.pdf [accessed: April 19 2011].

Ribeiro Hoffmann, A. and van der Vleuten, A. (eds). 2007. *Closing or Widening the Gap? Legitimacy and Democracy in Regional Integration Organizations*. Aldershot: Ashgate.

Rüland, J. 2009. Deepening ASEAN Cooperation through Democratization? The Indonesian Legislature and Foreign Policymaking. *International Relations of the Asia-Pacific*, 9(3), 373–402.

Sbragia, A. 2008. Review Article: Comparative Regionalism: What Might It Be? *Journal of Common Market Studies*, 46(1), 29–49.

Schimmelfennig, F. and Sedelmeier, U. 2002. Theorizing EU Enlargement: Research Focus, Hypotheses, and the State of Research. *Journal of European Public Policy*, 9(4), 500–528.

Shaw, T. M., Grant, J. A. and Cornelisson, S. (eds). 2011. *The Ashgate Research Companion to Regionalisms*. Aldershot: Ashgate.

Simmons, B. A. 1998. Compliance with International Agreements. *Annual Review of Political Science*, 1, 75–93.

Simmons, B. A. 2002. Capacity, Commitment, and Compliance: International Institutions and Territorial Disputes. *Journal of Conflict Resolution*, 46, 829–856.

Tallberg, J. 2002. Paths to Compliance: Enforcement, Management, and the European Union. *International Organization*, 56(3), 609–664.

Thomas, N. (ed.) 2008. *Governance and Regionalism in Asia*. London: Routledge.

UNU-CRIS. 2010. *Regional Integration Knowledge System*. [Online]. Available at: www.cris.unu.edu/riks/web/data [accessed: April 10, 2011].

Van der Vleuten, A. and Ribeiro Hoffmann, A. 2010. Explaining the Enforcement of Democracy by Regional Organizations: Comparing EU, Mercosur and SADC. *Journal of Common Market Studies*, 48(3), 737–758.

Van Langenhove, L. 2011. *Building Regions. The Regionalization of World Order*. Aldershot: Ashgate.

Vink, M. P. and Graziano, P. 2007. Challenges of a New Research Agenda, in *Europeanization. New Research Agendas*, edited by P. Graziano and M. P. Vink. Houndmills: Palgrave Macmillan, 3–22.

Warleigh-Lack, A. and Rosamond, B. 2010. Across the EU Studies–New Regionalism Frontier: Invitation to a Dialogue. *Journal of Common Market Studies*, 48(4), 993–1013.

Warleigh-Lack, A., Robinson, N. and Rosamond, B. (eds). 2011. *New Regionalism and the European Union: Dialogues, Comparisons and New Research Directions*. London: Routledge.

World Trade Organization. 2011a. *Regional Trade Agreements*. [Online]. Available at: www.wto.org/english/tratop_e/region_e/region_e.htm [accessed: April 11, 2011].

World Trade Organization. 2011b. *Regional Trade Agreements Information System (RTA-IS): List of all RTAs in Force*. [Online]. Available at: http://rtais.wto.org/UI/PublicMaintainRTAHome.aspx [accessed: April 11, 2011].

PART 2:
Genesis and Growth

Chapter 2
Ephemeral Regionalism: The Proliferation of (Failed) Regional Integration Initiatives in Post-Soviet Eurasia

Niklas Wirminghaus

Introduction

It was not until the end of the Cold War that one world region joined the global trend toward ever more regionalism: the area of the former Soviet Union. Amidst the turmoil of a crumbling Soviet superpower in late 1991, its "Slavic core" – comprising Russia, Ukraine and Belarus – signed the Belavezha Accords, thereby establishing the Commonwealth of Independent States (CIS): "a stunning surprise" (Church et al. 1991) since this move toward the pooling of state sovereignty seemed both unanticipated and counterintuitive for "newborn" nations.

After a decades-long incorporation into the Soviet super-state, the former republics had to put considerable effort into the establishment of exclusive national identities since most of them lacked any experience with independent statehood (Smith et al. 1998). It is against this background that it seems peculiar that the 15 Soviet successor states were so active in forming intergovernmental projects.

During the two decades between 1991 and 2010 one can count no less than 39 different initiatives of regional integration of which 36 organizations actually came into being.[1] Even when taking into account that many of them were rather enhancements of existing organizations than entirely new ones, 20 cases remain. Moreover, there were 14 instances in which organizations were re-modeled including a change of their name. Eighteen times organizations were either enlarged by the accession of new member states or lost member states. Regional integration activity was also more intense during the first decade of independence with 28 new foundations, probably because many problems had to be tackled after the dissolution of the Soviet Union (Collins 2009: 253, Nurmasheva 2008: 8). Yet, even after 2000, 11 new organizations were established.

Besides the apparent proliferation of regional initiatives and the frequent re-modeling of existing organizations, other phenomena can be observed. First, by and large these initiatives have not proven successful. Collins (2009: 252) deemed post-Soviet Eurasia as "one of many cases of stunted regionalism in the

---

[1] This and the following numbers are based on counts by the author, using material of List (2006), Collins (2009), Molchanov (2009), Pomfret (2009), Balayan (1996), Gleason (2001), Czakó (2005), Zhukov and Reznikova (2006) and Vinokurov (2007).

developing world."[2] Second, oftentimes the very same actors group together again and again, rendering a confusing picture that has been labeled "an 'alphabet soup' of organizations and groupings" (Nikitin 2007: 3) or a "spaghetti bowl" (Pomfret 2009: 51).

Therefore, the academic debate focuses on one crucial question: why is there a proliferation of (failed) regional integration schemes in the post-Soviet space? More precisely, this puzzle can be approached by seeking answers to two sub-questions: what motivated newly independent states to give up sovereignty at all? What led to the failure of so many initiatives?

Why are these questions relevant? First, they refer to a real-world puzzle that has no easy answer. Second, the existing literature is limited (Torjesen 2007: 18): the sub-region of Central Asia, for instance, is a popular topic, yet often treated in rather descriptive accounts.[3] Other scholars focus on the institutional aspects of post-Soviet regional integration[4] or a single country, usually Russia.[5] Accounts dealing with the entire post-Soviet space are rare[6] and often insufficient: when looking at a large number of cases, they often provide very little explanatory value (as in Zhukov and Reznikova 2006); when giving comprehensive explanations, they are usually limited to a small number of cases (as in Molchanov 2009). So far, there has been no systematic examination of the reasons accounting for the formation and failure of regional integration in the post-Soviet space.

This chapter is a first attempt to fill this gap by proceeding in three steps: it will propose a categorization of regional initiatives, review the existing literature to "collect" claims about their formation and failure, and finally conduct a preliminary weighting of explanatory factors to identify more and less plausible explanations.

Categorizing Post-Soviet Regionalism

Not all of the 39 post-Soviet regional organizations can be analyzed in detail within the scope of this chapter. A number of criteria for a selection are imaginable, for example, geographical proximity or a certain time frame, though that might lead to an analytical bias. I will therefore limit the examination to the most

---

2   See Table 2.1 for a comprehensive overview of status assessments drawn from the literature.

3   For accounts on Central Asia see Primbetov (1996), Spechler (2000), Muzafarov (2001), Gleason (2001), Green (2003), Bohr (2004), Czakó (2005), Geyikdagi (2005), Karaev (2005), Byrd et al. (2006), List (2006), Dadabaev (2007), Rakhmatullina (2007), Torjesen (2007), Allison (2008), Collins (2009), Pomfret (2009) and Rakhimov (2010).

4   On the institutional dimension, see Balayan (1996), Libman (2007) and Kembayev (2009).

5   For analyses centered on Russia, see Fischer (2007), Vinokurov (2007), Willerton and Beznosov (2007), Kazantsev (2008), Schmitz (2008), Freire (2009) and Smith (2009).

6   On regional integration in the entire post-Soviet space, see Grinberg (2003), Fischer (2006), Zhukov and Rezinkova (2006), Kobrinskaya (2007) and Molchanov (2009).

important categories of post-Soviet regionalism, based on the organizations' regional focus, issue areas, goals and actors involved.[7] For each category, I will focus on the most prominent members: the CIS as the original *post-Soviet regional integration*; the Eurasian Economic Community (EurAsEC) and the Common or Single Economic Space (CES/SES) in the category of *Russian-centered economic integration*; the Collective Security Treaty (CST) and the Collective Security Treaty Organization (CSTO) for *Russian-centered security integration*; the Central Asian Union (CAU), the Central Asian Economic Union (CAEU), the Central Asian Economic Community (CAEC) and the Central Asian Cooperation Organization (CACO), belonging to the group of *Central Asian regional integration*; and finally GUAM as a case of *anti-Russian regional integration*.[8]

As for the dependent variable, Mattli (1999: 12) proposed to measure the success and failure of regional initiatives "by the extent to which integration groups manage to match their stated integrations goals with subsequent achievements." Applying this approach to our cases, however, would yield rather unsatisfying results: compared to the glorious rhetoric and promises most regional integration agreements start out with, effective delivery of given promises is consistently weak. Almost no case would meet this standard. There is an ongoing discussion which dimensions best capture progress in regional integration, both among the development community (World Bank 2011) and among students of European Integration (Börzel 2005). For the benefit of this study, it will suffice to understand success as the formal cooperation between nation states. I will consider regionalism to have failed when organizations are described as being "mainly rhetorical," "dormant" or "defunct" (Collins 2009: 265). Due to the high number of ROs covered, this chapter cannot provide new empirical data, but rather will be based on relevant secondary literature.

---

7   For other categorizations, see Grinberg and Kosikova (1997: 32) and List (2006: 66).
8   The 2010 Customs Union of Belarus, Kazakhstan and Russia is not included since it emerged only recently (2007).

Table 2.1 Main regional integration projects in the post-Soviet space 1991–2009

Name	Date	Participants	Character	Current status
Original Post-Soviet regional integration				
Commonwealth of Independent States (CIS)	Dec 8, 1991 Dec 21, 1991 Jan 22, 1993	Belarus, Russia, Ukraine + Azerbaijan, Armenia, Kazakhstan, Kyrgyzstan, Moldova, Tajikistan, Turkmenistan, Uzbekistan + Georgia	economic, security, political	"mainly rhetorical" (Collins 2009: 265), "largely ceremonial" (Molchanov 2009: 336)
Russian-centered economic integration				
CIS Economic Union	Sep 24, 1993	Azerbaijan, Armenia, Belarus, Georgia, Kazakhstan, Kyrgyzstan, Moldova, Russia, Tajikistan, Turkmenistan, Ukraine, Uzbekistan	economic	Ratified by all states but Ukraine
Eurasian Economic Community (EurAsEC)	Oct 10, 2000 Jun 10, 2005 Oct 20, 2008	+ Uzbekistan - Uzbekistan	economic	"mainly rhetorical" (Collins 2009: 265)
Common Economic Space / United Economic Space /Single Economic Space (CES/SES)	Sep 19, 2003	Belarus, Kazakhstan, Russia, Ukraine	economic	"very little headway in integration" (Nurmasheva 2008: 33)

Russian-centered security integration				
Collective Security Treaty (CST)	May 15, 1992	Armenia, Kazakhstan, Kyrgyzstan, Russia, Tajikistan, Uzbekistan	security	"Dormant through most of 1990s" (Collins 2009: 265) "rarely implemented" (Collins 2009: 260)
	Sep-Dec 1993	+ Azerbaijan, Belarus, Georgia		
	Apr 2, 1999	- Azerbaijan, Georgia, Uzbekistan		
Collective Security Treaty Organization (CSTO)	Jul 10, 2002		security	"some military cooperation" (Collins 2009: 265)
	Jun 23, 2006	+ Uzbekistan		
Central Asian integration				
Central Asian Economic Union/ Central Asian Union (CAEU/ CAU)	Jul 8, 1994	Kazakhstan, Kyrgyzstan, Uzbekistan	economic, political	"defunct" (Collins 2009: 265), "dysfunctional" (Czakó 2005: 9), "rather ineffective" (Allison 2007: 264)
Central Asian Economic Community (CAEC)	1998	+ Tajikistan	economic	"took no further action" (Collins 2009: 260), "sluggish and inefficient superstructure" (Allison 2007: 264)
Central Asian Cooperation Organization (CACO/OCAC)	Feb 28, 2002 Oct 16, 2004	+ Russia	economic, security	"mainly rhetorical" (Collins 2009: 265), "dismal overall record" (Allison 2008: 191)
Anti-Russian regional integration				
GUAM	Oct 10, 1997	Azerbaijan, Georgia, Moldova, Ukraine	economic, security, political	"little substance" (Collins 2009: 275), "lowest integrational depth of all cooperations in the CIS space" (Clement et al. 2003: 54)
GUUAM	1999 Jun 7, 2001	+ Uzbekistan		
GUAM	2005	- Uzbekistan		

Source: Clement et al. (2003), Allison (2007, 2008), Nurmasheva (2008), Collins (2009), Molchanov (2009).

Explanations for Formation and Failure

In the next part, the existing explanations for the success and failure of post-Soviet regional initiatives will be reviewed. They are grouped according to their evaluation in the literature on post-Soviet regionalism, allowing for a classification as drivers of or obstacles to regionalism. A number of factors are considered in both regards – these will be called "ambiguous."

Factors Seen as Drivers of Regionalism

The literature identifies two key factors that strengthen regionalism. In this section, the effects of common problems and economic motives will be discussed.

Common problems The formation of the CIS is probably the most self-evident phenomenon among the various regionalist projects. The abrupt breakdown of the Soviet Union left open a wide range of issues for which the federal state of the Soviet Union had provided solutions. Now there was an "urgent necessity to solve myriads of problems resulting from the fall down of the single federal state" (Kembayev 2009: 90, also Fischer 2006: 134–140, Nurmasheva 2008: 5). The idea was to have a vehicle for a "civilized divorce" as then-Ukrainian president Kravchuk called it (cited in Molchanov 2009: 336).

With regard to the Central Asian region, it is widely argued that these countries share a wide array of issues that naturally require solutions on a regional level, such as labor migration (Zhukov and Reznikova 2006: 13), transit infrastructure (Czakó 2005: 6), inter-state water consumption, the drying up of the Aral Sea (Muzafarov 2001: 231, Nurmasheva 2008: 28), or border delimitation and control (Dadabaev 2007, Zhalimbetova and Gleason 2001).

Furthermore, most security threats in post-Soviet Eurasia were transnational (Collins 2009: 260, List 2006: 78). Dynamics such as religious extremism, terrorism, criminal networks, or social tensions and civil war in Afghanistan and Tajikistan (Czakó 2005: 9) have propelled Russian-led security integration.

Economic motives Most post-Soviet regional initiatives were justified economically. It was, for instance, argued that the former Soviet republics' goods could not compete on the world markets because of their technological backwardness. Globalization made the participation in integration structures "a sine qua non for the survival" (Kobrinskaya 2007: 21). Besides, the Soviet empire had been a highly integrated economic space with an internal market, coordinated economic policies, and a common currency (Ultanbaev 2003). This in turn also led to a highly specialized division of labor between the different republics (Nurmasheva 2008: 3). The CIS promised the "preservation of essential economic ties" (Molchanov 2009: 337). The CIS economic union was a direct reaction to the economic depression of 1993 (Gleason 2001: 1082). EurAsEC is significantly driven by the issue of energy which concerns almost all members in a distinct way since the organization unites "energy producers (Kazakhstan, Russia, Uzbekistan), transit countries (Belarus, Ukraine), and affiliates" (Molchanov 2009: 338). With the exception of Uzbekistan, the same was true for the CES.

Economic justifications were also employed for Central Asian regionalism. The Central Asian states are all landlocked countries; regionalism is needed to ensure easier trade and transit to world markets (Collins 2009: 258). Central Asia fears that otherwise international competition could turn them into a "raw material outskirt of the world economy" (Muzafarov 2001: 232, Geyikdagi 2005: 66). Moreover, economic development is truly necessary after the Central Asian economies have experienced deep crises, highly fluctuating GDP growth rates and still have poverty rates between 30 and 50 percent (Byrd et al. 2006, Geyikdagi 2005). By now, intra-regional trade is still low, which is partly due to the similar structures of Central Asian economies, lacking possibilities for complementary trade (Collins 2009: 257).[9]

As for anti-Russian integration, economic reasons are intertwined with power-based considerations. GUAM was intended to develop the region's transit potential that would make the countries more independent from Russia (Czakó 2005: 9, Kembayev 2009: 171, Nurmasheva 2008: 21). Meanwhile, the United States is interested in creating a strategic corridor through Azerbaijan, Georgia and Turkey (Zhukov and Reznikova 2006: 4).

Factors Seen as Obstacles to Regionalism

As seen in the previous section, there are good reasons for regional cooperation in the post-Soviet space. However, the literature on the area offers several explanatory factors to account for the frequent failure of such attempts. These are: the notion of success as failure, shortcomings in the organizational set-up, competition from alternatives to regionalism, and adverse economic preconditions.

Success as failure   One explanation for the failure of the CIS is that "after issues emerging from the Soviet collapse were solved, the organization had no clear raison d'être" (Kubicek 2009: 256). However, this interpretation is quite rare in the literature.

Organizational set-up   As for the failure of the CIS, it has been argued that from the start the organization's mandate and its institutional design were ambiguous. Within Russia, some saw it as a tool to restore Soviet supremacy, others as an EU-like liberal integration or simply as the vehicle needed for a "civilized divorce" (Rakhimov 2010: 97, Vinokurov 2007: 27, Webber 1996: 15). It had adopted an incoherent and "amorphous formation" (Muzafarov 2001: 231, Olcott et al. 1999). Even more importantly, the CIS also lacked effective management bodies.

---

9   Not all scholars doubt the prospects for economic integration because of this (see for instance Spechler 2000, Rakhmatullina 2007).

Furthermore, the CIS "exit option" which allowed each member state to determine for itself its level of engagement (Willerton and Beznosov 2007: 57) reduced member states' continuous commitment to the organization.

The failure of the CST is sometimes attributed to its structure that was flawed in one important aspect: the obligation to offer support to fellow member states only applied in the case of threats from third countries (List 2006: 79). However, the CST states rather suspected other former Soviet republics to be potential threats, not countries from outside.

Bilateral competition Bilateral relationships between former Soviet republics have proven to be more resilient than the CIS, particularly in the management of many contemporary security problems (Willerton and Beznosov 2007: 60). Russia, for instance, signed 77 bilateral security agreements between 1992 and 2004 with CIS states. Numerous bilateral trade and economic agreements have in effect resulted in the creation of a free trade area that has emerged "irrespective of the CIS" (Zhukov and Reznikova 2006: 3). Central Asian regionalism was increasingly constrained by both Russia and the United States that made use of bilateral agreements at the expense of multilateralism (Macfarlane 2004).

Multilateral competition In 1998, Kyrgyzstan was the first Soviet successor state to join the World Trade Organization, thus reducing its import tariffs to virtually zero. By allowing Kyrgyzstan this special status, the country has become "a 'Trojan horse' in the Eurasian space, a kind of window for duty-free inflow of goods from all over the world," constraining regional economic integration (Zhukov and Reznikova 2006: 3).

In a reiteration of the general pattern of post-Soviet regional integration, the CSTO has mostly the same members as EurAsEC, meaning that the respective representatives "at times have simply changed chairs when leaders who participate in both bodies have met in the same venue" (Allison 2008: 193). The same was true for CACO and EurAsEC.[10] Bilateral competition rendered the security benefit of the CSTO for Central Asia doubtful. "Obvious practical military and security benefits" (Allison 2008: 193) were in fact available through bilateral agreements with Russia.

Economic preconditions The move toward protectionism in times of crises in the 1990s caused a decline in intra-regional trading (List 2006: 72, Muzafarov 2001: 231). As Metcalf (1997: 530) sums up, "nowhere are the obstacles to integration more evident than in the former Soviet Union where fifteen states of varying sizes and levels of development determined to protect their newly gained sovereignty struggle with the disastrous consequences of the collapse of a unified market." Within EurAsEC, there are tangible differences regarding the structure, potential and orientation of the countries' economies, leading to

---

10 Consequently, the two organizations de facto merged in 2006.

increasing rivalries (Golovnin 2008: 40, List 2006: 91, Ultanbaev 2003). Overall, trade between EurAsEC members has even been declining (Golovnin 2008: 42). Moreover, there are a number of conditions that make market-based development in the post-Soviet states generally difficult. Several states are "landlocked"; others have difficult topographies, increasing the costs of economic exchange. All former Soviet republics have low or medium per capita income; yet, there are still "very wide gaps in development levels" (Zhukov and Reznikova 2006: 5–6). Usually, the driving force behind cross-border integration is the manufacturing industry. Throughout the former Soviet republics, however, "manufacturing (with the exception of metallurgy) is in a slump" (Zhukov and Reznikova 2006: 7). Moreover, most newly independent states are equally endowed with the very same factors of production, causing a lack of structural complementarity. Finally, the CIS-wide division of labor was the result of a year-long, planned, and geographically-oriented industrialization which often did not reflect comparative cost advantages (Nurmasheva 2008: 3).

Central Asian regionalism has faced similar problems. The demise of the Soviet Union hit the Central Asian countries particularly hard because their economic structures were hardly diversified and their peripheral position made it difficult to access foreign markets (Nurmasheva 2008: 28). Although the economic linkages between the Central Asian countries are more pronounced than between those of the overall CIS countries, this advantage has almost disappeared (Libman and Vinokurov 2010: 2). Moreover, the regimes' restrictions on cross-border movement have precluded the development of informal bottom-up regionalization (Collins 2009: 252). Together with protectionist trade policies, this has allowed for very little interaction of private business groups (Bohr 2004). Also, the regional infrastructure is poor (Allison 2007: 274, List 2006: 100) and the countries depend almost exclusively on trade in raw materials (Dadabaev 2007: 2).[11] Finally, the economies have similar structures, making them competing rather than complementary. In a nutshell: the Central Asian countries have "no objective prerequisites for more intensive cooperation" (Zhukov and Reznikova 2006: 9).

Moreover, the economic justification for GUAM turned out to be nothing more than rhetorical. Economists consider it largely artificial and solely driven by political motives: "The four countries have nothing to trade with each other" (Zhukov and Reznikova 2006: 9–10). Russia remains the most important trading partner for most GUAM members, despite all anti-Russian rhetoric (List 2006: 110).

---

11   This might, however, be helpful for solving budget problems (as hard currencies flow in) and giving a short-term impetus for the countries' economies, yet "it does not resolve the tasks of developing regionally-based processing industries, promoting trade in processed goods, facilitating the movement of labor and products across borders," by which their international competitiveness would be enhanced (Dadabaev 2007: 2).

Factors with Ambiguous Effects

Besides the aspects positively influencing regionalism or constituting obstacles, there are factors that affect regionalism depending on the respective context. According to the literature, power politics, identity politics and domestic factors can both facilitate and hinder regional integration.

Power politics For Russia, regional integration has for a long time been simply about upholding its regional dominance. During the early 1990s, Russia originally pushed for the formation of the CIS "as a principal means for obtaining greater control and power in the post-Soviet space" (Vinokurov 2007: 37).

Yet, it was the very same "great-power perspective" and its concentration on nation-state building that made Russia inhibit any further experiments with regional integration formats within the CIS (Kobrinskaya 2007: 20, Webber 1996: 15). Also, it undermined smaller member states' trust in Russia (Olcott et al. 1999: 11). Other member states took the CIS membership as a mere formality: Turkmenistan and Uzbekistan limited their participation "to the point of virtual boycott of the organization" (Molchanov 2009: 337). The fact that the CIS involved states both with pro-Russian and anti-Russian interests rendered the organization increasingly unable to develop further (Kuzio 2000).

Power politics also played an important role in the formation of Russian-centered economic integration schemes. A number of arrangements were, for instance, grounded on the strained relationship between Uzbekistan and other Central Asian states. Kazakhstan, Kyrgyzstan and Tajikistan fear Uzbekistan because of its capabilities and behavior that make it the local hegemon (Allison 2007: 260). Efforts to realize an exclusive Central Asian containment strategy through regional initiatives such as CAEU, CAEC or CACO were regarded as failed, leading to attempts to accommodate Uzbekistan within a larger framework. This explains why Russia is an integral part of groupings such as EurAsEC, providing a counterweight to the sub-regional hegemon Uzbekistan in a "bandwagoning" structure (Allison 2008: 192). The relatively small states of Kyrgyzstan and Tajikistan in particular have a keen interest in Russian involvement (Gleason et al. 2008). Russia, on the other side, was dissatisfied with the capabilities of CACO as a proper instrument of Russian influence in Central Asia (Allison 2007: 265, Vinokurov 2007: 34). It thus pushed for the creation of an integration structure in which Russia would be guaranteed to be the most powerful partner.[12] Within those integration structures, Russia obviously is by far the largest member state which creates an odd situation in which the other countries are concerned about Russia arbitrarily imposing its rules and eventually refuse to cede sovereignty which in turn hinders the integration process (Golovnin 2008: 42).

---

12 EurAsEC realizes this by allocating voting power in relation to financial contributions. Russia has thus 40 percent of voting power.

Ukraine in particular feared the influence of Russia, especially after the "Orange Revolution" in 2004 (Kembayev 2009: 124, Molchanov 2009: 340). The country was also worried about a possible incompatibility of the CES with an eventual integration into the European Union (Czakó 2005: 10, Nurmasheva 2008: 33, Vinokurov 2007: 34). In sum, the asymmetric power structure within Russian-centered economic integration frameworks is often held accountable for their failure.

Similar to economic integration, Russian-centered security frameworks such as CST and CSTO were driven by bandwagoning considerations. That explains why Central Asian states took part in CIS-based security integration that included Russia instead of creating their own schemes (Collins 2009: 275). They wanted Russia to maintain its presence, particularly in the face of the potential danger of China. At the same time, Central Asian states hoped to gain access to cheap Russian weaponry. For Russia, CST and CSTO were again mainly about yielding influence over the post-Soviet space (Allison 2007: 268). Thus, when the CST was to be prolonged for another five-year term in 1999, Azerbaijan, Georgia and Uzbekistan did not sign the treaty since they feared that Russia was merely interested in extending its sphere of influence (List 2006: 80). The three countries, together with Moldova and Ukraine, instead formed their own grouping, GUAM.

Central Asian dictatorships have also used regional integration to undermine the role of the United States and overall Western pro-democracy efforts in the region. A crucial actor for regionalism has been Kazakhstan that, in contrast to Uzbekistan, has used regional participation, not neutrality, to underscore its economic and political claims for leadership in Central Asia. As for CACO, an exclusively Central Asian organization until Russia joined in 2004, it has been argued that Russia's involvement was, again, driven by strategic interests in the region (Allison 2007: 265, Pomfret 2009: 54).

However, Central Asian regionalism is also fundamentally constrained by Russia's hegemonic ambitions (Allison 2007: 265, Collins 2009: 275, Czakó 2005: 7, Deyermond 2009: 159, Kubicek 1997). Overall, there is a polarizing pressure from Russia, China and the United States (Allison 2007: 275). Another key obstacle is the rivalry between Kazakhstan and Uzbekistan (Nurmasheva 2008: 28, Rakhimov 2010: 97).

All in all, power politics appear to play an important role in both Russian-centered and Central Asian regionalism. Interestingly, the anti-Russian organization of GUAM is driven by similar interests. Its member states wanted a rapprochement with the West, making GUAM an "anti-Russian geopolitical construct" (List 2006: 109, Clement et al. 2003: 53). For the smaller Central Asian states in particular, it was a way to balance the Russian influence (Collins 2009: 275). However, the interest in GUAM diminished after Uzbekistan withdrew from the organization in 2005 in another turn to reorient its integration policy (Nurmasheva 2008: 22).

Identity politics After the Soviet Union's demise, both political elites and the broad public experienced some kind of "post-imperial syndrome" (Kobrinskaya

2007: 15), expressing discontent with the present. Since most former Soviet republics were neither expected nor welcome in Europe, for them the CIS offered "an interstate community of belonging" (Molchanov 2009: 337). Moreover, there are some commonalities that make CIS states convenient partners for integration. This includes a common historical past, cultural similarities, the continued use of the Russian language as lingua franca as well as "close mentalities and similar business culture" (Zhukov and Reznikova 2006: 11, Nurmasheva 2008: 5). Since the early 1990s, Kazakh president Nazarbaev in particular has been very active pronouncing the idea of "Eurasianism," meaning a broad regional identity "with Central Asia and Russia at its heart" (Collins 2009: 259).

However, since the CIS was originally designed as a continuation of the Soviet Union, it was always in a way backwards-looking, not future-oriented, inhibiting the formation of a common identity (List 2006: 76). Moreover, there were neither common values nor shared interests as a basis for CIS integration. The CIS lacks an overarching idea or at least some kind of common threat with a potential to unite.

In contrast, the CES, with its member states Belarus, Ukraine and Russia, has the advantage of a shared history of being the industrial and political – and Slavic – core of the Soviet Union (Molchanov 2009: 338).

In Central Asia as well, identity politics have been used to push regional integration. Regional leaders have actively invoked a sense of regional identity, for instance by using semantic changes (Kubicek 1997). They thereby refer to the common Soviet legacy as well as to overlapping identities based on multilingualism, ethnic and kinship ties (Czakó 2005: 6, Primbetov 1996, Spechler 2002, Tolipov 2010, Ultanbaev 2003). Another common experience is Central Asia's treatment by the Soviet Union as a "unified economic space."

At the same time, however, Central Asian states have put considerable effort in the establishment of national identities and the feeling of belonging to a sovereign state. This has an adverse effect on any effort to form regional projects (Allison 2007: 274). Also, Central Asia is showing in fact fewer and fewer attributes of a homogenous region (Schrader 2010). Identity politics has also backed anti-Russian initiatives, by portraying Russia as "the other" (Kobrinskaya 2007: 19, Nurmasheva 2008: 21).

Domestic politics As early as in the 1990s, questions of domestic politics played into post-Soviet regionalism when Russia sabotaged integration efforts within the CIS on grounds of fiscal conservatism. A number of former Soviet republics were in general unwilling to cede sovereignty after only gaining it so recently (Olcott et al. 1999: 25). Later, the "color revolutions" and the subsequent regime changes in Georgia, Ukraine and Kyrgyzstan led to a reorientation of those countries' foreign policies – away from Russia and the Soviet past (Kobrinskaya 2007: 18).

The authoritarian nature of many post-Soviet governments also has explanatory power with regard to the changes in membership of Russian-centered economic integration schemes. Uzbekistan's rapprochement toward EurAsEC, culminating in its accession in 2005, was largely a move to secure Russian support for the regime of President Karimov (Allison 2007: 260, 267). The regime was under pressure after it shot at peaceful demonstrators in Andijan in May 2005. Most integration schemes, whether economic or security-oriented, can be seen as examples of regional structures that mainly fulfill a function of reinforcing regime security and legitimacy through a "virtual regionalism" (Allison 2008: 185) for authoritarian and neopatrimonial regimes. The state-centric integration process is largely controlled by authoritarian elites (Bohr 2004: 498). Rulers are often unwilling to agree to binding agreements (Collins 2009: 250) or inhibit their implementation. For them, economic regionalism – which implies economic liberalization – threatens personalist rule and patronage systems. If private sectors of the economy actually exist as they do in Kyrgyzstan and Kazakhstan, leaders "verbally promote regionalism so as to appease those communities" (Collins 2009: 251), leading to superficial and largely declarative regionalism (Allison 2007: 263).[13]

Regionalism, in particular in the security sphere, has also a domestic power dimension in that it allows authoritarian regimes to reassure each other. The Central Asian dictatorships have viewed security-oriented regionalism "as a mechanism for bolstering regime stability" (Collins 2009: 274). Through "defensive integration" (Allison 2007: 268) their power bases are not threatened. In fact, security cooperation can be a vehicle to oppress opposition threats (Collins 2009: 273).

Patterns of Explanations and Theories of Regional Integration

In the preceding section, the existing explanations for formation and failure of different initiatives were categorized. They will now be put into perspective by linking them to broader approaches to regionalism.

The CIS is associated with the requirement of responding to a double transition (political and economic); following this logic, it is possible to speak of *success as failure*, arguing that the CIS was no longer needed after completing the transition. The idea of a flawed *organizational set-up* seems to be relevant for an organization's failure in at least two cases (CIS and CST). These institutions either do not match cooperation problems or prove too weak to solve them. However, the structure of an organization might as well be intentionally built in a way that renders it weak or inefficient. Thus, other factors seem to drive this explanation – for instance, it may have to do with the "virtual regionalism" hypothesis or neo-realist assumptions.

At several points, the confusing picture of post-Soviet regional integration itself is mentioned as an explanation for weak outcomes. *Multilateral competition*

---

13 Overall, the degree of patrimonial control seems to influence the interest in regional integration. Less patrimonial control in Kyrgyzstan, Kazakhstan and Tajikistan means slightly more interest in regional integration whereas more control in Uzbekistan and Turkmenistan means less and no interest (Collins 2009: 272).

means that the sometimes redundant patterns of membership and competencies in different organizations become per se an inhibiting factor that is reinforcing itself (Fischer 2006). *Bilateral competition* which appears even more often has probably more to do with the hypocritical "virtual regionalism" which then means that states engage in regionalist initiatives pro forma while using bilateral channels to make substantial decisions.

Almost every regional organization is justified by *economic motives* and, as for its failure, has to be contrasted with the actual *economic preconditions*. International relations liberals have made a case for the idea of common economic interests as the backbone of regional integration (Doyle 1997). With regard to post-Soviet economic regionalism, processes of globalization are central factors, highlighted by the fear of becoming a "raw material outskirt." This is "new regionalism par excellence" (Molchanov 2009: 345) since it fits a global trend in which countries seek to implement economic regionalism at all costs in order not to lose out in the global competition. It seems that while in the beginning there is usually some enthusiasm for a project of economic regionalism, this vanishes as soon as unfavorable economic preconditions make it increasingly difficult to proceed. Again, more power-related factors may even better explain the subsequent reluctance in integration.

About half of the regional integration projects owe their existence at least partly to the idea of solving *common problems* collectively. This interpretation belongs to a family of neo-functionalist approaches that have been at the forefront of research on (Western European) regional integration (Schmitter 2004). The concept behind this is that states integrate in limited functional or technical areas, thereby triggering a self-sustaining spillover dynamic that leads to integration in neighboring areas. However, the whole mechanism relies on the pressure of interest groups and public opinion as well as the socialization of elites. That is why for post-Soviet Eurasia the approach is "less applicable" (Bohr 2004: 499). Authoritarian regimes that suppress the development of civil society prevent regionalization processes from below.

Another systemic theory – neorealism – has probably the greatest explanatory value for our cases. *Power politics* as explanation for formation and failure feature in every category of post-Soviet integration. Neorealism is about the "external configurations of power, the dynamics of power-political competition, and the constraining role of the international political system as a whole" (Hurrell 1995: 47). A number of mechanisms of forming alliances can be subsumed under this category, particularly the formation of alliances "to counter the power of another state or group of states within or outside the region" (Söderbaum 2005: 224): a local hegemon can use regional groupings to advance its interests as in the cases of Russian-centered economic and security integration. For smaller states, the participation can be beneficial as a form of bandwagoning, thereby assuring their own security. This explains for instance why the Central Asian states gave up on exclusive integration strategies and got Russia back involved. It also had to do with an interest to contain a local hegemon: EurAsEC balances the interests of smaller Central Asian states, Uzbekistan and Russia. The Shanghai Cooperation Organization (SCO) serves the same purpose for the regional powers of Russia and China. Regional groupings also emerge in response to a hegemon as was attempted with anti-Russian GUAM.

Neorealist power politics can also explain why organizations fail. Since the states' own interests are always the ultimate consideration, they frequently abandon regionalist initiatives they previously endorsed as soon as regionalism cedes to serve their interests. However, a power politics approach has difficulties explaining why there are so many integration schemes that are neither effective nor substantially endowed with competencies.

Identity politics, constructivist or *culturalist approaches* appear quite frequently throughout the analysis, yet they seem to play a minor role. Constructivist notions focus on "*regional awareness* and regional identity, on the shared sense of belonging to a particular regional community, and on what has been called 'cognitive regionalism'" (Hurrell 1995: 64). Politics of identity, common history and ideology have been subsumed under constructivist notions (Higgott 1998). These factors mainly serve as rhetorical justifications of regionalism but their role in actually driving regional integration is doubtful.

Finally, the influence of *domestic politics* has been included in most patterns of explanation. In the theoretical debate about regionalism, the idea to include domestic factors has been part of a group of approaches that criticize neorealist and other systemic theories (Mansfield and Milner 1999). It points to "the importance of domestic factors and the impact of democracy and democratization" (Hurrell 1995: 68). In turn, the authoritarian nature of a regime does influence its position toward regional integration. This factor has been important, adding explanations for the failure and formation of almost every case. Authoritarian regimes refuse to participate in substantial regional integration attempts since they endanger neopatrimonial power bases. The proliferation of initiatives is then a sign of a superficial "virtual regionalism" which can award legitimacy to authoritarian leaders.

Conclusion

This chapter started out with an empirical puzzle: despite only recently gaining independent statehood, the Soviet successor states have been very active in forming and participating in regional integration schemes during the last 20 years. Moreover, these attempts by and large proved inefficient or were abandoned entirely. The puzzle of the "ephemeral nature of many regional arrangements" (Pomfret 2009: 62) has certainly not been solved yet. However, a number of explanations yielded interesting and plausible results. Some approaches were also successfully applied to almost all of the cases under examination. It seems that, first and foremost, neorealist explanations and domestic politics approaches can best account for the dynamics of post-Soviet regional integration. Explanations regarding economic gains, common problems as well as constructivist or culturalist notions seem less applicable.

This chapter has taken a focus on individual organizations after categorizing them based on their purpose and involved actors. Alternatively, one could take the perspective of individual countries. Comparing their motives over time and in different organizations could possibly lead to a more accurate analysis of post-Soviet regionalism. After all, it may be that the best fitting model regarding the mechanisms of post-Soviet regional integration is a very parsimonious one that can, for instance, limit itself to one theoretical approach. For now, it is difficult to foresee such a model. As a starting point, however, this chapter has provided an overview of the broad range of explanatory factors that can be found throughout the literature.

References

Allison, R. 2007. Blockaden und Anreize. Autoritarismus und regionale Kooperation. *Osteuropa*, 57(8–9), 257–275.
Allison, R. 2008. Virtual Regionalism, Regional Structures and Regime Security in Central Asia. *Central Asian Survey*, 27(2), 185–202.
Balayan, O. M. 1996. *Institutionelle Struktur der Wirtschaftsintegration in der Gemeinschaft Unabhängiger Staaten (GUS). Eine rechtliche Untersuchung der Organstruktur der GUS im Vergleich zur Europäischen Gemeinschaft.* Berlin, Duncker & Humboldt.
Bohr, A. 2004. Regionalism in Central Asia: New Geopolitics, Old Regional Order. *International Affairs*, 80(3), 485–502.
Börzel, T. A. 2005. Mind the Gap! European Integration between Level and Scope. *Journal of European Public Policy*, 12(2), 217–236.
Byrd, W., Raiser, M. and Dobronogov, A. 2006. Economic Cooperation in the Wider Central Asia Region. *World Bank Working Paper No. 75*. Washington, DC: World Bank.
Church, G. J., Carney, J., Mader, W. and McAllister, J. F. O. 1991. The End of the U.S.S.R. *TIME Magazine*, 18–31.
Clement, H., Reppegather, A. and Troschke, M. 2003. Entwicklung der Handelsbeziehungen und handelspolitischen Regelungen zwischen den GUS-Staaten und ihre Rückwirkungen auf den Ost-West-Handel. *Working Paper Nr. 246*. München: Osteuropa-Institut.
Collins, K. 2009. Economic and Security Regionalism among Patrimonial Authoritarian Regimes: The Case of Central Asia. *Europe-Asia Studies*, 61(2), 249–281.
Czakó, V. 2005. The Prospects and Problems of Central Asian Integration. *ICEG EC Opinion VI*. Budapest: International Center for Economic Growth – European Center.

Dadabaev, T. 2007. Central Asian Regional Integration: Between Reality and Myth. *CACI Analyst 05/02/2007*. Washington, DC: Central Asia-Caucasus Institute.

Deyermond, R. 2009. Matrioshka Hegemony? Multi-levelled Hegemonic Competition and Security in Post-Soviet Central Asia. *Review of International Studies*, 35(1), 151–173.

Doyle, M. W. 1997. *Ways of War and Peace: Realism, Liberalism, and Socialism*. New York: W. W. Norton.

Fischer, S. 2006. Integrationsprozesse im post-sowjetischen Raum: Voraussetzungen, Erwartungen und Potenziale. *Internationale Politik und Gesellschaft*, 1, 134–149.

Fischer, S. 2007. Die russische Politik gegenüber der Ukraine und Weißrussland. *Aus Politik und Zeitgeschichte* (8–9), 16–23.

Freire, M. R. 2009. Russian Policy in Central Asia: Supporting, Balancing, Coercing or Imposing? *Asian Perspective*, 33(2), 125–149.

Geyikdagi, N. V. 2005. Regional Integration in Central Asia. *Journal of Asia-Pacific Business*, 6(4), 61–74.

Gleason, G. 2001. Inter-State Cooperation in Central Asia from the CIS to the Shanghai Forum. *Europe-Asia Studies*, 53(7), 1077–1095.

Gleason, G., Kerimbekova, A. and Kozhirova, S. 2008. Realism and the Small State: Evidence from Kyrgyzstan. *International Politics*, 45(1), 40–51.

Golovnin, M. 2008. Opportunities and Obstacles to EurAsEC Integration, in *Eurasian Integration Yearbook 2008*, edited by E. Vinokurov. Almaty: Eurasian Development Bank, 38–53.

Green, D. J. 2003. Regional Co-operation Policies in Central Asia. *Journal of International Development*, 13(8), 1151–1164.

Grinberg, R. 2003. Integration und Desintegration im postsowjetischen Wirtschaftsraum, in *Regionale Integration und Osterweiterung der Europäischen Union,* edited by D. Cassel and P. J. J. Welfens. Stuttgart: Lucius & Lucius, 339–347.

Grinberg, R. and Kosikova, L. 1997. *Rußland und die GUS: Auf der Suche nach einem neuen Modell wirtschaftlicher Zusammenarbeit*. Köln: Bundesinstitut für ostwissenschaftliche und internationale Studien.

Higgott, R. 1998. The International Political Economy of Regionalism: The Asia–Pacific and Europe Compared, in *Regionalism and Global Economic Integration: Europe, Asia, and the Americas*, edited by W. D. Coleman and G. R. D. Underhill. London: Routledge, 42–67.

Hurrell, A. 1995. Regionalism in Theoretical Perspective, in *Regionalism in World Politics. Regional Organization and International Order*, edited by L. Fawcett and A. Hurrell. Oxford: Oxford University Press, 37–73.

Karaev, Z. 2005. Border Disputes and Regional Integration in Central Asia. *Harvard Asia Quarterly*, 19(4), 1–15.

Kazantsev, A. 2008. Russian Policy in Central Asia and the Caspian Sea Region. *Europe-Asia Studies*, 60(6), 1073–1088.

Kembayev, Z. 2009. *Legal Aspects of the Regional Integration Processes in the Post-Soviet Area*. Berlin and Heidelberg: Springer.

Kobrinskaya, I. 2007. The Post-Soviet Space: From the USSR to the Commonwealth of Independent States and Beyond, in *The CIS, the EU and Russia. The Challenges of Integration*, edited by K. Malfliet, L. Verpoest and E. Vinokurov. Basingstoke: Palgrave Macmillan, 13–21.

Kubicek, P. 1997. Regionalism, Nationalism and Realpolitik in Central Asia. *Europe-Asia Studies*, 49(4), 637–655.

Kubicek, P. 2009. The Commonwealth of Independent States: An Example of Failed Regionalism? *Review of International Studies*, 35(S1), 237–256.

Kuzio, T. 2000. Geopolitical Pluralism in the CIS: The Emergence of GUUAM. *European Security*, 9(2), 81–114.

Libman, A. 2007. Regionalisation and Regionalism in the Post-Soviet Space: Current Status and Implications for Institutional Development. *Europe-Asia Studies*, 59(3), 401–430.

Libman, A. and Vinokurov, E. 2010. Is it Really Different? Patterns of Regionalization in the Post-Soviet Central Asia. *MPRA Working Paper No. 21062*.

List, D. 2006. *Regionale Kooperation in Zentralasien. Hindernisse und Möglichkeiten*. Frankfurt am Main: Peter Lang.

Mansfield, E. and Milner, H. 1999. The New Wave of Regionalism. *International Organization*, 53(3), 589–627.

Mattli, W. 1999. *The Logic of Regional Integration. Europe and beyond*. Cambridge: Cambridge University Press.

Macfarlane, S. N. 2004. The United States and Regionalism in Central Asia. *International Affairs*, 80(3), 447–461.

Metcalf, L. K. 1997. The (Re)Emergence of Regional Economic Integration in the Former Soviet Union. *Political Research Quarterly*, 50(3), 529–549.

Molchanov, M. A. 2009. Regionalism in Eurasia, in *Globalization and Security. An Encyclopedia*, edited by G. H. Fagan and R. Munck. Santa Barbara: Praeger Security International.

Muzafarov, D. R. 2001. Problems of Economic Integration in Central Asia. Economic Developments and Reforms in Cooperation Partner Countries: The Interrelationship between Regional Economic Cooperation, Security and Stability. *NATO Colloquium in Bucharest*. Bucharest.

Nikitin, A. 2007. The End of the "Post-Soviet Space". The Changing Geopolitical Orientations of the Newly Independent States. *Russia and Eurasia Briefing Paper 07/01*. London: Chatham House.

Nurmasheva, S. 2008. *Die Eurasec-Staaten im Spannungsfeld zwischen regionaler und multilateraler Integration*. Bamberg: Difo-Druck.

Olcott, M. B., Åslund, A. and Garnett, S. W. 1999. *Getting It Wrong. Regional Cooperation and the Commonwealth of Independent States*. Washington, DC, Carnegie Endowment for International Peace.

Pomfret, R. 2009. Regional Integration in Central Asia. *Economic Change and Restructuring*, 42(1–2), 47–68.
Primbetov, S. 1996. Central Asia. Prospects for Regional Integration, in *Economic Transition in Russia and the New States of Eurasia*, edited by B. Kaminski. Armonk and London: M. E. Sharpe, 159–170.
Rakhimov, M. 2010. Internal and External Dynamics of Regional Cooperation in Central Asia. *Journal of Eurasian Studies*, 1(2), 95–101.
Rakhmatullina, G. 2007. Central Asia: Economic Cooperation Potential. *Central Asia and the Caucasus*, 48(6), 136–142.
Schmitter, P. C. 2004. Neo-Neofunctionalism, in *European Integration Theory*, edited by A. Wiener and T. Diez. Oxford: Oxford University Press, 45–74.
Schmitz, A. 2008. Partner aus Kalkül. Russische Politik in Zentralasien. *SWP-Studie 2008/S 05*. Berlin: Stiftung Wissenschaft und Politik.
Schrader, H. 2010. Entwicklungsmodelle für und Entwicklungen in Zentralasien. *Arbeitsbericht Nr. 58*. Magdeburg: Otto von Guericke Universität Magdeburg.
Smith, G., Law, V., Wilson, A., Bohr, A. and Allworth, E. 1998. *Nation-building in the Post-Soviet Borderlands. The Politics of National Identities*. Cambridge: Cambridge University Press.
Smith, H. 2009. Russian Foreign Policy, Regional Cooperation and Northern Relations, in *The New Northern Dimension of the European Neighbourhood*, edited by P. Aalto, H. Blakkisrud and H. Smith. Brussels: Center for European Studies, 19–35.
Söderbaum, F. 2005. The International Political Economy of Regionalism, in *Globalising International Political Economy*, edited by N. Philips. Basingstoke: Palgrave, 221–245.
Spechler, M. C. 2000. Regional Cooperation in Central Asia: Promises and More Promises. *Praxis – The Fletcher Journal of Development Studies*, 16, 1–11.
Spechler, M. C. 2002. Regional Cooperation in Central Asia. *Problems of Post-Communism*, 49(6), 42–47.
Suzdaltsev, A. 2010. Politics Ahead of the Economy. Risks and Prospects of the EurAsEC Customs Union. *Russia in Global Affairs*, 8(1), 84–94.
Tolipov, F. 2010. Geopolitical Stipulation of Central Asian Integration. *Strategic Analysis*, 34(1), 104–113.
Torjesen, S. 2007. *Understanding Regional Co-operation in Central Asia, 1991–2004*. PhD dissertation. Oxford: University of Oxford.
Ultanbaev, R. 2003. Eurasian Economic Community: Thorny Path of Development. *Central Asia and the Caucasus*, 21(3), 129–139.
Vinokurov, E. 2007. Russian Approaches to Integration on the Post-Soviet Space in the 2000s, in *The EU, the CIS, and Russia: The Challenges of Integration*, edited by K. Malfliet, L. Verpoest and E. Vinokurov. Basingstoke: Palgrave Macmillan, 22–46.
Webber, M. 1996. *The International Politics of Russia and the Successor States*. Manchester: Manchester University Press.

Willerton, J. P. and Beznosov, M. A. 2007. Russia's Pursuit of its Eurasian Security Interests: Weighing the CIS and Alternative Bilateral-Multilateral Arrangements, in *The EU, the CIS, and Russia: The Challenges of Integration*, edited by K. Malfliet, L. Verpoest and E. Vinokurov. Basingstoke: Palgrave Macmillan, 47–70.

World Bank. 2011. *Q&As on Regional Integration in Africa*. [Online]. Available at: http://go.worldbank.org/N4QGVVAYO0 [accessed: April 27, 2011].

Zhalimbetova, R. and Gleason, G. 2001. Eurasian Economic Community (EEC) comes into being. *CACI Analyst*, June 20.

Zhukov, S. and Reznikova, O. 2006. Economic Interaction in the Post-Soviet Space. *The Caucus and Globalization*, 1(1), 1–14.

Chapter 3
Joining the Neighbors: The Accessions to ASEAN in the 1990s

Niklas Aschhoff

Introduction

In the period from 1995 to 1999, Cambodia, Laos, Myanmar, and Vietnam (CLMV) joined the Association of Southeast Asian Nations (ASEAN) and increased its size to 10 members. Former members of the Soviet bloc (Vietnam, Laos, and Cambodia), as well as the highly repressive authoritarian regime of Myanmar, are now part of a regional organization (RO), founded, at least implicitly, as a capitalist and pro-Western association in 1967.

Before 1990 some CLMV states had refused accession to ASEAN several times. This position changed completely in the mid-1990s. Based on this turn, the central research question of this chapter is as follows: why did CLMV join ASEAN in the 1990s, and not earlier?

This question will be answered by taking into account a theoretical background derived from the accessions of several states to the European Union (EU), especially the Central and Eastern European Countries (CEEC). The theoretical framework used in this chapter, thus, also seeks to address the question whether there are common patterns in the motivations of states to join an RO. As such, this chapter is a contribution to research on the accessions to ROs, an area of research that has scarcely been studied outside the EU context.

The central part of this chapter analyzes the accessions of CLMV to ASEAN based on three dimensions: general systemic conditions, organization-specific systemic conditions, and positional characteristics of states outside the RO. The end of the Cold War was a crucial systemic condition that enabled CLMV to cooperate with capitalist states and to seek membership. Their main motivations to join ASEAN were their expectations of receiving more foreign investments particularly from states outside ASEAN and to enhance their standing in international relations.

Why Countries (want to) Join Regional Organizations: Assumptions for the CLMV Case

The primary interest of this chapter is the analysis of countries' preference formation. Several theories of integration, in particular (neo)functionalism, transactionalism, and federalism, have originally been established to explain the deepening of integration once a community has been formed, yet were insufficient for the analysis of the formation of and accession to a regional organization. Even though the element of geographic expansion has been added to theory and research, the analysis of enlargement still has a very strong focus on the EU (Gstöhl 1996: 9–10, Schimmelfennig and Sedelmeier 2002).

Here, for the analysis of accessions to ASEAN, a rationalist approach is applied. According to rationalist theory, states join international organizations in order to pursue their interests more efficiently (Schimmelfennig and Sedelmeier 2002: 509). Their decision to join a group or not is informed by individual costs and benefits resulting from accession (Lamy 2006, Moravcsik and Vachudova 2003). Within rationalist theory, theoretical assumptions from neo-liberalism and neo-realism will be used with an emphasis on the former. Neo-liberalism is especially useful to explain economic cooperation. Neo-realism focuses on security interests and counterbalancing strong regional powers.

Schimmelfennig and Sedelmeier (2002: 512) differentiate among four "sources of enlargement preferences" of states outside an RO. The following three sources are analyzed:

1. general systemic conditions;
2. organization-specific systemic conditions; and
3. positional characteristics of states outside the RO.

The fourth source (sub-systemic conditions and domestic structures) is excluded on the grounds that this analytical category was primarily designed to study the behavior of different social actors in Western liberal democracies.

General Systemic Conditions

General systemic conditions are global changes that have impacts on single states. They include cardinal changes in the world economy, in technology, or the security environment. For instance, the end of the East–West conflict in 1990 meant a significant change in the global economic and security-political conditions. This change removed an obstacle for many neutral or Soviet-controlled states which could then join the EU. Finland, for example, oriented itself quickly toward the EU in terms of economic relations and security after the breakdown of the Soviet Union (Jenssen et al. 1998: 311).[1]

The systemic changes of 1990 could be considered a driving force for regional integration in at least two respects. Firstly, a large range of states were enabled to join the EU. For the formerly communist CEEC that joined the EU in 2004

---

1 Trade figures clarify the declining importance of the Soviet Union/Russia: while in the mid-1980s about 26 percent of all Finnish exports went to the Soviet Union, Russia (although not representing the whole USSR, of course) made up only 3 percent of Finnish trade in 1992. The EU's share of Finland's trade increased simultaneously (Finland 2010).

and 2007 the breakdown of the Soviet Union was a necessary precondition. In general, a substantial increase in institutionalized regional cooperation has taken place since the 1990s as a result of the end of the East–West conflict.

Secondly, the emergence of new regionalisms, in turn, induces a new systematic condition for accession: the creation of free trade zones, customs unions, and the integration of economies are felt in other parts of the world which gives states an incentive to create or join an RO. This holds for the EU as well as for ASEAN. The denationalization of the economy and the rise and expansion of ROs can thus be considered as two related phenomena that influence states to seek membership in an RO (Christiansen 2006: 591, 594, Schimmelfennig and Sedelmeier 2002: 512).

Organization-Specific Systemic Conditions

In contrast to general systemic conditions that stem from the global context, each RO exerts some external effects on, mostly neighboring, non-members. Especially negative externalities, such as trade and investment diversion, created by economic integration may evoke the need of outsiders to join this group. It can be assumed that the higher the level of economic integration, the more severe the negative externalities for outsiders. Organization-specific systemic conditions are part of what Mattli (1999) has called the demand side of regional integration. Demand in this context means the support for accession expressed by a country outside an organization in order to minimize negative externalities resulting from this group.[2]

Thus, a key motivation of the CEEC in favor of accession was to avoid the "uncertain and potentially catastrophic costs of being left behind as others move forward" (Moravcsik and Vachudova 2003: 43). These negative externalities are particularly high for former and current states bordering on the EU due to the Union's high degree of market integration. ASEAN-specific systemic conditions are operationalized by figures for trade and foreign direct investment (FDI) respectively.

Positional Characteristics of States Outside the RO

Beyond systematic conditions, there are other important reasons that influence a country's choice in favor of membership in an RO. Schimmelfennig and Sedelmeier (2002: 512) call them the positional characteristics of states. These are characteristics of single countries due to which accession becomes particularly desirable. Mostly related to economic gains, there are several different positional characteristics to each country.

The CEEC, for example, expected EU membership to be a means to re-integration into the world economy and economic restructuring (Bieler 2002: 588). They gained full market access which was anticipated to result in more trade

---

2   For an application of Mattli's framework to regional integration in MERCOSUR, see Chapter 4, this volume.

and investment. Furthermore, they could hope for budgetary receipts and transfers from EU funds as well as technical assistance by the EU (Bárta and Richter 1996: 18, Mattli and Plümper 2002: 557).

Another motivation to join ROs is the opportunity to gain influence in decision-making. Being part of a globally influential organization might boost a country's influence in international relations. For the CEEC, EU membership also meant a way out of the Russian sphere of influence and, thus, an enhancement of their sovereignty (Bieler 2002: 588, Holzinger et al. 2005: 71, Schimmelfennig and Sedelmeier 2002: 520). Yet, as far as the issue of sovereignty is concerned, there are also strong arguments against accession. In particular, a suspected loss of national sovereignty is the most prominent argument of accession opponents.[3] For the context of accession to the EU, this fear is to a large part due to the strict criteria that applicants have to fulfill, and the large adjustment costs these criteria translate into (Schimmelfennig and Sedelmeier 2002: 512).[4] The following section shows that these costs were considerably lower for states that joined ASEAN.

A further important positional characteristic of states in favor of accession is to benefit from membership in an RO through learning from incumbent member states, when "modernizing" economic and political systems. Again, this was an important argument for the CEEC to join the EU (Jacoby 2004). In some respects, security also played a role in the accessions of the CEEC. According to realist intergovernmentalism, EU membership was an attempt to, firstly, counterbalance Russia and, secondly, prevent a reassertion of Russian influence in the future (Bárta and Richter 1996: 16, Baun 2000: 10, Holzinger et al. 2005: 71).

Why CLMV Joined ASEAN in the 1990s, and Not Earlier

ASEAN is one of the oldest regional associations in the developing world. Within Southeast Asia, ASEAN is also the only regional association that has continued to exist from the Cold War period until today. In terms of size, ASEAN has become a heavyweight among ROs, with its 10 member countries having a total population of about 580 million.[5]

When ASEAN was founded, security aspects and the perception of a common threat played an important role. As a group of capitalist states in a volatile region surrounded by several communist states, security was an important issue for

---

3 Loss of sovereignty was the cardinal "contra" argument in the course of the debate on accession of the Nordic countries (Jenssen et al. 1998: 310). Sweden and Austria perceived membership to be incompatible with their status as neutral states (Bieler 2002: 576).

4 These criteria include considerable measures of liberalization and deregulation in the context of the acquis communautaire as well as the fulfillment of the Copenhagen criteria.

5 These are Indonesia, Malaysia, the Philippines, Singapore, Thailand, Brunei, Cambodia, Laos, Myanmar, and Vietnam.

ASEAN's founding members Indonesia, Malaysia, the Philippines, Singapore, and Thailand. In the first years, integration succeeded through promoting socio-economic development, strengthening stability and the relations between the member states as well as limiting the military influence of potential aggressors (Cockerham 2010: 171, Narine 2002). In the post-communist world order, circumstances changed for ASEAN. Economic cooperation became a priority in a period of increased global competition and regionalization taking place in several parts of the world (Narine 2002: 101, Witczynska 2009: 60).

It should be noted, however, that ASEAN never intended to be a supranational organization. In contrast, ASEAN members have openly declared their "aversion to European-style centralized bureaucracies and supranational entities" (Nesadurai 2008: 228). Instead of actively pooling sovereignty, ASEAN is rather seen as a forum to enhance the member states' national sovereignty (Narine 2002: 204).

The wave of ASEAN's expansion started with Vietnam's admission in 1995 followed by Myanmar in 1997 and Cambodia and Laos in 1999. The largest and most populous of all countries that joined ASEAN in the 1990s is Vietnam. The country's accession to ASEAN can be regarded as a considerable achievement when taking into account the security threat Vietnam posed to the association in the 1970s and 1980s. Overall, the integration of the former communist states into ASEAN proceeded relatively smoothly. Only Cambodia's membership of ASEAN was postponed for several months due to domestic political struggles. The most surprising and most disputed accession, however, was the case of Myanmar, a country governed by an oppressive military regime since 1990. During the Cold War, Myanmar had remained strategically neutral while it maintained good relations with China (McCarthy 2008: 913–915).

The expansion created a group of states that is today much larger than before in terms of geography and population. In terms of political systems, wealth, and economic structures, however, ASEAN has also become much more heterogeneous: the four new members are all more or less authoritarian states and are less developed than the original member states (Cockerham 2010: 176, Narine 2002: 101). The accession of CLMV has extended ASEAN's population by 36 percent, while it increased its aggregate wealth by only 4–5 percent (Guyot 1998: 191). The following section analyses the motivations of CLMV to join ASEAN in the 1990s, and not earlier, based on the three sources of integration mentioned above.

General Systemic Conditions

The general systemic conditions in the context of CLMV's accession to ASEAN are very similar to those encountered by the CEEC and formerly neutral states in the EU. Vietnam and Laos were strictly bound to their communist allies, the Soviet Union as well as China. While Myanmar had been a non-aligned state during the Cold War, it was always very committed to keeping good relations with China. As China suspected ASEAN to be an American-dominated organization, accession was not an option for Myanmar either. Apart from the strong geopolitical influences of the Soviet Union and China, the strong economic ties of CLMV with these two powers made any approach toward ASEAN unnecessary and would have been counterproductive (Economywatch 2011).

The importance of the end of the Cold War as a systemic condition that enabled CLMV's accession to ASEAN in the 1990s becomes clear when taking into account that Myanmar, Cambodia and Vietnam had refused ASEAN membership several times prior to 1990. Myanmar and Cambodia were invited to join the association already in the course of its establishment in 1967, but refused, however, as they were afraid of offending China as ASEAN members had not recognized the Chinese government. In particular Myanmar, which had traditionally close economic and strategic ties based on geographic proximity, did not want to provoke its big neighbor (McCarthy 2008: 915).

ASEAN's invitation to Vietnam after the communist victory in 1975 may have been an attempt to strengthen the association's neutrality. Vietnam, however, refused membership due to the association's perceived capitalist and pro-American bias (Anwar 2001: 27–28). For North Vietnam, ASEAN was a political fraud and part of the American policy of containment. On these grounds not only Vietnam but also Laos refused the observer status and adherence to the Treaty of Amity and Cooperation (TAC) (Emmers 2005: 72). Whereas diplomatic relations remained difficult, economic cooperation between Vietnam and ASEAN improved in the 1980s. Already at this time, Vietnam openly indicated its desire to eventually become an ASEAN member (Sutherland 2009: 328). In contrast, Laos continued to regard ASEAN with hostility until during the 1980s. Consequently, Laos' rapprochement toward ASEAN in the 1990s was initially much more hesitant than Vietnam's (Emmers 2005: 73).

In contrast to Vietnam and Laos, Cambodia was most of all concerned about neutrality as regards accession to ASEAN. After independence in 1953, King Norodom Sihanouk had adopted a foreign policy of non-alignment. Though not communist, the country rejected ASEAN membership in 1967 as it considered the RO to be pro-American and a danger to the country's neutrality (Emmers 2005: 73). Both the Khmer Rouge and the regime put into place by Vietnam after its invasion continued Cambodia's hostile stance toward ASEAN. The formation of a new coalition government after the general elections in 1993 led to a change in the country's foreign policy which was intended to bring the country out of its isolation. After improving relations with Vietnam, Laos, and Thailand, Cambodia expressed the desire to join ASEAN by signing the TAC in 1995 (Emmers 2005: 74).

The collapse of the Soviet Union translated into new opportunities for regional association in the 1990s. Furthermore, in order to prevent isolation in this period as Soviet economic support vanished, CLMV had to look elsewhere for trade and investment (Emmers 2005: 74). Thus, the fading East–West antagonism certainly had a strong impact on CLMV to approach ASEAN. For CLMV, not only the collapse of the Soviet Union was crucial. Moreover, softened attitudes of China as a key player in the region toward ASEAN dispelled in particular Myanmar's and Cambodia's worries of poisoning relations with the big power (Langhammer 2001: 102, McCarthy 2008: 915–916). By joining ASEAN, the Indochinese states avoided to be isolated in a "world of regions" as Katzenstein (2005) has characterized the contemporary order.

It can be argued that these systemic changes constitute a decisive condition for CLMV to join ASEAN. For Vietnam, accession was part of a wider strategy in response to the collapse of communism (Sutherland 2009: 328). The Soviet Union and the non-aligned states were its main trading partners until the late 1980s and the collapse of the Soviet Union was a key factor for Vietnam to direct trade relations toward Asian countries (Nguyen and Ezaki 2005: 200). A very supportive factor for Vietnam's relatively quick readiness to join ASEAN was the country's internal reform process starting in 1986.[6] These reforms created favorable conditions for ASEAN members and other states to trade with and invest in the country as well as for further political and economic reforms (Nguyen and Luan 2001). For instance, Vietnam also enhanced its relations with China in the course of its internal reforms (Sutherland 2009: 328).

Similar to Vietnam, Laos lost a major economic supporter after the breakdown of the Soviet Union and particularly improved its relations with China and Thailand which paved the way for ASEAN accession. However, little can be said about the immediate impact of the communist breakdown on Cambodia's and Myanmar's intention to join ASEAN. In the case of Myanmar, the strong advancement of China–ASEAN relations in the 1990s enabled the country's membership (McCarthy 2008: 916–917). General systemic conditions have played an important role in CLMV's accession to ASEAN. In the case of Vietnam and Laos the collapse of world communism as a general systemic condition has been crucial. This cannot be confirmed for Myanmar and Cambodia, however.

Organization-Specific Systemic Conditions

According to organization-specific systemic conditions and according to Mattli's demand side conditions, CLMV could not afford to stay outside ASEAN due to the negative externalities the association produced for these states, such as trade and FDI diversion. Severino (2007: 36) supports this view by stating that CLMV realized they could not afford to be successful in the international economy outside an RO.

In accordance with this assumption, it would be plausible that, first of all, intra-ASEAN trade and the trade of CLMV with ASEAN had strongly increased in the course of accession. This rise would indicate that there was indeed an urgent need to join. However, although intra-ASEAN trade has grown faster than ASEAN's trade with the rest of the world and despite the economic strength of ASEAN economies in the 1990s, the size of intra-ASEAN trade remained low and had only little impact

---

6 The so-called Doi Moi initiated the transition of the Vietnamese economy from central planning into a market-oriented economy (Emmers 2005: 73).

on the member states' economic developments. After the implementation of the ASEAN Free Trade Area (AFTA) in 1992, intra-ASEAN trade increased only from 20 to 25 percent. In 2008, it diminished to about 21 percent again. Hence, it is considerable lower than trade within other regional organizations (Kahler 2000, Katzenstein 2005, Nesadurai 2008, UN ESCAP 2009: 9).

While organization-specific systemic conditions as an explanation for accession may in fact hold for Laos and Myanmar which have a high share of trade with ASEAN of 83.7 and 51.6 percent respectively, they do not hold for Vietnam and Cambodia with 17.6 and 23.6 percent respectively (see Figure 3.1).

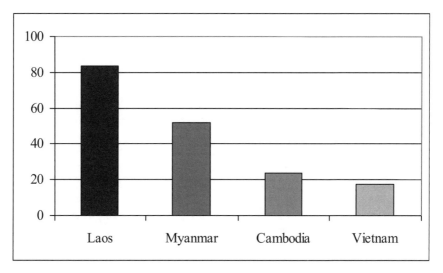

Figure 3.1 CLMV's share of trade with ASEAN in percent for 2009
Source: Own presentation based on data from ASEAN (ASEAN Statistics 2010).

In terms of FDI an overall low dependence on intra-ASEAN investments is even clearer. While 11.2 percent of all FDI in ASEAN comes from other ASEAN countries, this percentage is only 5.6 for Vietnam and 3.4 for Myanmar. Even 32.2 and 18 percent for Cambodia and Laos respectively do not show a high dependency on intra-ASEAN FDI (data for 2009 from ASEAN 2011). Taken together, the organization-specific systemic conditions that leave outsiders no alternative but to join due to negative externalities caused by the RO are only partially present in the case of CLMV. They can only be found as regards Laos' and Myanmar's relatively high trade dependence with other ASEAN countries. Particularly Vietnam, the largest of the CLMV countries, shows a low share of common trade and FDI with ASEAN. Although the aspect of ASEAN-related systemic conditions should not be rejected completely here, there must be other reasons for the accessions of CLMV.

Accordingly, Mattli's very generalizing view of a general logic on regional integration is rejected by a number of scholars dealing with ASEAN (Barichello et al. 2003, Emmers 2005, Langhammer 2001, Mirza and Giroud 2004, Narine 2002, Nguyen and Luan 2001, Sutherland 2009). They highlight the uniqueness of each regional integration process as well as the special conditions under which CLMV joined ASEAN. In their perception, the positional characteristics of states, especially the interests and motivations of national leaders, have been crucial for the decision in favor of accession.

Positional Characteristics of States

Apart from systemic conditions, we find a variety of positional characteristics of CLMV that encouraged support for ASEAN membership. Besides external reasons for accession, there are a number of individual incentives that motivated the countries to join ASEAN. Broadly speaking, CLMV hoped that accession would enhance their economic situation. Expectations as regards accession to ASEAN are very much based on the strong developments and achievements of the original ASEAN members, especially in economic terms. In the 1990s, CLMV expected to benefit from ASEAN membership in a similar way (Emmers 2005: 75). In particular, the greater access to world markets played a significant role in the countries' decision to become members of the regional organization. According to Barichello et al. (2003: 674), CLMV followed the "strong consensus among economists that developing countries ... have a great deal to gain from trade liberalization." Another major incentive for CLMV to join ASEAN was the assumption to benefit from more foreign investments. In particular, states hoped that in a stable and peaceful institutional environment conditions for external investors would improve (Emmers 2005: 75, Nguyen and Luan 2001: 189). Only as a less important consideration, CLMV hoped to receive increased investments from other ASEAN member states (Mirza and Giroud 2004: 233–234). In opposition to the CEEC, CLMV thus hoped for strong economic ties mainly with partners outside ASEAN. This is in line with the principle objective of AFTA to make ASEAN an attractive investment area rather than a promoter of intra-regional trade (Thongpakde 2001: 75).

The level of intra-ASEAN trade and FDI indeed remains relatively low. Intra-regional trade added up to only about 25 percent in 2006. The average FDI inflows coming from ASEAN countries were only 15 percent in the period of 2007 until 2009, whereas the EU contributed more than 20 percent of FDI over this period (ASEAN 2011). Between 1995 and 2008 total FDI inflows have even doubled, confirming the expectations of heightened investment (ASEAN 2011). From this, it can cautiously be assumed that ASEAN seeks to attract international FDI for its member states. It should be kept in mind, however, that the growth in FDI has taken place in the incumbent ASEAN members and Vietnam. In Cambodia, Laos, and Myanmar, in contrast, FDI remains on a relatively low level and only increases slowly (ASEAN 2011).

Also for Laos, economic aspects have been crucial for accession. The country could expect a rise in quantity and better quality of FDI in some sectors as a consequence of accession. Different from the other acceding countries, Laos' leadership also hoped to strengthen bilateral relations with individual ASEAN member states and to receive help with its nation-building efforts. Furthermore, an increase in quantity and quality of FDI in some sectors could be expected as a consequence of accession (Freeman 2001: 114). Lastly, Laos hoped to receive more foreign aid as an ASEAN member (Emmers 2005: 78–79).

Another major motivation for CLMV's accessions was the opportunity to strengthen their position and to gain voice and recognition internationally. Through ASEAN's standing in the Asia-Pacific region and globally, CLMV enhanced their geopolitical status and boosted their room for maneuver in relations with non-member states (Christiansen 2006: 592, Nguyen and Luan 2001, Severino 2007: 36). Accession was thus an attempt to enhance their international standing. This holds for Vietnam in particular, whose government intended to reconcile regionalism and nation-building for the purpose of strengthening domestic legitimacy and external sovereignty (Sutherland 2009: 316). Indeed, ASEAN has given Vietnam the opportunity to integrate into mainstream international affairs and to diversify its external relations, particularly with other states in the region (Emmers 2005: 76). By diversifying its external relations, Vietnam furthermore expected to decrease its dependence on big powers, especially China (Mirza and Giroud 2004).

Increasing influence in negotiations with major powers was also a main argument for Myanmar's military junta to seek accession to ASEAN. For example, as a member of the association the country gained access to Asia-Europe Meeting (ASEM) through which it could directly influence the agenda of this high-level inter-regional forum. However, Myanmar's reasons for joining ASEAN differ partially from those of the other applicant states. Accession became attractive for Myanmar in the 1990s due to diplomatic isolation and punitive sanctions from Western countries. Much more than the other new member states, Myanmar had high expectations that ASEAN membership would enhance its international legitimacy. ASEAN's principle of non-interference in the domestic affairs of its member states is very attractive for the regime, possibly even more than for all other ASEAN members (Guyot 1998: 190, McCarthy 2008: 917–918). McCarthy (2008: 934) doubts that the regime seriously intends to introduce substantial economic reforms. Instead, he assumes that "the generals were in search of quick friends" when joining the association.

As in the EU accession process, security issues were also present, yet not predominant reasons for CLMV to join ASEAN. In particular, CLMV leaders hoped that potential conflicts could be dealt with on the regional level and, hence, domestic efforts could be put into economic development and human welfare issues (Nguyen and Luan 2001: 188). Furthermore, Vietnam expected better leverage regarding its territorial disputes with Beijing over the South China Sea (Emmers 2005: 76). Indeed, accession in order to counterbalance China's military power and its potential threat is the main argument brought forward by realist scholars (Gudisch 2009).

In contrast to the demanding accession criteria of the EU which have been perceived as a threat to national sovereignty by some European political leaders, accession criteria are very low for ASEAN membership applicants. In fact, the absence of specific political and economic conditions for admission enabled the candidates to rapidly enter the association (Emmers 2005: 71). As Langhammer (2001: 163) put it, ASEAN enlargement resembled a "Las Vegas jump start wedding." Certainly, the notion of giving away sovereignty does not apply for ASEAN. Narine (2002: 204) thus argued that accession to ASEAN was a process of enhancing rather than pooling sovereignty. The set-up of ASEAN allows its members to keep their domestic political system and to preserve their national independence and identity while cooperating with countries of different regimes and ideologies (Nguyen 2007: 496, Nguyen and Luan 2001: 194).

Conclusion

This chapter analyzed the accessions of CLMV to ASEAN in the 1990s from the perspective of the applicant states. For this purpose, an analytical framework was used initially developed for accession processes in the EU differentiating among three different sources of integration. Particular attention was given to the timing of accession and the question why CLMV did not join until the mid-1990s. It was found that for CLMV's accessions to ASEAN, general systemic conditions as well as positional characteristics of the acceding countries were crucial whereas ASEAN-specific systemic conditions were less important.

A key explanation for the timing is the end of the Cold War. CLMV were allies of the Soviet Union or were strongly dependent on communist allies. In times of the East–West antagonism, the capitalist ASEAN was considered an enemy. Thus, CLMV refused invitations to join ASEAN prior to 1990. In the 1990s, CLMV were in a similar situation as the CEEC. In both cases, the breakdown of the Soviet empire was been a crucial factor that enabled states to join ROs. Beyond that, the specific preconditions of CLMV, particularly in economic terms, were an important factor for accession.

In terms of economic benefits, the outlook on foreign investments was a key concern for CLMV. They hoped to benefit from ASEAN as a successful investment area. In particular, countries outside ASEAN were expected to invest in CLMV following their accession. The strong economic performance of the incumbent member states before ASEAN's enlargement was an additional incentive to join the organization. Impressed by high growth rates, CLMV hoped to benefit from an economic boom in a similar way as a part of ASEAN. As regards intra-regional trade, however, CLMV's expectations were not very high. Indeed, intra-ASEAN trade still remains on a low level today.

Apart from economic interests, the ability to influence the decision-making of an aspiring RO, and, consequently, to gain more international leverage, was another central motivation for CLMV in favor of accession. This was supported by the lack of serious affiliation criteria, which meant that the accessions did not mean a loss of sovereignty for CLMV. Particularly for Myanmar, accession was an attempt to gain international credibility and legitimacy, while not having to engage in domestic political reforms.

References

Anwar, D. F. 2001. ASEAN's Enlargement: Political, Security, and Institutional Perspectives, in *ASEAN Enlargement: Impacts and Implications*, edited by M. Than and C. L. Gates. Singapore: Institute of Southeast Asian Studies, 26–44.

ASEAN. 2011. *ASEAN Statistics*. [Online]. Available at: www.aseansec.org/19230.htm [accessed: March 15, 2011].

ASEAN Statistics. 2010. *Intra- and Extra-ASEAN trade, 2009*. [Online]. Available at: www.aseansec.org/stat/Table18.pdf [accessed: May 31, 2011].

Barichello, R. R., McCalla, A. and Valdes, A. 2003. Developing Countries and the World Trade Organization Negotiations. *American Journal of Agricultural Economics*, 85(3), 674–678.

Bárta, V. and Richter, S. 1996. *Eastern Enlargement of the European Union from a Western and an Eastern Perspective*. Research Report No. 227. Vienna, The Vienna Institute for Comparative Economic Studies (WIIW).

Baun, M. J. 2000. *A Wider Europe – The Process and Politics of European Union Enlargement*. Lanham: Rowman & Littlefield.

Bieler, A. 2002. The Struggle over EU Enlargement: A Historical Materialist Analysis of European Integration. *Journal of European Public Policy*, 9(4), 575–597.

Christiansen, T. 2006. European Integration and Regional Cooperation, in *The Globalization of World Politics. An Introduction to International Relations*, edited by J. Baylis and S. Smith. Oxford and New York: Oxford University Press, 579–597.

Cockerham, G. 2010. Regional Integration in ASEAN: Institutional Design and the ASEAN Way. *East Asia*, 27(2), 165–185.

Economywatch. 2011. *Vietnam Economic Statistics and Indicators*. [Online]. Available at: www.economywatch.com/economic-statistics/country/Vietnam [accessed: April 13, 2011].

Emmers, R. 2005. The Indochinese Enlargement of ASEAN: Security Expectations and Outcomes. *Australian Journal of International Affairs*, 59(1), 71–88.

Finland. 2010. *Finnish Customs*. [Online]. Available at: www.tulli.fi/en/finnish_customs/statistics/publications/pocket_statistics/index.jsp [accessed: September 30, 2010].

Freeman, N. 2001. The Rise and Fall of Foreign Direct Investment in Laos, 1988–2000. *Post-Communist Economies*, 13(1), 101–119.

Gstöhl, S. 1996. *Switzerland, Norway and the EU – The Odd Ones Out?* Genève: Institut européen de l'Université de Genève.

Gudisch, D. 2009. *Regionale Handelsabkommen in einer globalisierten Weltwirtschaft – ASEAN, AFTA und die WTO*. [Online]. Berlin. Available at: http://aussenpolitik.net/themen/weltwirtschaft/regionale_handelsabkommen_in_einer_globalisierten_weltwirtschaft-asean-afta_und_die_wto [accessed: April 3, 2011].

Guyot, J. 1998. Burma in 1997. From Empire to ASEAN. *ASEAN Survey*, 38(2), 190–195.

Holzinger, K., Knill, C., Peters, D., Rittberger, B., Schimmelfennig, F. and Wagner, W. (eds). 2005. *Die Europäische Union – Theorien und Analysekonzepte*. Paderborn: Schöningh.

Jacoby, W. 2004. *The Enlargement of the European Union and NATO. Ordering from the Menu in Central Europe*. Cambridge: Cambridge University Press.

Jenssen, A. T., Personen, P. and Gilljam, M. 1998. *To Join or Not to Join – 3 Nordic Referendums in the European Union*. Oslo: Scandinavian University Press.

Kahler, M. 2000. Legalization as Strategy: The Asia-Pacific Case. *International Organization*, 54(3), 549–571.

Katzenstein, P. J. 2005. *A World of Regions: Asia and Europe in the American Imperium*. Ithaca: Cornell University Press.

Lamy, S. L. 2006. Contemporary Mainstream Approaches: Neo-realism and Neo-liberalism, in *The Globalization of World Politics. An Introduction to International Relations*, edited by J. Baylis and S. Smith. Oxford and New York: Oxford University Press, 124–141.

Langhammer, R. 2001. European Union Enlargement: Lessons for ASEAN, in *ASEAN Enlargement: Impacts and Implications*, edited by M. Than and C. L. Gates. Singapore: Institute of Southeast Asian Studies, 102–127.

Mattli, W. 1999. *The Logic of Regional Integration. Europe and Beyond*. Cambridge: Cambridge University Press.

Mattli, W. and Plümper, T. 2002. The Demand-side Politics of EU Enlargement: Democracy and the Application for EU Membership. *Journal of European Public Policy*, 9(4), 550–574.

McCarthy, S. 2008. Burma and ASEAN. Estanged Bedfellows. *ASEAN Survey*, 48(6), 911–935.

Mirza, H. and Giroud, A. 2004. Regionalization, Foreign Direct Investment and Poverty Reduction. Lessons from Vietnam in ASEAN. *Journal of the Asia Pacific Economy*, 9(2), 223–248.

Moravcsik, A. and Vachudova, M. A. 2003. National Interests, State Power, and EU Enlargement. *East European Politics and Societies*, 17(1), 42–57.

Narine, S. 2002. *Explaining ASEAN. Regionalism in Southeast Asia*. Boulder: Lynne Rienner.

Nesadurai, H. E. S. 2008. The Association of Southeast Asian Nations (ASEAN). *New Political Economy*, 13(2), 225–239.

Nguyen, P. B. and Luan, T. D. 2001. Expectations and Experiences of the New Members. A Vietnamese Perspective, in *Reinventing ASEAN*, edited by S. Tay, J. Estanislao and H. Soestra. Singapore: Institute of Southeast Asian Studies, 185–205.

Nguyen, T. D. and Ezaki, M. 2005. Regional Economic Integration and its Impacts on Growth, Poverty and Income Distribution: The Case of Vietnam. *Review of Urban & Regional Development Studies*, 17(3), 197–215.

Nguyen, V. T. 2007. Vietnam's Membership of ASEAN. A Constructivist Interpretation. *Contemporary Sotheast Asia*, 29(3), 483–505.

Schimmelfennig, F. and Sedelmeier, U. 2002. Theorizing EU Enlargement: Research Focus, Hypotheses, and the State of Research. *Journal of European Public Policy*, 9(4), 500–528.

Severino, R. C. 2007. The ASEAN Developmental Divide and the Initiative for ASEAN Integration. *ASEAN Economic Bulletin*, 24(1), 35–44.

Sutherland, C. 2009. Reconciling Nation and Region: Vietnamese Nation Building and ASEAN Regionalism. *Political Studies*, 57(2), 316–336.

Thongpakde, N. 2001. Impacts and Implications of ASEAN Enlargement on Trade, in *ASEAN Enlargement: Impacts and Implications*, edited by M. Than and C. L. Gates. Singapore: Institute of Southeast Asian Studies, 1–25.

UN ESCAP. 2009. *ASEAN and Trade Integration*. United Nations Economic Commission for Asia and the Pacific, Trade and Investment Division, Staff Working paper 1/09, April.

Witczynska, K. 2009. Integrationsprozesse in Ostasien. *Osteuropa-Wirtschaft*, 54(1–2), 58–65.

Chapter 4
MERCOSUR:
Integration through Presidents and Paymasters

Felix Hummel and Mathis Lohaus

Introduction

Which factors evoke attempts toward regional integration and influence their rate of success? In the case of the Southern Common Market (MERCOSUR), the most prominent theories in this regard seem to lack explanatory power. Neither the emergence nor the institutional development and outcomes of MERCOSUR are consistent with the assumptions made by intergovernmentalism and neofunctionalism. As one scholar puts it, "the sequence of interdependence–integration–institutions simply did not take place" (Malamud 2003: 59–61), thus limiting the applicability of the major theories. To account for regional integration in this case, a different approach appears to be necessary.

According to our hypothesis, Mattli's (1999) framework for regional integration will prove suitable. With regard to the emergence of MERCOSUR, the organization can be seen as a counter-union to balance external influences like the US-led Free Trade Area of the Americas (FTAA) or bilateral agreements. The subsequent (lack of) regional integration is best explained by a mixture of demand- and supply-side factors, combining arguments from economics and political science. Our main explanatory factors are the Latin American particularity of interpresidentialism and Brazil's role as a paymaster. These two factors supplement the supply side of Mattli's framework and explain MERCOSUR's relative success – despite limited demand and a low level of legalization. We will illustrate our argument with the examples of two major crises of MERCOSUR, namely the 1995 automobile crisis and the 2001 external tariff crisis.

A Framework to Analyze Regional Integration

With his analytical framework, Mattli sheds light on two phenomena related to regional integration: First, why do some attempts at it fail, while others succeed? In this context, the degree of success is defined as "the extent to which integration groups manage to match their stated integration goals with subsequent achievements." Second, how can we explain the process of outsiders becoming insiders? Regional integration evokes external effects on non-members, who can either try to gain membership or to constitute a group of their own. To resolve the shortcomings identified within strictly neofunctionalist or strictly intergovernmentalist explanations, Mattli (1999: 10–12) wants to account for regional integration by "bridging political science and economics."

Turning first to what Mattli calls the second puzzle of regional integration, we will briefly discuss the framework's assumptions about the effects of regional integration on outsiders (non-members). It is assumed that any successful process of integration between a group of countries will bring disadvantages to others. Examples include the loss of market access resulting from discriminatory trade policies, or the diversion of investment which is likely to concentrate within the group. When these "external effects are felt or are bound to be felt" by outsiders, they have two possibilities to react (Mattli 1999: 61). The first is to apply for membership. The second integrative response sees the outsiders create their own regional group. Mattli argues that the Latin American Free Trade Association and others were triggered by the establishment of the European Community, and that the subsequent deepening of European integration led to a "tidal wave of integration projects throughout the world in the late 1980s" (Mattli 1999: 61). Whenever countries choose to "experiment with their own regional schemes" they face the same conditions for success or failure that apply to the original group (Mattli 1999: 62–63).

What is called the "demand for integration" in the framework is a consequence of the logic of economic gains. Technological progress, economics of scale, and competitive or location-based advantages will encourage transactions across national borders. Those, in turn, entail different types of costs, for example, uncertainty about public order in foreign countries or problematic behavior by commercial partners. As private contractual measures may not cover these risks sufficiently, the demand for an external safeguard, namely integrated governance, grows. A new governance structure is then likely to lead to more market integration, again pushing for increased political integration. However, this mechanism is not sufficient to evoke regional integration on its own: "If demand is not met by supply, no change will occur" (Mattli 1999: 47–50).

Generally, governments are most likely to sacrifice sovereignty in times of economic struggle, when further regional integration promises overall payoffs that outweigh special interests (Mattli 1999: 50–51). Given the uncertainty about member states' behavior in a regional organization, success then depends on so-called commitment institutions: Mattli's first condition of supply is that countries striving for sustained integration need to establish institutions responsible for "centralized monitoring and third party enforcement" (Mattli 1999: 53–54).

Whenever coordination is needed to share distributional costs, the choice between equally efficient options will be easier if there is one undisputed leader whose policies become the new standard because they require the "least costly change within the group." This leader is likely to act as "regional paymaster, easing distributional tensions and thus smoothing the path of integration" (Mattli

1999: 56). Hence, the existence of an undisputed leader is Mattli's second, and stronger, supply condition.

Accounting for the Emergence of MERCOSUR

When Argentina and Brazil began negotiating the terms of closer economic cooperation and regional integration in the middle of the 1980s, they were able to build on earlier attempts, namely LAFTA and LAIA[1] (Vervaele 2005: 390). However, the area did not provide them with a successful experience of regional economic integration, but rather daunting examples of "how NOT to create an economic integration organization or a common market" (Porrata-Doria Jr. 2005: 10).

Low Level of Interdependence

According to intergovernmentalist and neofunctionalist strands of theory, the foundation of a regional organization would likely be motivated by an increase in trade flows, then leading to more interdependence and either a conscious decision by leaders to institutionalize cooperation or a functional demand for increasing integration (Malamud 2003: 59–60). The MERCOSUR experience contradicts these expectations.

On the one hand, the economies of the founding members of MERCOSUR were, in principle, more compatible than those in the case of earlier, unsuccessful attempts at integration (Bieling 2007: 191). On the other hand, there were only minor trade and investment flows between them at the beginning of the 1990s. One could argue that "in a context of relatively low interdependence the primary purpose of MERCOSUR was to raise economic intercourse rather than to administer its effects" (Bouzas and Soltz 2001: 14).

In the 1980s, regional trade represented only a minimal share in the balances of those states that would later constitute MERCOSUR. In 1986, trade within the region equated to 1.5 percent of Argentina's GDP, or 0.9 percent in the case of Brazil. Economic exchange between Argentina and Brazil had declined from 1.8 to 1.1 billion US dollars between 1980 and 1985, then reaching 1980 levels again in 1990 (Malamud 2003: 62). A closer look at the "intra-regional trade share" supports the impression that trade within the region was not very important. This indicator is defined as "intra-regional trade as a percentage share of the region's total trade (regional total imports plus regional total exports)," thus ranging from 0 to 100 (UNU-CRIS 2008: 5). In the decade before MERCOSUR was established, the share of intra-regional trade had stagnated and then moderately increased – a development that was by all means far from spectacular (see Table 4.1).

---

1 The Latin American Free Trade Association was created in 1960 and superseded by the Latin American Integration Association in 1980.

Table 4.1 Intra-regional trade share before the foundation of MERCOSUR

Year	1981	1982	1983	1984	1985	1986	1987	1988	1989	1990
ITS	8.57	8.19	6.78	7.98	7.17	10.3	9.00	9.00	10.95	11.28

Source: Regional Integration Knowledge System (UNU-CRIS 2010).
Note: Intra-regional trade share (ITS) in percent for MERCOSUR founding members.

Comparing MERCOSUR to other world regions, the low level of interdependence as indicated by the data is striking. At the end of the 1980s, the share of trade within the region was far smaller than elsewhere. A moderately positive trend after 1991 seems to support the argument that it was MERCOSUR's primary purpose to create trade in the first place (for a detailed comparison, see Capannelli et al. 2009).

MERCOSUR: The Second Integrative Response

According to Mattli, MERCOSUR can be interpreted as a response to developments in the Americas and Europe. The enlargement and deepening of the European Union, the costs of German reunification, and the new situation in Eastern Europe were important factors: Latin American countries feared that deeper integration in Europe would hamper the chances for their imports and draw European investment and aid toward Eastern and Central European countries. Regarding both aid and investment, Europe had been a more important player than the United States. Concerning trade, it was the other way round: 20 percent of the Latin American exports at the end of the 1980s went to Europe, with twice as much going to the United States (Mattli 1999: 152–153). Not surprisingly, two US-led initiatives triggered Southern American responses: negotiations on the North American Free Trade Agreement (NAFTA) in 1990 coincided with the formation of MERCOSUR, and talks about the FTAA "stimulated" MERCOSUR's common external tariff (Bouzas and Soltz 2001: 13).

Regional integration in South America has been described as "defensive developmental response," with MERCOSUR and North America competing for the leading role: while the Andean Community did not sustain a concerted policy, culminating in Venezuela's withdrawal after several members had started bilateral negotiations with the United States in 2006, MERCOSUR resisted both the FTAA and bilateral offers (see Tussie 2009: 181–182). This may be seen as an indicator of how important the balancing of US interests has been and still is within MERCOSUR. The thesis that external events "played a key role in shaping the evolution of regional co-operation" (Bouzas and Soltz 2001: 13) is also supported by the preamble to the Treaty of Asunción. It states that the founding members have considered "international trends, particularly the integration of large economic areas, and the importance of securing their countries a proper place in the international economy," and that they believe "that this integration process is an appropriate response to such trends" (MERCOSUR 1991: 319).

Furthermore, negative domestic developments added to the perceived threat of other integration projects, as "external events coincided with a period of general economic decline in Latin America" (Mattli 1999: 154). External debt, technological and financial problems, declining trade volumes and plummeting prices for important commodities had led to a fear of marginalization and isolation: "In sum, the new regionalism in Latin America can be understood as an effort to reverse a decade of economic decline and to fend off the negative externalities of bloc formation elsewhere" (Mattli 1999: 155).[2]

Analyzing the Development of MERCOSUR

The next section deals with the organization's institutional design and evaluates to what extent the goals set in the treaties have been reached. This assessment will provide the point of departure for the analysis using Mattli's demand and supply conditions. Additionally, the important role played by interpresidentialism will be examined in order to provide a more comprehensive account of how MERCOSUR has developed.

Institutional Design (Formal Integration)

After MERCOSUR was established by the Treaty of Asunción in 1991, several amendments have been made to its set-up. It was the Protocol of Ouro Preto in 1994 that gave the organization its institutional structure and legal personality. Next to those, which are the most important documents, there are the Protocol of Brasilia that established the first dispute settlement mechanism in 1991, the Protocol of Ushuaia that introduced a democratic clause in 1998, and the Protocol of Olivos to reform dispute settlement in 2002.

MERCOSUR's set-up can be characterized as strictly intergovernmental. There are three bodies relevant for regional decision-making, the highest being the Common Market Council (CMC), where the heads of states and ministers make the strategic decisions. It is supported by the Common Market Group (CMG), responsible for the executive aspects and comprised of national officials from ministries and central banks. The CMG also supervises many specialized working groups and committees (Pena and Rozemberg 2005: 2). A number of issues, for example, competition and consumer protection, are handled by the MERCOSUR

---

2 In addition, MERCOSUR can be seen as "pluralistic security community" following Karl Deutsch (Malamud 2003: 63), although security matters are handled in separate treaties. Another factor is the policy convergence taking place in the region (see Domínguez 2010: 29–31). Both aspects are necessary preconditions for integration, but should be distinguished from the driving forces.

Trade Commission (MTC), which also consists of delegates from the member states. Taken together, the decisions, resolutions, and directives of those three bodies constitute the binding secondary law in MERCOSUR. Thus, the right of initiative lies exclusively with the member states, as they are the ones submitting proposals to the decision-making bodies (Vervaele 2005: 392). Decisions have to be taken by consensus, making them binding for member states to implement into national law (Vervaele 2005: 393–394).

Contrary to the EU and the role played by the European Commission, the MERCOSUR Secretariat is limited to administrative and technical tasks (Vervaele 2005: 392). Furthermore, there is the MERCOSUR Parliament, which occupies a consultative role. A recent initiative to furnish it with more authority and responsibilities has been turned down by the heads of state (Elsner and Alabor 2009: 3), and the mode of electing its delegates is due to be revised by 2012 (INTAL 2009: 94–97). Several consultative bodies are comprised of national officials and delegates from the private sector (see Pena and Rozemberg 2005: 3–4).

Remarkably, there is no supremacy or direct effect of MERCOSUR law (Porrata-Doria Jr. 2005: 78), but a "de facto form of superiority" (Duina 2006: 251–216) since member states are obliged to transpose decisions into domestic law. The only exclusion to the rule of consensus and national implementation is the dispute settlement, "although the mechanisms established by the Protocol of Brasilia have been called upon only ten times in 15 years" (Malamud and Schmitter 2007: 16). With the 2002 Protocol of Olivos, the Permanent Review Court was established as the ultimate level of jurisdiction, allowing claims by private or commercial actors from the member states. However, both parties of every settlement procedure will be represented by their respective national branch of the CMG, which is also responsible for bringing the case to charges. Under these circumstances, it seems very unlikely that any actor will be able to enforce MERCOSUR law against their own government (Azevedo Cunha 2007: 14).

According to the concept of legalization, international organizations can be characterized along a set of properties divided into obligation, precision, and delegation (Abbott et al. 2000: 401–402). Applied to a regional organization, obligation means that community rules can be more or less binding for member states. As MERCOSUR members are obliged to implement law domestically while there is no direct effect, a dynamic has developed that "has made the effectiveness of the decisions ... dependent on domestic mechanisms and interests" (Motta Veiga 2004: 13–14). In theory, MERCOSUR produces binding law, but in practice, member states defect frequently. We will return to this issue in the next section.

Regarding the aspect of precision, the initial Treaty of Asunción was characterized as a "framework agreement" (Motta Veiga 2004: 11), with secondary law regulating the details. The initial mode of reducing tariffs is an important exception, because it determined "precise, obligatory [and] nearly universal" schedules (Domínguez 2010: 31).

With respect to the matter of delegation, member states display a strong "reluctance to cede political sovereignty," keeping control of the process through their representatives at all times (Arieti 2006: 764). Even more so, the institutional provisions are characterized as "particularly weak," with many decisions being made at occasional meetings (Preusse 2004: 138). In fact, the organization also "depends exclusively on the national governments for enforcement, compliance and, in most cases, adjudication" (Malamud 2008: 127). As there is no full-fledged court of justice or any legislative body of supranational character, it is safe to say that the overall level of delegation is low.

Achievements (Informal Integration)

Let us now turn from formal integration, the institutional framework, to what may be called informal integration: the actual interactions and economic exchange in the region (see Mattli 1999: 72). The Treaty of Asunción states as its goal the establishment of a common market, consisting of four elements: free movement of goods, services, and factors of production; a common external tariff; coordination of relevant policies between member states; harmonization of legislation (MERCOSUR 1991: 319–320).

With Annex I of the treaty, an initial Trade Liberalization Programme was introduced (MERCOSUR 1991: 326–329), which has already been mentioned under the aspect of precision. This part of the agreement was effective, accounting for the "most remarkable achievements of MERCOSUR" (Bouzas et al. 2002: 108). A very important aspect was its universal approach, allowing only some exceptions. It has been pointed out that by 1996, "99.4 percent of all trade items had been liberalized between Argentina and Brazil" (Domínguez 2010: 31).

Indeed, during the first years of the automatic tariff reductions, intra-regional trade grew by about 27 percent annually, much faster than trade with the rest of the world (Mattli 1999: 159). The share of intra-MERCOSUR trade over total trade rose significantly. Of course, this is reflected in the volume of trade: before 1991, trade within MERCOSUR added up to about 7 percent of combined GDP – by 1998 it grew to more than 11 percent: "The period 1991–98 may in the future be called the 'Golden Age' of MERCOSUR" (Malamud 2008: 120). Reaching the end of the 1990s, however, the growth of intra-regional trade was reversed due to "crises in the region" and Brazil's focus on trade with partners outside of MERCOSUR (European Commission 2007: 10–11).

Furthermore, the attempt to introduce a common external tariff (CET) for a wide range of goods, as planned in the 1995 Protocol of Ouro Preto, proved problematic as member states were allowed to define exceptions. Thus, the most important industries were excluded and the agreements were "imperfect and riddled with exceptions, so much so that leaders agreed to aim for 2006 as a target date for full deployment" (Duina 2006: 20–21). Again, this target has not been met, adding to MERCOSUR's failures regarding the liberalization of services, economic policy harmonization, and coordination of policies on foreign direct investments (Domínguez 2007: 110).

With a CET regime that is best described as "barely existing" (Domínguez 2010: 38) when it should be a key component of MERCOSUR, what can be said about the other aspects of MERCOSUR's external relations? Recalling that the Treaty of Asunción identified the necessity of securing a good position in the international economy (MERCOSUR 1991: 319), there is evidence of some success. MERCOSUR was perceived to have "done much to help its members feature on the world's map for the new century" fairly early in the process (Malamud 2003: 58). One indicator of diplomatic clout may be the free trade agreement with the European Union that is currently back on the agenda (see European Commission 2010). Moreover, MERCOSUR successfully acted to prevent an FTAA that would not have served the interests of the Southern American states (Tussie 2009: 182).

Last but not least, because most decisions have to be transposed into domestic law by all member states in order for them to come into effect, the issue of domestic ratification becomes relevant. Considering CMC decisions, CMG resolutions, and MTC directives, the record gives cause for concern. In the period from 1991 to March 2006, roughly half of the norms requiring transposition to national law were not properly implemented by all member states. Thus, a regulation may be approved by the Council and several parliaments – but will only come into force once approved by the last national parliament (Malamud 2008: 129–130). In essence, this constitutes a second veto opportunity for governments, with different veto priorities leading to another counterproductive effect: while the average *individual* rate of implementation for CMG resolutions was between 71 and 79 percent, the *overall* rate reached only 49 percent (Bouzas 2008: 360). This implementation gap hampers integration in MERCOSUR and seems to be the organization's most problematic shortcoming.

Demand Side – Increasing, and then Stagnating

How can we now try to account for the state of things as presented above? First of all, the initial level of interdependence in the region was extremely low. During the first years of MERCOSUR, however, increasing interdependence led to more demand, as uncertainty about "[a]mbiguous and unilaterally changeable rules" and disputes about the conditions for investment became problematic (Bouzas and Soltz 2001: 15). Indeed, the early years of MERCOSUR saw the emergence of a "powerful lobby in the private sector for deeper integration," displeased about the organization's shortcomings (Mattli 1999: 159). One early observer of the process concludes that "[in contrast to] previous Latin American attempts at integration, where the private sector deferred to government leadership, some entrepreneurial sectors have taken the lead in this integration effort" (Manzetti 1993: 115–116).

Nevertheless, the overall demand for deeper integration was weak, mostly due to asymmetries in size. In the case of Brazil, the biggest economy by far, trade within the region represented an even lower share than in the other member states, thus limiting the appeal of "more formal and procedural institutions" as opposed to flexibility (Bouzas and Soltz 2001: 15). To make matters worse, MERCOSUR countries have experienced stagnating or decreasing levels of interdependence since 1999, while their share of the world market is limited. Thus, "the prospects for further regional integration are very limited by a relatively small market size and a relatively narrow export basis" (Malamud 2008: 118). Recent trends suggest that economic exchange with the rest of the world will continue to grow faster than trade within the region, further reducing interdependence. This tendency manifests itself most visibly in Brazil, where the share of intra-regional trade has almost fallen to the pre-MERCOSUR level of 1990 (Malamud 2008: 121). All in all, the low level of interdependence, also in comparison to other regions, helps to account for MERCOSUR's "lean institutional design" (Bouzas and Soltz 2001: 15).

Supply Side – Reluctance and Crises

As the governments in South America faced the "major challenge of restructuring their economies along market-oriented principles" at the start of the 1990s, the issue of trade liberalization was of great importance (Perales 2003: 93). First of all, political leaders needed to increase the credibility of their measures, which meant solving the problem that most of their proposals would normally be weakened by compromises in response to domestic pressure. Second, they needed to improve their bargaining position in general, because a good share of the private sector was "relatively unreceptive" to trade liberalization (Perales 2003: 93–94). Credibility of economic policy reform was increased by fixing the exchange rates in Argentina (1991) and Brazil (1993): with monetary policy taken away from the government's day-to-day control, economic policy became more predictable. The second aspect of credible reform, trade policy, was then taken to another level. By committing on the regional level, the governments facilitated predictions about trade policy and increased their credibility. At the same time, they addressed this problem by establishing a reciprocal regime in the region, which was meant to reduce the opposition in the private sector (Perales 2003: 94–95). Indeed, the major steps of integration taken in 1991 and 1994 occurred in the context of macroeconomic crises and domestic bargaining processes between business and governments in Argentina and Brazil (Perales 2003: 96), supporting Mattli's presumptions. This pattern re-emerged a decade later. After the economic crises in Argentina and Brazil, and the following electoral success of the political left in both countries, there was a new round of development in MERCOSUR. From 2003 onwards, the secretariat's competencies were somewhat extended, and the MERCOSUR Parliament was established. This can be seen as a new approach toward integration in the region (Bieling 2007: 194), again reflecting domestic political developments in reaction to crises.

Turning to Mattli's first supply condition, the creation of commitment institutions, it seems obvious that such bodies do not exist in MERCOSUR. Given the historical experiences in the region, it may have been a conscious choice not to adopt a highly institutionalized model of integration, as this could have raised problems of legitimacy (Malamud and Schmitter 2007: 24). Others believe that the lack of institutions is a result of Brazil's preference to "leave MERCOSUR in a state of latent institutionalization" (Flemes and Westermann 2009: 7).[3] Weak regional institutions allowed the major players, Argentina and Brazil, to cooperate bilaterally and keep the process under executive control, again improving their bargaining position against domestic pressures (Perales 2003: 95). Moreover, the asymmetric composition of the bloc impedes the set-up of institutions more supranational in character: the MERCOSUR Parliament, for example, currently includes the same number of delegates from every member state. At the end of the transitional period in 2014, a direct election is planned to take place in all member states. However, the final composition of the body still needs to be discussed: if Brazil were to send delegates according to its share of population, it would hold a permanent majority in the Parliament, which would certainly lead to dissent. Leaving the parliament without any decision-making power may be the only way to avoid a dispute about its composition (Malamud 2008: 126).

Contrary to the European experience, MERCOSUR's dispute settlement mechanism is very far from being a driver of integration. Seemingly, it does not even serve its core function of resolving disputes, as not one of the 283 disputes between 1995 and 1997 was settled via the rule-based mechanisms. During the years of economic troubles from 1998 to 2003, only nine out of 201 cases were solved using the institutionalized mechanism. Even after the Permanent Review Court was established in 2002, Argentina has continued to file claims against Brazil with the World Trade Organization, instead of using MERCOSUR's own bodies (Domínguez 2010: 35).

This lack of strong regional institutions could, however, be mitigated by another supply condition: according to Mattli, the existence of undisputed leadership in the region is a stronger condition for success than commitment institutions. After all, it was a lack of leadership that "crippled the Andean Pact," as none of the members "was willing to compromise or willing to bribe the others into acquiescence" (Mattli 1999: 64). Going one step further than the original framework, we want to analyze four possible types of leadership. Two of them focus on institutions: first, regional bodies can act as a broker; second, intergovernmental diplomacy can help to reach agreement. The next pair concerns leadership by financial means: third, a hegemonic member state can act as paymaster; fourth, regional funds can be used to steer the process of integration (Malamud 2008: 122–123).

The idea of a supranational institution as a broker largely overlaps with Mattli's argument on commitment institutions. While the Commission and Court of Justice play important roles in European integration, and consequently also in theories on the subject, there is no such dynamic in MERCOSUR (Malamud 2008: 124–126). A similar observation can be made regarding regional funds, the fourth

---

3   Interestingly, the United States' dominant position in NAFTA did not produce a similar result (see Chapter 5, this volume).

type of leadership. Although MERCOSUR has recently established a so-called regional convergence fund (FOCEM), it is much smaller than the billions of euros redistributed annually by the European Union. The overall budget of the FOCEM is set to reach 400 million US dollars in 2010, with slightly more than a quarter of the money already allocated to running projects (MERCOSUR 2009: 4). Given the huge difference in size, scholars argue that "regional payoffs in MERCOSUR look little promising as an engine for integration" (Malamud 2008: 124).

Regarding the third type of leadership, Brazil is the potential paymaster to cover "a disproportionate share of the integration costs," similar to Germany in the EU (Malamud 2008: 122). However, it seems that during the first years of MERCOSUR, the country was "reluctant to use its economic and political position to assume active regional leadership." Short-term domestic interests were given priority over regional projects, for example, in the case of trade barriers leading to disputes with other members of the bloc, and the Brazilian government opposed to the creation of regional redistributive funds (Mattli 1999: 160). It has been argued that this changed under Lula, who seemed more willing to take the financial lead than his predecessors (Malamud and Schmitter 2007: 22). Concerning the measure of redistributive funds, however, the hegemonic commitment remains relatively weak. In 2008, Brazil provided 0.007 percent of its gross national income to FOCEM, in contrast to Germany committing 0.39 percent to the several European funds (Malamud 2008: 123).

Because of asymmetries between and within member states, financial transfers are "difficult to justify in the eyes of the underprivileged that live in the contributor countries" (Malamud and Schmitter 2007: 23). Low GDP per capita, high poverty rate and huge inequality in Brazil provide good arguments against transfers to the better-off neighbors in Argentina and Uruguay. But without the discretion to withhold or grant financial incentives, Brazil seems unable to steer the course of integration. As external donors give aid regardless of regional policy and Venezuela's petro-dollars are added to the equation, the situation seems unlikely to develop favorable to deeper integration (Malamud 2008: 123–124). Nevertheless, as we will discuss in the next section, presidential initiatives and the benevolence of an (indirect) paymaster in times of crises seem to have sustained MERCOSUR so far. Thus, we regard the second and (to a lesser extent) the third type of leadership as crucial for the case of MERCOSUR.

The Particular Role of Interpresidentialism

Most students of MERCOSUR have not only put emphasis on its intergovernmental character, but also stressed the importance of presidential diplomacy, leading to a "highly personalized decision-making process" that worked well in the early years (Preusse 2004: 138). As the heads of states have played the dominant role in both the creation and day-to-day business of MERCOSUR, at the same time publicly stressing the huge importance of their endeavor, this "extreme type of intergovernmentalism" has been called "interpresidentialism" (Tussie 2009: 175–176).

Rules have been changed to accommodate special interests or circumstances, and "economic matters that got in the way" were disregarded for the sake of MERCOSUR's importance as strategic project, especially between Argentina and Brazil (Domínguez 2010: 34–35). Andrés Malamud, one of the proponents of the interpresidentialism thesis, argues that it is in fact the "hidden cause" for the success of MERCOSUR (Malamud 2003). In the context of Mattli's framework for regional integration, interpresidentialism adds to the supply side as one type of leadership via governmental diplomacy.

Without the presidents' dominant role in agenda-setting, the organization would not have been founded under circumstances of low interdependence and a reluctant private sector, and its development would have stalled completely (Malamud 2003: 63). Cooperation can be seen as the product of "executive preferences and political entrepreneurship," meaning that success is highly dependent on the presidents' initiative (Perales 2003: 93). The highly influential position of the heads of state is hardly a surprise, given that presidential decrees dominated domestic economic policy in Argentina and Brazil (Perales 2003: 96–98). Furthermore, Latin American presidents have always been heavily involved in shaping foreign policy, a pattern that was "reinforced by the new democratic regimes" in the years prior to the foundation of MERCOSUR – which explains why the political dimension of integration has dominated the economic one (Malamud 2003: 66).

Let us now further illustrate how MERCOSUR presidents gave political interests priority over economic ones, resulting in interpresidentialism as a driving force of regionalism. We will do so by drawing on two important conflicts in MERCOSUR's history: the automobile crisis and the external tariff crisis.[4]

The Automobile Crisis

The 1995 automobile crisis can be seen as the first major clash of interests between the Brazilian and the Argentine government since the establishment of MERCOSUR. The automobile sector was given extraordinary importance in the negotiations to the Treaty of Asunción and the additional Protocol of Ouro Preto. Both agreements include a special clause that explicitly excludes the car industry from the greater liberalization process in the region. Instead, the member states agreed for the time being in decision 29/94 of the MERCOSUR Common Market Council on recognizing each other's domestic trade policies (Gómez Mera 2009: 20). Additionally, a common policy for the automobile industry should be established by the year 2000 (Wrobel 1999: 86).

---

4   Other examples indicating the importance of interpresidentialism can be found in Malamud 2003.

However, in 1995, the aftermaths of the Mexican economic crisis demonstrated their impact on other Latin American countries (the so-called Tequila Effect) and caused a decline in the Brazilian and Argentine economy. The Brazilian government reacted by unilaterally lowering trade barriers for raw materials and technology while at the same time raising tariffs for car imports, including those from its MERCOSUR partners and therefore Argentina. This change in Brazil's automobile policy constituted a breach of decision 29/94 and caused the biggest crisis of MERCOSUR to date (Malamud 2005: 143).

Although Brazil tried to justify its policies as adjustments to existing agreements that had favored the Argentine car industry, both Argentine officials and producers argued that the Brazilian behavior meant a breach of the Protocol of Ouro Preto. To support his car industry, Argentine president Menem decided to threaten his Brazilian counterpart with the boycott of a long planned presidential summit in Brazil (Malamud 2005: 145).

Menem's threat had the intended effect. Not only did the president of Paraguay and Uruguay offer to mediate between the conflicting parties, but Brazilian president Cardoso also postponed his plans to reduce car imports to his country by 50 percent in the second half of 1995 and contacted Menem personally, trying to convince him to attend the presidential summit (Malamud 2005: 145).

In the first bilateral talks between the presidents, Cardoso hoped to convince Menem to lower his objections "in order to restore a balance between the parts" (Malamud 2005: 145). However, with one of his strongest industries breathing down his neck, Menem did not buckle under the demands of his partner and insisted that the negotiations on a solution in the automobile regime could only take place on the basis of the earlier agreements between the two countries, namely Commission Decision 29/94.

The next day a solution was found. Argentina admitted that Brazil had been disadvantaged by the earlier agreements. In exchange Brazil committed to not implementing quotas for Argentine car imports. Furthermore, both parties agreed to establish a "definitive common regime that would last until 2000" (Malamud 2005: 146).

The automobile crisis illustrates well how a conflict that was caused by domestic economic short-term interests could be resolved through presidential diplomacy and the political will in Brazil to serve as paymaster for the sake of the continuation of MERCOSUR. After the start of a recession caused by the Mexican economic crisis and an unstable Brazilian economy, the domestic car industry pressured its government to lower the tariffs for technology and resources and raise the ones for car imports. The automobile branch, being one of Argentina's most important industries, was highly affected by this breach of decision 29/94. It now pressured its government on its own part to regain access to one of its biggest selling markets. This disagreement on a trade issue brought MERCOSUR to the brink of collapse.

However, in the end the dispute was solved through presidential diplomacy and the willingness of Brazil to bear the costs. The presidents of Brazil and

Argentina agreed on policies that guaranteed the survival of MERCOSUR as a political project even though they conflicted with the powerful economic interest in Brazil since the quotas on Argentine cars were not established.

The External Tariff Crisis

At the beginning of the year 2000, the development of MERCOSUR generated optimism amongst supporters of the project. This was first and foremost because the Brazilian economy seemed to be recovering from an economic breakdown that had been caused by the earlier mentioned Tequila Effect. Therefore, it was commonly believed that the crisis of the Southern Cone had been overcome. The member states boosted this notion by announcing the relaunch of MERCOSUR in a meeting of the CMC. However, in the second half of the year Argentina started to suffer from setbacks that caused a recession in the national economy and threw the country into a deep crisis. Furthermore, Argentine producers were still suffering from the consequences of devaluation of the Real and the resulting competitive disadvantages. At the end of the year, Argentina could only be saved from bankruptcy with an international aid package of 39.7 billion US dollars by the International Monetary Fund and major changes in its external tariff policy (Carranza 2003: 84).

In the course of this policy change, the Argentine government raised tariffs on imported consumer goods like textiles and farming products, while at the same time eliminating those for capital investments from outside MERCOSUR, thereby breaking with the common external tariff of the organization. Furthermore, the Argentine Minister for Economic Affairs Domingo Cavallo repeatedly expressed his desire to downgrade MERCOSUR into a free trade area during the crisis, which would have allowed his country to take unilateral measures to boost the economy (Gómez Mera 2005: 30).

A Brazilian-style devaluation of the Argentine currency to foster the competitiveness of domestic producers was not an option for the de la Rúa administration because of the earlier adopted convertibility plan that kept the Peso on a fixed exchange rate with the US dollar. Furthermore, most big Argentine firms had received credits in US dollars and a devaluation of the Peso would have driven many of them into insolvency. In this context it is important to note that it was not one dominant economic interest group that called for help, but that the entire economy of Argentina was affected. Consequently, measures were implemented to rescue the domestic economy as a whole both on the investment and the production side (Carranza 2003: 84–86).

In the beginning of the economic crisis in Argentina, the Brazilian government was tolerant toward its neighbor's policies to rescue its economy, knowing that a collapse of the Argentine economy would also mean a major strike for its own companies. Not only did Brazil import many industrial and agricultural goods from Argentina but, with over 11 percent of all Brazilian exports going to its biggest neighbor, the collapse of the Argentine economy would have meant the loss of an important selling market as well. Therefore, president Cardoso allowed the Argentine government the temporary elimination of tariffs on financial goods to attract foreign capital from outside MERCOSUR. Brazil seemed to accept its role of being the paymaster of the organization because integration in the Southern Cone served Brazilian interests.

However, when Argentina decided to include telecommunication and technology products such as mobile phones and computers in the new tariff policy, products that many Brazilian firms had been selling to Argentina, the Brazilian producers protested heavily, fearing a large decline in Brazilian exports through the loss of the advantage MERCOSUR had provided (Gómez Mera 2005: 33).

Furthermore, with a new recession starting in Brazil in 2001 the Real underwent a second heavy devaluation, this time declining by another 32 percent. Additionally, Argentine economic minister Cavallo's idea to downgrade MERCOSUR into a free trade area caused a lot of anger amongst Brazilian officials who were hoping that a strong MERCOSUR would strengthen their bargaining position in bilateral talks with the United States and the European Union (Carranza 2003: 85).

At the peak of the crisis, Brazil pressured Argentina by "suspending negotiations over the common automobile regime and threatening to resort to retaliatory measures, this time by restricting imports of Argentine wheat and petroleum" (Gómez Mera 2005: 30). The Argentine government, on the other hand, replied with the threat of blocking MERCOSUR and accused Brazil of deliberately devaluating its currency and speculating on Argentine bankruptcy. Brazilian president Cardoso reacted to this insult with the cancellation of his planned trip to Argentina.

Finally, in the fall of 2001, both presidents met to resolve the disputes between their two countries. Eventually, both countries had to make concessions to keep the project alive. Brazil had to accept Argentina's need of keeping the tariffs for financial goods low and agreed to create a common safeguard regime in accordance with the directives of the World Trade Organization that it had rejected two years earlier. Argentina, on the other hand, was forced to exclude telecommunication and technological goods from tariff reduction (Carranza 2003: 85).

Concluding Remarks

Just as in the case of the automobile crisis, the external tariff crisis could again be solved through bilateral talks between the presidents of Argentina and Brazil, which led to concessions by both countries for the sake of the survival of MERCOSUR. Apparently, Brazil was willing to pay the price for Argentina breaking the CET rules, and even after the crisis had expanded into the technology sector, an agreement was reached between the heads of state.

All in all, we argue that MERCOSUR has proven more successful than conventional theories on regional integration lead us to expect, but displays certain particularities, such as its very limited institutional design and a troublesome record regarding the domestic implementation of regional decisions. The dominant role of presidents, especially those of Argentina and Brazil, and the low levels of economic interdependence help to understand these outcomes. It appears to have been presidential initiatives that allowed the regional organization to form despite adverse economic conditions, and to carry on throughout major crises. The latter were also mitigated by the third type of regional leadership, the role of dominant states as paymasters. Rather than through regional funds, Brazil appears to fulfill this duty indirectly, by making political concessions against its economic interests in critical situations.

What can be said about the compatibility of Mattli's framework with MERCOSUR? Although there has been little demand for integration and commitment institutions were not installed, the organization was more successful than predicted. Serving as a unique variant of regional leadership, interpresidentialism appears to have compensated for the lack of commitment institutions in MERCOSUR. In fact, interpresidentialism may be classified as a functional equivalent to regional institutions (Malamud 2003: 56). Given that there was just the Argentine–Brazilian axis for bargaining and presidential agreements, presidential power helped more than it could have in the face of "cross-cutting cleavages" such as in Europe (Malamud 2003: 67).

Turning to the chances for deeper integration, MERCOSUR's modus operandi of very light institutionalization has entailed the disadvantages of erratic implementation and dependence on diplomacy. The organization can neither rely on the help of centralized monitoring and enforcement, nor on the dynamics of spillover. Furthermore, there are reasons to believe that interpresidentialism and the paymaster effect may have lost momentum: first, the admission of Venezuela could weaken the power of interpresidentialism, as it adds a potential new cleavage and complicates the balance of powers. Second, Brazil's shift in trade priorities away from the region reduces the hegemon's incentive to invest in MERCOSUR. Considering that several previous efforts to renew the process of integration have been dismissed as a resort to "parchment institutions and rhetoric as a substitute for effectiveness and deepening" (Domínguez 2010: 38), there seems to be reason for doubt about MERCOSUR's future.

References

Abbott, K. W., Keohane, R. O., Moravcsik, A., Slaughter, A.-M. and Snidal, D. 2000. The Concept of Legalization. *International Organization*, 54(3), 401–419.

Arieti, S. A. 2006. The Role of Mercosur as a Vehicle for Latin American Integration. *Chicago Journal of International Law*, 6(2), 761–773.

Azevedo Cunha, M. V. d. 2007. *The Judicial System of MERCOSUR: Is there Administrative Justice?* [Online]. Available at: www.iilj.org/GAL/documents/cunha.pdf [accessed: March 22, 2011].

Bieling, H.-J. 2007. *Internationale Politische Ökonomie. Eine Einführung.* Wiesbaden: VS Verlag für Sozialwissenschaften.

Bouzas, R. 2008. Regional Governance Institutions, Asymmetries, and Deeper Integration in MERCOSUR, in *Deepening Integration in MERCOSUR. Dealing with Disparities*, edited by J. S. Blyde, E. Fernández-Arias and P. Giordano. Washington, DC: Inter-American Development Bank, 355–379.

Bouzas, R. and Soltz, H. 2001. Institutions and Regional Integration: The Case of MERCOSUR, in *Regional Integration in Latin Amrica and the Carribean: The Political Economy of Open Regionalism*, edited by V. Bulmer-Thomas. London: Institute of Latin American Studies, 98–118.

Bouzas, R., Motta Veiga, P. d. and Torrent, R. 2002. *In-Depth Analysis of Mercosur Integration, its Prospectives and the Effects Thereof on the Market Access of EU Goods, Services and Investment, Report*. [Online]. Barcelona: Observatory of Globalisation. Available at: http://madb.europa.eu/madb_barriers/viewDoc.htm?type=study&filename=32.doc [accessed: March 20, 2011].

Capannelli, G., Lee, J.-W. and Petri, P. 2009. Developing Indicators for Regional Economic Integration and Cooperation. *UNU-CRIS Working Papers W-2009/22* [Online]. Available at: www.cris.unu.edu/fileadmin/workingpapers/W-2009-22.pdf [accessed: March 20, 2011].

Carranza, M. E. 2003. Can Mercosur Survive? Domestic and International Constraints on Mercosur. *Latin American Politics and Society*, 45(2), 67–103.

Domínguez, J. I. 2007. International Cooperation in Latin America. The Design of Regional Institutions by Slow Accretion, in *Crafting Cooperation. Regional International Institutions in Comparative Perspective*, edited by A. Acharya and A. I. Johnston. Cambridge: Cambridge University Press, 83–128.

Domínguez, J. I. 2010. Regional Economic Institutions in Latin America. Politics, Profits, and Peace. *The Annual Meeting of the American Political Science Association.*

Duina, F. 2006. *The Social Construction of Free Trade. The European Union, NAFTA, and MERCOSUR*. Princeton: Princeton University Press.

Elsner, G. and Alabor, C. 2009. *Gipfel der (Un-)Möglichkeiten. Uruguay übernimmt die pro tempore-Präsidentschaft des MERCOSUR. Länderbericht Uruguay*. [Online]. Available at: www.kas.de/wf/doc/kas_17299-544-1-30.pdf [accessed: March 25, 2011].

European Commission. 2007. *Mercosur Regional Strategy Paper 2007–2013.* Brussels.

European Commission. 2010. *EU Trade Commissioner Karel De Gucht travels to Argentina and Brazil to discuss EU-Mercosur trade negotiations. Press release, September 13, 2010*. Brussels.

Flemes, D. and Westermann, L. 2009. Konkurrierender Regionalismus. Fünf Jahre UNASUR und ALBA. *GIGA Focus Lateinamerika* [Online]. Available at: www.giga-hamburg.de/dl/download.php?d=/content/publikationen/pdf/gf_lateinamerika_0912.pdf [accessed: March 15, 2011].

Gómez Mera, L. 2005. Explaining MERCOSUR's Survival: Strategic Sources of Argentine-Brazilian Convergence. *Latin American Studies*, 37, 109–140.

Gómez Mera, L. 2009. Domestic Constraints on Regional Cooperation: Explaining Trade Conflict in MERCOSUR. *Review of International Political Economy*, 16(5), 746–777.

INTAL. 2009. *MERCOSUR Report N° 13 (2007–2008)*. [Online]. Buenos Aires: IDB-INTAL. Available at: www.iadb.org/intal/aplicaciones/uploads/publicaciones/i_MERCOSUR_Report_13.pdf [accessed: April 5, 2011].

Malamud, A. 2003. Presidentialism and Mercosur. A Hidden Cause for a Successful Experience, in *Comparative Regional Integration. Theoretical Perspectives*, edited by F. Laursen. Aldershot: Ashgate, 53–73.

Malamud, A. 2005. Presidential Diplomacy and the Institutional Underpinnings of MERCOSUR: An Experimental Examination. *Latin American Research Review*, 40(1), 138–164.

Malamud, A. 2008. The Internal Agenda of Mercosur. Interdependence, Leadership and Institutionalization, in *Los nuevos enfoques de la integración: más allá del regionalismo*, edited by G. Jaramillo. Quito: FLACSO, 115–135.

Malamud, A. and Schmitter, P. C. 2007. The Experience of European Integration and the Potential for Integration in South America. *IBEI Working Paper 2007/6* [Online]. Available at: http://ssrn.com/abstract=965798 [accessed: March 5, 2011].

Manzetti, L. 1993. The Political Economy of Mercosur. *Journal of Interamerican Studies and World Affairs*, 35(4), 101–141.

Mattli, W. 1999. *The Logic of Regional Integration. Europe and Beyond*. Cambridge: Cambridge University Press.

MERCOSUR. 1991. Treaty of Asunción. *United Nations Treaty Series No. 2140* [Online]. Available at: http://untreaty.un.org/unts/144078_158780/11/9/4261.pdf [accessed: September 20, 2010].

MERCOSUR. 2009. *Common Market Council Decision 16/2009. "Fondo para la convergencia estructural del Mercosur. Presupuesto 2010"*. Montevideo.

Motta Veiga, P. d. 2004. MERCOSUR's Institutionalization Agenda. The Challenges of a Project in Crisis. *INTAL-ITD Working Paper 06E/2004*. Buenos Aires: IDB-INTAL.

Pena, C. and Rozemberg, R. 2005. MERCOSUR. A Different Approach to Institutional Development. *FOCAL Policy Paper*. Ottawa: FOCAL.

Perales, J. R. 2003. A Supply-Side Theory of International Economic Institutions for the Mercosur, in *Comparative Regional Integration. Theoretical Perspectives*, edited by F. Laursen. Aldershot: Ashgate, 75–101.

Porrata-Doria Jr., R. A. 2005. *Mercosur. The Common Market of the Southern Cone*. Durham: Carolina Academic Press.

Preusse, H. G. 2004. *The New American Regionalism*. Cheltenham: Edward Elgar.

Tussie, D. 2009. Latin America. Contrasting Motivations for Regional Projects. *Review of International Studies*, 35(S1), 169–188.

UNU-CRIS. 2008. *Technical Notes. Regional Integration Knowledge System.* [Online]. Available at: www.cris.unu.edu/uploads/Technical_notes_may_2008.doc [accessed: April 10, 2011].

UNU-CRIS. 2010. *Regional Integration Knowledge System.* [Online]. Available at: www.cris.unu.edu/riks/web/data [accessed: April 10, 2011].

Vervaele, J. A. 2005. Mercosur and Regional Integration in South America. *International and Comparative Law Quarterly*, 54(2), 387–410.

Wrobel, P. S. 1999. MERCOSUR after the Brazilian Financial Turmoil. *The International Spectator*, 34(3), 81–89.

PART 3
Institutional Design

Chapter 5

Explaining Differences in the Institutional Design of ASEAN and NAFTA

Leon Kanthak

Introduction

The aim of this chapter is to analyze and explain institutional variance by providing a comparison of two examples of non-European regionalism: the Association of Southeast Asian Nations (ASEAN) and the North American Free Trade Agreement (NAFTA). Both of these organizations can be seen as alternatives to the EU model of regional integration, being, arguably, more intergovernmental and more restricted in their approach. However, the aim of this chapter is to show major differences in the institutional design of these two cases and to provide an explanation for it.

The basic argument of this chapter is that divergence of institutional design can be explained by the different vulnerabilities countries may face when they create regional organizations. If their vulnerabilities are regional in nature, and can be controlled by binding the behavior of regional actors (e.g. states, companies), they will choose a model of high legalism. If the vulnerabilities are non-regional (e.g. global), they will rather prefer a model of high flexibility. In this chapter, the focus will be on the dimension of trade. Theoretically speaking, it seems, however, possible to apply it to further policy dimensions.

This analysis begins with a short overview of regional integration within ASEAN and NAFTA. Thereafter, the scope is narrowed to two crucial dimensions: legalism and flexibility. Then, to provide an explanation for the divergence, a theoretical model is developed which suggests that the type of institutional design depends upon the relative strength of regional and global vulnerabilities. In a last step, this theoretical model is applied to the cases, providing a test as to whether its predictions are correct.

ASEAN, NAFTA, and Regional Integration

This section will focus on the general outlook of ASEAN and NAFTA as examples of regionalism in their respective regions, Southeast Asia and North America. Before proceeding, it seems advisable to clarify some definitions. Regions will be understood as geographically contiguous spaces that are also perceived as regions by relevant actors (Hurrell 1995). Regionalism, then, will be defined as "state-led projects of cooperation [within regions] that emerge as a result of intergovernmental dialogues and treaties" (Breslin and Higgott 2000: 344). This definition is purposely state-centric, being contrasted with the concept of regionalization which describes the non-state-led mechanisms of regional integration. This separation is analytically important because it allows for establishing causal connections differences in institutional design of inter-state regional organizations (examples of regionalism) and the degree or kind of regionalization.

ASEAN, founded with the Bangkok Declaration of 1967, is one of the oldest regional organizations in the world and one of the most prominent in Asia (Cockerham 2009). At its inception, the founding members were mainly concerned with dealing with domestic communist threats and reducing the risk of armed conflict between them (Narine 1997). Accordingly, though the non-binding declaration "advocated collaboration in economic, social, cultural, technical, scientific, and administrative fields" (Cockerham 2009: 170), security issues were prevalent during this time (Akrasanee 2001, Bowles and MacLean 1996).

Eventually, ASEAN embarked on an incremental and demand-driven path of regional integration and institutionalization (Cockerham 2009, Kahler 2000). This path was characterized by a set of certain norms subsumed under the term ASEAN Way, which "describes the informality of cooperation, the adherence to the principle of non-interference, the greater reliance on personal relations than on institutions and the decision-making through consultation and consensus" (Volkmann 2008: 79). Particularly after the Cold War—earlier attempts were largely unsuccessful (Akrasanee 2001)—ASEAN expanded in the economic sphere. The Singapore Declaration of 1992 envisaged an ASEAN Free Trade Area (AFTA), which was incrementally institutionalized and modified in the course of the following years. The Bali Concord II of 2003 suggested the establishment of "a single market and production base" (ASEAN 2003). In 2007, the ASEAN Charter was signed, its most significant achievements being the institutionalization of existing principles and practices, the expression of a commitment to democracy and human rights, and the attribution of a legal personality for ASEAN (ASEAN 2007b).

Regionalism in North America took its current shape in 1994, when NAFTA entered into force superseding the previously existing Canada-US Free Trade Agreement (CUFTA) of 1988. It was complemented by two supplementary agreements, the North American Agreement on Environmental Cooperation (NAAEC) and the North American Agreement on Labor Cooperation (NAALC). NAFTA's initial institutional design has not undergone significant changes since its creation.

As Abbott notes, "NAFTA is among the most highly detailed international trade agreements ever negotiated between governments" (Abbott 2000: 524). It follows a clear primary objective: the elimination of all tariff and many non-tariff barriers to trade of goods and services as well as the promotion of conditions of fair competition (NAFTA 1994: Chapter 1 Article 102). While its scope is clearly restricted to issues associated with trade and investment, it does cover comprehensively certain aspects of the economic and socio-cultural sphere: regulations in the domains of competition and industry (rules of origin, customs, standards, etc.), economic freedoms (capital liberalization, trade in goods and services), energy and transport, and agriculture (including subsidies) in the former; regulation on consumer protection (through means of standards and complaints), and research and development (by regulating investment and intellectual property issues) in the latter case.

Narrowing the Scope of Analysis: Legalism and Flexibility

The decisive argument made in this section is that ASEAN and NAFTA follow two distinct, partly converse logics of regional integration. The former could be described as flexible regionalism, relying on processes of learning and adjustment and starting with non-binding and imprecise measures. In contrast, the latter could be described as fixed regionalism, setting clear and binding rules and minimizing uncertainty for the future institutional development. Five variables subdivided in two categories are used to describe this contrast. The first category concerns legalism and includes the variables of obligation, precision, and enforcement. These variables are borrowed from the legalization concept (Abbott et al. 2000). Basically, obligation refers to the degree to which international rules are binding for states and other actors subjected to them. Precision is defined as the degree to which the room for alternative explanations is narrowed. Cases in which both of these variables take a high value are examples of high legalism. The most important difference between the concept of legalization developed in the literature (see Abbott and Snidal 2000) and the concept of legalism used here is that the latter restricts the dimension of delegation to (delegated) enforcement. This restriction is made in order to focus on the legal status of a rule which remains, technically speaking, unaffected by whether or not it provides for *further* rule-making (i.e. secondary legislation). The second category concerns and encompasses the variables adaptive flexibility, that is the degree to which the institutions of an international arrangement provide room for different or changing preferences of (single) member states (for example, escape clauses) and transformative flexibility, that is the degree to which an international institution is able to change as a whole (Koremenos et al. 2001). Cases in which both of these variables take a high value are examples of high flexibility. Importantly, delegation of further rule-making may serve as a tool to increase transformative flexibility in the sense that it may *create* an authority for transforming existing rules to meet future demands. This adds a practical reason to the theoretical one mentioned above to distinguish between delegation and legalism.

Of course the model for highlighting the differences in institutional design between ASEAN and NAFTA is both simplifying (leaving out other important features of institutional design) and ideal typical (contrasting two objects of comparison more sharply than is actually empirically the case). ASEAN is not entirely non-binding and NAFTA is not always inflexible: for example, ASEAN has continuously moved to more strongly legalized dispute settlement (Cockerham

2009) whereas NAFTA has adapted to new standard procedures provided by the WTO (Clarkson et al. 2002). Nevertheless, ASEAN continues to state its preference for flexible engagement and open dialogue (ASEAN 2007b: Preamble) whilst NAFTA's adjustments are marginal at best and are of technical rather than political nature (Clarkson et al. 2002).

Legalism: Obligation and Precision

Applying the legalization concept to the Asia-Pacific macroregion, Kahler finds that there is a general aversion to binding and precise rules (Kahler 2000). ASEAN has, however, experienced an incremental development toward more obligation and precision though it still remains at a low level (Kahler 2000).

The Bangkok Declaration of 1967 was, in the strict legal sense, a non-binding document (Cockerham 2009). In terms of codification of the three founding documents of AFTA, one was a non-binding declaration (Singapore Declaration) whilst the other two were legally binding under international law. Initially, however, the agreements did not create binding rules (Nesadurai 2008). In particular, the degree of enforcement was low. At first, AFTA did not include a formal dispute settlement mechanism. The only mechanism available to member states in case of non-compliance of another member state were open consultations unable to bind the party complained against (ASEAN 1992: Article 8). This lack of enforcement encouraged non-compliance, which eventually—towards the end of the 1990s—contributed to the establishment of somewhat more binding rules (Nesadurai 2008, Ravenhill 2009).

Concerning precision, AFTA ranks low. As most of the documents issued by ASEAN, the three documents are not very detailed in their provisions and leave room for interpretation. Exact tariff rates are not specified. The CEPT Scheme envisages a tariff reduction to a value between 0 and 5 percent. Given that AFTA, thus, does not necessarily require member states to abolish tariffs, it has been suggested that "ASEAN's definition of free trade was an unusual one" (Ravenhill 2009: 226). There are no lists of specific commodities for which the CEPT applies other than the 15 products that were designated for accelerated tariff reduction. Furthermore, the rules on non-tariff barriers to trade as well as the rules of origin remain unclear (Soesastro 2005). The lack of precision was criticized for undermining potential gains (Ravenhill 2009). Countries eventually backtracked as their obligations were not precisely articulated. Already in 1994, it was consequently decided to expand and clarify the list of goods covered as well as introduce the aim of zero tariff rates (Bowles and MacLean 1996).

NAFTA, on the other hand, is codified as a binding agreement under international law. In terms of obligation, NAFTA rates high as well. Abbott, applying the legalization concept, comes to the same conclusion pointing to the definite and widely non-permissive language used (parties "give effect"; "shall") in combination with its legal standard and the express terms of the agreement (Abbott 2000).

There are three different NAFTA dispute resolution mechanisms. The first (Chapter 11) concerns investment (NAFTA 1994: Chapter 11 Section B). It allows private investors to challenge member state interventions on the basis of their accordance to NAFTA. As a result, the state may be forced to restore property or pay arbitrary awards to the investor. Significantly, it thus allows private individuals to sue member state governments (Abbott 2000). The second mechanism (Chapter 19) allows member states to challenge other members' application of their regulations concerning anti-dumping and countervailing duties (NAFTA 1994: Chapter 19). Such panel decisions are directly binding (NAFTA 1994: Chapter 19 Article 1904.9). The third dispute settlement procedure (Chapter 20), the generally applicable mechanism, provides for government-to-government consultations and, if these are unsuccessful, for panel review of a specific measure/policy of a member state suspected to be inconsistent with NAFTA by another member state. If non-compliance is found and the party complained against does not make the recommended adjustments, the complaining party may suspend benefits (NAFTA 1994: Chapter 20 Section B). This comprehensive system of dispute resolution points to a high degree of enforcement.

Concerning precision, NAFTA rates high as well (Abbott 2000). Actually, according to Abbott, NAFTA is more precise than the WTO agreement and the EC treaty, thus qualifying as one of the most precise international trade agreements ever concluded (Abbott 2000). NAFTA covers comprehensively, in 22 chapters, almost every aspect of international trade. It provides clear and detailed rules for the different commodities.

Summing up, obligation and enforcement are high in NAFTA whilst they are low in ASEAN. Even more striking is the difference between the two in terms of precision. Kahler juxtaposes AFTA's original 15 pages (Framework Agreement, CEPT Scheme) with NAFTA's more than 1,000 (Kahler 2000). Recently, however, ASEAN has begun to move toward more binding and detailed rules. Nevertheless, as of now, obligation and precision remain at a significantly lower level than in NAFTA and there are few signs that ASEAN is giving up its general preference for non-binding and imprecise rules (Nesadurai 2008).

Flexibility: Adaptive and Transformative

In terms of adaptive flexibility, that is the ability to accommodate changing preferences of member states, ASEAN is a very flexible organization. Recently it developed the ASEAN Minus X formula, introduced first for integration concerning trade in services, which was explicitly mentioned in the ASEAN Charter (ASEAN 2007a, 2007b). It allows unwilling states to refuse cooperation without impeding further and faster integration among other member states.

Additionally, the CEPT Scheme allows for groups of countries to increase the speed of integration with each other beyond the requirements of the treaties (ASEAN 1992: Article 4.1c). This provision already came very close to the ASEAN Minus X formula, as it also allowed a subset of member countries to push integration further. AFTA includes flexible arrangements also for countries which consider the speed or scope of integration as harmful or belief that it may be inflicting damage on their domestic economy, their security, or their national independence. Countries are allowed to exclude products or product lists from the CEPT Scheme (ASEAN 1992: Article 2). Also, countries may suspend tariff reduction in entire sectors when they consider such a measure to be effective in protecting domestic producers (ASEAN 1992: Article 6).

ASEAN's ability to change and adapt, referred to as transformative flexibility, is also remarkable. First, ASEAN has, over the course of the years, significantly altered its scope from an organization mainly occupied with security-related issues to one that covers a wide array of policy fields and features the deepest degree of integration in the economic sphere (Cockerham 2009, Nesadurai 2008). Thus, ASEAN's ability to transform is hard to deny, but it is more difficult to find out what specific feature of ASEAN's institutional design is responsible for this flexibility. Certain signs of transformative flexibility may be found in the treaties. For example, the postponing of further rule-making in the future may indirectly strengthen transformative flexibility and, as much as imprecision allows for different interpretations among members, it may also empower the organization as a whole to readjust its goals in the face of changing circumstances. ASEAN, therefore, has a built-in mechanism for change in its ability to issue secondary legislation, though this ability is exclusively intergovernmental.

NAFTA, on the other hand, is characterized by a rather low level of flexibility. Concerning adaptive flexibility, the treaty does not include opt-in or opt-out clauses. Countries are only able to accede to or withdraw from the agreement as a whole; picking certain provisions while leaving out others is not possible. There are certain sector-specific exceptions in the treaty, for example, concerning Mexico's energy sector (NAFTA 1994: Chapter 6 Annexes 602.3; 603.6; 605; 607) or Canada's cultural industries (CUFTA 1989: Chapter 20 Article 2005, NAFTA 1994: Chapter 21 Annex 2106). However, these exceptions are, in contrast to those of ASEAN, restricted to a certain issue, applicable only to a certain country, and determined a priori. They do not improve member states' ability to "respond to unanticipated shocks" (Koremenos et al. 2001: 773) and, therefore, do not increase the adaptive flexibility of the treaty.

The level of transformative flexibility provided for by NAFTA is low, as well. Since its creation, it has only undergone minor and purely technical changes. NAFTA is apolitical in the sense that none of its bodies is empowered to take political decisions and issue (secondary) legislation. While the power of "policy-making" is delegated to the regional level in ASEAN (ASEAN 2007b: Chapter 4 Article 7), even the chief intergovernmental body of NAFTA, the FTC, is far from being given the right to develop its own policies. Instead, it is only delegated the power to "supervise" and "oversee" the implementation and elaboration of the existing agreement (NAFTA 1994: Chapter 20 Article 2001.2).

Summing up, flexibility is high in ASEAN whereas NAFTA is rather inflexible. NAFTA rules leave little room for adjustments to changed needs and preferences in the future, neither of individual countries nor of the organization as a whole. ASEAN, on the other hand, allows its member states to adjust to changes. They may increase the speed of integration, slow it down, or even suspend it entirely if necessary. Flexible formulas allow individual countries to do so without holding up the integration process as a whole. In addition to that, also ASEAN as a whole has proven its ability to transform its institutional structure.

Explaining the Divergence

Why are ASEAN's and NAFTA's institutional design opposites in terms of the integration of legalism and flexibility in their approach? In order to answer this question, the following section aims to develop a theoretical approach that can be, in a final step, applied to the two cases.

Theoretical Approach

Three basic assumptions of my explanatory approach, fairly common among rational institutionalist scholars (see Koremenos et al. 2001), are made before further exploring this question. First, it is assumed that institutions matter. They may change actions, for example, by changing incentives, preference structures, or values. The second assumption is that actors are rational. Pertaining to institution building this means that they rationally calculate costs and benefits of a specific design and choose between different alternatives on the basis of what seems most profitable to them. Third, it is assumed that states are the decisive actors when it comes to inter-state treaties fostering integration. The states may be influenced by other domestic or international factors but when trying to understand inter-state institution building it is decisive to understand the states.

In terms of policy goals there are good reasons to pursue legalism as well as flexibility. Legalism, first and foremost, reduces uncertainty about future actors' behavior. Binding and precise rules make future behavior comparatively more predictable as their preference structures are altered (usually in the direction of fulfilling the precise obligations set forth by the institution). Risk-averse actors have a strong preference to minimize uncertainty, making legalism in international institutions a desirable policy goal. A preference for flexibility can also be explained as a way to deal with uncertainty. When states are faced with uncertainties about the future, it may be rational for them to design institutions that hinder as little as possible the states' ability to respond effectively to unexpected developments and that are also able to adapt when faced with such changes.

If both legalism and flexibility are rational goals for states to pursue the question arises as to why they do not design institutions that are both legalized and flexible? The argument here is that there is actually also a trade-off between the two categories. Highly binding and precise rules cannot provide much flexibility whereas highly flexible arrangements cannot allow for a high degree of legalism. Thus, countries have to choose between them.

How can this choice be explained? As mentioned earlier, both legalism and flexibility can be identified as ways to deal with uncertainty. Scholars of rational design (Koremenos et al. 2001) recognize uncertainty as one of the independent variables influencing the institutional set-up of international organizations. They distinguish between uncertainty about the state of the world, uncertainty about others' behavior, and uncertainty about others' preferences. The distinction used here will be slightly different: it will be between uncertainties controllable by the regional organization, that is uncertainties about the behavior of the actors involved, and uncertainties beyond its scope, that is uncertainties about the behavior of actors not involved in, and not committed to, the regional institution. On the basis of this distinction, it will be argued that a difference in the *kind* of uncertainty may be the reason why some states choose one model of institutional design whilst others choose another. As the rational design scholars have argued, flexibility may alleviate the vulnerability to uncertainties about developments that have their roots outside the region and, thus, cannot be regionally controlled (Koremenos et al. 2001). However, the argument here is that this is only one side of the coin: legalism may be an attractive option (even at the price of a loss of flexibility) to deal with uncertainties as well when these are about the actions of the regional actors involved.

According to this model, ASEAN states are expected to be relatively more vulnerable to outside forces, whereas the design of NAFTA should be motivated by a relatively high vulnerability to actions from within the region.

Alternative Explanations

Before engaging in an application of the theoretical model to the cases two other explanations will be reviewed in order to show why, concerning the focus of this work, they seem less promising than the one elaborated above.

First, it may seem plausible to point to cultural differences to account for the differences in the institutional design of ASEAN and NAFTA. One could say that ASEAN's flexibility is, first and foremost, caused by the Southeast Asian norms and values as expressed in the ASEAN Way, whereas NAFTA's legalism is shaped by a Western preference for binding and legal rules. The strand of cultural explanations cannot be dismissed entirely. Culture certainly matters even when assuming rational actors, as their preferences will at least partly be shaped by their specific cultural background. However, there are strong hints that it does not provide a sufficient explanation as it can neither explain the large degree of variance in regional integration in different institutional schemes of Southeast Asia (see Kahler 2000) or of North America (see Abbott 2000). Examples which would contradict the expectations of cultural explanations are provided by the ASEAN Charter of 2007 and NAFTA's side agreements. It may, therefore, be worthwhile to look at other factors, such as the specific strategic setting of the actors.

Another way of explaining both Southeast Asian and North American regionalism rests on global pressures as explanatory factors. Actually, European integration (Single European Act 1987) has served as an explanation, characterizing integration elsewhere as "second integrative response" (Mattli 1999). Also, the end of the Cold War and pressures arising from globalization have been used as explanatory factors to explain both the creation of AFTA and that of NAFTA (Kim 2004, Schirm 2002). Yet, global factors suggest uniform effects and are thus not useful when trying to explain inter-regional divergence. This is, however, far from saying that these explanations are false. The factors mentioned have explanatory value, especially when the question is asked as to why so many regions turned to regionalism in the early 1990s. Yet, when asking for an explanation for the differences between the regional approaches, global explanations are insufficient.

Finally, some approaches attempted to provide historical explanations for regionalism. They pointed to the past experience of being colonized and subjected to foreign powers and the involvement of the United States during the Cold War as explanatory factors for the high value attributed to sovereignty and the lack of pressures for further, more legalized and less flexible integration (Aggarwal and Koo 2008). For NAFTA, the conflictual history with and the fear of being dominated by the much larger neighbor have been used as explanatory factors for the hostility toward regional integration present in Canada and Mexico for much of the twentieth century (Golob 2003). The shift away from this hostility, explained by the economic and political crises of the 1980s, is then described as a critical juncture. Whereas one cannot wholly dismiss historical institutionalist explanations, their strength lies in explaining continuity (by pointing to path dependency) rather than change (which always must be explained by critical junctures outside the theoretical framework).

Empirical Application

In the following the approach outlined above will be tested. There are several advantages that distinguish an approach based on vulnerabilities from other possible explanations. First, it does not ignore the specific issues that are covered. Countries may be more vulnerable concerning some issues than they are in others. Therefore, different kinds of integration in different agreements among the same countries (for example, NAFTA and its side agreements) can be explained. Second, vulnerabilities can change over time. Therefore, it is not necessary to assume that regional institutions basically remain static and the transformation of regional organizations (for example, ASEAN) can be accounted for. Third, vulnerabilities may diverge inter-regionally as the strategic setting of the countries may be different, as well. Therefore, vulnerabilities may potentially serve as an explanatory factor for divergence across issues (at one time and within one region), across time (with the same issue within one region), and across regions (with the same issue and at one time). This analysis mainly focuses on the latter.

Table 5.1 Selected trade statistics for ASEAN and NAFTA members

Country (Year)	GDP (in PPP, in bn USD)	Imports (in bn USD)	Exports (in bn USD)	Total Trade (in bn USD)	Trade/GDP	Intraregional trade (2009)
Brunei (2008)	20.0	2.6	10.7	13.3	66.5 %	27.90 %
Cambodia (2009, 2010)	28.7 30.1	5.9 6.0	4.2 4.7	10.1 10.7	35.2 % 35.5 %	23.63 %
Indonesia (2009, 2010)	974.6 1,003.0	84.4 111.1	119.5 146.3	203.9 257.4	20.9 % 25.7 %	24.52 %
Laos (2009, 2010)	14.6 15.7	1.3 1.5	1.1 2.0	2.4 3.5	16.9 % 22.0 %	61.02 %
Malaysia (2009, 2010)	388.8 416.7	128.3 174.3	163.2 210.3	291.5 384.6	74.9 % 92.3 %	25.49 %
Myanmar (2009, 2010)	58.3 60.1	4.0 4.5	6.9 7.8	10.9 12.3	18.7 % 20.5 %	46.34 %
Philippines (2009, 2010)	329.2 353.2	46.4 59.9	37.6 50.7	84.0 110.6	25.5 % 31.3 %	20.70 %

Singapore (2009, 2010)	255.0 292.4	245 310.4	268.9 351.2	513.9 661.6	201.5 % 226.3 %	27.24 %
Thailand (2009, 2010)	539.3 580.3	118 156.9	151.9 191.3	269.9 348.2	50.0 % 60.0 %	19.97 %
Vietnam (2009, 2010)	260.3 278.1	65.4 84.3	57.1 72.0	122.5 156.3	47.1 % 56.2 %	17.64 %
Canada (2009, 2010)	1,297.0 1,335.0	327.3 406.4	323.3 406.8	650.6 813.2	50.2 % 60.1 %	65.49 %
Mexico (2009, 2010)	1,485.0 1,560.0	234.4 306.0	229.8 303.0	464.2 609.0	31.3 % 39.0 %	67.47 %
United States (2009, 2010)	14,330.0 14,720.0	1575.0 1903.0	1,069.0 1,270.0	2,644.0 3,173.0	18.5 % 21.6 %	27.83 %

Sources: CIA World Factbook and International Monetary Fund (CIA annual, IMF 2010).

Table 5.2 Main trading partners for ASEAN and NAFTA members

Country	Main trading partners (imports in percent)	Main trading partners (exports in percent)
Brunei (2009)	Singapore 38.4, Malaysia 18.7, Japan 7.2, China 5.4, Thailand 5.2, US 4.5, UK 4.3	Japan 38, Indonesia 26, South Korea 14, Australia 7.2
Cambodia (2009)	Thailand 24.8, Vietnam 19.7, China 14.1, Singapore 11.3, Hong Kong 7.4, Taiwan 5.1, S. Korea 4.1	US 45.3, Singapore 9.5, Germany 7.5, UK 7.1, Canada 6.3, Vietnam 4.1
Indonesia (2009)	Singapore 25, China 12.5, Japan 8.9, Malaysia 5.9, South Korea 5.6, US 4.9, Thailand 4.5	Japan 17.3, Singapore 11.3, US 10.8, China 7.6, South Korea 5.5, India 4.4, Taiwan 4.1, Malaysia 4
Laos (2009)	Thailand 66.2, China 11.45, Vietnam 5.3	Thailand 29.2, China 15, Vietnam 15, UK 4.3
Malaysia (2010 est.)	China 12.6, Japan 12.6, Singapore 11.4, US 10.7, Thailand 6.2, Indonesia 5.6	Singapore 13.4, China 12.6, Japan 10.4, US 9.5, Thailand 5.3, Hong Kong 5.1
Myanmar (2009)	China 33.1, Thailand 26.3, Singapore 15.2	Thailand 46.6, India 13, China 9, Japan 5.7
Philippines (2009 est.)	Japan 12.5, US 12, China 8.8, Singapore 8.7, South Korea 7.9, Taiwan 7.1, Thailand 5.7	US 17.6, Japan 16.2, Netherl. 9.8, Hong Kong 8.6, China 7.7, Germany 6.5, Singapore 6.2, S. Korea 4.8
Singapore (2009 est.)	US 14.7, Malaysia 11.6, China 10.5, Japan 7.6, Indonesia 5.8, South Korea 5.7	Hong Kong 11.6, Malaysia 11.5, US 11.2, Indonesia 9.7, China 9.7, Japan 4.6, Hong Kong 11.6

Thailand (2009 est.)	Japan 18.7, China 12.7, Malaysia 6.4, US 6.3, UAE 5, Singapore 4.3, South Korea 4.1	US 10.9, China 10.6, Japan 10.3, Hong Kong 6.2, Australia 5.6, Malaysia 5
Vietnam (2010 est.)	China 23.8, South Korea 11.6, Japan 10.8, Taiwan 8.4, Thailand 6.7, Singapore 4.9	US 20, Japan 10.7, China 9.8, South Korea 4.3
Canada (2009)	US 51.1, China 10.9, Mexico 4.6	US 75, UK 3.4, China 3.1
Mexico (2009 est.)	US 48, China 13.5, Japan 4.8, South Korea 4.6, Germany 4.1	US 80.5, Canada 3.6, Germany 1.4
US (2009)	China 19.3, Canada 14.2, Mexico 11.1, Japan 6.1	Canada 19.4, Mexico 12.2, China 6.6, Japan 4.8

Source: CIA World Factbook (CIA annual).

As ASEAN's degree of legalism is low while its flexibility is high, the theoretical approach suggests that within ASEAN the vulnerability to outside forces was greater than the vulnerability to actions of regional actors. Indeed, there is evidence supporting this claim. Intra-ASEAN trade only played a secondary role in the past. Even when AFTA was created it did not rise significantly (Nesadurai 2008). This is explained by the fact that "the ultimate objective of AFTA is to increase ASEAN's competitive edge as a production base geared for the world market. Stimulating intra-ASEAN trade is secondary" (Tan 2004: 939). This perspective helps to understand why ASEAN was relatively "tolerant of abuses and backtracking" (Tan 2004: 941). It can also be assumed that, concerning trade, this specific setting leads to a comparatively more important role of global trade relative to regional trade. As trade may create vulnerabilities, changes of global trade may have serious impacts on ASEAN member states that cannot be controlled for regionally. Given this setting, reducing flexibility in order to decrease uncertainties on the regional level may not seem like a good deal. Additionally, the slow rise of the share of intra-ASEAN trade (Nesadurai 2008) corresponds with an incremental rise of legalism within ASEAN, although a monocausal explanation for this rise would be overly simplifying. However, even after the recent rise, the importance of intra-ASEAN trade accounts for only 24.5 percent of total trade on average, and the number becomes even smaller when the two extreme outlier cases, Laos and Myanmar, are excluded (ASEAN 2010).

As Table 5.1 shows, ASEAN countries are still more dependent on global trade patterns than on regional ones. Intra-ASEAN trade accounts for less than one-fourth of the accumulated total trade of ASEAN countries (IMF 2010).

Furthermore, some ASEAN countries are tightly integrated in, and extremely dependent on, world trade. Singapore's total trade volume is more than twice as large as its GDP, even in a year of crisis such as 2009, but it is an outlier in that respect (and a special case as a city state). However, data for Malaysia, Thailand, and Vietnam indicate a high dependence on trade as well. In terms of these countries' top trading partners (see Table 5.2), the shares are either fairly evenly spread among a list of countries including ASEAN and non-ASEAN states (Malaysia) or, where larger shares of singular countries are present, indicate extra-ASEAN dependencies (Vietnam: highest shares for imports from China and exports to the United States). This means that they are vulnerable either to large patterns of world trade or to the behavior of specific non-ASEAN countries. Therefore, flexibility appears preferable to legalism.

There are certainly countries with a relatively large share of intra-ASEAN trade, most remarkably the aforementioned Laos and Myanmar (both countries' most important trade partner is Thailand). However, for both these countries trade is of lower salience as the comparatively low ratio of total trade volume and GDP indicates and they are, therefore, less vulnerable to changes in regional and world trade policy in the first place.

In what may seem like another contradiction, Brunei has a high trade/GDP ratio, yet its most important import partners are two ASEAN members (Singapore and Malaysia), which together account for over half of its imports. However, the value of exports, consisting mainly in crude oil and natural gas, is four times as high as the value of imports. Of the top four destinations for these exports mentioned in the *World Factbook*, only one, Indonesia, is an ASEAN member. Given this data, it becomes obvious that the country is, in its trade, at least as vulnerable to global developments (for example, the oil price) as it is to those that are regionally controllable. Overall, the empirical results therefore conform to the expectations of the theoretical approach for the case of ASEAN.

According to the theoretical approach, and given NAFTA's high degree of legalism and low flexibility, one would expect that the strategic setting of states within North America is characterized by a relatively high vulnerability to other regional actors' actions in comparison to the vulnerability to outside forces.

When it comes to trade, the relationship between the three North American nations is very dense. Table 5.1 shows that intra-regional trade is high and important for all countries. Particularly for Canada and Mexico in their respective relation to the United States this argument is strong. It suggests a stronger dependence on the region than on the rest of the world, both as a producer of imports and a consumer of exports. The data confirms this, as these countries' trade within NAFTA accounts for about two-thirds of their total trade, total trade having a moderate (Mexico) to relatively high salience (Canada). More precisely, it is trade with the United States that accounts for the lion's share of both countries' total trade (CIA annual). Consequently, Canada and Mexico are more vulnerable to changes in the trade policy of the United States than to changes in that policy of any other country—or even all others combined. For the Canadian case it is striking that at least nine out of 10 Canadian provinces export more to the United States than to the other provinces (Public Policy Forum 2003). In the Mexican case, the share of the products produced by *Maquiladora* industries—manufacturing sites along the US–Mexico border focused on producing for export to the United States—alone provides for more than half of Mexico's total exports (Clarkson et al. 2002). The suggestion that high vulnerability is an effect rather than a potential determinant of NAFTA's institutional design can be refuted on the basis of pre-NAFTA and pre-CUFTA data (CIA 1987), which reveals a comparable degree of vulnerability before their creation.

In the case of the United States, a relatively great dependence in trade on its neighbors can be noted as well. Canada and Mexico are among the United States' top trading partners: though more recent data accounts for a relative increase of the role of China, now the chief importer to the United States, Canada and Mexico remain strong, taking the first and third place regarding the value of overall trade (U.S. Census Bureau 2011). Table 5.1 reports an overall lower regional trade share for the United States than for Canada and Mexico, yet it is still higher than the accumulated share within ASEAN (IMF 2010). As there is, thus, some vulnerability to regional trade in the case of the United States and great regional vulnerability in the case of Canada and Mexico, the prediction of the model, high legalism, conforms to the empirical results found for the institutional design of NAFTA.

Yet, as foreshadowed, the vulnerabilities of North American countries diverge. This is highlighted by the extreme asymmetrical setting in North America. Thus, market access means, for Canada and Mexico, access to a market many times greater than their domestic ones. Furthermore, two facts revealed by the table are of importance. First, US trade is more diversified in terms of partners than that of its neighbors. None of its trading partners has a share of over 20 percent of total US trade. Second, the United States is much less dependent on foreign trade as such. This is highlighted by the small size of its total trade volume relative to its GDP (less than 1 to 5), compared to Canada's (about 1 to 2) and Mexico's (about 1 to 3) relative trade volume. Thus, for the United States, market access to Canada and Mexico combined was, and is, of much less significance. Consequently, Canada and Mexico are much more vulnerable to the United States than the other way round. So why did the United States join?

The traditional view, inspired by realism, is that large and powerful countries will not agree to submit to binding and precise rules as they present an obstruction to their sovereignty. The answer given here to this potential critique is that the realist notion—large and powerful countries can basically act as they please—exaggerates the actual circumstances. As using their greater power continuously to press for preferable outcomes is costly even for the most powerful states, they may prefer to embody their preferences in legalized rules (Abbott and Snidal 2000). NAFTA embodies US preferences in several ways. First, the agreement in effect forces Canada and Mexico to adapt to US rules and trade policy preferences, which long before expressed a preference for free trade. Already in 1979, during his presidential campaign, Ronald Reagan proposed free trade with Canada and Mexico (Reagan 1979). Second, NAFTA may be regarded as foreign policy tool with only minor impact on the US economy but with major impacts in helping friendly governments succeed (Krugman 1993). Third, NAFTA provided a blueprint of the US vision for future hemispheric or global governance of trade (Floudas and Rojas 2000). Fourth, the United States had little reason to insist on maximizing flexibility as its general vulnerability to outside forces, whether regional or global, was significantly lower than in smaller economies. Relating to globalization pressures, Schirm notes that the United States, far from being subjected to them, often was the real originator of these pressures (Schirm 2002).

Conclusion

ASEAN and NAFTA are two very different models of regionalism. Nevertheless, this approach has attempted to compare their respective institutional designs in a consistent and meaningful way that is profitable for the understanding of both.

ASEAN and NAFTA are both examples of regionalism outside of Europe and certainly they are both very different from the EU. However, concerning their ability to develop rules that are effectively binding and their ability to change and adapt, the two organizations are very different from each other as well. This difference can be expressed in their respective placement along two broad subdivided categories: legalism and flexibility. For a rational actor, both high legalism and high flexibility provide important advantages. However, as there is a trade-off between them, these cannot be attained together. Therefore, it becomes necessary to choose between them. But how can member states' choices be explained?

The theoretical model developed here allocates preferences for either legalism or flexibility to different kinds of uncertainties: uncertainty about the outside forces tends to lead to a preference for flexibility, whereas uncertainty about regional actors' behavior tends to induce a preference for legalism. In all real-world situations, actors will be faced with both kinds of uncertainty. However, they may weigh them differently according to their vulnerability to actions of either regionally containable or global factors. Overall, the empirical test seems to conform to the predictions of the model. The vulnerabilities in the field of trade in Southeast Asia are global rather than regional in nature, whereas trade vulnerabilities within North America, particularly of Canada and Mexico facing the United States, are extremely strong. It may be worthwhile to engage in further testing of the model, for example, by applying it to other regional organizations.

This chapter does not take sides on the question of whether flexible or legalized regionalism is superior. The analysis has shown that there may be good reasons for rational actors to pursue both types. Therefore, as long as the conditions of uncertainty remain differentiated between regions, a global convergence of institutional designs of regionalism is not to be expected and the number of different designs lending themselves to comparative analysis will remain high.

References

Abbott, F. M. 2000. NAFTA and the Legalization of World Politics: A Case Study. *International Organization*, 54(3), 519–547.

Abbott, K. W. and Snidal, D. 2000. Hard and Soft Law in International Governance. *International Organization*, 54(3), 421–456.

Abbott, K. W., Keohane, R. O., Moravcsik, A., Slaughter, A.-M. and Snidal, D. 2000. The Concept of Legalization. *International Organization*, 54(3), 401–419.

Aggarwal, V. and Koo, M. G. 2008. Asia's New Institutional Archictecture: Evolving Structures for Managing Trade, Financial, and Security Relations, in *Asia's New Institutional Architecture*, edited by V. Aggarwal and M. G. Koo. Berlin: Springer, 1–34.

Akrasanee, N. 2001. ASEAN in the Past Thirty-Three Years. Lessons for Economic Co-operation, in *Reinventing ASEAN*, edited by S. S. C. Tay, J. P. Estanislao and H. Soesastro. Singapore: Institute of Southeast Asian Studies, 35–41.

ASEAN. 1992. *Agreement On The Common Effective Preferential Tariff (CEPT) Scheme For The ASEAN Free Trade Area*. Singapore.

ASEAN. 2003. *Declaration of ASEAN Concord II (Bali Concord II)*. Bali.

ASEAN. 2007a. *ASEAN Economic Blueprint*. Singapore.

ASEAN. 2007b. *Charter of the Association of Southeast Asian Nations (ASEAN Charter)*. Singapore.

ASEAN. 2010. *External Trade Statistics: Intra- and extra-ASEAN trade, 2009*.

Bowles, P. and MacLean, B. 1996. Understanding Trade Bloc Formation: The Case of the ASEAN Free Trade Area. *Review of International Political Economy*, 3(2), 319–348.

Breslin, S. and Higgott, R. 2000. Studying Regions: Learning from the Old, Constructing the New. *New Political Economy*, 5(3), 333–352.

CIA. 1987. *The World Factbook*. Washington, DC: Central Intelligence Agency.

CIA. annual. *The World Factbook*. Washington, DC: Central Intelligence Agency.

Clarkson, S., Davidson Ladly, S. and Thorne, C. 2002. De-Institutionalizing North America: NAFTA's Committees and Working Groups. *Third EnviReform Conference*. Toronto.

Cockerham, G. 2009. Regional Integration in ASEAN: Institutional Design and the ASEAN Way. *East Asia*, 27(2), 165–185.

CUFTA. 1989. *Free Trade Agreement between Canada and the United States of America*. Ottawa and Washington, DC.

Floudas, D. and Rojas, L. F. 2000. Some Thoughts on NAFTA and Trade Integration in the American Continent. *International Problems*, LII(4), 1–11.

Golob, S. R. 2003. Beyond the Policy Frontier: Canada, Mexico, and the Ideological Origins of NAFTA. *World Politics*, 55(3), 361–398.

Hurrell, A. 1995. Explaining the Resurgence of Regionalism in World Politics. *Review of International Studies*, 21(4), 331–358.

IMF. 2010. *Direction of Trade Statistics. Yearbook 2010*. Washington, DC: International Monetary Fund.

Kahler, M. 2000. Legalization as Strategy: The Asia-Pacific Case. *International Organization*, 54(3), 549–571.

Kim, S. S. 2004. Regionalization and Regionalism in East Asia. *Journal of East Asian Studies*, 4(1), 39–68.

Koremenos, B., Lipson, C. and Snidal, D. 2001. The Rational Design of International Institutions. *International Organization*, 55(4), 761–799.

Krugman, P. 1993. The Uncomfortable Truth about NAFTA: It's Foreign Policy, Stupid. *Foreign Affairs*, 72(5), 13–19.

Mattli, W. 1999. *The Logic of Regional Integration*. Cambridge: Cambridge University Press.

NAFTA. 1994. *North American Free Trade Agreement*. Mexico City, Ottawa and Washington, DC.

Narine, S. 1997. ASEAN and the ARF: The Limits of the "ASEAN Way." *Asian Survey*, 37(10), 961–978.

Nesadurai, H. 2008. The Association of Southeast Asian Nations (ASEAN). *New Political Economy*, 13(2), 225–239.

Public Policy Forum. 2003. *PPF Symposium: Rethinking North American Integration*. [Online]. Ottawa: Public Policy Forum. Available at: www.ppforum.ca/sites/default/files/na_outcomes_final.pdf [accessed: September 17, 2010].

Ravenhill, J. 2009. East Asian Regionalism: Much Ado about Nothing. *Review of International Studies*, 35(S1), 215–235.

Reagan, R. 1979. *Ronald Reagan's Announcement for Presidential Candidacy*. [Online]. New York, November 13: Ronald Reagan Presidential Library. Available at: www.reagan.utexas.edu/archives/reference/11.13.79.html [accessed: September 17, 2010].

Schirm, S. A. 2002. *Globalization and the New Regionalism: Global Markets, Domestic Politics and Regional Co-operation*. Cambridge: Polity Press.

Soesastro, H. 2005. Accelerating ASEAN Economic Integration: Moving Beyond AFTA. *Second ASEAN Leadership Forum*. Kuala Lumpur.

Tan, L. H. 2004. Will Asean Economic Integration Progress beyond a Free Trade Area? *The International and Comparative Law Quarterly*, 53(4), 935–967.

U.S. Census Bureau. 2011. *Foreign Trade: Top Ten Countries with which the U.S. Trades (for the month of January 2011)*. [Online]. Available at: www.census.gov/foreign-trade/top/dst/2011/01/balance.html [accessed: April 11, 2011].

Volkmann, R. 2008. Why does ASEAN need a Charter? Pushing Actors and their National Interests. *Asien*, 109, 78–87.

Chapter 6
Why Did NAFTA and ASEAN Set Up Dispute Settlement Procedures?

Annika Korte

Introduction

Over the past decades many regional organizations have been established. Since the 1990s, this development has even accelerated. Despite various differences in their institutional designs, major regional organizations have one thing in common: all of them have established some kind of dispute settlement procedure (DSP). These procedures often focus on economic aspects of regional integration, such as issues related to trade and investment.

This finding itself is not surprising since states getting involved in a process of deepening integration presumably need some venue to deal with conflicts that inevitably arise out of greater interdependence. One interesting finding is that some regional organizations rarely, if at all, use their DSPs. For example, the Court of Justice of ECOWAS received its first case in 2004, nine years after the Revised Treaty of ECOWAS entered into force (AICT 2011). The DSP of MERCOSUR has arbitrated only 13 cases since the Protocol of Brasilia in 1993 (Krapohl et al. 2009: 23). The DSP of ASEAN has not arbitrated any case to date (Koesrianti 2005: 287). Instead, conflicts are often either solved at an intergovernmental level by conciliation or at the international level, for example, through the venues of the World Trade Organization (WTO). Sometimes they are not solved at all, as in the case of ASEAN. Consequently, this chapter seeks to address the question of why regional organizations set up DSPs if they hardly make use of them, or not at all. This chapter finds that functional considerations are not the only explanation for the creation and utilization of DSPs. While in the case of NAFTA a DSP was created in order to solve confrontational trade and investment disputes, ASEAN's DSP mainly serves the purpose of increasing the association's international legitimacy.

In the first part of this chapter, the theoretical background is specified. It is largely based on a theory developed by Stone Sweet which assumes that an increase in intra-regional trade leads to an increase in the demand for DSPs. In the second part, this theory and its relevance for this chapter are discussed in greater detail, leading to the development of a hypothesis about the creation of DSPs. The third section focuses on the North American Free Trade Agreement (NAFTA). I then proceed with the analysis of the Association of Southeast Asian Nations (ASEAN) in the fourth section. The DSP of ASEAN has never been used, thus the fifth section briefly discusses alternative reasons for the establishment of a DSP in the case of ASEAN.

Theoretical Background

According to Stone Sweet the process of deepening integration is characterized by an evolving system of governance. Governance is a mechanism "through which the rule structures in place in any community are adapted, on an ongoing basis, to the needs and purposes of those who live under them" (Stone Sweet 2004: 3). This mechanism can be explained in four stages. First, there is the normative structure, which provides individuals with rules of behavior. This structure can prevent disputes among individuals since it gives normative guidance to them (Stone Sweet 2003: 60). Examples for this normative structure are the Treaty of Lisbon in the case of the EU or the NAFTA treaty and the ASEAN Charter.

The normative structure provides individuals with rules of behavior and leads to the second stage of dyadic contracting because these rules facilitate the exchange of goods and services. The facilitation of exchange that generates dyadic contracting is, for example, a commercial contract between a car producer and a car seller. The increase in dyadic contracting directs us to the third stage of the governance mechanism. As exchange increases and gets more complex, disputes arise and create a demand for impartial third-party dispute resolution in the form of rule-interpretation (Stone Sweet 2003: 61). Consequently, a dyad transforms into a triad because the dyad decides to delegate the task to solve a conflict to a third party (Stone Sweet 2003: 61). The delegation of a conflict to a third party is led by cost-benefit decisions. Consequently, if the costs for third-party dispute resolution are assumed to be higher than refraining from exchange, there will not be any delegation to third-party actors. This chapter identifies DSPs as a form of triadic dispute settlement resolution, for example, through the establishment of a panel for dispute resolution or of a court. Consequently, conciliation and mediation among two parties, without delegating the arbitration of the conflict to a third party, does not constitute a formal DSP. The process of third-party dispute resolution leads us to the last stage of the governance mechanism. The third party interprets the normative structure that has been established at the first stage and develops new rules by settling disputes (Stone Sweet 2003: 64). At this point we come full circle: as legal security is increased, more trade is encouraged, which brings us back to the second stage of dyadic contracting. The adjudicative process from third-party dispute resolution back to the normative structure is an important component of Stone Sweet's complete theory, but is less relevant for our research question and is consequently of marginal importance for the chapter.

Stone Sweet's theory provides us with important information about why regions establish DSPs. In particular, the process from the normative structure to third-party dispute resolution is insightful for the purposes of this chapter, since it explains how the demand for third-party dispute resolution evolves. As our research question deals with DSPs for solving trade disputes, we focus on trade as a variable for exchange between individuals within a community. In this context, the theory of Stone Sweet asserts firstly that a normative structure, for example, a free trade agreement, facilitates an increase in intra-regional trade. Secondly, this increase in trade gives rise to the demand for impartial DSPs. Thus, we can derive the hypothesis that increasing intra-regional trade creates a demand for third-party dispute resolution. This hypothesis will be tested in the cases of NAFTA and ASEAN in the course of this chapter, and will help to find out why regional organizations establish DSPs.

NAFTA

NAFTA went into force on January 1, 1994, with the primary objective to eliminate barriers to trade in goods and services as well as to promote fair competition (NAFTA 1994: Article 102). The agreement establishes several organs in order to implement the treaty's obligations. The most important ones are the Free Trade Commission, the Secretariat and the DSPs. The institutions which have a larger scope of action are the DSPs. Due to the high intra-regional trade and the strongly deployed DSP, NAFTA is well suited for this case study.

Trade in the NAFTA Region

Intra-regional trade can be measured in different ways. An indicator commonly used is the intra-regional trade share. This indicator assesses the portion of the intra-regional trade (exports plus imports) in the region's total trade. However, the indicator of intra-regional trade share has been criticized for many reasons. One critique important for this chapter concerns the size of a region in terms of the trade volume. According to Lelio Iapadre (2006: 66) "the intra-regional trade share is positively influenced by the size of a region"; thus larger regions have higher intra-regional trade shares only because of their larger trade volume. This finding is not only important for comparing different regions, but also for examining one region over a period of time because a region's trade volume increases or decreases over time due to economic growth or decline. Consequently, a decrease in the intra-regional trade share does not necessarily indicate a lower regional concentration of trade flows, but may simply be the effect of a decline in the region's relative size in world trade (Iapadre 2006: 67). In fact, the trade volume of NAFTA has been in decline since 2001. The total merchandise exports of NAFTA made up 19 percent of the total world merchandise exports in 2001. In 2008, NAFTA only had a share of 13 percent on the total world merchandise exports (WTO 2009a, 2009b).

Iapadre developed an indicator that circumvents this flaw. The trade introversion index relates the regional trade share with the extra-regional trade share in total world trade. According to this, the indicator is independent of the size of a region and not susceptible to cyclic fluctuations (Iapadre 2006: 71). The index ranges from zero to one, with zero indicating no concentration of trade within a region and one indicating a complete concentration of trade (Iapadre 2006: 71).

The symmetric trade introversion index depicts a different picture of trade within NAFTA, because it takes the decline of NAFTA's share in total world trade into account. In terms of this index, the intra-regional trade increased from 0.6 in 1994 to 0.7 in 2007, as illustrated by Figure 6.1.

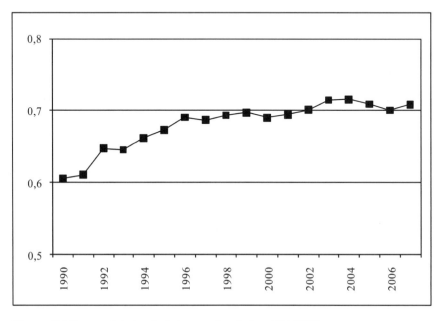

Figure 6.1 Symmetric trade introversion index (NAFTA)
Source: Data from the Regional Integration Knowledge System (UNU-CRIS 2011).

As a consequence, the establishment of NAFTA can be assumed to be a considerable factor for the increase in intra-regional trade. Nevertheless, the intra-regional trade already tended to increase before the establishment of NAFTA in 1994. This might be due to the Canada–United States Free Trade Agreement (CUFTA) that preceded NAFTA or to a generally stronger orientation on regional trade within North America before 1994. The limited increase or stagnation in intra-regional trade after 2001 might be due to the terrorist attacks on the World Trade Center. It can be assumed, however, that the negative effects of the attacks on intra-regional trade might have been worse without the NAFTA treaty.

Institutional Design of the DSP

NAFTA is said to be one of the most precise free trade agreements in the world as well as a treaty with a high level of obligation for its signatories (Abbott 2000: 519). Consequently, the DSPs are extensively specified in the agreement. The NAFTA treaty includes three different DSPs defined in Chapter 11, Chapter 19, and Chapter 20 of the agreement. The member states have not delegated authority for the adoption of secondary legislation to any of these procedures. Accordingly, "the NAFTA parties maintain effective control over the selection of arbitrators and the implementation of dispute-settlement decisions, and NAFTA rules are not directly applicable in the law of Canada or the United States" (Abbott 2000: 535). The DSPs of NAFTA assume that the conflicting parties must take all necessary measures to resolve conflicts by means of consultations. Only if the conflict cannot be settled by consultation, can the DSPs be invoked.

The DSPs of Chapter 20 deal with disputes regarding the interpretation of the NAFTA treaty (NAFTA 1994: Article 2004). Chapter 20 is supposed to resolve a dispute between two countries by conciliation. The decisions, however, are not centrally enforceable. Due to this limitation, many scholars regard Chapter 20 as ineffective (for more information see Clarkson 2008, Thomure 1997). The DSP under Chapter 11 deals with disputes between a government and a foreign investor. A NAFTA investor who claims that a host government breached its investment obligations under Chapter 11 can file a complaint. Many scholars assume the DSP of Chapter 11 to be the most effective one since its decisions are binding to the member states (for more information see Clarkson 2008, Gaines 2007).

Panels under Chapter 19 can be filed by each NAFTA Party and deals with the review of Antidumping (AD) and Countervailing Duty (CVD) determinations. The panels review AD and CVD determinations to decide whether the relevant administrative agency applied its law correctly. The administrative agencies are the authorities of each member state, which make dumping and subsidy determinations and conduct injury inquiries as to whether or not the dumping or subsidy has caused injury to the domestic industry. The panels' decisions are technically binding (NAFTA 1994: Article 1904 (1–2, 9)). There are some limitations to this, however, because the decision of final compliance remains at the national level. The panel just remands a determination that is not in accordance with NAFTA. In the event of remand, the national administrative agency reconsiders its determination in the light of the panel's decision (NAFTA 1994: Article 1904 (8)). The DSPs of Chapter 19 are generally seen as more effective than the procedures of Chapter 20 and more than 130 panel reviews have been initiated (Knox 2006, NAFTA Secretariat 2010). Most of the disputes brought to Chapter 19 have been resolved smoothly with the member states complying with the decisions.

NAFTA: DSP as Anticipation of Increasing Trade

Our hypothesis states that increasing intra-regional trade creates a demand for third-party dispute resolution. The case of NAFTA seems to confirm this assumption. While negotiating the agreement, the three North American states expected intra-regional trade to increase, since the main goal of the agreement was "to facilitate the cross-border movement of goods and service between the territories of the parties" (NAFTA 1994: Article 102). According to these expectations, the member states established procedures to settle disputes arising through NAFTA. The symmetric trade introversion index indicates that the expectations of the member parties have been met: due to NAFTA, the intra-regional trade has increased since 1994.

The analysis of cases filed under Chapter 19 depicts an intermingled picture.

Figure 6.2 illustrates that in the period between 1994 and 2000 the demand for the DSP under Chapter 19 was high, with just one outlier in 1996 counting only five cases. The demand reached its peak in 2000 with 18 filed cases. This overall increase in the demand for the DSP supports our hypothesis. However, the decline in the demand for DSP in 2001, followed by a period of unstable demand until 2006 and concluding in a decrease by 2010 does not correlate with the hypothesis, at least at first glance. Yet, the symmetric trade introversion index indicates a flattening out of intra-regional trade since the beginning of the twenty-first century. Consequently, a decline in the demand for DSP is a reaction to the stagnation of intra-regional trade. This supports the hypothesis since stagnation in intra-regional trade leads to stagnation in demand for DSP. The stagnation of intra-regional trade dates back to the year 2001. In this year, the terrorist attacks of 9/11 had major influences on international and regional trade. This is supported by Clarkson (2008: 369–370) who argued that the terrorist attacks of 9/11 were the main reason for a process of backward development of the North American region.

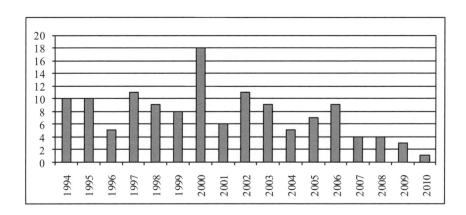

Figure 6.2 Number of cases filed under Chapter 19

Source: Data from the NAFTA Secretariat (2010): Status Report of Dispute Settlements.

Another reason for the decrease in demand for the DSP of Chapter 19 after 2006 could be the rising skepticism toward the procedure since the member states did not always comply with decisions made by Chapter 19 panels. There have been a few (but important) cases in which Chapter 19 was not able to solve disputes. The most discussed dispute is the decades-long Softwood Lumber Dispute between the United States and Canada. In this case, the United States decided not to comply with the panels' decisions (for more information about the case see Anderson 2006, Charmony 2006, Quayat 2009).

To sum up the intermediate findings, the member states of NAFTA established DSPs to solve trade disputes due to an increase in regional interdependence. The North American governments expected trade disputes to arise and took this into consideration when creating the free trade agreement. The fractional inefficiencies and flaws discovered after the establishment of the DSP are due to unexpected developments and are not linked to the initial decision to establish DSPs. Consequently, NAFTA confirms the hypothesis that increasing regional trade necessitates the establishment of DSPs.

ASEAN

ASEAN was established in 1967 with the Bangkok Declaration and pursued the goal of creating regional peace and security within Southeast Asia (Nesadurai 2008: 225, Bangkok Declaration 1967). ASEAN's most important organ is the ASEAN Summit, in which the heads of governments convene. After the end of the Cold War, ASEAN's initial focus on security shifted to economic cooperation (Cockerham 2010: 173). Accordingly, in 1992 the Singapore Declaration pursued the establishment of a free trade area within 15 years. In 1996, a formal DSP for trade disputes was established. The developments within the region led to an increase in intra-regional trade and made ASEAN the third largest regional organization in terms of intra-regional trade. The DSP of ASEAN, however, has never been activated since its formal establishment in 1996. This finding makes ASEAN an interesting second case for this chapter.

Trade in the ASEAN Region

The intra-regional trade within ASEAN increased from 1990 to 2008. This is proven by the intra-regional trade share and the symmetric trade introversion index. The trade share (exports + imports) of ASEAN in total world trade is much lower than the trade share of NAFTA. This returns us to the critique on the indicator of intra-regional trade share. NAFTA is a far larger region in terms of trade volume than ASEAN. In 2008, NAFTA had a share of 12 percent on the world merchandise exports while ASEAN only accounted for 6 percent.

In order to compare the two regions, we need to take a look at the symmetric trade introversion index. According to this index, the intra-regional trade of

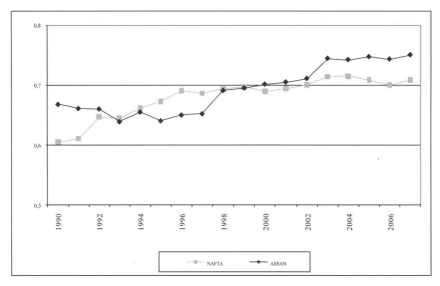

Figure 6.3 Symmetric trade introversion index (ASEAN)
Source: Data from the Regional Integration Knowledge System (UNU-CRIS 2011).

ASEAN is at the same level as NAFTA's intra-regional trade. Contrary to NAFTA, the intra-regional trade within ASEAN has increased steadily since 1995. One of the main reasons for this increase is the implementation of the ASEAN Free Trade Area (AFTA). AFTA was adopted with the Singapore Declaration in 1992. The actual implementation of the free trade area, however, only made slow progress during the first years, since many governments continued to pursue a protectionist approach. It took around three years until ASEAN member states reinstated their liberalization goals and put stronger effort into the implementation of AFTA (Nesadurai 2008: 230). The consequent phasing out of trade barriers and tariffs facilitated an increase of intra-regional trade. According to our hypothesis, an increase of intra-regional trade requires institutions to coordinate these trade flows and settle arising disputes. Correspondingly, ASEAN established a DSP in 1996.

Institutional Design of the DSP

ASEAN is characterized by an approach to intergovernmental interaction and an institutional design which is often seen as in opposition to Western decision-making processes. This approach is commonly discussed in literature as the ASEAN Way. According to Acharya (1998: 58), the ASEAN Way is "associated with a high degree of discreteness, informality, pragmatism, expediency, consensus building, and non-confrontational bargaining styles." Furthermore, Cockerham (2010: 167) emphasized that the most important elements of the ASEAN Way were informality and an aversion to institutionalization. This approach to intergovernmental bargaining appears to govern the overall institutional design of ASEAN.

The institutional design of the DSP seems to constitute a departure from the traditional approach. The DSP was established in 1996 with the Protocol on Dispute Settlement Mechanism (PDSM). It provides for the establishment of a panel if informal consultations between member states fail to resolve a dispute (ASEAN 1996: Article 4). Consequently, the settlement of disputes is transferred from an informal to a formal sphere and provides for third-party dispute resolution. The DSP covers inter-state disputes arising under every economic agreement adopted by ASEAN. This includes among others trade and investment disputes (ASEAN 1996: Appendix 1). However, the establishment of a panel requires unanimity of all ASEAN member states as represented in the Senior Economic Officials Meeting (SEOM). The meeting "may decide to deal with the dispute to achieve an amicable settlement without appointing a panel" (ASEAN 1996: Article 4). Furthermore, the panel's decisions are not directly binding for the member states. Instead, the panel delivers a report to the SEOM which will then be included it in its considerations (ASEAN 1996: Article 7). Finally, the SEOM rules about the dispute by simple majority. The parties to the dispute can appeal the ruling to the ASEAN Economic Ministers Meeting (AEM). The ruling of the AEM is binding and final for the parties. If the member states fail to comply with the SEOM's or AEM's ruling, the complainant may suspend concessions made to the accused party (ASEAN 1996: Article 8 and 9). The rule of simple majority voting and the possibility to suspend concessions is a departure from the ASEAN Way and bears resemblance to the DSPs of NAFTA and the WTO. Nevertheless, the influence of ASEAN member states in this DSP was clearly manifested through the SEOM.

In 2004, ASEAN adopted the Protocol on Enhanced Dispute Settlement Mechanism (PEDSM) which substituted the protocol of 1996. The protocol of 2004 is more precise and comprehensive than its predecessor. Article 5 of the protocol requires the establishment of a panel by the SEOM if informal consultation fails to solve the dispute, unless there is a consensus against its establishment. Likewise, the SEOM must adopt the panel's report unless there is a consensus against its adoption (ASEAN 2004: Article 9). This decision-making procedure is directly borrowed from the WTO and is commonly referred to as negative or reverse consensus. The introduction of the negative consensus as a decision-making rule signifies a departure from the ASEAN Way which is traditionally characterized by consensual decision-making procedures. Furthermore, a permanent appellate body was established by the AEM, based on the standing appellate body of the WTO. For example, Article 12 of the PEDSM, which establishes the appellate body, is largely identical to Article 17 of the Understanding on Rules and Procedures Governing the Settlement of Disputes (Uruguay Round Agreements), which established the WTO appellate body. Neither the appellate body, nor the DSP have been invoked by any member state to date. Consequently, the hypothesis that DSPs are the result of an increase in demand for these procedures does not appear to have explanatory power for the ASEAN DSP.

ASEAN's Idle DSP

When AFTA was established, the member states did not necessarily expect intra-regional trade to increase, since the primary goal of AFTA was not to facilitate trade within the region but to attract foreign direct investment (Nesadurai 2008: 230). This is also probably the reason why ASEAN did not set up a DSP with AFTA in 1992. When ASEAN actually started to implement AFTA in the mid-1990s, the intra-regional trade increased due to the withdrawal of regional trade barriers. Data about an increase in the demand for DSPs, due to the increase in intra-regional trade, is difficult to obtain. Only a single officially recorded trade dispute arose between the ASEAN member states during the 1990s. In 1995, Singapore charged Malaysia with the prohibition of imports of petrochemical products, which is one of Singapore's major exports. This constituted a breach of the agreement within AFTA to lower tariffs by 2003 (Kahler 2000: 565). AFTA did not possess any venue to resolve this dispute and hence Singapore filed a WTO complaint against Malaysia. The case has been withdrawn due to a "mutually agreed solution" (WTO 2010a). According to Kahler (2000: 565), "bringing an intra-ASEAN trade dispute to the WTO was an embarrassment to the organization and its members; it also sparked a realization that disputes of this kind were likely to increase as economic integration deepened among the ASEAN economies." Accordingly, it could be assumed that the Protocol on Dispute Settlement Mechanism was adopted due to an expected increase in intra-regional trade disputes. The member states established their own DSP in order to deal with future disputes independently. Nevertheless, there are many arguments against this assumption that indicate that the member states of ASEAN never intended to actually use the DSP. On the one hand, the weak institutional structure and the impreciseness of the 1996 Protocol suggest that the DSP did not have bright prospects for realization. On the other hand, the Protocol delegated a great deal of power to the SEOM which is able to block every attempt to form a panel. Consequently, the settlement of disputes remained at the informal level or was transferred to other venues.[1]

There are a few cases in which member countries (or investors that are nationals of one of the member countries) filed complaints to other venues. One case was initiated by a Singaporean investor against Myanmar in 2000 under the rules of the ICSID. The tribunal, however, rejected the claim as the dispute did not fall under its jurisdiction (Tan 2004: 949). Another case was initiated by a Singaporean investor against Indonesia in 2004 under the rules of the ICSID. The tribunal abstained from delivering a decision due to an informal settlement of the dispute ahead of schedule (UNCTAD 2010). A third case was filed by the Thai

---

1 The DSP Protocols do not exclude the use of other venues (for instance WTO) to solve trade disputes. Investment disputes may be brought before the ASEAN DSP, the International Centre for Settlement of Investment Disputes (ICSID), the United Nations Commission on International Trade Law (UNCITRAL) and the Regional Centre for Arbitration at Kuala Lumpur (ASEAN 1987: Article X).

government against the Philippines under the WTO in 2008. A panel was formed to solve the dispute and a final decision is pending (WTO 2010b). Generally, however, the usage of formal DSPs at the international level by ASEAN member states is at a low level. This would suggest that the ASEAN states do not have an interest in formal dispute settlement. Therefore, the demand for DSPs is limited irrespective of the increase in intra-regional trade.

This suggests that the 2004 Protocol on Enhanced Dispute Settlement Mechanism seems to be a case of "traveled governance."[2] The Protocol bears a strong resemblance to the WTO DSPs and evidently departs from the ASEAN Way. This raises the question of whether ASEAN ever intended to use this enhanced DSP at all. This leads us back to the initial question as to why ASEAN set up DSPs. Obviously, the hypothesis that the DSP was set up due to an increase in trade disputes cannot explain ASEAN's decision to establish a DSP. An attempt to answer this question will be pursued in the following section.

ASEAN: DSP to increase FDI and International Legitimacy

When establishing the DSP, ASEAN seemingly did not have the intention to actually invoke this procedure. Consequently, the member states of ASEAN might have had different reasons for setting up DSPs within their region to those the EU or NAFTA had. This section suggests possible reasons for the establishment of such a procedure in ASEAN.

Regional organizations are not in any way isolated from each other but find themselves in a similar context and are subjected to the diffusion of ideas and norms. The concept of diffusion refers to the "process through which ideas are spread across time and space" (Strang and Meyer 1993, as quoted in Börzel and Risse 2009: 6). The strongest driver of the diffusion of ideas about regional integration is arguably the EU which often serves as a template for other regional organizations wanting to achieve similar levels of security and economic growth. One of the leading recipients of these ideas appears to be ASEAN. According to Jetschke "Southeast Asian governments have mimicked the steps of the European integration process since the European Economic Community (EEC) began in 1957" (Jetschke 2009: 409). In fact, ASEAN does feature many characteristics of the EU. The most recent example of this is the 2007 ASEAN Charter which "downloads important parts of the EU's constitutional structure" (Börzel and Risse 2009: 13) and aims at the establishment of three pillars, the first one being an ASEAN single market, the second one building an ASEAN Political-Security Community and the third one establishing an ASEAN Socio-Cultural Community. Mimicry of the EU serves as an explanation for the gap between "ASEAN's 'oversized' projects and its subsequent implementation failures" (Jetschke 2009: 409).

---

2 The term "traveled governance" indicates that certain modes of governances developed in the Western world are adopted in other parts of the world. For more information see Risse and Lehmkuhl (2010).

The DSP of ASEAN, however, has not been copied from the EU since the procedure does not feature characteristics of the ECJ. Instead, the DSP closely resembles the WTO DSP. Already the 1996 Protocol on Dispute Settlement Mechanism included elements of the WTO DSP, even though in a more limited scale than the 2004 protocol. The 2004 Protocol on Enhanced Dispute Settlement Mechanism copied important parts of the WTO DSP, as laid out in the Understanding on Rules and Procedures Governing the Settlement of Disputes (Annex II of the WTO agreement). Consequently, it can be assumed that WTO norms of dispute settlement diffused to ASEAN. The observation that the implementation of the ASEAN DSP was a radical departure from the ASEAN Way (Ravenhill 2008: 480) supports this assumption.

Nevertheless, ASEAN did not only form their DSP according to WTO standards because they assumed them to be the most efficient ones. The driving forces of the adoption of WTO standards were the constitution of international legitimacy and recognition as well as the establishment of an attractive region for foreign direct investments (FDI). The member state's decision was "driven by a concern for legitimacy rather than a preoccupation with efficiency" (Jetschke 2009: 409). With the end of the Cold War, the international political climate changed significantly and ASEAN needed to adapt to these new challenges (Cockerham 2010: 174). ASEAN did not only face legitimacy problems in the sense of international credibility but was also increasingly challenged by economic constraints. The ASEAN member states realized that processes of regional integration in other parts of the world, such as the Single European Market implemented in 1992, and NAFTA, could lead to the diversion of FDI from ASEAN (Nesadurai 2008: 230). Furthermore, the process of economic liberalization in China added to these concerns. Consequently, ASEAN experienced heavy pressure to increase its level of regional integration and to create a more stable regional market. The decision to establish a regional free trade area in 1992 and the establishment of a DSP in 1996 was based on the expectation that foreign investors would be attracted to the enlarged and stable market in Southeast Asia (Kahler 2000: 553, Nesadurai 2008: 230). The Southeast Asian states found themselves in competition with other free trade areas.

In regards to the DSP, however, the institutional design faced problems of credibility. The DSP has not been used once since its establishment. According to Kahler (2000: 554), ASEAN's "half-hearted attempts at regional trade liberalization in the past and the informal institutional preferences of ASEAN members produced skepticism on the part of many observers." The introduction of an institutional design that is internationally well-proven and recognized would lessen the skepticism of the international community and increase ASEAN's legitimacy. Consequently, the adoption of the 2004 Protocol on Enhanced Dispute Settlement Mechanism was the logical consequence of this mindset, since it was more formalized and rule-based than its predecessor.

In conclusion, it can be assumed that ASEAN established a DSP by "downloading" WTO standards for two distinct functional reasons. On the one hand, a well-developed DSP contributes to the international recognition of the region, resulting in other regional organizations, countries, and investors taking the process of economic regional integration in ASEAN more seriously. On the other hand, it was thought that the DSP would increase economic stability in the region. With a DSP as highly institutionalized as the WTO DSP, the member states of ASEAN should be able to solve trade disputes independently.

The Driving Forces for the Establishment of DSPs

This chapter examined different approaches to the question of why regions establish DSPs. The most obvious approach seemed to be that an increase in intra-regional trade, resulting from free trade agreements, creates a demand for DSP. This hypothesis was confirmed by the case of NAFTA. The member states of NAFTA expected intra-regional trade to increase and thus established appropriate procedures to settle disputes arising through the increasing economic interdependence among the three member states.

Nevertheless, the hypothesis does not hold for every regional organization, as shown in the case of ASEAN. When AFTA was adopted, it did not come along with a DSP. The member states did not expect a rise in intra-regional trade disputes as a result of their free trade area. Neither did they expect the intra-regional trade to increase significantly since the reasons for the adoption of AFTA were rather to attract FDI and to gain international legitimacy than to enhance intra-regional interdependence. The regional organization adopted the DSP to satisfy international demands and not to solve trade disputes.

In conclusion, ASEAN and NAFTA can be seen as regional organizations that pursue two opposing approaches to third-party dispute settlement. NAFTA adopted DSPs in order to solve confrontational disputes while ASEAN adopted DSPs in order to increase its legitimacy. The findings of this case study illustrate different approaches to the establishment of DSPs in regional organizations and provide two contrasting answers to the question of why regions set up DSPs.

References

Abbott, F. M. 2000. NAFTA and the Legalization of World Politics: A Case Study. *International Organization*, 54(3), 519–547.

Acharya, A. 1998. Culture, Security, Multilateralism: The "ASEAN Way" and Regional Order. *Contemporary Security Policy*, 19(1), 55–84.

AICT. 2011. *Court of Justice of the Economic Community of West African States*. [Online]. Available at: www.aict-ctia.org/courts_subreg/ecowas/ecowas_home.html [accessed: April 14, 2011].

Anderson, G. 2006. Can Someone Please Settle This Dispute? Canadian Softwood Lumber and the Dispute Settlement Mechanisms of the NAFTA and the WTO. *World Economy*, 29(5), 585–610.

ASEAN. 1987. *Agreement for the Promotion and Protection of Investments.* [Online]. Available at: www.aseansec.org/1370.htm [accessed: July 28, 2010].

ASEAN. 1996. *Protocol on Dispute Settlement Mechanism.* [Online]. Available at: www.aseansec.org/16654.htm [accessed: July 26, 2010].

ASEAN. 2004. *Protocol on Enhanced Dispute Settlement Mechanism.* [Online]. Available at: www.aseansec.org/16754.htm [accessed: July 26, 2010].

Börzel, T. and Risse, T. 2009. Diffusing (Inter-) Regionalism. The EU as a Model of Regional Integration. *KFG Working Paper 7*. Berlin.

Charmony, C. 2006. Softwood Lumber Dispute (2001–2006). *The American Journal of International Law*, 100(3), 664–674.

Clarkson, S. 2008. *Does North America Exist? Governing the Continent after NAFTA and 9/11*. Toronto, Buffalo and London: University of Toronto Press.

Cockerham, G. 2010. Regional Integration in ASEAN: Institutional Design and the ASEAN Way. *East Asia*, 27(2), 165–185.

Gaines, S. 2007. Environmental Policy Implications of Investor-State Arbitration under NAFTA Chapter 11. *International Environmental Agreements: Politics, Law and Economics*, 7(2), 171–201.

Iapadre, L. 2006. Regional Integration Agreements and the Geography of World Trade. Statistical Indicators and Empirical Evidence, in *Assessment and Measurement of Regional Integration*, edited by P. d. Lombaerde. New York: Routledge, 65–85.

Jetschke, A. 2009. Institutionalizing ASEAN: Celebrating Europe through Network Governance. *Cambridge Review of International Affairs*, 22(3), 407–426.

Kahler, M. 2000. Legalization as Strategy: The Asia-Pacific Case. *International Organization*, 54(03), 549–571.

Knox, J. 2006. The 2005 Activity of the NAFTA Tribunals. *The American Journal of International Law*, 100(2), 429–442.

Koesrianti, K. 2005. *The Development of the ASEAN Trade Dispute Settlement Mechanism: From Diplomacy to Legalism*. Thesis. University of New South Wales.

Krapohl, S., Dinkel, J. and Faude, B. 2009. Judicial Integration in the Americas? A Comparison of Dispute Settlement in NAFTA and MERCOSUR. Paper prepared for the 21st IPSA World Congress of Political Science, July 16–19, 2009 in Santiago, Chile. [Online]. Available at: www.uni-bamberg.de/fileadmin/uni/fakultaeten/sowi_professuren/politikwissenschaft_insb_int/Dateien/Mitarbeiter/Forschungsp._region._Integration/BOPIR4-2009.pdf [accessed: October 21, 2011].

NAFTA. 1994. *North American Free Trade Agreement*. [Online]. Mexico City, Ottawa and Washington, DC. Available at: www.nafta-sec-alena.org/en/view.aspx?conID=590 [accessed: April 14, 2011].

NAFTA Secretariat. 2010. *Status Report of Dispute Settlements*. [Online]. Available at: www.nafta-sec-alena.org/en/StatusReport.aspx [accessed: July 24, 2010].

Nesadurai, H. E. S. 2008. The Association of Southeast Asian Nations (ASEAN). *New Political Economy*, 13(2), 225–239.

Quayat, D. 2009. The Forest for the Trees: A Roadmap to Canada's Litigation Experience in Lumber IV. *Journal of International Economic Law*, 12(1), 115–151.

Ravenhill, J. 2008. Fighting Irrelevance: An Economic Community "with ASEAN Characteristics." *Pacific Review*, 21(4), 469–488.

Risse, T. and Lehmkuhl, U. (eds). 2010. *Governance Without a State? Policies and Politics in Areas of Limited Statehood*. New York: Columbia University Press.

Stone Sweet, A. 2003. Judicialization and the Construction of Governance, in *On Law Politics, and Judicialization*, edited by M. Shapiro and A. Stone Sweet. New York: Oxford University Press, 55–89.

Stone Sweet, A. 2004. *The Judicial Construction of Europe*. New York: Oxford University Press.

Tan, L. H. 2004. Will Asean Economic Integration Progress beyond a Free Trade Area? *The International and Comparative Law Quarterly*, 53(4), 935–967.

Thomure, J. C. 1997. Star Chamber Accountability. Appellate Review of Chapter 20 Panel Decisions. *The University of Miami Inter-American Law Review*, 28(3), 629–659.

UNCTAD. 2010. *Database of Treaty-Based Investor-State Dispute Settlement Cases: Trinh Vinh Binh and Binh Chau Joint stock Company v. Socialist Republic of Viet Nam*. [Online]. Available at: www.unctad.org/iia-dbcases/jurisprudence.aspx?id=186 [accessed: July 27, 2010].

UNU-CRIS. 2011. *Regional Integration Knowledge System: Databases. Regional Indicators*. [Online]. Available at: www.cris.unu.edu/riks/web/data [accessed: April 14, 2011].

WTO. 2009a. *International Trade Statistics 2009. Appendix Table A6: World Merchandise Exports by Region and Selected Economy, 1998–2008*. [Online]. Available at: www.wto.org/english/res_e/statis_e/its2009_e/appendix_e/a06.xls [accessed: April 14, 2011].

WTO. 2009b. *WTO: International Trade Statistics 2009. Appendix Table A3: Merchandise Trade of Selected Regional Integration Arrangements, 2000–08*. [Online]. Available at: www.wto.org/english/res_e/statis_e/its2009_e/appendix_e/a03.xls [accessed: April 14, 2011].

WTO. 2010a. *Dispute DS 1. Malaysia – Prohibition of Imports of Polyethylene and Polypropylene*. [Online]. Available at: www.wto.org/english/tratop_e/dispu_e/cases_e/ds1_e.htm [accessed: April 14, 2011].

WTO. 2010b. *Dispute DS 371. Thailand – Customs and Fiscal Measures on Cigarettes from the Philippines*. [Online]. Available at: www.wto.org/english/tratop_e/dispu_e/cases_e/ds371_e.htm [accessed: April 14, 2011].

Chapter 7
Institutional Similarities Between Regional Organizations: An Analysis of ECOWAS and the Arab League

Constanze Koitzsch

Introduction

The pursuit of peace, stability and economic development are the main objectives of numerous regional organizations. Over the last decades, comparative approaches to regional phenomena received increasing attention but were often Eurocentric (Breslin and Higgott 2000: 343, Sbragia 2008: 33). In contrast, this chapter focuses on two regional organizations, which are less often considered in cross-regional analysis: the League of Arab States (LAS)[1] and the Economic Community of West African States (ECOWAS).

Apart from their date of establishment both organizations depict cultural, political and most obviously geographical differences. Also regarding the League's ineffectiveness in comparison to the adoption of supranational characteristics within the West African Community (Lehmann 2004: 225), the outcomes of regional integration seem to be completely different. But the institutional outcomes of reform processes in both organizations are similar. For that reason, it is the purpose of this chapter to provide an answer to the question of why such different regional organizations have developed similar reform plans of their institutional designs. In particular, this chapter will investigate why ECOWAS revised its treaty in 1993 and why the Arab League continuously expresses its intention to carry out reforms. Moreover, this chapter aims to clarify why *both* regional organizations decided to create bodies like a parliament or a court of justice, which illustrates a trend toward structural convergence.

In regard to this empirical focus, several comparative studies examining the LAS and the Organization of African Unity (OAU) (for example Boutros-Ghali 1975) as well as studies analyzing ECOWAS in comparison to other African regional organizations are useful (for instance Bach 1983, Mair and Peters-Berries 2001, Ntumba 1997). This literature mainly deals with dispute settlement procedures (Honegger 1983), collective security systems (Adwan 1987, Zacher 1979) or economic matters (Kühn and Seelow 1979). Moreover, Mattli (1999)

---

1 In the following, the terms Arab League or League are used synonymously.

and Laursen (2004) presented systematic comparative analyses of regional integration schemes. However, while Mattli (1999) examined integration efforts in different regions outside Europe, he did not elaborate on the West African or Arab regions. A comparative examination of ECOWAS and the Arab League has not been attempted and literature on the organizational design of both regional organizations is hard to find.[2] A study by Acharya and Johnston (2007c) included contributions to African as well as Arab approaches to regional cooperation but institutional design is treated as a dependent variable as well as an independent variable. In this chapter *institutional design* (dependent variable) refers to formal institutions (in terms of bodies) established by a treaty or protocol.[3]

This chapter shows that power and interest based approaches are poorly equipped for explaining institutional similarities. Instead mechanisms of diffusion are explored. This adds another perspective to reform processes of regional organizations and to the proliferation of institutional designs of regional organizations (also Bilal 2005: 18–26).

Similarities in the Institutional Design of ECOWAS and the Arab League

While ECOWAS and the LAS are generally regarded as very different regional organizations, this chapter argues that they gradually converge with regard to their structures. A large amount of scholarly work points to differences in the institutional designs of regional organizations (Acharya and Johnston 2007a, Laursen 2004: 283). This work, however, intends to reconsider those assumptions by revealing similarities in the organizational set-up of ECOWAS and the LAS after both organizations have attempted reforms. More precisely, this research addresses structural changes that occurred with the ECOWAS treaty revision in 1993[4] and the reform proposal for the Arab League in 2004.[5] Obviously, by

---

2   Structural reforms in ECOWAS are addressed in some publications (Lavergne 1997, Mair and Peters-Berries 2001), but it is particularly challenging to gain information on reform plans in the LAS.

3   Subsequently, terms like organizational design/set-up, structural design/set-up or institutional set-up are utilized synonymously.

4   The Cotonou Treaty (1993) revised the Treaty of Lagos (1975). The Protocol relating to the Mechanism for Conflict Prevention, Management, Resolution, Peacekeeping and Security (PMCS) is included in the analysis because the revised treaty calls for the establishment of a mechanism to prevent and solve conflicts (ECOWAS 1993: Article 58). The recent replacement of the ECOWAS Secretariat by a Commission is not considered since it was not part of the 1993 reform.

5   The LAS's founding document is the Pact of the League of Arab States (1945). Although reform initiatives were sporadically put forward throughout the League's history, the focus is on a recent reform plan that was issued by A. Moussa, Secretary General of the LAS, in 2004. Besides, public discourse is considered (Arab Reform Bulletin 2004, Blanford 2008, Ezzat 2003, Faath 2005: 67–92, Moussa 2010, Wittes 2004).

implementing the reforms, ECOWAS has undertaken a considerable step that has not been accomplished by the LAS so far. However, instead of comparing different projects of regionalism in the same time period and determining that they are dissimilar, it is more beneficial to include the reform plans of the Arab League in order to consider comparable logical instances (De Lombaerde et al. 2009: 11). The explicit and iterated discourse on reform initiatives in the Arab League allows for a comparative analysis with the already realized reform initiatives of ECOWAS. Both organizations have a similar perception of further developing their institutional structures, irrespective of whether or not these structures have been fully implemented, are not fully operational or have only been proposed.

Table 7.1 depicts structural similarities between ECOWAS and the LAS. First of all, it is obvious that both organizations feature some form of an executive, legislative and judicial branch. The League's General Secretariat and the Executive Secretariat of ECOWAS present permanent administrative bodies that are responsible for carrying out the day-to-day politics of their organization (Al-Ramadhani 1974: 159, ECOWAS 1993: Article 19). The League's Secretary General and the Executive Secretary of ECOWAS personify the principle executive officer since they implement the Council's as well as the Authority's[6] provisions (ECOWAS 1993: Article 19.3a, LAS 1953: Article 1). Neither has any decision-making power but they influence the agenda of the Council/Authority, coordinate various activities and represent their organization externally (ECOWAS 1993: Article 19, LAS 1953: Article 3–8). The Council of the Arab League and ECOWAS's Authority are both composed of representatives from all member states and present the principle decision-making organ of their organizations (ECOWAS 1993: Article 7.1, LAS 1945: Article 3.1).

Furthermore, both regional organizations envisioned the establishment of a judicial body since the start of their integration process. ECOWAS foresaw the creation of a Tribunal of the Community (ECOWAS 1975: Article 4, 11) and the LAS the formation of an Arab Tribunal of Arbitration (LAS 1945: Article 19); however neither institution has become operational. Although the judicial mechanism of ECOWAS is already more developed (ECOWAS 1993: Article 15, 16, 76), it is noteworthy that with a treaty revision, both organizations institute judicial bodies which will settle disputes among member states and ensure compliance with the treaty (Gans 2006: 66–67, Samoleit and Mattes 2008: 4–5). Moreover, in the beginning of their integration process, neither ECOWAS nor the Arab League considered the creation of a parliamentary body. But, with the treaty revision in 1993 and the LAS's reform plans, the ECOWAS Community Parliament as well as an Arab Transitional Parliament were established. Considering that the parliaments are endowed with consultative rather than legislative competencies (Dean and Matthews 2009: 1414, Mair and Peters-Berries 2001: 198, Samoleit and Mattes 2008: 5), one could certainly challenge the efficacy of both parliamentary bodies. Nevertheless, it is intriguing that both regional organizations have

---

6   This refers to the Authority of Heads of State and Government of ECOWAS.

Table 7.1 Institutional design of the Arab League and the Economic Community of West African States

	League of Arab States	ECOWAS
Executive branch	**General Secretariat** (General Secretary, Assistant Secretaries, several departments)	**Executive Secretariat** (Executive Secretary, Deputy Secretaries for Administration and Economic Affairs, one Financial Controller)
Legislative branch	**Council of the League** **Political Committee** **16 Permanent Committees**	**Authority of Heads of State and Government** **Council of Ministers** **Eight Specialized Technical Commissions** (1993)
Judicial branch	**Arab Court of Justice** Arab Tribunal of Arbitration (never realized) Administrative Tribunal of the Arab League	**Community Court of Justice** Community Tribunal (1975, never operational) Arbitration Tribunal
Military or security related bodies	Bodies established by the **Joint Defense and Economic Cooperation Treaty** (1950) - Arab Unified Military Command - Economic Council - Joint Defence Council - Permanent Military Commission **Arab Peace and Security Council** Arab Peace Keeping Force	Defence Council (Defence Commission) Mediation and Security Council (MSC) ECOWAS Monitoring Group (ECOMOG)
Financial body	**Arab Fund for Economic and Social Development (AFESD)** (affiliated body) **Investment and Development Bank**	**ECOWAS Fund** (for Co-operation, Compensation and Development) **ECOWAS Bank for Investment and Development (EBID)**
AOB	**Arab Transitional Parliament** **Economic and Social Council** Specialized Organizations, for example, Arab League Educational, Cultural, and Scientific Organization (ALESCO)	**ECOWAS Parliament** **Economic and Social Council** Specialized Agencies, for example, West African Health Organisation (WAHO)

Source: Own composition based on the LAS Pact, the Joint Defense and Economic Cooperation Treaty, the 2004 reform plan and the ECOWAS treaties from 1975 and 1993 as well as the PMCS.

Note: bold print designates organizational similarities.

established a parliamentary assembly, at a time when the majority of their member states' domestic political systems were not based on democratic rule. Concluding, this overview shows that structural similarities between both organizations can be found. This is not only depicted by a similar labeling of bodies, but in some cases also by the assignment of similar functions. The latter point, however, is not further elaborated within the scope of this chapter.

Explaining Reform Initiatives in ECOWAS and the Arab League

There is a great variety of theoretical approaches that can to some extent explain institutional similarities and differences. In particular neo-functionalist and intergovernmental approaches have dominated debates about regional integration (Hurrell 1995, Rosamond 2000). It might be problematic to solely rely on theoretical approaches, which were developed to account for the European integration process (De Lombaerde et al. 2009: 12ff.). Neo-liberal institutionalism also addressed the process of European integration, but was originally developed without an explicit emphasis on regional integration efforts (Hurrell 1995: 62f.). Since authors like Baldwin (1993), Hurrell (1995) and Keohane (1984) have already extensively scrutinized these theoretical approaches, a comprehensive portrayal is omitted. Instead, propositions derived from different strands of theory will be introduced and tested against the background of ECOWAS and the LAS.

First, drawing on assumptions of intergovernmentalism (Pollack 1996: 430) the pace of integration, and thus the onset of reform processes, is determined by calculated interests and preferences of member states through intergovernmental bargaining (Cockerham 2010: 180). Therefore, institutional choices are made rationally in order to capture mutual benefits from cooperation, to reduce transaction costs but to simultaneously limit the delegation of authority to regional entities (Acharya and Johnston 2007b: 266).

While it would be very difficult to retrace and examine each member's attitude towards the reform process, it is possible to identify whether reforms are the result of intergovernmental bargaining between the Heads of State and Government. Even if benefits from cooperation as well as transaction costs are hard to quantify (Aryeetey 2001: 26), it needs to be analyzed whether institutions were created to facilitate communication and to improve the provision of information (Hurrell 1995: 64) or whether concerns over the preservation of national sovereignty determine the results of intergovernmental, regional conferences and summits.

Second, in a functionalist line of thought, the increase of regional economic interdependencies among member states creates a demand for enhanced regional cooperation in other areas and therefore triggers reform initiatives.

The growth of regional economic interdependencies can certainly be gauged by various yardsticks. Here, the overall economic situation in the period before the respective reform initiative is taken into consideration and information on intra-regional trade and (non-)tariff barriers to trade are provided. Although this proposition also points to the logic of spillover (Hurrell 1995: 59), the "classic" definition must be put into perspective: the impact of elites as agents of integration, as well as the dynamic and independent role of supranational institutions, is less relevant in the case of ECOWAS and the LAS. Recalling the first proposition, the argument of Keohane and Hoffmann (1991: 19), "that spillover leads to task expansion in the wake of a major intergovernmental bargain," is of avail. The authors acknowledged that spillover only occurs under certain conditions. Therefore, spillover effects must not necessarily derive from the economic sector but could equally be the result of an insecure environment (Keohane and Hoffmann 1991: 20).

Third, according to the Rational Design of International Institutions concept (RDII) (Koremenos et al. 2001), reform processes occur if there is a functional necessity to overcome collective action problems and/or to manage changes in external as well as systemic pressures. Thereby, member states of regional organizations purposefully modify existing or thoroughly design new institutions (Koremenos et al. 2001: 76–77).

Subsequently, shared problems emerge due to an insecure and unstable (political) environment and/or due to unfavorable economic developments. Besides, coming close to neo-realist thinking, reform efforts in regional organizations are promoted by powerful external actors as well as geopolitical challenges (Hurrell 1995: 47–48). For instance, the end of the Cold War presented a turning point for regional organizations (Keohane and Hoffmann 1991: 19). Moreover, globalization can stimulate regional integration if global challenges as well as international pressures for competitiveness and economic efficiency are better handled on a regional level (Hurrell 1995: 56–58).

Fourth, from a neo-realist point of view, the leading role of a particular state is a decisive catalyst for regional integration (Hurrell 1995: 50). It is thus the commitment and capability of a regional hegemon which incites reform processes. This chapter will therefore determine if the preponderance of a state has an impact on processes of regional integration, although reforms can also be initiated in order to confine hegemonic power (Solingen 2008: 263).

The ECOWAS Treaty Revision in 1993

In order to reinvigorate the stagnating integration process, the ECOWAS Summit of Heads of State and Government appointed and assigned a Committee of Eminent Persons to make recommendations for a treaty reform in 1991 (Gans 2006: 41). According to Bundu (1997: 43), "in carrying out its assignment, the Committee interpreted its mandate to include the consideration of institutional matters." The Committee (un)intentionally enlarged its actual task. This, however, would limit the proposition that the onset of reform processes is a calculated and strategic move of the member states which is characterized by a sequence of interstate negotiations and results in the convergence of member states' preferences. Such negotiations can hardly be seen as an intergovernmental bargaining. Political leaders often lack negotiating power at the national, as well as the regional, level, because they are generally confronted with recurrent changes of government which inhibits sustainable and secure conditions for bargaining (Anadi 2005: 142). The assumption that institutions are created systematically and according to the member states' interests must be further challenged if one considers that during negotiations West African states perceived the recommended creation of a parliament or a court of justice as an infringement on their sovereignty and independence (van den Boom 1996: 84). Even if this did not avert the adoption of the revised treaty by the Heads of State and Government in 1993, it is questionable if the document really reflected member states' preferences, since scholars repeatedly highlight that national interests are still of prime importance (Bundu 1997: 38, Dennis and Brown 2004: 231). Nonetheless, the subsequent creation of the ECOWAS Mediation and Security Council (MSC) exemplifies that ECOWAS member states value cooperation if it meets national interests and potentially reduces costs (Herbst 2007: 144). Whereas the creation of a parliament or a court could reduce transaction costs, provide information or facilitate communication, it is doubted that those benefits outweigh the costs of transferring authority to the respective regional body. Hence, this indicates that institutional choices cannot always be explained by strategic behavior.

Invoking the second proposition, progress in economic integration was rather poor although the two ROs have been founded as economic communities. Community programs for trade liberalization were insufficiently realized (Cernicky 2007: 83), and throughout the 1980s West African states were generally affected by economic instability (Bundu 1997: 40). Trade statistics show that between 1975 and 1990 intra-regional exports grew only marginally, from 3 to 5 percent, and intra-regional imports from 2 to 7 percent (Anadi 2005: 115, Aryeetey 2001: 21). Consequently, an increase in regional economic interdependencies cannot explain the reform efforts.

However, unfavorable economic conditions present a collective problem that could be solved by enhanced cooperation. Being confronted with an insufficient infrastructure, a lack of coherent national economic policies, the absence of comparative advantages as well as barriers to trade (Anadi 2005: 111–117, Aryeetey 2001: 25, 28–29), a revision of the treaty was necessary to revitalize economic integration (Bach 2005: 178, ECOWAS 1993: Preamble).

In addition, political instability in the whole region constituted a further collective problem faced by member states of ECOWAS in the early 1990s. Thus, the outbreak of the civil war in Liberia was a major driver for reform plans (Dennis and Brown 2004: 229, Mair and Peters-Berries 2001: 191).

Considering the third proposition, the end of the Cold War is a decisive turning point for ECOWAS, because West Africa lost its geostrategic importance and was economically and politically marginalized (Bach 1997: 78, van den Boom 1996: 113). Furthermore, some highlight the fact that integration efforts were accelerated because of growing international market forces as well as greater pressure from Western donors (Cernicky 2007: 82, Dapaah-Agyemang 2003: 19). Last but not least, as a regional hegemon during the formation of ECOWAS (Gambari 1991: 46–47, van den Boom 1996: 67–70), Nigeria played an important role in the initiation of the reform process. The active role of Nigeria in the formation of a peacekeeping force for Liberia continued in Nigeria's ambition to stimulate—at least partially—the overall reform process. However, Senegal, Ghana and Côte d'Ivoire equally played a stabilizing and important role for the region and attempted to restrict Nigeria's influence (Aryeetey 2001: 33).

The Arab League's Reform Plan in 2004

Since 2001 the member states of the Arab League have issued several proposals on an institutional reform (Samoleit and Mattes 2008: 3–6). These were discussed during summit meetings and consultations among the foreign ministers (Ezzat 2003).

The 2004 plan is hardly the result of converging preferences of the LAS's member states. Genuine intergovernmental bargaining did not take place. Attendance at meetings was rather poor and talks often focused exclusively on national affairs. Reform processes were not driven by the calculated interests of member states, as the so far unrealized nature of the reform plans suggests that anticipated costs for the organization's reform still exceed expected benefits from cooperation.

Furthermore, an increase in regional economic interdependencies did not trigger reform initiatives in the Arab case. Since the League's inception, various initiatives to foster regional economic integration, for instance the establishment of an Arab Common Market in 1964, have failed (Englert 2000: 2–3). Among other things this has been caused by an underdeveloped infrastructure for transport and communication, a lack of complementarity in production structures, persistently high barriers to trade as well as generally low economic diversification (World Bank 2008: 52). As the level of economic interdependence among members of the Arab League remains comparatively low until today (ESCWA 2008: ix), the creation of the Greater Arab Free Trade Area (GAFTA), as well as the intent to create an Arab Customs Union and an Arab Common Market (Kalpakian 2007: 227, Moussa 2010), were to a certain extent stimulated by a desire to improve the performance of Arab economies.

Regional insecurity contributed to reform processes in the Arab League, which was frequently confronted with regional crises, for example with the Israeli-Palestinian conflict. The League reacted to the Iraq-Kuwait crisis in 1990 with a plan to revise the Charter (Engelhardt 1997: 89). Facing numerous challenges deriving from, among others, the US intervention in Iraq in 2003, the situation in Palestine, Iran and Lebanon (Al Zohairy 2009, Moussa 2010), the lack of regional stability required the creation of a regional security system. Consequently, an Arab Peace Keeping Force and the Arab Peace and Security Council were proposed (Ezzat 2003, Moussa 2010). On the other hand, it is difficult to assess whether Arab states are really committed to solving these issues collectively (Hamzeh 2004) or whether they were pushed to avert genuine political reforms (Wittes 2004).

Even if authors also point to the fact that the end of the Cold War influenced the LAS (Thompson 2008), other external factors are more relevant in driving reform. Such factors include changes to the global economy and challenges of the twenty-first century (Samoleit and Mattes 2008: 3), reform pressures from Western countries (Kalpakian 2007: 222) as well as the implementation of the United States' Greater Middle East Initiative (Al Zohairy 2009, Moussa 2010). While collective action problems are difficult to identify, the whole reform process is not only the result of unintentional actions, but a (somehow) controlled answer to growing internal and external pressures. It is an attempt at political renewal, while maintaining the pre-eminence of state sovereignty in order to avert an empowerment of regional entities (Barnett and Solingen 2007: 181).

Finally, reverting to the fourth proposition, the existence of a hegemon who decisively triggered the reform process is difficult to determine. Although Egypt still has a considerable impact on the LAS, its regional position declined in comparison to the 1950s or 1960s (Gomaa and GumAa 1977: 50, Samoleit and Mattes 2008: 6).

To sum up the findings so far, calculated interests and negotiated preferences were not constitutive factors for reforms, neither in the LAS, nor ECOWAS. Increased regional economic interdependencies also did not prompt reforms. Whereas in the case of ECOWAS, the genesis of reforms can be explained by a desire for regional stability and enhanced economic development, this variable only has limited explanatory power in the Arab case. By referring to the first, second and partially to the third proposition, explanatory variables are either absent in both cases or take on different values. Hence, they cannot explain the observed institutional similarity. Although the analysis shows that in both organizations the regional hegemon plays a special role, it is not a sufficient explanatory variable for the phenomenon examined. The roles of external actors as well as geopolitical challenges are essential for the onset of reform processes in both regional organizations. In sum, the latter factors are necessary conditions but do not have sufficient explanatory power for the observed institutional convergence.

Explaining Institutional Similarity: Inter-regional Diffusion

The previous analysis reveals that neo-liberal institutionalism partially explains the inception of reform processes, but cannot provide a satisfying explanation to the observed structural similarity between ECOWAS and the LAS. In addition, a power- and interest-based perspective cannot completely elucidate why reform efforts in both organizations entail the establishment of bodies like a peacekeeping force, a security council, a court of justice or a parliament. Whereas the emergence of the first two bodies is explained with a functional necessity to overcome collective problems of regional insecurity, it is particularly challenging to account for the creation of a regional court and a parliament. Even if democratic developments within the organization's member states were partly prior to the reform efforts (Dapaah-Agyemang 2003: 13, ECOWAS 1991, Faath 2005: 69), member states were not committed to enhance decision-making procedures or interested in democratic institutions.

Table 7.2 Status of political rights (PR) in ECOWAS (1990–1992)

	1990	1991	1992
Benin	6 (PF)	2 (F)	2 (F)
Burkina Faso	6 (NF)	6 (NF)	5 (PF)
Cape Verde	5 (PF)	2 (F)	1 (F)
Côte d'Ivoire	6 (PF)	6 (PF)	6 (PF)
Gambia	2 (F)	2 (F)	1 (F)
Ghana	6 (NF)	6 (NF)	5 (PF)
Guinea	6 (NF)	6 (NF)	6 (PF)
Guinea-Bissau	6 (NF)	6 (PF)	6 (PF)
Liberia	7 (NF)	7 (NF)	7 (NF)
Mali	6 (NF)	6 (PF)	2 (F)
Mauretania	7 (NF)	7 (NF)	7 (NF)
Niger	6 (NF)	6 (PF)	5 (PF)
Nigeria	5 (PF)	5 (PF)	5 (PF)
Senegal	4 (PF)	4 (PF)	4 (PF)
Sierra Leone	6 (PF)	6 (PF)	7 (NF)
Togo	6 (NF)	6 (NF)	6 (NF)

Source: Freedom House 2011.
Note: F means "free", PF "partly free," NF "not free" according to the Freedom House classification.

Table 7.3 Status of political rights (PR) in the Arab League (2001–2003)

	2001	2002	2003
Algeria	6 (NF)	6 (NF)	6 (NF)
Bahrain	6 (NF)	5 (PF)	5 (PF)
Comoros	6 (PF)	5 (PF)	5 (PF)
Djibouti	4 (PF)	4 (PF)	5 (PF)
Egypt	6 (NF)	6 (NF)	6 (NF)
Iraq	7 (NF)	7 (NF)	7 (NF)
Jordan	5 (PF)	6 (PF)	5 (PF)
Kuwait	4 (PF)	4 (PF)	4 (PF)
Lebanon	6 (NF)	6 (NF)	6 (NF)
Libya	7 (NF)	7 (NF)	7 (NF)

Mauritania	5 (PF)	6 (NF)	6 (NF)
Morocco	5 (PF)	5 (PF)	5 (PF)
Oman	6 (NF)	6 (NF)	6 (NF)
Palestinian Authority	-	-	-
Qatar	6 (NF)	6 (NF)	6 (NF)
Saudi Arabia	7 (NF)	7 (NF)	7 (NF)
Somalia	6 (NF)	6 (NF)	6 (NF)
Sudan	7 (NF)	7 (NF)	7 (NF)
Syria	7 (NF)	7 (NF)	7 (NF)
Tunisia	6 (NF)	6 (NF)	6 (NF)
United Arab Emirates	6 (NF)	6 (NF)	6 (NF)
Yemen	6 (NF)	6 (NF)	5 (PF)

Source: Freedom House 2011.

Analyzing data from the Freedom House database for the period 1990–1992, prior to the reforms, a significant majority of ECOWAS member states were either not free or only partly free (see Table 7.2). Hence, the creation of a parliament did not occur due to a sudden commitment to democracy by West African states. In the three years before the LAS reform plan was published in 2004, the majority of member states were assessed as not free (see Table 7.3). Furthermore, it seems unlikely that member states, which are strongly committed to their national sovereignty, would purposefully create a court which makes binding decisions. In order to fill this explanatory gap, the concept of diffusion will be introduced.[7]

In a world of growing interdependencies, *change*, which is caused by a certain action of a particular actor, is spread to a network of actors who carefully monitor each other and who might successively adopt that action (Levi-Faur 2005). The notion that certain ideas are (directly or indirectly) communicated between members of a social system, and adopted by recording actors, is not a new phenomenon (Holzinger et al. 2007b: 11, Tews et al. 2003: 572). Consequently, literature on diffusion and its mechanisms is ample and has already been extensively analyzed (Börzel and Risse 2009: 6–7, Braun et al. 2007: 39, 42–45, Elkins and Simmons 2005: 38, Holzinger et al. 2007b: 25). As diffusion processes are neither one-dimensional nor coincidental (Börzel and Risse 2009: 5), this chapter argues that *emulation*, as one mechanism of diffusion, narrows the explanatory gap for the institutional similarity between ECOWAS and the LAS. This mechanism is relevant since there seems to be no intentional action of a policy- or norm-entrepreneur (here: the active promotion of an organization's institutional set-up); it is rather based on indirect mechanisms.

---

7   Throughout this chapter diffusion is regarded as one mechanism whose outcome could be convergence. For a discussion on the concept of policy diffusion in comparison to policy transfer and convergence see Holzinger et al. (2007a).

Although the use of emulation in political science has been limited, several rationales for emulating behavior can be discerned. First of all, actors who are confronted with a particular problem look at other actors that have already successfully managed that challenge. It is possible that actors simply copy ideas and practices because their utility is taken for granted (Börzel and Risse 2009: 12). The actor also aims to improve its performance without incurring too many (information) costs (Polillo and Guillen 2005: 1772).[8] Besides, through "uncoordinated interdependence" (Elkins and Simmons 2005: 38) an actor's behavior is influenced as more and more actors adopt a particular solution (Braun et al. 2007: 39).[9] Second, from a normative point of view, actors seek to gain legitimacy for their behavior by symbolically imitating successful actors (Jetschke 2009: 409, Tews et al. 2003: 594).[10]

The Case of ECOWAS

In analyzing the West African reform process, indications of institutional imitation of the EU can be identified (Marfaing and Schulz 1993: 277, Nivet 2006: 13) but there are also voices that are critical in how far the EU really served as an institutional model. Kivimäki and Laakso (2002) and Gambari (1991) argued that the European model is not completely applicable for ECOWAS. In contrast, Bourenane (1997) emphasized that ECOWAS clearly emulated the EU's structural design. Furthermore, scholars highlighted that the seemingly simple causal mechanism between economic growth and progress in regional integration increased the inclination of West African states to learn from the European project (Asante 1982: 309, Obasanjo 1990: ix–xii). Considering that the ECOWAS reform process was also stimulated by a desire for improved economic integration, the appearance of an exceptional event—the completion of the European internal market—prompted ECOWAS to partially emulate the structures of the EU (Asante 1982: 307). The ECOWAS member states chose the European path in order to increase their own economic performance and competitiveness in comparison to the European, as well as the global, market (Obasanjo 1990). Consequently, ECOWAS simply adopted bodies because their benefit was taken for granted; the bodies were labeled according to the European pattern but not endowed with similar functions (Bourenane 1997: 55).

---

8   Braun et al. point to two processes that could be involved: rational and bounded learning (Braun et al. 2007: 42).

9   Elaborating on the effects of international institutions Börzel and Risse argue that the legitimacy of a particular solution increases as more actors adopt it. As a result, the likelihood of another actor following the same solution also increases (Börzel and Risse 2002: 151).

10   The different rationales present ideal types. With regard to empirical cases they are likely to appear simultaneously or together with other mechanisms of diffusion.

The Case of the Arab League

Rationales for emulation are also traceable with regard to the LAS. The possible establishment of a parliament or a court is neither accompanied by an increased commitment of Arab governments to democratic policy-making, nor a functional necessity. Instead, it is an instrument of legitimization. To some extent it might also be true that Arab states looked for ways to successfully settle their regional conflicts, as well as to increase their economic performance. However, considering that the region has always been hit by conflicts and has historically suffered from an imbalanced economic performance, it is more plausible that external pressures prompted Arab states to initiate reforms, thereby increasing their international legitimacy. In the Arab case, it is more difficult to identify a reference object being emulated. Even if the Moroccan king supported the idea of gradual economic development according to the European model (Faath 2005: 83), a simple copying of EU structures is hardly conceivable. As a result, it is necessary to extend the view beyond the EU.

A Global Script for the Institutional Design of Regional Organizations?

Every regional organization has some sort of parliamentary body and a judicial branch that are partially institutionalized (Bilal 2005: 18–26). This organizational convergence cannot be explained by *only* reverting to the European model. ECOWAS and the LAS have (independently of each other) emulated their organizational design from a global script which was (un-)consciously developed and used by various social actors (such as states, institutions, organizations) and diverse global processes.[11] Without being able to analyze the precise emergence and transmission of such a template within the scope of this chapter, the EU and the United Nations (UN) certainly represent important actors. From early on, various forms of cooperation have been established between the UN and regional organizations. Through its regional commissions, such as the Economic Commission for Africa (ECA) or the Economic and Social Commission for Western Asia (ESCWA), the UN undeniably exerts influence on processes of regional integration. For instance, many authors argue that the creation of ECOWAS was encouraged by ECA (Okolo 1985: 124, van den Boom 1996: 50, Yansane 1977: 50). Above all because of the Israeli-Palestinian conflict, the LAS was persistently involved in UN politics and regional crises strengthened the coordination between the two actors (Maksoud 1995: 584). Further considering that, over the last decades, regional organizations increasingly gained importance within the international system and extended

---

11 For a similar argument see Meyer et al. (1997: 144–145) and Boli and Thomas (1999). Whether both organizations acted completely independent of each other is only assumed at this point in time. In the future it would be interesting, for example, to pursue the role of the African Union (AU) comprising member states of ECOWAS and the LAS.

their functional scope to, for example, matters of peace and security, cooperation between the UN system and regional organizations increased, too.

The examples of ECOWAS and the Arab League illustrate that bodies for peacekeeping and security seem, at least according to the designation of respective institutions, to be primarily oriented toward the UN system. It is possible that, without currently specifying mechanisms, certain ideas of an institutional design of regional organizations are diffused by the UN system. Considering that the international system is characterized by increasing interlinkages at the global, regional and national level, it seems plausible that, in course of time, principles, norms and concepts of dominant actors determine the shape of such a global script. This would then function as an appropriate reference object for other actors. As a tentative conclusion that still requires further analysis, such a global script can therefore be seen as another set of formal and informal rules that prescribes modes of actions, constrains behavior and shapes expectations on the organizational set-up of regional organizations (Keohane 1988: 383).

This so far very vague idea would certainly challenge some prevailing assumptions. First of all, further research on diffusion could stimulate the debate on conditions for the convergence of institutional designs of regional organizations. Second, it endorses the notion that the organizational design does not only mirror a rational or functional necessity of a regional grouping. Third, the debate about the EU's capacity for external diffusion (Börzel and Risse 2009) as well as its portrayed and perceived role as a model for regional integration is advanced. For example, even if the EU actively promotes its concept of regional integration and is eventually emulated by other regional organizations like the AU or the Association of Southeast Asian Nations (ASEAN) (Bilal 2005, Jetschke 2009, Navarro 2010), it must not necessarily be the sole reference object. Besides, without questioning that each project of regional integration bears distinctive features, with the existence of a global script, the structures of regional organizations might converge over time. But, being aware that a small-N comparative research design is prone to inferential inaccuracy, the results of this research cannot be generalized at this stage. Nevertheless, the observations and inferences made encourage further research on the institutional set-up of regional organizations as well as on inter-regional processes of diffusion.

Conclusion

In sum, this chapter researched the institutional outcome of regional integration efforts in the West African as well as Arab region and thereby examined two seemingly most different points of reference. By reflecting on the 1993 reform efforts of ECOWAS, and recent reform debates within the Arab League, structural similarities between the regional organizations became evident. It was the aim of this work to explain why both organizations initiated reforms, which led to the creation of particular institutions. The comparative analysis revealed that in both cases, the influence of external actors, as well as geopolitical challenges, induce organizational changes. However, since cases seldom differ in all but one variable, this argument cannot be generalized at this stage. A combination of several factors causing ECOWAS's treaty revision, as well as the reform debate within the LAS, cannot be precluded. It became apparent that a neo-liberal institutionalist approach to regional integration can partially account for the *why* and possibly *when* of reform processes. Identifying *how* the phenomenon of institutional similarity developed, diffusion processes provide further insight and stimulate the concept of a global script.

Analyzing the West African reform process, indications for emulative behavior of the EU's structural design were highlighted. It was argued that the European path was followed in order to improve ECOWAS's economic performance, as well as to increase its international legitimacy. In the Arab case, the desire for greater legitimacy within the global community presented the most important rationale but it was much more difficult to identify a reference object being emulated. Further considering that the establishment of bodies like a security council or a peacekeeping force in both organizations cannot be explained by only referring to the EU, the view was extended beyond the EU's capacity for external diffusion. Consequently, the notion of a global script that is developed and used by various actors and diverse global processes and that also prescribes modes of actions and shapes expectations on the institutional design of regional organizations was contemplated. Although the notion of a global script certainly applies only by including so far unrealized reform plans by the LAS, converging processes can hardly be neglected. Thus, to further elaborate on the idea of a global script, more research is required. For example, if there is a globally shared concept of a regional organization's institutional design, it needs to be clarified which actors and mechanisms contribute to its development and dissemination. The idea of "neighbor emulation" (Brinks and Coppedge 2006: 464) might present one starting point for further research. Being part of a network, it is imaginable that regional organizations look at their neighbors when considering an action. In the long run, this might support the perception that the more regional organizations are moving in one direction, the more will follow. Besides it would be necessary to identify when and why regional organizations decide to follow that script. To what extent do they emulate the global script? Do they mimic particular actors? Which roles do the EU and the UN have?

This analysis shows that diffusion processes can be used to explain why ECOWAS and the LAS decided to incite reforms; why they were increasingly pressured to realize them; why *both* regional organizations created particular bodies; and why institutional similarities can be observed.

References

Acharya, A. and Johnston, A. I. 2007a. Comparing Regional Institutions: An Introduction, in *Crafting Cooperation: Regional International Institutions in Comparative Perspective*, edited by A. Acharya and A. I. Johnston. Cambridge: Cambridge University Press, 1–31.

Acharya, A. and Johnston, A. I. 2007b. Conclusion: Institutional Features, Cooperation Effects, and the Agenda for Further Research on Comparative Regionalism, in *Crafting Cooperation: Regional International Institutions in Comparative Perspective*, edited by A. Acharya and A. I. Johnston. Cambridge: Cambridge University Press, 244–278.

Acharya, A. and Johnston, A. I. 2007c. *Crafting Cooperation: Regional International Institutions in Comparative Perspective*. Cambridge: Cambridge University Press.

Adwan, S. Y. 1987. *The League of Arab States and Regional Collective Security*. Claremont, Graduate School, Diss., 1987.

Al-Ramadhani, M. I. 1974. *Die Liga der arabischen Staaten (LAS). Studie zu ihrer Entstehung, Organisation und ihren Aktivitäten*. Freiburg (Breisgau), Univ. Diss., 1974.

Al Zohairy, D. 2009. *Regional Crises Hound Arab League*. [Online]. Available at: http://english.aljazeera.net/focus/2009/03/200932210293629611.html [accessed: June 10, 2010].

Anadi, S. K. M. 2005. *Regional Integration in Africa. The Case of ECOWAS*. Zurich: University of Zurich.

Arab Reform Bulletin. 2004. *Reforming the Arab League?* [Online]. Available at: https://carnegieendowment.org/arb/?fa=show&article=21310 [accessed: June 7, 2010].

Aryeetey, E. 2001. *Regional Integration in West Africa*. Working Paper No. 170.

Asante, S. K. B. 1982. The Experience of EEC: Relevant or Impediment to ECOWAS Regional Self-Reliance Objective? *Africa Spectrum*, 17(3), 307–323.

Bach, D. C. 1983. The Politics of West-African Economic Co-Operation – Ceao and Ecowas. *Journal of Modern African Studies*, 21(4), 605–623.

Bach, D. C. 1997. Institutional Crisis and the Search for New Models, in *Regional Integration and Cooperation in West Africa. A Multidimensional Perspective*, edited by R. Lavergne. Trenton: Africa World Press, 77–101.

Bach, D. C. 2005. The Global Politics of Regionalism: Africa, in *Global Politics of Regionalism. Theory and Practice*, edited by M. Farell, B. Hettne and L. van Langenhove. London: Pluto Press, 171–186.

Baldwin, D. A. 1993. *Neorealism and Neoliberalism: The Contemporary Debate*. New York: Columbia University Press.

Barnett, M. and Solingen, E. 2007. Designed to Fail or Failure of Design? The Origins and Legacy of the Arab League, in *Crafting Cooperation: Regional*

International Institutions in Comparative Perspective, edited by A. Acharya and A. I. Johnston. Cambridge: Cambridge University Press, 180–220.

Bilal, S. 2005. Can the EU Be a Model of Regional Integration? Risks and Challenges for Developing Countries. *ACP-EU Joint Parliamentary Assembly's Committee on Political Affairs Discussion on the Issue of "Lessons to be Learnt from the European Model of Regional Integration for the ACP Countries."* Brussels.

Blanford, N. 2008. *The Arab League and Political Reform: A Vague Commitment.* [Online]. Available at: www.carnegieendowment.org/arb/?fa=show&article=21271 [accessed: May 28, 2010].

Boli, J. and Thomas, G. M. 1999. *Constructing World Culture International Nongovernmental Organizations since 1875.* Stanford: Stanford University Press.

Börzel, T. A. and Risse, T. 2002. Die Wirkung internationaler Institutionen. Von der Normerkennung zur Normeinhaltung, in *Regieren in internationalen Institutionen*, edited by M. Jachtenfuchs and M. Knodt. Opladen: Leske und Budrich, 141–182.

Börzel, T. A. and Risse, T. 2009. *The Transformative Power of Europe the European Union and the Diffusion of Ideas.* KFG Working Paper Series, No. 1, May 2009, Kolleg-Forschergruppe (KFG) "The Transformative Power of Europe," Berlin, Freie Universität Berlin.

Bourenane, N. 1997. Theoretical and Strategic Approaches, in *Regional Integration and Cooperation in West Africa. A Multidimensional Perspective*, edited by R. Lavergne. Trenton: Africa World Press, 49–63.

Boutros-Ghali, B. 1975. The League of Arab States and the Organization of African Unity, in *The Organization of African Unity After Ten Years. Comparative Perspectives*, edited by Y. El-Ayouty. New York: Praeger, 47–78.

Braun, D., Gilardi, F., Füglister, K. and Luyet, S. 2007. Ex Pluribus Unum: Integrating the Different Strands of Policy Diffusion Theory, in *Transfer, Diffusion und Konvergenz. Politische Vierteljahresschrift. Sonderheft 38*, edited by K. Holzinger, H. Jörgens and C. Knill. Wiesbaden: VS Verlag für Sozialwissenschaften, 39–55.

Breslin, S. and Higgott, R. 2000. Learning from the Old, Constructing the New. *New Political Economy*, 5(3), 333–352.

Brinks, D. and Coppedge, M. 2006. Diffusion is no Illusion – Neighbor Emulation in the Third Wave of Democracy. *Comparative Political Studies*, 39(4), 463–489.

Bundu, A. 1997. ECOWAS and the Future of Regional Integration in West Africa, in *Regional Integration and Cooperation in West Africa. A Multidimensional Perspective*, edited by R. Lavergne. Trenton: Africa World Press, 29–47.

Cernicky, J. 2007. Was nützt die ECOWAS? *KAS Auslandsinformationen*, 8, 78–111.

Cockerham, G. 2010. Regional Integration in ASEAN: Institutional Design and the ASEAN Way. *East Asia*, 27(2), 165–185.

Dapaah-Agyemang, J. 2003. Transformation of ECOWAS as a Security Apparatus and its Implications in Ghana's Political Orientation, 1999–2000. *African and Asian Studies*, 2(1), 3–36.

De Lombaerde, P., Söderbaum, F., Van Langenhove, L. and Baert, F. 2009. *The Problem of Comparison in Comparative Regionalism*. [Online]. Available at: www6.miami.edu/eucenter/publications/DeLombardeEtAlLong09edi.pdf [accessed: May 27, 2010].

Dean, L. and Matthews, C. 2009. *The Middle East and North Africa 2010*. 56th Edition. London: Routledge.

Dennis, P. M. and Brown, M. L. 2004. The ECOWAS: From Regional Economic Organization to Regional Peacekeeper, in *Comparative Regional Integration. Theoretical Perspectives*, edited by F. Laursen. Aldershot: Ashgate, 229–249.

ECOWAS 1975. Treaty of the Economic Community of West African States, in *Political and Comparative Dimensions of Regional Integration: The Case of ECOWAS*, edited by I. A. Gambari. Atlantic Highlands: Humanities Press International, 139–165.

ECOWAS. 1991. *Declaration of Political Principles of the Economic Community of West African States*. [Online]. Available at: www.afrimap.org/english/images/treaty/file423b0220808e6.pdf [accessed: July 3, 2010].

ECOWAS. 1993. *Treaty of the Economic Community of West African States*. [Online]. Available at: www.comm.ecowas.int/sec/index.php?id=treaty&lang=en [accessed: January 14, 2010].

Elkins, Z. and Simmons, B. 2005. On Waves, Clusters, and Diffusion: A Conceptual Framework. *Annals of the American Academy of Political and Social Science*, 598, 33–51.

Engelhardt, K. 1997. Macht und Ohnmacht der Arabischen Liga, in *Probleme der Süd-Süd-Kooperation*, edited by D. van den Boom. Hamburg: Verlag Dr. Kovac, 81–95.

Englert, A. 2000. *Die große arabische Freihandelszone Motive und Erfolgsaussichten der neuen Initiative für eine intra-arabische Integration aus arabischer Sicht*. Diskussionspapier Nr. 73, Freie Universität Berlin, Fachbereich Wirtschaftswissenschaft, Fachgebiet Volkswirtschaft des Vorderen Orients. Berlin, Das Arabische Buch.

ESCWA. 2008. *Annual Review of Developments in Globalization and Regional Integration in the Arab Countries*. New York: United Nations.

Ezzat, D. 2003. *It's all about Political Will. Has the Fall of Baghdad Contributed to the Decline of the Arab League?* [Online]. Available at: http://weekly.ahram.org.eg/2003/636/re2.htm [accessed: May 28, 2010].

Faath, S. (ed.). 2005. *Demokratisierung durch externen Druck? Perspektiven politischen Wandels in Nordafrika / Nahost*. Hamburg: Deutsches Orient-Institut.

Freedom House. 2011. Freedom in the World Country Rankings 1972–2011. [Online]. Available at: www.freedomhouse.org/images/File/fiw/historical/FIWAllScoresCountries1973-2011.xls [accessed: October 20, 2011].

Gambari, I. A. 1991. *Political and Comparative Dimensions of Regional Integration: The Case of ECOWAS*. Atlantic Highlands: Humanities Press.

Gans, C. 2006. *Die ECOWAS: Wirtschaftsintegration in Westafrika*. Berlin: Lit Verlag.

Gomaa, A. M. H. and GumAa, A. h. M. 1977. *The Foundation of the League of Arab States: Wartime Diplomacy and Inter-Arab Politics 1941 to 1945*. London: Longman.

Hamzeh, A. S. 2004. *Leaders Adopt Reform Plan*. [Online]. Available at: www.jordanembassyus.org/05242004001.htm [accessed: May 11, 2010].

Herbst, J. 2007. Crafting Regional Cooperation in Africa, in *Crafting Cooperation: Regional International Institutions in Comparative Perspective*, edited by A. Acharya and A. I. Johnston. Cambridge: Cambridge University Press, 129–144.

Holzinger, K., Jörgens, H. and Knill, C. (eds.). 2007a. *Transfer, Diffusion und Konvergenz von Politiken*. Wiesbaden: VS Verlag für Sozialwissenschaften.

Holzinger, K., Jörgens, H. and Knill, C. 2007b. Transfer, Diffusion und Konvergenz. Konzepte und Kausalmechanismen, in *Transfer, Diffusion und Konvergenz. Politische Vierteljahresschrift. Sonderheft 38*, edited by K. Holzinger, H. Jörgens and C. Knill. Wiesbaden: VS Verlag für Sozialwissenschaften, 11–35.

Honegger, C. 1983. *Friedliche Streitbeilegung durch regionale Organisationen: Theorie und Praxis der Friedenssicherungs-Systeme der OAS, der Liga der Arabischen Staaten und der OAU im Vergleich*. Zürich: Schulthess.

Hurrell, A. 1995. Regionalism in Theoretical Perspective, in *Regionalism in World Politics: Regional Organization and International Order*, edited by L. Fawcett and A. Hurrell. Oxford: Oxford University Press, 283–308.

Jetschke, A. 2009. Institutionalizing ASEAN: Celebrating Europe through Network Governance. *Cambridge Review of International Affairs*, 22(3), 407–426.

Kalpakian, J. 2007. The United States and the Arab League, in *Strategic Interests in the Middle East. Opposition and Support for US Foreign Policy*, edited by J. Covarrubias and T. Lansford. Aldershot: Ashgate, 217–228.

Keohane, R. O. 1984. *After Hegemony: Cooperation and Discord in the World Political Economy*. Princeton: Princeton University Press.

Keohane, R. O. 1988. International Institutions: Two Approaches. *International Studies Quarterly*, 32(4), 379–396.

Keohane, R. O. and Hoffmann, S. 1991. Institutional Change in Europe in 1980s, in *The New European Community*, edited by R. O. Keohane and S. Hoffmann. Boulder: Westview Press, 1–40.

Kivimäki, T. and Laakso, L. 2002. Conclusions and Recommendations, in *Regional Integration for Conflict Prevention and Peace Building in Africa. Europe, SADC and ECOWAS*, edited by L. Laakso. University of Helsinki: Department of Political Science, 170–177.

Koremenos, B., Lipson, C. and Snidal, D. 2001. The Rational Design of International Institutions. *International Organization*, 55(4), 761–799.

Kühn, R. and Seelow, F. 1979. Regionale Wirtschaftsintegration in Westafrika: CEAO und ECOWAS. *Africa Spectrum*, 14(2), 135–149.

LAS 1945. The Pact of the League of Arab States, in *The League of Arab States and Regional Disputes. A Study of Middle East Conflicts*, edited by H. A. Hassouna. New York: Oceana Publications, 403–410.

LAS 1953. Internal Regulations of the Secretariat-General of the League, in *The League of Arab States. A Study in the Dynamics of Regional Organization*, edited by R. W. MacDonald. Princeton: Princeton University Press, 344–347.

Laursen, F. (ed.). 2004. *Comparative Regional Integration: Theoretical Perspectives*. Aldershot: Ashgate.

Lavergne, R. (ed.) 1997. *Regional Integration and Cooperation in West Africa: A Multidimensional Perspective*. Trenton: Africa World Press.

Lehmann, J. 2004. *Wirtschaftsintegration und Streitbeilegung außerhalb Europas*. Zugl Berlin, Freie Univ. Diss., 2003. Baden-Baden: Nomos.

Levi-Faur, D. 2005. The Global Diffusion of Regulatory Capitalism. *Annals of the American Academy of Political and Social Science*, 598, 12–32.

Mair, S. and Peters-Berries, C. 2001. *Regionale Integration und Kooperation in Afrika südlich der Sahara EAC, ECOWAS und SADC im Vergleich*. Forschungsberichte des Bundesministeriums für Wirtschaftliche Zusammenarbeit und Entwicklung, Deutschland. Bonn, Weltforum-Verlag.

Maksoud, C. 1995. Diminished Sovereignity, Enhanced Sovereignity: United Nations-Arab League Relations at 50. *Middle East Journal*, 49(4), 582–594.

Marfaing, L. and Schulz, C. 1993. Internationale Konferenz über Integration in Westafrika (Konferenzbericht). *Africa Spectrum*, 28(2), 273–8.

Mattli, W. 1999. *The Logic of Regional Integration: Europe and Beyond*. Cambridge: Cambridge University Press.

Meyer, J. W., Boli, J., Thomas, G. M. and Ramirez, F. O. 1997. World Society and the Nation-state. *American Journal of Sociology*, 103(1), 144–181.

Moussa, A. 2010. *The Situation in the Middle East: Aspects of a Vision for the Future*. [Online]. Available at: www.arableagueonline.org/lasimages/picture_gallery/Moussa21--2-2010.doc [accessed: September 4, 2010].

Navarro, J. 2010. The Creation and Transformation of Regional Parliamentary Assemblies: Lessons from the Pan-African Parliament. *The Journal of Legislative Studies*, 16(2), 195–214.

Nivet, B. 2006. *Security by Proxy? The EU and (Sub-)Regional Organisations: The Case of ECOWAS*. Occasional paper No. 63. Paris, European Union Institute for Security Studies.

Ntumba, L. L. 1997. Institutional Similarities and Differences: ECOWAS, ECCAS, and PTA, in *Regional Integration and Cooperation in West Africa. A Multidimensional Perspective*, edited by R. Lavergne. Trenton: Africa World Press, 303–320.

Obasanjo, O. 1990. *The Impact of Europe in 1992 on West Africa*. New York: Crane Russak.

Okolo, J. E. 1985. Integrative and Cooperative Regionalism: The Economic Community of West African States. *International Organization*, 39(1), 121–153.

Polillo, S. and Guillen, M. F. 2005. Globalization Pressures and the State: The Worldwide Spread of Central Bank Independence. *American Journal of Sociology*, 110(6), 1764–1802.

Pollack, M. A. 1996. The New Institutionalism and EC Governance: The Promise and Limits of Institutional Analysis. *Governance: An International Journal of Policy and Administration*, 9(4), 429–458.

Rosamond, B. 2000. *Theories of European Integration*. Houndmills: Palgrave Macmillan.

Samoleit, A. and Mattes, H. 2008. Die blockierte Reform der Arabischen Liga. *GIGA Focus Nahost* [Online]. Available at: www.giga-hamburg.de/dl/download.php?d=/content/publikationen/pdf/gf_nahost_0802.pdf [accessed: July 5, 2010].

Sbragia, A. 2008. Comparative Regionalism: What might it be? *Journal of Common Market Studies*, 46(1), 29–49.

Solingen, E. 2008. The Genesis, Design and Effects of Regional Institutions: Lessons from East Asia and the Middle East. *International Studies Quarterly*, 52(2), 261–294.

Tews, K., Busch, P. O. and Jörgens, H. 2003. The Diffusion of New Environmental Policy Instruments. *European Journal of Political Research*, 42(4), 569–600.

Thompson, R. 2008. Secretary General, Arab League. *MEED: Middle East Economic Digest*, 52(16), 26–28.

van den Boom, D. 1996. *Regionale Kooperation in Westafrika Politik und Probleme der ECOWAS*. Hamburg: Institut für Afrika-Kunde.

Wittes, T. C. 2004. *Arab League Has Proposed Reform, But Will It Happen?* [Online]. Available at: www.cfr.org/publication.html?id=7056 [accessed: May 28, 2010].

World Bank. 2008. *Middle East and North Africa Region: 2008 Economic Developments and Prospects: Regional Integration for Global Competitiveness*. [Online]. Available at: http://siteresources.worldbank.org/INTMENA/Resources/EDP2008_Chap_2.pdf [accessed: August 3, 2010].

Yansane, A. 1977. West African Economic Integration: Is ECOWAS the Answer? *Africa Today*, 24(3), 43–59.

Zacher, M. W. 1979. *International Conflicts and Collective Security, 1946–77: The United Nations, Organization of American States, Organization of African Unity, and Arab League*. New York: Praeger.

PART 4
Member States' Behavior

Chapter 8
Does Regime Type Matter? Regional Integration from the Nation States' Perspectives in ECOWAS

Veronika Kirschner and Sören Stapel

Introduction

Regional integration is not a new phenomenon in Africa. Shortly after independence, the first African president, Kwame Nkrumah from Ghana, spread the idea that Africa must unite. Regional unity in Africa has been seen as a possible solution to the continent's deep and prolonged economic and social crisis (Gans 2006, Mouendou 2009). Integration is believed to be crucial for the socio-economic transformation of Africa (Kufuor 2006). The largest West African regional organization, the Economic Community of West African States (ECOWAS), is often named as the most complex, active, intricate and advanced sub-region on the African continent (Edi 2007, Nkiranuye 2007, Okafor-Obasi 1995).

ECOWAS is confronted with several problematic issues mainly in political and economic terms. West African states are mostly countries with small economies, which are characterized by their dependence on imports, high state indebtedness and the dependence on the export of primary goods. Especially the political situation raises concerns as the West African sub-region has to face post-colonial problems, multiple security threats and instable political realities such as state fragility. Since ECOWAS was established in 1975, a lot of regime changes and political transformations have taken place in the region.

However, these political processes are rarely taken into account when examining regional organizations (ROs) in Africa and particularly in West Africa. Although this seems to be especially interesting compared to the EU or NAFTA, where relatively constant regimes can be observed in every member state. While influences of regional organizations on the processes within member states have been studied, there is very little research on the reverse correlation. Systematic research to determine the effects of regime types on regional integration is hardly available. This also holds true for the effects of neopatrimonialism which seems to negatively influence the regional integration process according to the literature. Neopatrimonialism is referred to as dominant in many West African countries (Pitcher et al. 2009, van de Walle 2001).

For us it seems worth questioning whether the regime type or neopatrimonial features of integrating states influence the integration process as such. These causalities have only been taken into account recently, but regionally they have been limited to other areas (Allison 2008, Collins 2009, Rüland 2009). Neither the influence of the regime types of member states nor the effects of neopatrimonialism on West African regional schemes have been systematically investigated. Therefore, we seek to detect whether there are differences among member states according to these characteristics. In other words: does the regime type of a member state or neopatrimonial rule affect the country's positions toward regional integration? Our results show that both regime type and neopatrimonial rule have a significant influence on a member state's commitment on the regional level. While democracies are the quickest to ratify regional protocols, autocracies and neopatrimonial regimes take considerably longer.

After an introductory overview of the political developments in the region we introduce the basic concepts that we are referring to, democracy and neopatrimonialism. As these concepts often overlap in many countries we also delineate their theoretical boundaries. We review the best-known studies of regional integration that have integrated these concepts into their respective approaches. Afterwards, we present four hypotheses about the regime types' and neopatrimonialism's effects on regional integration which form the basis for our empirical investigation.

Political Developments in ECOWAS and its Member States

The ECOWAS revised treaty of 1993 led to significant changes both concerning the structure and the character of the regional organization. Interestingly, these changes occurred at the time when the so-called third wave of democratization brought considerable challenges and opportunities to West African countries in the 1990s (Edi 2007, Francis 1999: 139). It has been argued that when a government's foreign politics open up, these developments lead to deeper integration, especially in the political sector (Mair 2001). Ernest Aryeetey even speaks about a "wind of political change blowing through the sub-region responsible for the increasing discussion among ECOWAS members on a number of issues like the new governing institutions that allow for pluralism and tolerance in decision-making" (Aryeetey 2001: 30).

Widespread support for democracy already swept through the region in the late 1980s. Political leaders have been obliged to concede reform born in crisis, and elected civilian regimes have succeeded in replacing military dictatorship in some countries, such as Niger, Mali and later Nigeria. Ever since, the region has been constantly faced new socio-political dynamics developing from political changes (Diamond and Plattner 1999, Nwokedi 1995, Solomon and Liebenberg 2000). A decade after 1990, significantly greater political freedom and more space for civil society have developed in many African countries. A new ideological and intellectual climate has emerged, while political ideologies, illusions and excuses have fallen into disrepute (Diamond 1999). Moreover, considerable structural changes in political institutions have taken place, establishing democratic standards (Edi 2007). One-third of countries have become electoral democracies, such as for instance Ghana or Benin, and the number of political parties has risen at an exponential rate. With a renewed interest in constitutionalism and constitutional government, most countries have adopted new constitutions or revised their existing ones. Both the media and civil society have gained an important and active role (Gyimah-Boadi 1999). Nevertheless, neopatrimonialism, which has been undermining state structures, still persists in certain West African countries.

While before 1990 autocracies made up the vast majority of regime types, this number has decreased considerably since the end of the Cold War and has settled down to a constant low level. Meanwhile the number of democracies is increasing right up to today. Since 1991 the so-called anocracies, defined as "mixed, or incoherent, authority regimes" (see below), have been the most widespread type of regime. However, since the 2000s their number has been decreasing steadily, whereas the number of democracies has grown (see Polity IV Project 2011).

Nevertheless, the discourse about political regimes in Sub-Saharan Africa is ambivalent and generalizations are common (Gyimah-Boadi 1999, Nwokedi 1995). A central question in the post-1990 literature concerns the appropriateness of talking about "democracy" in Africa. These depreciative tones reinforce the vision of a permanent inability of African political systems to develop into democracies like those in Europe or North America (Edi 2007). We do not share these unassertive approaches and argue that we can indeed refer to democratic regimes in Sub-Saharan Africa.

Democracy, Autocracy and Neopatrimonialism in Sub-Saharan Africa

In the following we define the main concepts used in this chapter. As we are mainly interested in democracy and its influences, we first focus on this concept and then delineate other regime types. Next, the phenomenon of neopatrimonialism is described which then leads to a contextualization of all the concepts mentioned.

Defining democracy has attracted the attention of many thinkers and scholars, but there is no universally accepted definition of the concept. Some underline the importance of freedom, while others emphasize certain features of the institutional set-up. Often democracy is reduced to certain formal procedures like elections. But even though elections indeed represent an important condition, it is not a sufficient one.

Democracy is often measured in quantitative terms, for instance in the data sets of Freedom House's Freedom in the World Index or the World Bank's World Governance Indicators. All of these data sets certainly have their advantages. In the following, we focus on the Polity IV data (Polity IV Project 2011) and their definitions which distinguish three regime categories: democracy, anocracy and autocracy. The data contain key qualities of executive recruitment, constraints on executive authority, and political competition. They also record changes in the institutionalized qualities of governing authority. While one of the most important features of a democracy is "institutionalized procedures for open, competitive, and deliberative political participation," in autocracies restrictions or even suppression of citizen's participation are common. Voters in democracies choose and replace their chief executives in open, competitive elections and substantial checks and balances on the powers of the executive are in place. In an autocracy, however, "chief executives are selected according to clearly defined (usually hereditary) rules of succession from within the established political elite"; they are not confronted with any meaningful control institutions. Anocracies are regimes with "institutions and political elites that are far less capable of performing fundamental tasks and ensuring their own continuity." They are instable, ineffective and especially vulnerable to new political events. Here, anocracy is used as a middling category rather than a distinct form of regime type (Marshall and Cole 2009: 9–10). The Polity IV data emphasize institutional and formal aspects, but the most important advantage is the distinction between regime types.

Many African states also have to deal with neopatrimonialism, which is still a widely dominant phenomenon, although it has decreased quantitatively and qualitatively. Neopatrimonialism refers to "an entire system of authoritarian rule defined by concentration of power in a personalistic leader and his ties, rather than formal institutions and legality" (Bratton and van de Walle 1997: 62). Whereas patrimonialism always implies personal relations, neopatrimonialism at least formally acknowledges the separation of public and private spheres. Formal structures and regulations exist although they may de facto be riddled with private relations and thus informal policies may penetrate formal institutions (Erdmann and Engel 2006, 2007). Therefore, formal structure is often weak in practice and neopatrimonialism is characterized by uncertainty concerning the behavior of state institutions and their staff. These systems are characterized by particular attributes, and severe consequences may arise: actions of institutions are unpredictable, formal institutions do not fulfill their functions and lose legitimacy among the people. Policies and politics are marked by particular (vested) interests, to the point of the institutionalization of informal politics (Erdmann and Engel 2007).

Whether a state is a democracy, an anocracy or an autocracy needs to be treated independent of its characterization as being neopatrimonial. The concept neopatrimonialism represents yet another dimension which rather indicates a form of exerting dominance. In the majority of cases the appearance of neopatrimonialism might coincide with an autocratic regime. Nevertheless, it can also occur in formally democratic and semi-democratic regimes, although then the question arises if and to what extent neopatrimonial rule dominates the state structures. In many instances state institutions are undermined by patrimonial practices where officeholders utilize public resources for private ends and political authority frequently supports clientelist networks. Where there is major state intervention in the economy, or where there is weak resistance from non-state actors, patron-client networks serve to provide patronage and favors, using instruments such as import licenses and the granting of quotas.

Regime Type, Neopatrimonialism and Regional Integration

While there is almost no work on neopatrimonial states in ROs, the relation between democracy and regional integration has been increasingly studied in recent years (see Chapter 11, this volume). It is widely assumed that international or regional organizations play a decisive role in democratizing their member states and consolidating the respective democracies. According to Pevehouse (2005), regional organizations can facilitate transitions to democracy and ensure its survival because regional institutions can pressure member states to democratize. He argues that the more democratic a regional organization's membership, the more likely it is to pressure autocratic governments to liberalize. Imposing and enforcing conditions on membership, these more homogeneous organizations can supply the necessary political will and may support member states to legitimize transitional regimes (Pevehouse 2005). These effects are also examined in the literature about the European Union. One strand of literature on the concept of Europeanization, which studies the diffusion of EU norms to member and accession states, takes democracy as the dependent variable as well (Schimmelfennig and Sedelmeier 2005, Schimmelfennig et al. 2003).

The connection between the effects of regime type or neopatrimonialism on state behavior on the regional level is as yet under-researched for the ECOWAS region. Nevertheless, we infer four hypotheses regarding this connection from the literature.

Democracies and Regional Integration

The first hypothesis derives from the strand of literature that examines why states accede to regional organizations by exploring the domestic factors affecting interstate economic cooperation, but can also be used in our line of thought. Mansfield et al. (2008) argue that the likelihood that states will cooperate on trade policies depends crucially on their regime type. As states become more democratic, they are more likely to conclude trade agreements. Statistically, democratic countries are about twice as likely as autocratic countries to form trade agreements. In this regard, the voters' influence and their ability to control political leaders are decisive. In democracies, voters can make their judgement on the political leaders' performance through elections. In autocratic regimes however, leaders do not depend on the voters' choices and thus have less incentive to act transparently and enter international agreements. Even if democracy is not the only reason to promote such agreements, the findings of Mansfield et al. affirm that the regime type, next to systemic and economic factors, strongly influences a state's decision about joining trade agreements (Mansfield et al. 2002). This argumentation should still hold once a regime has entered a regional organization as they still face their voters' judgement.

Furthermore, democracies are able to make credible international commitments. Gaubatz (1996) found strong empirical evidence that alliances between liberal democratic states have proved more durable than alliances between non-democratic states or alliances between democratic and non-democratic states. Regularized leadership transitions and institutional stability ensure a certain degree of policy continuity. Thus, due to their transparent and stable domestic order of preference, democracies can maintain their commitment on the international level (Gaubatz 1996). Finally, a state's legitimacy plays a role regarding its ability or willingness to agree on regional arrangements. Democracies find it easier to share power regionally than autocracies do, as democratic leaders usually enjoy a greater legitimacy through elections and other democratic elements. By contrast, autocratic leaders lack authorization and have much less support from the population. Additionally, they are often constrained by their principals like influential clans (Pedersen 2002).

As democratic regimes are dependent on their citizens' voting decisions, it is in their interest to act as transparently as possible. Thus, countries with stable democratic institutions are more likely to be committed on a regional level because they are based on legitimate power structures. Autocratic regimes have to take much more care about internal developments to safeguard their own power and therefore cannot make major concessions on the regional level which in some cases would even contradict their own style of government. Thus, on the contrary, autocratic regimes express less commitment on the regional level.

> H1: A democratic regime is likely to be more committed on the regional level than other regimes.

Concerning the second hypothesis, we draw upon the approach by Mansfield et al. (2002) stated above. We endeavor to prove their findings about democracies being more likely to cooperate on trade policies for ECOWAS. Due to the resulting benefits for voters, democracies are more likely to take part in regional integration projects than autocracies. Such agreements mostly mean economic growth for the country and this is likely to benefit the median voter. Moreover, the performance in regional integration projects is believed to prove the leaders' competence to the voters. So, political leaders in democracies have a strong incentive to join regional organizations in order to enhance their political support (Mansfield et al. 2008). ECOWAS was originally founded in 1975 as an economic community aiming to promote cooperation and development in all fields of economic activity. The majority of the signed protocols and conventions concerns economic issues. We assume that democratic regimes are faster than autocratic ones to ratify these protocols and conventions because they depend on their voters' choices. Joining regional agreements can either mean overall positive economic development for the respective regimes or they may serve as culprits for unpopular decisions. As already mentioned above, regional agreements can make policy choices of political leaders more transparent to voters and decentralize political responsibilities. Autocratic regimes are supposedly less dependent on voters and mainly intend to enhance the political elite's benefit, making them less interested in regional economic policies (Mansfield et al. 2008).

> H2: If a regime is democratic, it will be more committed on economic issues on the regional level than in other policy sectors.

Neopatrimonialism and Regional Integration

Regarding the heterogeneous political systems in West Africa it is also relevant to consider the effects of neopatrimonialism on regional integration. This influence has been further examined in other regions. Foremost in Central Asia where ROs are substantially affected by protective integration, shadow regionalism and the survival motive of neopatrimonial systems. This strand of literature deals mostly with the motivations of states to join regional organizations.

Collins (2009) introduced the concept of a "survival motive" to the study of neopatrimonialism's impact on ROs. She assumes that leaders of such regimes basically pursue two goals: protecting the status quo and maximizing personal enrichment. In economic terms, only those measures that will lead to personal enrichment are taken. She describes a process of co-optation with the aim of appeasing internal as well as external actors: it is a *de jure* commitment to integration which lacks effective implementation (Collins 2009). In addition to this, Allison (2008) introduces "protective integration." The term describes the dominant political function of ROs, which is to secure the neopatrimonial regime and gain legitimacy among the people. Protective integration thus serves as a measure to appease external actors and their policies of good governance and market liberalization, but also to undermine arising internal demands for, for example, democratization (Allison 2008).

Bach (2006) and others provide yet another similar explanation. Neopatrimonial leaders perform a "shadow regionalism," limiting their efforts toward regional integration to symbolic and discursive actions. Similar to the "protective integration" approach, states are not committed to the process of regional integration and leaders are unwilling to implement formally agreed policies. Contrary to "protective integration," they not only seek to gain legitimacy among their people, but also among international corporations and donor organizations (Bach 2006, Griffiths 1996, Mair 2001). The latter two arguments of "protective integration" and "shadow regionalism" could be assessed as being rather specified forms of a "survival motive" because their intention is also to secure the regime's existence and to enrich the regime's leader. Following this line of argumentation, neopatrimonialism will lead to the effect that once having entered the regional integration scheme, neopatrimonial states will not show any commitment to the

RO anymore as they will already have achieved their aims. Thus, they take much more time for ratification—if they indeed ratify at all.

> H3: Regimes with neopatrimonial features are likely to be less committed on the regional level.

Following Mair's (2001) argumentation, neopatrimonial systems render two effects possible. ROs offer attractive incentives for patrons as integration means access to other member states' resources as well as access to prestigious and reputable positions in the RO. But integration also poses a risk in the rulers' perspective as national resources may decline and thus clients may not be compensated for their loyalty. National revenues have been the major source of income for patrons, and Mair therefore argues that customs policies will be at the center of attention in regional negotiation and cooperation processes (Mair 2001). Mair finds that neopatrimonialism is a huge obstacle to integration. Deeper political and economic integration is unlikely to happen as economic shortcuts jeopardize the clients' loyalty. Yet, according to Collins (2009), integration would be possible in security issues if a common (external) threat was perceived by the member states. ROs affected by neopatrimonialism deal with these issues by balancing or bandwagoning with the regional hegemon, e.g. in the ECOWAS case with Nigeria (Collins 2009).

Given these two aspects, we infer that neopatrimonial states resist pooling or delegating sovereignty rights in the economic sector and thus we expect to see a rather low commitment in these issues. Furthermore, it also seems plausible that neopatrimonial states would tend to prefer to integrate in the security sector if this would safeguard their regime. If they cooperate on the regional level they do so mainly in security issues in order to create a supportive network to ensure their own political regime and to protect it against internal resistance or external interventions. In hazardous times they can expect the support of their regional partners. Thus, the amount of time neopatrimonial states need to ratify security-related protocols and conventions should be less than they need for economic ones.

> H4: If a regime possesses neopatrimonial features, it will be less committed in economics-related policies than in other policy sectors.

Member States' Commitment toward ECOWAS Policies

As already mentioned above, in order to classify the countries according to their regime type we work with the Polity IV data. Various regime categories are recorded on a scale between -10 and 10. This represents a spectrum of forms of governance on a continuum from fully institutionalized autocracies (-10 to -6) through mixed authority regimes (named "anocracies," -5 to 5) to fully institutionalized democracies (6 to 10). It must be borne in mind that the data only include information on the institutions of the central government and on political groups acting, or reacting, within the scope of that authority. We treat a regime type as constant if it has not changed between the date of signature and the date of ratification of the respective document. A regime type is counted as being constant even when values change within a single category, i.e. if it changes between -7 and -9 it still will be counted as autocratic. This distinction is necessary as we are only interested in the ratification time of regime types but not in the countries' performances as such. Furthermore, if we had not omitted changing regime types, a sound argument regarding the differences between democratic and autocratic regimes would not have been possible.

The focus of our analysis is the commitment of member states within ECOWAS. We try to find out if, according to the country's regime type, there are differences regarding their commitment on the regional level. By commitment we mean member states' interest and dedication toward their obligations to regional integration in West Africa. Borrowed from organization theory, commitment toward organizations expresses the level of identification of members. The higher the commitment the more employees, or in this case member states, identify and feel attached to the organization (Allen and Meyer 1990). According to Senghor (2007: 147) "one source of evidence on the extent of commitment is the status of ratification of the Revised Treaty, protocols, the conventions and decisions of the ECOWAS legislative organs." Other indicators could be the rate of active correspondence of a member state with the regional secretariat, the level of representation of delegates in ministerial and technical meetings, or the financial contributions of a member state. Furthermore, scholars examine public speeches and official statements using discourse analysis in order to quantify the relevance of ECOWAS in national politics. Yet, the ample gap between rhetoric and action, especially in neopatrimonial states, makes this indicator invalid for our aims.

After a treaty has been signed by the heads of state, ratification by the proper decision-making body within the member states is the initial action-point before implementation, monitoring and evaluation (Senghor 2007). Thus, the level of ratification indicates how seriously a member state complies with the decisions made at the regional level (van den Boom 2010). Senghor (2007) argues here that while signing a new protocol there is usually unanimity, problems arise when these acts have to be incorporated in national legislation through ratification. Being aware that this might not be the ideal indicator due to data availability and technical feasibility, we operationalize commitment by calculating the time member states take for ratification of ECOWAS protocols and conventions after their signature. We refer here to data from the ECOWAS about signing and ratification processes of all 53 ECOWAS protocols, additional protocols and conventions from 1975 until 2009 (ECOWAS 2009). We assigned these official documents to four categories: economic, security, institutional and others.

Given these 53 policy decisions and the 15 current ECOWAS members, we use a data set of 795 observations. Out of this, 258 observations have to be omitted as the respective document has not been ratified yet by the country concerned, the date of ratification has not been available or the member state has not signed the preceding protocol. As Polity IV does not provide data about Cape Verde we cannot use its ratification processes either. Yet another 105 observations are not viable because the regime type was not constant. Thus, we examine 379 events, 82 of which are counted as democratic, 83 as anocratic and 214 as autocratic regime types. But we should keep in mind two limitations: first, the standard deviation of all means that are presented below lies at a value of about 25 months and the variation is also high. Second, the observations qualified as autocratic potentially bias the results as the number of autocracies surmounts the number of anocracies and democracies.

We proceed as follows: in a first step we present and interpret box plots that visualize the distributions of and the relations between the variables. But this can only give a first impression because descripitve statistics are not suitable to prove causal relations. Therefore, in a second step, we also apply statistical non-parametric tests (Kolmogorov-Smirnov-Z-Test; Kruskal-Wallis-H-Test) in order to determine the significance of the results. We choose these tests because they allow for comparison between nominal and metric scaled variables that are not normally distributed in the sample. In every test we apply a null hypothesis that would not assume a relation between the variables. The following significance levels always refer to the null hypotheses implicating that the smaller the value, the higher the significance of our research hypotheses.

As the figures show, our data analysis indicates that the assumed relation between regime type and commitment on the regional level will hold true if we take for instance the mean time to ratification. Whereas democratic regimes need 28 months on average to ratify policies, the autocracies take yet another nine months to do so as well. Interestingly, the amount of time anocracies take to ratify lies between the two at an average time of about 32 months. This is especially interesting as it prompts the assumption that the relation between (more) democracy and (more) commitment might be a linear one. Also other statistical indicators visualized in Figure 8.1, such as the median and the 0.25 and 0.75 percentiles, support the hypothesis because democracies do better in all aspects when it comes to commitment. Here the null hypothesis stipulates that there would be no difference between democratic and autocratic regimes concerning the time needed to ratify ECOWAS documents. As the result is significant when p=0.027, we reject the null hypothesis and can therefore accept our hypothesis. Even if this result is not highly significant, it still provides strong support for the assumption that the regime type influences the member state's commitment on the regional level.

In order to be able to make a statement about the policy type's influence, we also control for the regime type (see Figure 8.2). On average, democracies need about 28 to 30 months to ratify economic and other policies, whereas they need much less time regarding security-related policies (about 18 months), and much more time for institutional issues (about 40 months). Therefore, our second hypothesis would

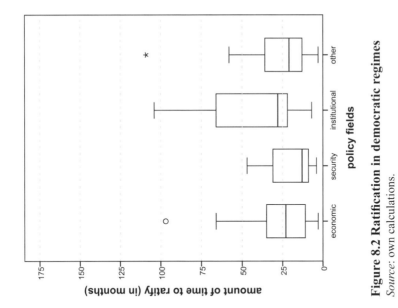

Figure 8.2 Ratification in democratic regimes
Source: own calculations.

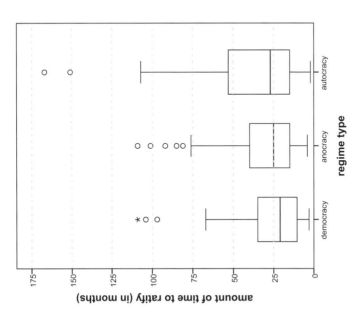

Figure 8.1 Ratification according to regime type

be partly rejected: while an influence of the policy type can be observed, contrary to our expectations democracies seem to be more committed to security-related issues than to economic ones. Ratification processes for institutional policies even take the longest time. This possibly happens due to the democracy's expectations of the policy's content and the (non-)problem to eventually comply with the regulations. By pursuing this line of argument as suggested by Rüland, democratic regimes seek to stipulate extensive democratic standards on the regional level and of the RO's institutions and mechanisms. If their concerns are not met in the negotiations, they will hamper the ratification process (Rüland 2009). Moreover, as the (median) voter problem is still relevant, unlike autocratic regimes they need to comply with, for instance, the regional court's jurisdictions. Yet it should be considered here that our sample only contains limited data. With a significance of $p=0.225$ the test also underlines these observations. This does not show any positive relation between regime type and commitment toward economic policies in ECOWAS and thus the second hypothesis does not hold.

We examine the influence of neopatrimonial features in regimes as well. The countries are categorized as neopatrimonial or not neopatrimonial according to secondary literature (Bratton and van de Walle 1994, 1997, Pitcher et al. 2009, Snyder 1992, van de Walle 2001). Due to missing data, we have omitted several events because clear statements are missing about the state of neopatrimonialism in the respective countries (such as Guinea and Liberia). It should be mentioned that the literature mostly provides information if states are considered neopatrimonial, but there is little data available about the opposite. Therefore, we have a total number of 318 events whereof 243 are neopatrimonial and 75 are counted as not neopatrimonial.

With regard to neopatrimonial states and their commitment on the regional level, the data supports the assumed relation (Figure 8.3): on average, neopatrimonial states need about 40 months in order to ratify. Countries without any neopatrimonial affiliation ratify within 25 months. Interestingly, while almost 75 percent of non-neopatrimonial states have ratified a policy, only one out of four neopatrimonial ones have done so. One extreme case supporting our assumption is Guinea-Bissau that has not ratified any policy since 1994. The visualized effect can be recognized in the test result being highly significant at $p=0.000$, indicating a strong relation between neopatrimonialism and their lack of comittment toward regional integration.

More specifically, we also need to dive into the neopatrimonal states' varying ratification processes with respect to different types of policies. All in all, neopatrimonial states ratify institutional policies faster (36 months) than economic and security ones. Additionally, the amount of time to ratify security policies (45 months) lies above the value for economic issues (39 months). Thus, the assumption about the neopatrimonial regime's preferences with respect to ratifying policies is not supported. Interestingly, neopatrimonial regimes always needed at least 10 months to ratify institutional policies, but once this period was over these countries do act. Even more interesting: economic issues take longer in

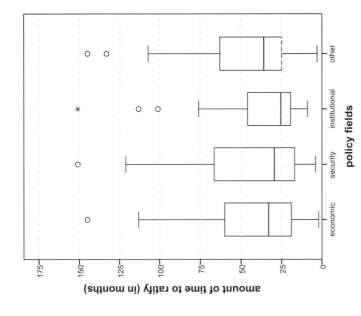

Figure 8.4 Ratification in neopatrimonial states
Source: own calculations.

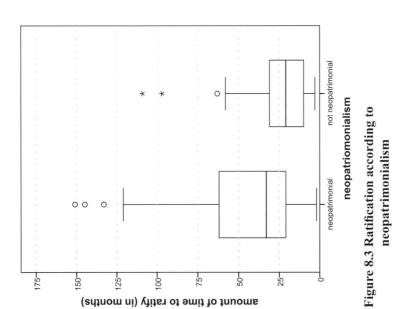

Figure 8.3 Ratification according to neopatrimonialism

the ratification process than security related policies. The statistical analysis also leads to the conclusion that neopatrimonialism seems not to make a difference as regards the time needed to ratify specific policies in ECOWAS as p=0.175 exceeds the significance level p=0.05.

Nevertheless, the data only indicates trends but not causalities. In fact, one should bear in mind that the comprehensive integration in the security sector in ECOWAS exceed the measures in most of the regional organizations in the world, for instance regarding the option to externally intervene in domestic crises.

To sum it up, the statistical analysis provides revealing findings about the influence of regime type and neopatrimonialism on the comittment toward regional integration. In line with the literature, we find significant results supporting the research hypotheses: democracies are more committed on the regional level than autocracies and the same holds true for non-neopatrimonial states compared to neopatrimonial ones. However, with regard to the other two research hypotheses our findings do not suggest that democratic and neopatrimonial states would be more comitted to specific policy fields.

Concluding Remarks

All in all, we can assume that there is a relation between the regime type and the respective commitment on the regional level, although some of our findings remain ambiguous. The analysis indicates that autocratic states as well as neopatrimonial regimes are less committed than democracies and non-neopatrimonial regimes. Regarding the concerned policies, empirical proof is not as clear as theoretical assumptions might have suggested. The findings provide valuable insights to the integration process of ECOWAS but are not comprehensive enough. More detailed information would be needed to strengthen our argument(s). Furthermore, competing approaches such as socialization of integrating states may challenge our findings as they may address learning processes that will change the member states' and thus the regimes' commitment on the regional level. We are still a long way from detecting any causal relationship and the issue at hand will need to be examined further. At this point we are only able to see tendencies, and generalizations should at least be limited to the ECOWAS region.

These tendencies scratch the surface of much more work that needs to be addressed in the literature and in empirical studies (both quantitative and qualitative). First, forthcoming theoretical work should discuss the competing arguments in much more depth and assumptions need to be inferred from theory more systematically. Second, case studies that take into account a small number of cases help us to understand how the regime type and neopatrimonialism influences the member states' position toward the regional organization and the integration process. Such approaches do not necessarily need to be limited to the ratification of policies; they can question the member state's position during negotiations or the implementation of ratified policies as well. Third, in the study of regional organizations the member states' regime types have been under-researched for various reasons. Thus, the limited scope and lack of comparative work constitute another valid starting point for further research. Democratic transitions have occurred in several regions such as Latin America, Asia and Africa. Likewise, in these regions neopatrimonialism has persisted long enough to be included in the study of regionalism. If the influence of regime type and neopatrimonialism is also identified in a cross-region comparison, this will support our argument.

References

Allen, N. J. and Meyer, J. P. 1990. The Measurement and Antecedents of Affective, Continuance and Normative Commitment to the Organization. *Journal of Occupational Psychology*, 63(1), 1–18.

Allison, R. 2008. Virtual Regionalism, Regional Structures and Regime Security in Central Asia. *Central Asian Survey*, 27(2), 185–202.

Aryeetey, E. 2001. *Regional Integration in West Africa*. OECD Development Center. Working Paper No. 170.

Bach, D. C. 2006. *Regional Governance and State Reconstruction in Africa*. African Center for Peace and Development Studies. Working Paper Series No. 6. Kyoto.

Bratton, M. and van de Walle, N. 1994. Neopatrimonial Regimes and Political Transition in Africa. *World Politics*, 46(4), 453–489.

Bratton, M. and van de Walle, N. 1997. *Democratic Experiments in Africa: Regime Transition in Comparative Perspective*. Cambridge: Cambridge University Press.

Collins, K. 2009. Economic and Security Regionalism among Patrimonial Authoritarion Regimes: The Case of Central Asia. *Europe-Asia Studies*, 61(2), 249–281.

Diamond, L. J. 1999. Introduction, in *Democratization in Africa*, edited by L. J. Diamond and M. F. Plattner. Baltimore: Johns Hopkins University Press, ix–xxvii.

Diamond, L. J. and Plattner, M. F. (eds). 1999. *Democratization in Africa*. Baltimore: Johns Hopkins University Press.

ECOWAS. 2009. *Status of Ratification of the ECOWAS Revised Treaty, Protocols and Conventions as of 18th December 2009*. Abuja: ECOWAS Commission.

Edi, E. M. 2007. *Globalization and Politics in the ECOWAS*. Durham, NC: Carolina Academic Press.

Erdmann, G. and Engel, U. 2006. Neopatrimonialism Revisited. Beyond a Catch-All Concept. *GIGA Working Paper 16* [Online]. Available at: www.giga-hamburg.de/dl/download.php?d=/content/publikationen/pdf/wp16_erdmann-engel.pdf [accessed: April 10, 2011].

Erdmann, G. and Engel, U. 2007. Neopatrimonialism Reconsidered. Critical Review and Elabortation of an Elusive Concept. *Journal of Commonwealth and Comparative Studies*, 45(1), 95–119.

Francis, D. J. 1999. The Economic Community of West African States, the Defence of Democracy in Sierra Leone and Future Prospects. *Democratization*, 6(4), 139–165.

Gans, C. 2006. *Die ECOWAS – Wirtschaftsintegration in Westafrika*. Berlin: Lit Verlag.

Gaubatz, K. T. 1996. Democratic States and Commitment in International Relations. *International Organization*, 50(1), 109–139.

Griffiths, I. 1996. Permeable Boundaries in Africa, in *African Boundaries, Barriers, Conduits, and Opportunities*, edited by P. Nugent and A. I. Asiwaju. London: Pinter, 68–83.

Gyimah-Boadi, E. 1999. The Rebirth of African Liberalism, in *Democratization in Africa*, edited by L. J. Diamond and M. F. Plattner. Baltimore: Johns Hopkins University Press, 34–47.

Kufuor, K. O. 2006. *The Institutional Transformation of The Economic Community of West African States*. Hampshire: Ashgate.

Mair, S. 2001. *Regionale Integration und Kooperation in Afrika südlich der Sahara. Synopse der Fallstudien EAC, ECOWAS und SADC*. SWP Studie 2001/17. Berlin.

Mansfield, E. D., Milner, H. V. and Pevehouse, J. C. 2008. Democracy, Veto Players and the Depth of Regional Integration. *The World Economy*, 31(1), 67–96.

Mansfield, E. D., Milner, H. V. and Rosendorff, B. P. 2002. Why Democracies Cooperate More: Electoral Control and International Trade Agreements. *International Organization*, 56(3), 477–513.

Marshall, M. G. and Cole, B. R. 2009. Global Report 2009 – Conflict, Governance, and State Fragility. Center for Systemic Peace and Center for Global Policy. [Online]. Available at: www.systemicpeace.org/Global%20Report%202009.pdf [accessed: April 10, 2011].

Mouendou, H. N. 2009. *Regionale Integration und Entwicklung in West- und Zentralafrika. Politische Analyse einer Lethargie afrikanischer Entwicklungsprozesse*. Marburg: Tectum Verlag.

Nkiranuye, J. E. 2007. ECOWAS: Current State and Perspectives, in *Global Voices on Regional Integration*, edited by A. Kösler and M. Zimmek. Bonn: ZEI Discussion Paper C176, 51–57.

Nwokedi, E. 1995. *Politics of Democratization – Changing Authoritarian Regimes in Sub-Saharan Africa*. Münster: Lit Verlag.

Okafor-Obasi, O. 1995. *Wirtschaftsgemeinschaft Westafrikanischer Staaten (ECOWAS) – Hintergrund, rechtliche Probleme und Lösungsvorschläge*. Gießen, Materialien des Zentrums für Regionale Entwicklungsforschung der Justus-Liebig-Universität Gießen Nr. 35.

Pedersen, T. 2002. Cooperative Hegemony: Power, Ideas and Institutions in Regional Integration. *Review of International Studies*, 28(4), 677–696.

Pevehouse, J. C. 2005. *Democracy from Above: Regional Organizations and Democratization*. Cambridge and New York: Cambridge University Press.

Pitcher, A., Moran, M. H. and Johnston, M. 2009. Rethinking Patrimonialism and Neopatrimonialism in Africa. *The African Studies Review*, 52(1), 125–156.

Polity IV Project. 2011. Political Regime Characteristics and Transitions, 1800–2009. [Online]. Available at: www.systemicpeace.org/polity/polity4.htm [accessed: March 16, 2011].

Rüland, J. 2009. Deepening ASEAN Cooperation through Democratization? The Indonesian Legislature and Foreign Policymaking. *International Relations of the Asia-Pacific*, 9(3), 373–402.

Schimmelfennig, F. and Sedelmeier, U. (eds). 2005. *The Europeanization of Central and Eastern Europe*. Ithaca, NY: Cornell University Press.

Schimmelfennig, F., Engert, S. and Knobel, H. 2003. Costs, Commitment and Compliance. The Impact of EU Democratic Conditionality on Latvia, Slovakia and Turkey. *Journal of Common Market Studies*, 41(3), 495–518.

Senghor, J. C. 2007. Institutional Architecture for Managing Integration in the ECOWAS Region: An Empirical Investigation, in *Towards Africa's Renewal*, edited by J. C. Senghor and N. K. Poku. Aldershot: Ashgate, 143–179.

Snyder, R. 1992. Explaining Transitions from Neopatrimonial Dictatorships. *Comparative Politics*, 24(4), 379–399.

Solomon, H. and Liebenberg, I. (eds). 2000. *Consolidation of Democracy in Africa – a View from the South*. Burlingtion: Ashgate.

van de Walle, N. 2001. *African Economies and the Politics of Permanent Crises, 1979–1999*. Cambridge: Cambridge University Press.

van den Boom, D. 2010. *ECOWAS. How Regional Integration Works in West Africa*. Berlin.

Chapter 9
State Capacity and Compliance in ASEAN

Lukas Goltermann

Introduction

> ASEAN's problem is not one of lack of vision, ideas, or action plans. The problem is one of ensuring compliance and effective implementation.
>
> (ASEAN Secretariat 2006: 4)

The Association of Southeast Asian Nations (ASEAN) is changing since its members have committed themselves to the establishment of a single market and production base by 2015. ASEAN's Economic Community (AEC) requires its member states to adapt parts of their economic, financial and legal frameworks to common rules and standards. Whether or not the association can live up to its new ambitions, however, is disputed. Despite the great enthusiasm with which the AEC was proclaimed in 2009, progress toward a single market and production base is falling behind schedule. In particular, the question arises if ASEAN can cope with enforcement problems. Many important projects are not implemented fully, on time or at all. A common explanation for this failure is the absence of appropriate institutions at the regional level (Caballero-Anthony 2008, Stahl 2010). Much less attention has been given to the ways in which member states cope with regional commitments.

This chapter sets out to analyze and evaluate the progress of the most challenging regional policies so far. At the focus of the inquiry is the question whether the slow implementation progress and low levels of legal compliance can be better explained by member states' interests in establishing a single market or the differences in state capacity. While most orthodox accounts of Southeast Asian regionalism hold that compliance variation can be explained by member states' preferences, this chapter argues that state capacity offers more explanatory power for the shortcomings in the implementation of regional commitments. More precisely, the more state capacity member states have, the easier it is for them to adapt their economic, legal and financial systems to the requirements of regional integration.

The chapter proceeds as follows. In a first step, recent developments in Southeast Asia as well as their academic evaluation are outlined. This is followed by a discussion of compliance theory and an operationalization of the concept of state capacity. Lastly, the implementation of member states' obligations in the AEC for the period 2008–2010 is studied and the findings presented. The empirical basis for the analysis is provided by two case studies of the most demanding regional projects so far: the standardizing customs procedures and harmonizing cosmetics regulation.

The ASEAN Economic Community

Originally formed in 1967 as a diplomatic forum to foster peace and stability in the region, ASEAN has increased its economic and political significance over the past 40 years. In this process, the expectation of economic gains was generally a driving force behind deeper integration.

In 2003, the association declared it would establish an ASEAN Economic Community (AEC) as one of the three pillars of an ASEAN Community by 2020 (ASEAN 2003b). With the Hanoi Plan of Action and the Vientiane Action Programme the idea was beginning to take shape and 11 priority sectors were identified for accelerated integration.

In 2007, faced with increasing competition from its neighbors India and China the target date of the ASEAN Economic Community was moved to 2015. In the same year, the ASEAN Charter was presented to the public, outlining the institutional and legal framework within which integration should take place. A departure from previous regional agreements was marked by the provisions for ASEAN's Economic Community. The Charter boldly declared that the ultimate goal was the creation of a single market and production base. To this end, free flows of goods, services, investment and skilled labor as well as freer flows of capital were agreed to be achieved by 2015 (ASEAN 2007). New instruments and rules were also designed to aid implementation. Primarily, the ASEAN Secretariat has been given more powers to oversee the implementation process. For example, the Secretariat now issues annual scorecards which evaluate the overall progress made. At the same time, the ASEAN approach of regional integration remained characterized by non-confrontational intergovernmentalism with a minimal degree of delegation to supranational institutions.

In 2009, the association published a *Roadmap for an ASEAN Community 2009–2015* containing the schedule for achieving the aims outlined in the Charter (ASEAN 2009). Some of the 176 priority actions identified in the document contain clear policy instructions and deadlines for implementation. In particular in the economic sphere, governments have agreed to several coordinated liberalization and harmonization efforts, putting—for the first time—adaptational pressure on member states. With the adoption of the Blueprint it was hoped that the previously slow process of implementing regional agreements would turn into "process-driven integration [with] clearly defined goals and timeframes" (Soesastro 2008: 48). Although the Blueprint contains many flexible arrangements in sensitive areas, its precise timeframes and deadlines in other sections enable researchers to study the AEC's implementation progress. This feature makes the Blueprint the single most important document against which regional integration progress in Southeast Asia can be evaluated.

Evaluating ASEAN's Integration Process

In the face of implementation delays many scholars are skeptical that the organization can live up to its ambitions. ASEAN has always been prone to "making grand declarations, but follow-up has been much more difficult" (Narine 2002: 162). With regards to the AEC, this chapter argues that state capacity can be a useful concept for explaining this phenomenon.

Such a view contrasts with traditional accounts of Southeast Asian integration. Commonly, the reluctance of ASEAN member states to commit themselves to deeper regional integration is explained by conflicting national interests and a historical aversion to pooling sovereignty (Möller 1998, Ravenhill 2008). Some have already condemned the association to "the limited purpose of maintaining regional order" (Jones and Smith 2007: 149). Particular blame falls on Cambodia, Laos, Myanmar and Vietnam (CLMV), which "joined ASEAN with absolutely no expectation that their domestic politics would be subject to regional scrutiny, and there is no indication that they have changed their minds on this point" (Narine 2009: 378).[1] In other words, the costs of pooling sovereignty are thought to exceed the benefits of increasing the level of regional integration.

While this line of argument certainly captures some peculiarities of regional integration in Southeast Asia, it proves less useful for explaining the undeniable process of institutional change over the past decade. In particular when economic gains were expected there has been a greater willingness to commit to deeper integration. Since the region's governments pledged to create a single market and production base by 2015, they find themselves confronted with obligations for adapting their economic, legal and regulatory framework to some common standards. ASEAN has identified several priority sectors for integration (ASEAN Secretariat 2004). In some of these sectors the need has emerged to harmonize regulations and standards.

The harmonization of cosmetics standards has been more or less completed, harmonizing electronic equipment standards is still ongoing, and similar measures in many other sectors are currently being negotiated. Another challenge is the modernization of customs procedures in the region under the so-called National Single Window plans. These initiatives do not only impose some financial costs, but also require changes in national laws, new competencies for regulatory agencies, equipment, testing facilities, monitoring capabilities and expertise.

To complicate matters, the ASEAN Secretariat suddenly finds itself confronted with issues of non-compliance. Low levels of obligation and precision in previous

---

1 For a detailed account of CLMV's motivation for joining ASEAN, see Chapter 3 in this volume.

agreements have meant that issues of non-compliance simply were not on the association's agenda in the past. Despite the association's relatively old age of over 40 years it is inexperienced with handling the coordination and monitoring of complex obligations. Already in the first year after the ratification of the ASEAN Charter it became apparent that non-compliance with agreed rules and procedures is widespread.

Making use of its new monitoring powers, the ASEAN Secretariat issued its first scorecard for the implementation progress for the year 2008–2009. The report warned that "several areas need to be addressed by ASEAN Member States for timely implementation to avoid a backlog of unimplemented commitments with the onset of more commitments and measures" (ASEAN Secretariat 2010: 17). After a meeting of the ASEAN Economic Ministers in February 2010, the Malaysian Trade Minister openly complained that there were some gaps in the implementation of regional commitments. The streamlining of customs procedures, the elimination of non-tariff barriers and the harmonization of standards were reported as particularly problematic (Malaysian Ministry of International Trade and Industry 2010).

With the important exception of Hamilton-Hart (2003), the literature has not used state capacity as an explanatory factor for the outcomes of regional integration in Southeast Asia. The standard response in the existing literature is to recommend a higher degree of delegation and a stronger institutional structure at the regional level (Hew 2007: 218). Findings of this sort, however, are based on the implicit assumption that member state's compliance is merely a result of cost-benefit calculations. So far, this claim is persistently reproduced in the literature without having been challenged by other plausible explanations.

Compliance Theory

The central question in this respect is whether or not the observed non-compliance of member states is involuntary because some states lack the capacity to comply or, instead, primarily a form of strategic defection, that is avoiding the costs of compliance.

In the past two decades, compliance with international rules has been a hotly debated topic (Checkel 2001, Haas 1998, Keohane et al. 2000, Tallberg 2002). In this debate, managerial approaches have competed with enforcement approaches on explaining the sources of non-compliance. While enforcement approaches highlight the importance of cost-benefit analysis and the threat of punishment (Dorn and Fulton 1997, Downs et al. 1996, Martin 1992), managerial approaches have consistently argued that usually non-compliance "is not ... the result of deliberate defiance of the legal standard" (Chayes and Chayes 1991: 302). To the contrary, Chayes and Chayes have argued that reasons for non-compliance are to be found in imprecise treaties, lack of state capacity or uncontrollable social or economic forces (Downs et al. 1996). In other words, while the enforcement approach is geared toward the institutional design at the international level, the managerial approach is also concerned with the capacities found at the national level. From these two perspectives follow drastically different conclusions on how to address non-compliance issues. Enforcement approaches highlight the importance of monitoring and sanctioning to alter cost-benefit calculations. In contrast, the managerial school finds any form of punishment inappropriate and even a risk to future cooperation. Consequently, persuasion and argument, transparency and capacity-building are advocated as solutions to non-compliance (Haas 1998, Jacobson and Brown Weiss 1995). The core assumptions of both approaches are reflected in various assessments of the ASEAN integration progress.

The Enforcement Approach

From an enforcement perspective, it can be criticized that low levels of delegation to supranational authorities are a characteristic feature of regional integration in Southeast Asia. In the case of ASEAN's dispute settlement mechanism, which remains the only instance where we find a high level of delegation, institutions have never been utilized. Furthermore, it seems somewhat surprising that despite a recent increase in highly precise obligations for its member states—as in the case of the harmonization initiatives—ASEAN still lacks a protocol on how to handle infringements of obligations.

Consequently, the costs associated with defecting from regional commitments are relatively low. In the absence of a regional court or other sanctioning methods enforcement theory holds that states are less likely to conform to international rules and norms (Horne and Cutlip 2002). Scholars following this logic have often proposed monitoring and sanctioning measures at the regional level as a method to alter the cost-benefit calculations of states (Hew 2007: 218).

So far, the only response was to grant the Secretariat new monitoring powers. In line with its tradition of strict non-interference, ASEAN members have refrained from formulating sanctioning mechanisms. Some regional observers such as Ravenhill (2008) have argued that this is the decisive shortcoming of the Charter and hold little hope that in the absence of such measures economic integration can be completed successfully. The enforcement hypothesis—governments will only comply with their commitments when the benefits of compliance outweigh the benefits of non-compliance—is tested by using intra-regional trade dependence as an indicator for economic gains. Indeed, intra-regional trade patterns reveal that some countries are more reliant on trade interdependence than others. While Thailand and Vietnam only export roughly 20 percent to other ASEAN economies, Laos exports 85 percent of its goods to the region (United States International Trade Commission 2010: Chapter 2, 5). From this follows:

> H1: Higher intra-regional trade dependence of ASEAN member states translates into a higher implementation rate of legal commitments under the AEC.

The Managerial Approach

In the context of ASEAN, the enforcement approach seems somewhat unsatisfying as an explanation for non-compliance: decisions are taken by consensus and are usually preceded by extensive and mostly secretive negotiations. As a result, member states cannot be forced to implement inconvenient rules and standards. Instead, whenever politically sensitive agreements are made, regional agreements opt for low levels of precision and/or obligation. Consequently, it seems unlikely that *intentional* defection from regional commitments is a particularly eminent problem in the region.

The managerial approach holds that there is a general willingness to comply with commonly agreed rules. Non-compliance is primarily a result of lacking resources such as manpower, technology or expertise to do so (Downs et al. 1996, Haas 1998, Tallberg 2002). This is not to say that involuntary non-compliance is restricted to comparatively poor regions. Studies on non-compliance in the EU have also shown that state capacity plays a crucial role in accounting for compliance variation (Börzel et al. 2007).

Hamilton-Hart (2003) has suggested that some ASEAN governments lack sufficient capacity to engage in complex regional integration projects. Similarly, Narine (2002: 131) has argued that the "semi-institutionalized approach to AFTA … may be appropriate to the ASEAN context. The limited institutional capacity of key ASEAN states means that they would have difficulty in implementing a binding legal arrangement."

Indeed, member states are often granted extensive flexibility in the implementation process in order "to meet the domestic needs of ASEAN's diverse membership" (Nesadurai 2008: 237). Particularly the development gap between the older ASEAN-6[2] and the newer CLMV[3] is often considered to be "a major hindrance to economic integration" (Salazar and Das 2007: 2). Consequently, this chapter considers the hypothesis that:

> H2: Less state capacity means more involuntary infringements of AEC commitments.

This hypothesis would expect that the newer members face more compliance problems than ASEAN's older member states.

State Capacity

Since the 1980s the concept of state capacity has been frequently utilized in development studies (Evans et al. 1985, Geddes 1994). Publications in this field

---

2 ASEAN-6: Brunei Darussalam, Indonesia, Malaysia, Philippines, Singapore, Thailand.
3 CLMV: Cambodia, Laos, Myanmar, Vietnam.

have used the concept, for example, to show that there is a relationship between the quality of state institutions and economic growth (Evans and Rauch 1999). Despite the concept's popularity in development studies it has rarely been used for the study of regional integration and there is no consensus on how to operationalize it.

In the most general sense, state capacity can be defined as "the ability of the state to formulate and implement strategies to achieve economic and social goals in society" (Kjær and Hansen 2002). In the context of Southeast Asia, administrative capacity assumes a pivotal role for the fulfillment of regional commitments (Hamilton-Hart 2003). Administrative capacity can be measured both quantitatively and qualitatively. While the former includes financial and human resources (Haas 1998, Simmons 1998), the latter can be measured in terms of government effectiveness and regulatory quality (Evans et al. 1985).

The human resources available to a government are usually measured in terms of public sector employment as a percentage of total employment or percentage of GDP spent on the civil service. While this seems a plausible measurement for a Western bureaucracy, it is of little utility in the context of Southeast Asia. Many of the countries in the region are currently in the process of restructuring their civil service. Multilateral and bilateral donors have identified the quality to be a much bigger constraining factor than the resources available. In fact, many countries in the region have been urged by donors to downsize their civil service. A recent report on Cambodia, for example, stated that rather than a lack of staff "the inefficiency of the civil service may have more to do with such factors as the distribution of staff among ministries, the lack of meritocracy, low salaries, entrenched attitudes, and unqualified staff" (Wescon 2001: 12–14). The qualitative differences in administrative capacity are, thus, at the forefront of this investigation. Two indicators from Kaufmann's *Governance Indicators* are utilized in this chapter to represent state capacity: *Government Effectiveness* and *Regulatory Quality* (Kaufmann et al. 2009).[4] Although this perception-based index cannot be regarded as an exact representation of state capacity as the number of its sources varies between countries, it is used in this study as an approximation because it is one of the few indices that cover all countries of Southeast Asia.

Government Effectiveness measures the perceptions of the "quality of the civil service and the degree of its independence from political pressures" (Kaufmann et al. 2009). The adherence to formal rules is an important element of the bureaucracy, because it contributes to "administrative objectivity and hence restrain[s] arbitrary and impulsive action" (Nee and Opper 2009). Bureaucratic independence and rules-based conduct also impact on the administration's technical efficiency, its expert control and precision. Government Effectiveness is also intended to capture "the quality of policy formulation and implementation, and the credibility of the government's commitment to such policies" (Kaufmann et al. 2009: 6).

---

4 The data covers 212 countries and has been collected through surveys on an annual basis since 2002.

The quality of public administration is crucial for regional integration because it requires "a state's commitment to long-term goals and policies, despite change in the composition of political leadership" (Nee and Opper 2009).

Regulatory Quality captures perceptions of the government's capacity "to formulate and implement sound policies and regulations that permit and promote private sector development." The ability to do so is essential for a country to participate in a single market. Building the ASEAN Economic Community requires many of its member states to transform their regulatory systems. Taken together the average score of these two indicators will be used as the qualitative measurement of our state capacity concept.

Table 9.1 Overview of operationalization

Theoretical approach	Variable	Measurement	Source
Enforcement approach	Trade dependence	Intra-regional trade as percentage of global trade	ASEAN Statistics
Managerial approach	State capacity	Government effectiveness, regulatory quality	World Bank Governance Indicators

Source: Own compilation.

The Capacity Gap in ASEAN

According to our measurement of state capacity the capacity gap in ASEAN is larger than in any other major regional organization. The spectrum ranges from Singapore's well-trained, highly efficient and career oriented bureaucracy, to Myanmar's poorly equipped and often corrupt administration, in which the problems are "so severe that the bureaucracy has difficulty accomplishing even basic tasks necessary to maintain the regime" (Engelhaart 2005: 623).

Particularly striking is the capacity gap between the CLMV and the ASEAN-6 members. Among the ASEAN-6 Singapore, Brunei and Malaysia score the highest, while the Philippines and Thailand form a middle group. Indonesia's state capacity score is closer to the CLMV than to the older member states. Indeed, it has been pointed out that Indonesia's civil service is "badly in need of reform" and has been described as "slow; lacks transparency, accountability, and initiative; and is sometimes corrupt" (Tjiptoherijanto 2007: 31).

The reasons for the stark contrast in capacity can be found in the recent history of the newer member states. The CLMV are still engaged in the process of state-building, as they have only recently changed their economic systems from central planning to market-oriented capitalism. There is also a general scarcity of (highly) qualified personnel and expertise which significantly reduces the administrative capacity in these countries (Caballero-Anthony 2006). Consequently, some ASEAN members are not in a position to fulfill increasingly complex and ambitious regional initiatives. Although there have been some efforts in the past decade to address capacity gaps in the region, such as the Initiative for ASEAN Integration (ASEAN 2000), these have been largely ineffective in bringing about substantial improvements (Salazar and Das 2007, Severino 2007).

Case Studies

The case selection for testing our hypotheses comes from the Roadmap published by the ASEAN Secretariat. It is the central document against which the compliance with ASEAN agreements can be measured. While some commitments are based on rather vague formulations, ASEAN is also experimenting with more precise obligations and fixed deadlines. The most extensive requirements found in the document for the period 2008–2010 are concerned with the harmonization of cosmetics regulations as well as the streamlining of customs procedures. The success of these projects is vital for paving the way for the establishment of the AEC by 2015. Not only does a failure potentially create a "backlog of unimplemented commitments" (ASEAN Secretariat 2010: 17), but the experience with these initial measures could also influence the scope of further actions, such as harmonization initiatives currently under negotiation.

Although the Secretariat also publishes a Scorecard to monitor the process of implementation itself, the version available to the public does not name and shame individual member states. Instead, the overall progress made over a year is measured. The Scorecard published for the two-year period 2008–2009, for example, has noted that overall 73.6 percent of all targets have been achieved. Unfortunately, the ASEAN Statistical Office also does not collect data on the process of implementation, but only outcome-based indicators. To conduct comparative research on the implementation effort made by individual member states, data has been collected from official reports, press releases, online media and academic research. The first case study deals with the legal implementation of the ASEAN's National Single Window (NSW) initiative. It is followed by an evaluation of the harmonization of cosmetics regulations.

The ASEAN Single Window Initiative

The Single Window initiative has confronted the region with a challenging project for the facilitation of trade in goods. According to ASEAN's economic ministers the Single Window will "facilitate the speedy clearance of imports through electronic processing of trade documents at national and regional level" (ASEAN 2005). At least the economic ministers of the region hold it to be "the single most important initiative of customs" (ASEAN 2005). After all, the member states expect tangible benefits from a region-wide customs modernization. The overall goal is to accelerate customs clearance of goods through streamlining procedures and standardizing the handling of data. At the moment, the speed and ease of customs procedures varies widely among ASEAN member states. By reducing the time needed for customs clearance a considerable amount of money could be saved in the region (The Nation 2009).

First, however, the member states will have to bring their own customs procedures and regulations into line in a so-called National Single Window system. To this end, measures will have to be taken to simplify, harmonize and standardize trade and customs processes and procedures. According to the Roadmap, the ASEAN-6 have agreed to operationalize their National Single Windows by 2008, while the CLMV are granted a further four years to fully complete their NSWs (ASEAN 2005).

Reviewing the current status of the National Single Window reveals that despite the potential benefits associated with this initiative almost all ASEAN-6 countries have fallen behind schedule.

Table 9.2 Implementation of ASEAN Single Window

Member state	Activation of National Single Window	State capacity score	Trade dependence
Singapore	2008	2.23	27.3%
Brunei	Partially in 2008	0.86	25.8%
Malaysia	End of 2008	0.70	25.1%
Thailand	Partially in late 2009	0.19	20.7%
Philippines	Partially in late 2009	-0.03	20.7%
Indonesia	Early 2010	-0.28	24.5%
Vietnam	Expected in late 2011	-0.42	17.6%
Cambodia	Scheduled for 2012	-0.64	23.6%
Laos	Scheduled for 2012	-1.05	83.7%
Myanmar	Scheduled for 2012	-1.96	51.6%

Sources: Various (Antara News 2010, ASEAN Statistics 2010, Brunei FM 2009, Dee 2009, Kaufmann et al. 2009, The Nation 2009, SunStar Manila 2010, Thailand Customs Department 2008).

According to the US Trade Commission not one of the ASEAN member states has effectively met the deadline for operationalizing their National Single Window. In March 2010 Singapore was reported to be the only country to have fully implemented its NSW (United States International Trade Commission 2010: Chapter 2, 24). The other ASEAN-6 countries have only managed to partly activate their NSWs. Looking at the date the NSW was activated, we can see that apart from Singapore only Brunei managed to activate (although not fully) its National Single Window on time. These countries also have a high state capacity score, but also the highest trade dependence of the older ASEAN members. While Malaysia was able to implement its program with a delay of almost a year, it took Thailand, the Philippines and Indonesia considerably more time to do so. In the case of Indonesia, it seems difficult to attribute the delay of two years to a lack of interest in the project. With the fourth highest intra-regional trade dependence the country can expect significant material gains from this project.

Although the CLMV were granted until 2012 to streamline their customs procedures, there are indicators that these countries too will face difficulties to activate their NSW on time. Some qualitative differences in the adaptational process can also be seen. Vietnam is the only country to date to have completed a NSW Master Plan and has piloted an "E-Customs system" (United States International Trade Commission 2010: Chapter 2, 24). Cambodia, Laos and Myanmar have made the least progress so far.

It has been pointed out that many of the region's countries are "facing challenges, especially the differences in regulations on transport, customs clearance for commodities, administrative procedures and technical standards" (ASEAN 2010). The NSW project has resulted in huge costs for the member states, as new personnel, offices and IT infrastructure (data storage, security provisions) are required. Furthermore, a variety of legal problems relating to the sharing of data between government agencies and across borders also have to be addressed. The availability of ICT expertise remains another weakness. Although Brunei has recently offered to help other member states with the operationalization of the E-Customs systems, it is unclear whether this ad hoc measure of help will be sufficient to overcome the current obstacles in the implementation process. So far, most of the assistance for modernizing customs procedures comes from multilateral and bilateral donors, such as the World Bank in Laos and Vietnam or the US Agency for International Development in the Philippines (United States International Trade Commission 2010: Chapter 2, 26).

Trade dependence might have also played a role in the speed of the implementation process. The only two countries which managed to operationalize their National Single Window on time also have the greatest intra-ASEAN trade dependence of the ASEAN-6. Indonesia, however, is the outlier case, which seemed to face most difficulties during the implementation process, despite its relatively high trade dependence of 24.5 percent. From an enforcement perspective this is surprising since higher trade dependence suggests that the potential gains from the NSW project are also much greater.

Considering the complex nature of this project state capacity seems to offer more explanatory power than the cost-benefit argument of the enforcement approach. At the same time, however, the discussion has highlighted that the reliance on external donors might also translate into qualitative differences in the implementation process depending on the donor's scope of assistance.

Future research on compliance in ASEAN should include external support as an intervening variable.

The ASEAN Cosmetics Directive

In several product categories ASEAN countries will harmonize standards and regulations: healthcare, electrical and electronic equipment, forest products, automotive, food processing, medical equipment, rubber products, fishery products, and agricultural products. Although the aim is to either have common standards and regulations or mutual recognition agreements in these sectors across the region, to date only limited progress has been made (United States International Trade Commission 2010: Chapter 6, 1).

Specifically the healthcare sector is an important segment of ASEAN economies. Regional trade volume of healthcare goods has increased by 23 percent per year and reached the $2 billion mark in 2008 (United States International Trade Commission 2010: Chapter 6, 1). A sub-sector which is of particular importance for both internal and external trade is the market for cosmetics. In order to remain a competitive location for cosmetic companies, ASEAN governments decided to harmonize the region's cosmetics regulation. After six years of negotiations, ASEAN economic ministers finally agreed on a single regulatory scheme for cosmetics goods in 2003 (ASEAN 2003a). The deadline for full implementation of the so-called ASEAN Cosmetics Directive (ACD) was scheduled for January 1, 2008 (ASEAN 2003a: Article 2.3). Unlike many other regional initiatives, CLMV were not granted additional time for the implementation. All countries were also required to change their regulatory systems, so as to significantly shorten the time span for the approval of new cosmetic products.

In order for regionally produced cosmetics to continue to have access to the European market, the ASEAN Directive has been closely modeled after the European Union's Cosmetic Directive.[5] The region also received extensive assistance from the European Committee for Standardization in drawing up the regulatory requirements. Considering ASEAN's high dependence on the European market for exports ASEAN's alignment with European standards certainly makes sense. A comparison of the progress toward implementing the regulatory scheme ordered by date of implementation is presented in Table 9.3.

As we can see, only five countries managed to implement the directive in a timely manner, and a total of six countries were able to implement the directive in 2008. Among the laggards are three of the CLMV which exceeded the target date by more than a year. Vietnam performs surprisingly well, while Indonesia is again the outlier case. Trade dependence does not seem to significantly affect the speed of implementation, suggesting again that limits in administrative capacity are an important factor for the observed delays.

---

5 It should also be noted that ASEAN does not usually issue "directives."

Table 9.3 Implementation of ACD (ranked by date of implementation)

Member state	Implementation of notification procedures	State capacity score	Trade dependence
Singapore	Early 2008	2.23	27.3%
Malaysia	Early 2008	0.70	25.7%
Philippines	Early 2008	-0.03	20.7%
Vietnam	Early 2008	-0.42	17.6%
Brunei	Early 2008	0.86	25.8%
Thailand	Mid 2008	0.19	20.7%
Cambodia	Mid 2009	-0.64	23.6%
Laos	Mid 2009	-1.25	83.7%
Myanmar	Mid 2009	-1.96	51.6%
Indonesia	End 2010	-0.28	24.5%

Source: Kaufmann et al. (2009); ASEAN Statistics (2010) and own research.

Harmonization of cosmetics standards has been challenging for ASEAN member states, because it "meant a change in regulatory dogma from registration to notification, as such from pre-market approval to post-market surveillance of cosmetic products" (Struessmann 2009). In other words, rather than having to approve a product prior to marketing, the administration has to monitor whether or not the products on sale satisfy the quality and ingredient standards outlined in the ACD. The monitoring process is conducted using a notification process, which can be used by companies and consumers alike. It has been reported that major challenges during and after the implementation process were "a lack of manpower due to the large quantities of notifications and the fact that additional professional skills are needed" (Struessmann 2009). In other words, capacity limitations can be seen as an obstacle for fulfilling the ACD requirements. While the state capacity measurement used in this study manages to broadly account for the variance in the implementation process, it cannot account for Indonesia's particularly poor performance.

Findings

In the past decade, ASEAN has gradually stepped up its efforts to harness the potential economic and political benefits of increased regional integration. Although the institutional design on the regional level has not been radically changed, the ASEAN Community is an ambitious plan to achieve a significantly higher level of regional cooperation and economic integration. Building a single market and production base requires the member states to adapt parts of their legal and economic system. This is certainly a new aspect of regionalism in Southeast Asia, which has so far not been studied extensively. It not only poses a challenge to the member states, but also to ASEAN's central institutions as compliance issues have suddenly appeared on the agenda. At the same time, it has emerged that the development gap in ASEAN is also a capacity gap that needs to be taken seriously.

As a result of the confidential, non-confrontational and consensual decision-making process, regional commitments are arguably overall less demanding than, for example, in the European Union. That does not mean, however, that compliance problems do not exist. Instead, most countries have not met their obligations in the two cases under investigation.

While the correlation between the state capacity score and compliance was highest in the case of the ASEAN Single Window initiative, it was less pronounced in the harmonization case. While Vietnam scored better than expected, Indonesia performed worse than the state capacity hypothesis would expect.

In the cases studied, state capacity offers more explanatory power for the observed compliance variation than regional trade dependence. Although the nature of this study does not allow for making generalizations about the relationship between non-compliance and state capacity, the pattern found in the cases under investigation would suggest that state capacity has to be taken into account when evaluating compliance with regional commitments. Of course, the two concepts are not mutually exclusive. Nevertheless, taking state capacity into account captures an important aspect of compliance issues in regional integration that is currently under-represented in the literature on regionalism outside the European Union.

Furthermore, the often articulated assumption that the outcome of regional integration in Southeast Asia is primarily shaped by concerns about the member states' sovereignty could not be substantiated. Of course, the institutions chosen at the regional level differ significantly from the supranational framework chosen by European governments. Nevertheless, the project of establishing a single market and production base shows that its member states are willing to open up parts of their economic and legal system to common regional norms and standards. As far as compliance with regional agreements is concerned, the cases studied in this chapter do not indicate that cost-benefit calculations have so far impeded this process.

Instead, it appears that the capacity gap in the region is a more serious impediment to fully meeting the target date of 2015. Moreover, Indonesia's relatively poor performance indicates that not only the CLMV should be the target of regional assistance. This finding is interesting because in the past the differences in organizational capacity were mostly conceived of as the difference between the less developed newer member states and the old ASEAN-6. That compliance and capacity problems can also be found in some of the ASEAN-6 countries suggests that public sector capacity building efforts should not be restricted to the CLMV.

Conclusion

In comparison with the traditional approach to regional integration in Southeast Asia, the focus on state capacity gives us a more detailed and slightly different picture of the processes and outcomes. On a general level, we can see that the rational actor model applied by many observers of regional integration to account for the behavior of states is often too crude to explain enforcement problems. One should be careful not to assume that all states participating in regional organizations are on an equal footing. There are great differences in the capacity of states to fulfill the regional integration agenda. More specifically, we can observe that regionalism in Southeast Asia has gradually become more demanding. As far as (non-)compliance with regional commitments is concerned the assumption of our first hypothesis (H1) that the choices of ASEAN's member states purely follow a cost-benefit analysis could not be substantiated. Instead, the findings of this study lend more explanatory power to our second hypothesis (H2) that the overall poor compliance with regional initiatives is largely a result of a lack of capacity of the member states.

Whether or not future projects will be equally delayed largely depends on ASEAN's response to the problems encountered in the past two years. As ASEAN has repeatedly shied away from supranational enforcement mechanisms, the management approach would suggest responding to compliance problems by focusing on capacity building in some of the weakest member states, including Indonesia.

Many of ASEAN's current projects, such as the harmonization of regulation or the modernization of customs procedures, are achieved with the help of a variety of different development agencies. To what extent the high influence of external donors impacts on state capacity improvements as well as on the drafting and implementation of regional commitments would certainly be an interesting point for further research.

To conclude, regionalism in Southeast Asia is increasingly shaped by the capacity of the participants to fulfill ambitious regional projects. While all ASEAN member states have identified a variety of projects for cooperation which would greatly benefit the region as a whole, some limitations and delays can be traced back to administrative weaknesses found in some of the countries. To complicate matters, ASEAN finds it almost impossible to respond adequately to compliance problems. A growing backlog of commitments will make the 2015 deadline increasingly difficult to meet. Without addressing capacity issues in several member states, ASEAN will fail to live up to its new ambitions for deeper regional integration.

References

Antara News. 2010. *News Focus: RI Adopts Single Window System to Smooth Exim Traffic*. [Online]. Available at: www.antaranews.com/en/news/1264805560/news-focus-ri-adopts-single-window-system-to-smooth-exim-traffic [accessed: September 20, 2010].

ASEAN. 2000. *Initiave for ASEAN Integration (IAI) Work Plan for the CLMV Countries*. Singapore.

ASEAN. 2003a. *Agreement on the ASEAN Harmonized Cosmetics Regulatory System*. Phnom Penh, Cambodia.

ASEAN. 2003b. *Declaration of ASEAN Concord II*. Bali.

ASEAN. 2005. *Agreement to Establish and Implement the ASEAN Single Window*. [Online]. Kuala Lumpur. Available at: www.aseansec.org/18005.htm [accessed: September 20, 2010].

ASEAN. 2007. *Charter of the Association of Southeast Asian Nations*. Singapore.

ASEAN. 2009. *Roadmap for an ASEAN Community 2009 – 2015*. Jakarta: ASEAN Secretariat.

ASEAN. 2010. *ASEAN Nations Move to Gear up Logistics Integration*. [Online]. Available at: http://asean2010.vn/asean_en/news/36/2DA94C/ASEAN-nations-move-to-gear-up-logistics-integration [accessed: September 20, 2010].

ASEAN Secretariat. 2004. *ASEAN Accelerates Integration of Priority Sectors*. [Online]. Available at: www.aseansec.org/16620.htm [accessed: September 20, 2010].

ASEAN Secretariat. 2006. *Report of the Eminent Persons Group on the ASEAN Charter*. [Online]. Available at: www.asean.org/19247.pdf [accessed September 20, 2010].

ASEAN Secretariat. 2010. *ASEAN Economic Community Scorecard*. [Online]. Available at: www.asean.org/publications/AEC%20Scorecard.pdf [accessed: September 1, 2010].

ASEAN Statistics. 2010. *Intra- and Extra-ASEAN Trade, 2009*. [Online]. Available at: www.aseansec.org/stat/Table18.pdf [accessed: May 31, 2011].

Börzel, T. A., Dudziak, M., Hofmann, T., Panke, D. and Sprungk, C. 2007. *Recalcitrance, Inefficiency, and Support for European Integration: Why Member States Do (Not) Comply with European Law*. Center for European Studies Working Paper Series No. 151. Berlin, Center for European Studies.

Brunei FM. 2009. *e-Customs Change for the Better*. [Online]. Available at: http://news.brunei.fm/2009/09/16/ecustoms-change-for-the-better [accessed: September 20, 2010].

Caballero-Anthony, M. 2006. Bridging Development Gaps in Southeast Asia: Towards an ASEAN Community. *UNISCI Discussion Papers* [Online], 11, 37–48. Available at: www.ucm.es/info/unisci/revistas/UNISCI11FULL.pdf [accessed: September 20, 2010].

Caballero-Anthony, M. 2008. The ASEAN Charter – An Opportunity Missed or One that Cannot be Missed? *Southeast Asian Affairs*, 71–85.

Chayes, A. and Chayes, A. H. 1991. Compliance without Enforcement: State Behaviour under Regulatory Treaties. *Negotiation Journal*, 7(3), 311–330.

Checkel, J. T. 2001. Why Comply? Social Learning and European Identity Change. *International Organization*, 55(3), 553–588.

Dee, P. 2009. Services Liberalization Toward the ASEAN Economic Community, in *Tracing the Progress Toward the ASEAN Economic Community, ERIA Research Project Report 2008, No. 1*, edited by J. Corbett and S. Umezaki, 58–96. [Online]. Available at: www.eria.org/pdf/research/y2008/no1/DEI-Ch02.pdf [accessed: April 28, 2011].

Dorn, A. W. and Fulton, A. 1997. Securing Compliance with Disarmament Treaties: Carrots, Sticks, and the Case of North Korea. *Global Governance*, 3, 17–40.

Downs, G. W., Rocke, D. M. and Barsoom, P. N. 1996. Is the Good News about Compliance Good News about Cooperation? *International Organization*, 50(3), 379–406.

Engelhaart, N. A. 2005. Is Regime Change Enough for Burma? The Problem of State Capacity. *Asian Survey*, 45(4), 622–644.

Evans, P. and Rauch, J. E. 1999. Bureaucracy and Growth: A Cross-National Analysis of the Effects of "Weberian" State Structures on Economic Growth. *American Sociological Review*, 64(5), 748–765.

Evans, P., Rueschemeyer, D. and Skocpol, T. (eds). 1985. *Bringing the State back in*. Cambridge: Cambridge University Press.

Geddes, B. 1994. *Politician's Dilemma: Building State Capacity in Latin America*. Los Angeles: University of California Press.

Haas, P. M. 1998. Compliance with EU Directives: Insights from International Relations and Comparative Politics. *Journal of European Public Policy*, 5(1), 17–37.

Hamilton-Hart, N. 2003. Asia's New Regionalism: Government Capacity and Cooperation in the Western Pacific. *Review of International Political Economy*, 10(2), 222–45.

Hew, D. (ed.). 2007. *Conclusion: Towards an ASEAN Economic Community by 2015*. Jakarta: Asia Pacific Press.

Horne, C. and Cutlip, A. 2002. Sanctioning Costs and Norm Enforcement. *Rationality and Society*, 14(3), 285–307.

Jacobson, H. K. and Brown Weiss, E. 1995. Strengthening Compliance with International Environmental Accords: Preliminary Observations from a Collaborative Project. *Global Governance*, (1), 119–148.

Jones, D. M. and Smith, M. L. R. 2007. Making Process, Not Progress. *International Security*, 32(1), 148–184.

Kaufmann, D., Kraay, A. and Mastruzzi, M. 2009. *Governance Matters VIII: Aggregate and Individual Governance Indicators 1996–2008*. World Bank Policy Research Working Paper 4978. Washington, DC.

Keohane, R. O., Moravcsik, A. and Slaughter, A.-M. 2000. Legalized Dispute Resolution: Interstate and Transnational. *International Organization*, 54(3), 457–488.

Kjær, M. and Hansen, O. H. 2002. *Conceptualizing State Capacity*. DEMSTAR Research Report No. 6, April 2002. Aarthus.

Malaysian Ministry of International Trade and Industry. 2010. *Media Release. 16th ASEAN Economic Ministers' Retreat*. [Online]. Available at: www.miti.gov.my/cms/contentPrint.jsp?id=com.tms.cms.article.Article_14d32d58-c0a81573-2f1d2f1d-4e630e07&paging=0 [accessed: September 1, 2010].

Martin, L. M. 1992. *Coercive Cooperation: Explaining Multilateral Economic Sanctions*. Princeton: Princeton University Press.

Möller, K. 1998. Cambodia and Burma: The ASEAN Way Ends Here. *Asian Survey*, 38(12), 1087–1104.

Narine, S. 2002. *Explaining ASEAN: Regionalism in Southeast Asia*. London: Lynne Rienner.

Narine, S. 2009. ASEAN in the Twenty-first Century: A Sceptical Review. *Cambridge Review of International Affairs*, 22(3), 369–386.

The Nation. 2009. *National Single Window Nears Reality*. [Online]. Available at: www.nationmultimedia.com/worldhotnews/30115908/National-Single-Window-nears-reality [accessed: September 20, 2010].

Nee, V. and Opper, S. 2009. Bureaucracy and Financial Markets. *Kyklos: International Review for Social Sciences*, 62(2), 293–315.

Nesadurai, H. E. S. (ed.) 2008. *Southeast Asia's New Institutional Architecture for Cooperation in Trade and Finance*. Hamburg: Springer.

Ravenhill, J. 2008. Fighting Irrelevance: An Economic Community "with ASEAN Characteristics." *The Pacific Review*, 21(4), 469–488.

Salazar, L. C. and Das, S. B. 2007. Bridgning the ASEAN Developmental Divide – Challenges and Prospects. *ASEAN Economic Bulletin*, 24(1), 1–14.

Severino, R. 2007. The ASEAN Developmental Divide and the Initiative for ASEAN Integration. *ASEAN Economic Bulletin*, 24(1), 35–44.

Simmons, B. A. 1998. Compliance with International Agreements. *Annual Review of Political Science*, (1), 75–93.

Soesastro, H. 2008. *Implementing the ASEAN Economic Community (AEC) Blueprint*. ERIA Research Project Report 2007 1–2, Economic Research Institute for ASEAN and East Asia. Jakarta.

Stahl, B. 2010. Die Gemeinschaft südostasiatischer Staaten (ASEAN): Erfolge und Probleme einer überforderten Institution, in *Multilaterale Institutionen in Ostasien-Pazifik*, edited by D. Nabers. Wiesbaden: VS-Verlag für Sozialwissenschaften, 17–53.

Struessmann, A. 2009. *ASEAN Cosmetic Directive – Status on Implementation in the Various Member States*. [Online]. Special Chem. Available at: www.specialchem4cosmetics.com/services/articles.aspx?id=4041&lr=tfcos09008&li=100023332 [accessed: May 25, 2010].

SunStar Manila. 2010. *Customs Single Window System*. [Online]. Available at: www.sunstar.com.ph/manila/customs%E2%80%99-single-window-system [accessed: September 20, 2010].

Tallberg, J. 2002. Paths to Compliance: Enforcement, Management, and the European Union. *International Organization*, 56(3), 609–664.

Thailand Customs Department. 2008. *Cargo Clearance*. [Online]. Available at: www.customs.go.th/Customs-Eng/CargoClearance/CargoClearance.jsp?menuNme=Cargo [accessed: September 20, 2010].

Tjiptoherijanto, P. 2007. Civil Service Reform in Indonesia. *International Public Management Review*, 8(2), 31–44.

United States International Trade Commission. 2010. *ASEAN: Regional Trends in Economic Integration, Export Competitiveness, and Inbound Investment for Selected Industries*. Investigation No. 332-511, USITC Publication 4176. Washington, DC.

Wescon, C. G. (ed.). 2001. *Key Governance Issues in Cambodia, Lao PDR, Thailand, and Viet Nam*. Manila: Asian Development Bank.

Chapter 10

When Pigs Fly:
ECOWAS and the Protection of Constitutional Order in Events of Coups d'État

Kai Striebinger

West Africa is *the* region of coups d'état. Almost every second African military coup d'état takes place in its western region (McGowan 2003: 355). For a long time, this source of political instability was not of concern to neighboring states. After independence, African countries established non-interference in domestic affairs as a constitutive principle of inter-state relations (Clapham 1996: 110). Continental and regional organizations did not officially comment on a case of unconstitutional change of government in a member state. They were not willing to intervene in order to protect the country's constitution and enforce a particular political system.

After the end of the Cold War, something unexpected happened: "pigs started to fly." In Africa, the continent where one-party systems and authoritarian dictatorships were in the majority, state leaders replaced the norm of non-interference by a norm of non-indifference with the long-term goal of establishing democracy in their states (Williams 2007).

Over the last two decades, member states of the Economic Community of West African States (ECOWAS) have given their regional organization (RO) a full-fledged political mandate to safeguard democratic constitutions, especially in cases of coups d'état.[1] But ECOWAS has not reacted uniformly to the continued incidence of coups.

Why has ECOWAS intervened in some cases of military coups d'état against democratic governments and not in others? And, why has ECOWAS, when it intervened, used different means to do so?

This research question addresses several aspects—both on a theoretical and a practical level. First, the issue of intervention has mainly been addressed by the realist school of international relations. Countries would intervene militarily in the domestic affairs of a third state to maximize their power. Inspired by a social-constructivist approach, this chapter seeks to establish if other motivations also have an impact on the decision to intervene. Second, the present chapter enlightens one prominent example of international norm evolution. In Africa, the guarantee

---

1 For a comparable development in MERCOSUR, see Chapter 11, this volume.

of sovereignty was a cornerstone of inter-state relations after independence. During the last two decades non-indifference replaced non-interference. Third, the chapter addresses the question of a possible "actor quality" of international organizations. Are ROs merely the agents of the powerful states or do they also have an independent impact on member states? Finally, the chapter contributes to the question under what conditions ROs will react to unconstitutional power changes and can therefore inspire practical solutions in other regions.

Theoretical Background

In the realm of democracy promotion, ECOWAS's main focus lies on the unconstitutional access to or prolongation of power. For our purposes a coup is defined as the (1) illegal seizure of power by a small fraction of the elite or (2) the illegal maintenance of power by a democratically elected executive that result in (3) the violation and/or suspension of the constitution (Marshall et al. 2010, Zimmermann 1981). Coups against the constitutional order are our pool of possible cases where interventions could take place. Constitutional order is understood as a democratic political system characterized by a minimal form of popular participation: the existence of elections. In order to avoid including extremely unfair elections, international observer mission reports will be consulted to determine if a government has actually been democratically elected.

Interventions by ECOWAS

This chapter wants to explain the type of intervention by ECOWAS (our dependent variable). Finnemore defines intervention as "compromises of sovereignty by other states that are exceptional in some way" (2003: 9). Or simply put: "the interference in the domestic affairs of a member state" (Van der Vleuten 2007: 155). Here, "intervention" is understood in a nuanced way, going beyond military intervention. It will be measured on a four-step scale, from low to high-intensity interventions, inspired by Nolte (2006: 13):

1. no intervention
2. political dialogue with the goal of influencing the domestic affairs in the target state
   a. low-intensity intervention: publicly voiced condemnation and demands
   b. low- to medium-intensity intervention: formalized meetings and negotiations
3. medium-intensity intervention: economic and/ or political sanctions
4. high-intensity intervention: military intervention.

Factors Favoring and Obstructing Interventions by ROs

But what causes the regional organization to conduct or abstain from an intervention? The following, functionally equivalent explanations are based on social-constructivist and realist international relations theory (Jong Choi and Caporaso 2002, Van der Vleuten 2007, Van der Vleuten and Ribeiro Hoffmann 2010). One objective of this research is to determine which independent variable provides more explanatory power.

The degree of democratic identity of ECOWAS "There is no reason why a regional organization with a weak democratic identity would intervene in the domestic affairs of a Member State whose democracy is threatened" (Van der Vleuten and Ribeiro Hoffmann 2010: 740). The democratic identity of a RO consists of three distinct aspects: (1) homogeneity of democratic membership, (2) the strength of pro-intervention norms and (3) democratic norm congruence with continental intervention norms.

The homogeneity of membership argument is based on the assumption that only those countries that are democratic themselves or want to democratize are willing to intervene in cases of democratic dilemmas in their neighboring countries.

The strength of the norms to protect democracy and intervene in cases of norm violations is constitutive for any action by the RO (Van der Vleuten 2007: 157). If the norms are very precise and prescribe specific action, then an intervention is more likely.

The democratic identity is also strengthened through norm congruence between regional and continental norms (Acharya 2004: 239, Checkel 1999: 84). Here, the congruence of the two norms sets will be examined—if norms match, then their enforcement is more likely because actors will not have the possibility to choose the norm they prefer.

> H1: The stronger the democratic identity of the regional organization, the more likely is a high-intensity democracy-preserving intervention in a member state.

Van der Vleuten and Ribeiro Hoffmann have proposed the following indicators to measure the degree of democratic identity: (1) the existence of a "democratic clause requiring applicant countries to be democracies"; (2) "whether there is a rule specifying modes of intervention in case of threat to democracy"; (3) the homogeneity of membership measured through the Freedom House Index (FHI) (2010: 740).

For our purposes, the three parts of the democratic identity will be measured step-by-step. Membership homogeneity is assessed with the FHI; the concept of legalization allows assessing the strength (the precision, obligation and delegation) of a pro-intervention norm (Abbott et al. 2000); this will be compared with the level of legalization of a pro-intervention norm on the continental level as defined by the Organization of African Unity (OAU) and the successor organization, the African Union (AU).

Table 10.1 Measuring democratic identity

Degree of membership homogeneity	Level of legalization of democracy standards (adapted from Abbott et al. 2000)			Legalization-level of AU pro-intervention norm	Strength of democratic identity
	Degree of precision	Degree of obligation	Degree of delegation		
> 50% of members "not free"	Impossible to determine if conduct complies	Norms without law-making authority (recommendations)	Forum for negotiations	low	Weak
> 50% of members "partly free"	Substantial but limited issues of interpretation	Contingent obligations	Legitimation of decentralized enforcement	moderate	Moderate
> 50% of members "free"	Determinate rules, narrow issues of interpretation	Unconditional obligation	Centralized enforcement	strong	Strong

Source: own compilation.

The degree of membership homogeneity is the most important factor in a RO where member states control the decision-making process. A moderate or strong democratic identity is possible only when a small minority of states is "not free" and the level of legalization is between moderate and high. The continental norm development moderates the democratic identity in one direction or another.

The degree of domestic non-state and international pressure The idea of this argument, also rooted in social-constructivist thinking, is that domestic non-state and international state actors can influence the decision-making process through political pressure for intervention (Pevehouse 2005: 19). If the RO does not react to this pressure, its identity as a safeguard for democracy might be damaged (Van der Vleuten 2007: 157).

If the target actors claim to belong to a common community that embodies certain norms, pressure can be more successful (Keck and Sikkink 1998: 29). It should be expected that an increase in the strength of democratic identity of the regional organization goes hand-in-hand with increased success chances for domestic non-state and international, other than continental, pressure for interference (Van der Vleuten and Ribeiro Hoffmann 2010: 752–753).

> H2: The higher the degree of domestic non-state and international pressure for intervention, the more likely is a high-intensity democracy-preserving intervention in a member state.

Actors can build up pressure from two sides, from "above" and from "below." Domestic non-governmental organizations (NGO) and other political actors can try to build up pressure on the streets, through demonstrations or other activities. Also, NGOs can look for transnational partners who will then pressure their own governments who might influence the target-RO or other states through the regular channels of international relations (Keck and Sikkink 1998: 12). In the latter case, states put pressure on other states. Therefore state behavior will be analyzed ignoring its underlying causes.

The existence of either pressure will be assessed through an analysis of relevant newspaper articles, literature and publications. Especially, the behavior of actors who are historically relevant in the region (United States, France, UK, EU) will be analyzed.

The interest of the regional hegemon for or against intervention   Rooted in a realist understanding of international relations, this variable assumes that a regional hegemon has more bearing on the decision to intervene than a less powerful state (Mearsheimer 1994). This argument acknowledges that more powerful states are in the position to cover more costs, making a higher intensity intervention more probable (Pedersen 2002, Pevehouse 2005).

> H3: The stronger the interest of the regional hegemon for an intervention, the more likely is a high-intensity democracy-preserving intervention in a member state.

In order to test this hypothesis, first the regional power has to be determined, and then its interest has to be analyzed. For our purposes, the regional hegemon will be defined as the state that unites an important share of the military, economic and demographic power in the region (Nolte 2006: 28). In West Africa, the first country to consider is Nigeria. With over 150 million inhabitants it is the most heavily populated country in Africa. It unites about 75 percent of the total West African Gross National Product (GNP) and sustains an army of almost 100,000 soldiers, making it by far the largest in the region (Salomon 2008: 246). Since Nigeria is a member of ECOWAS and the RO might intervene in Nigeria as well, other powerful players in the region like Senegal and Côte d'Ivoire will be considered (Edi 2007).

Methods and Case Selection

In order to assess the explanatory power of each of the variables, case studies will be conducted. These will follow the congruence method, which consists of looking at the values of the independent variables and then determining if the predicted outcome is congruent with the real outcome (George and Bennett 2005: 181). In order to further increase the plausibility of determining the existence of a causal relationship, we trace the decision-making process leading up to an intervention (George and Bennett 2005: 210).

In the 16 (from 2001: 15) ECOWAS member states, 37 coups have taken place from 1991 to 2008; 12 were successful, leading to a change in government (Marshall et al. 2010).[2] A preliminary analysis allows determining whether a coup was an unconstitutional power accession or prolongation, and thereby might have warranted a reaction by ECOWAS.

Out of these 12 coups, eight can be considered as relevant for our analysis because they have put an end to a democratically elected government as defined above. For these eight cases, the yearbooks also indicate values of each variable.

The three independent variables show evolution over time in one case and rather unstable patterns of change in the other two cases. The interest of the regional hegemon, in conjunction with realist theory, does not change significantly over time. The degree of pressure also varies from case to case without showing a tendency in one direction or in another.

The democratic identity evolved, however, in three phases. During the first phase, from 1991 to 1998, democratic identity was weak (homogenous undemocratic membership, neither regional nor continental legalized pro-intervention norms). During the second phase, from 1999 to 2007, democratic identity was moderate (mixed membership, slowly evolving regional and continental legalized pro-intervention norms). During the third phase, from 2008 on, democratic identity is strong (mixed membership but highly legalized regional and continental pro-intervention norms).

In order to plausibly argue for a causal influence of an independent variable on the outcome, it makes sense to select the cases with the highest variance on the independent variables (Evera 1997: 78–79). This leaves us with three cases: (1) the coup in Nigeria (1993) where only high domestic and international pressures are present and accordingly an intervention should be expected; (2) the coup in Sierra Leone (1997) where the regional hegemon has a high interest in intervening and therefore a high-intensity intervention should be expected; (3) the coup in Guinea (2008) where the democratic identity is strong but only a weak hegemonic interest is present and thus a low-intensity intervention is to be expected.

---

2   The coup on July 9, 1994 in Liberia is listed in the data. The event will not be considered here because the civil war effectively suspended any form of constitutionality.

Table 10.2 Successful coups, 1991–2008

Date	Country	Suitable for analysis?
04/30/1992	Sierra Leone	No. Military ruler Joseph Saidu Momoh who received power from long-time ruler Siaka Stevens was ousted by military Captain Valentine E. Strasser.
06/12/1993 11/17/1993	Nigeria	Yes, unconstitutional power prolongation. Babangida illegally annulled the election and thereby stopped the transition process. The military coup in November was a consequence of the first political coup.
07/23/1994	Gambia	Yes, unconstitutional power accession. Long-time president Dawda K. Jawara was re-elected in 1992. The coup by unsatisfied military personnel brought democracy to an abrupt end.
01/27/1996	Niger	Yes, unconstitutional power accession. President Mahamane Ousmane was elected on March 27, 1993 and ousted by the military coup led by Ibrahim Baré Maïnassara.
01/16/1996	Sierra Leone	No. The military coup was directed at military ruler Strasser who was replaced by General Julius Maada Bio.
05/25/1997	Sierra Leone	Yes, unconstitutional power accession. Kabbah was democratically elected and illegally overthrown by the military.
12/24/1999	Côte d'Ivoire	Yes, unconstitutional power accession. Henri Konan Bédié was elected in 1995 and ousted by the military.
05/07/1999	Guinea-Bissau	Yes, unconstitutional power accession. The military coup against João Bernardo Vieira challenged the transition process.
04/09/1999	Niger	No. President Maïnassara came to power in a coup (1996) and was killed in the coup in 1999.
09/14/2003	Guinea-Bissau	No. President Kumba Yalá was not elected democratically and the military decided to dispose of him.
02/05/2005	Togo	Yes, unconstitutional power accession. When Togo's longtime ruler Eyadéma Gnassingbé died, the army and Faure Gnassingbé prevented the legal successor, the president of the parliament, Fambaré Natchaba Ouattara, from taking office and suspended the constitution.
12/23/2008	Guinea	Yes, unconstitutional power accession. Guinea's long-time ruler Lansana Conté died. The constitution stipulates that the president of the parliament should succeed. But young military officers led by Dadis Camara took power.

Source: Own compilation based on Afrika Jahrbücher (from 1991 to 2003) and then the successor publication Africa Yearbooks (from 2004 to 2008).

A Coup without Intervention (Nigeria 1993)

Failed democratization attempts have shaped Nigerian history for a long time. The democratization process initiated by General Babangida led to presidential elections on June 12, 1993. However, Babangida put a halt to the peaceful transition to a democratically elected government by annulling the release of election results (Osaghae 1998: 239). ECOWAS did not react to this unconstitutional power prolongation by Babangida.

A Weak Democratic Identity

In June 1993 the democratic identity of ECOWAS was weak. Freedom House considers almost 50 percent of member states "not free" at the time of the coup. Nine member states were considered "partly free" or "free."

If the level of legalization of democracy standards were high, the democratic identity might still be considered weak to moderate. This is not the case. In June 1993, only one officially adopted document on the regional level refers to democratic standards.[3] The Declaration of Political Principles signed on July 6, 1991, has two relevant clauses, which could have had an impact on a decision to preserve democracy. One affirms the member states' commitment to democracy (ECOWAS 1991: preamble), the other indirectly promotes elections (ECOWAS 1991: point 6). The formulations are, however, imprecise, non-binding, and do not institute a third body tasked with supervision and enforcement. The level of legalization of democracy standards is therefore low. On the continental level, the OAU considered questions of changes of government in its member states in a declaration adopted in 1990. It states: "[Member states] reaffirm the right of [their] countries to determine, in all sovereignty, [their] system of democracy" (OAU 1990: point 10). In this respect there is high congruence of a *non*-intervention norm.

Considering the high number of undemocratic states in the region, the overall low level of legalization and the inexistence of a continental pro-intervention norm, the democratic identity of ECOWAS is "weak" at the time of the coup and the hypothesis is therefore confirmed.

A High Degree of Domestic Non-State and International Pressure

The second hypothesis is, however, not confirmed. Although there was a high pressure from "below" and from "above" no intervention took place. The annulment-decision by Babandiga and the subsequent dissolution of the National Electoral Commission (NEC) caused nation-wide protests leading Nigeria to be

---

3   The revised treaty was signed in July 1993 but only entered into force in 1995. So it is not applicable here.

"on the brink of anarchy" (Falola and Heaton 2008: 228). Even violent terrorist attacks occurred in the following months (Osaghae 1998: 256).

The international community supported these protests. After the cancellation of the election, the United States, the UK and France imposed limited sanctions on Nigeria: visa restrictions were introduced for military personnel and their families, military cooperation was suspended, non-humanitarian assistance was cut off and the United States issued statements advising their citizens to avoid traveling to Nigeria (Suberu 1997: 284).

The pressure "from above" was fairly intense since it attacked the military elite and delegitimized Babangida internationally. Nigeria was soon perceived as a "pariah state" (Osaghae 1998: 251). However, this was not sufficient to cause an intervention by ECOWAS.

No Interest of the Regional Hegemon

The absence of a powerful regional hegemon interested in an intervention contributed to the decision not to intervene. Neither Senegal nor Côte d'Ivoire as representatives of the francophone West Africa took up the challenge to push for a democratic transition in Nigeria. Such action would have led to a further destabilization of the whole region. Therefore, it was in the interest of the remaining big powers to remain silent.

The case study of the Nigerian coup in June 1993 shows that high domestic non-state and international pressure alone are not sufficient to cause an intervention by the regional organization.

A Coup with Military Intervention (Sierra Leone 1997)

In Sierra Leone, instability and civil war characterized the political landscape in the early 1990s. On March 16, 1996, relatively free and fair elections brought Ahmad Tejan Kabbah of the Sierra Leone People's Party to power. The military removed Kabbah in a coup d'état on May 25, 1997. In response, ECOWAS and its Committee of Four (C4), consisting of Nigeria, Ghana, Guinea and Côte d'Ivoire, continuously increased pressure on the junta. On August 28, the ECOWAS Authority decided to enlarge the ECOWAS Cease-Fire Monitoring Group's (ECOMOG) mandate originally only covering Liberia to include Sierra Leone. ECOMOGII was supposed to bring Kabbah back to power.

A Weak Democratic Identity

The democratic identity can hardly explain this high-intensity intervention. The FHI only shows slight changes to the situation in 1993. In May 1997, the number of "free" or "partly free" countries is still very low.

Considering the overall stagnation of democratic membership, an important normative shift would be surprising. The revised treaty of July 24, 1993, led to important revisions regarding the institutional set-up but only two articles mention democracy-related issues. While the objective to promote and consolidate a "democratic system of governance" has a high obligation attached to it, it remains imprecise on what such a system should look like (ECOWAS 1993: article 4j). The regional organization itself is only tasked with assisting member states (at their request) in the conduct of democratic elections (ECOWAS 1993: article 58). Despite this slight progress toward more binding and independently enforced standards, the overall level of legalization remains low. On the continental level, no important norm change can be observed with regard to unconstitutional power accession either.

Considering the low number of democratic member countries, the overall low level of legalization and the non-intervention norm congruence, the democratic identity of ECOWAS remains weak. The value of this variable cannot explain the high-intensity intervention.

A Mixed Degree of Domestic Non-State and International Political Pressure

The analysis of domestic and international pressure reveals an ambiguous picture. Domestic pressure from "below" was largely inexistent. By contrast, regional and international actors pushed for ECOWAS involvement. Protests were rare—also because of the extreme hardships the population had been facing in the past. Neither the junta nor the Nigerian involvement were greeted with "sympathy" (Körner 1998: 168). The perception of Nigerian soldiers was largely shaped by their participation in the war economy through allegedly protecting illegal diamond mining activities (Akude 2009: 243).

On the international scene, the United Nations (UN) and the OAU, among others, expected a concerted action by ECOWAS. The UN Security Council declared that "[i]t strongly deplores this attempt to overthrow the democratically elected government" (UN Security Council 1997b) and tasked ECOMOG with the enforcement of an oil embargo (UN Security Council 1997a). The OAU council appealed, in its first session after the coup, "to the leaders of ECOWAS to assist the people of Sierra Leone to restore constitutional order to the country" (OAU Council of Ministers 1997).

The actions by international actors put pressure on ECOWAS to intervene in Sierra Leone. But, in order to fully understand the dynamic that led to a *military* intervention, the interest and actions of Nigeria have to be considered.

A Strong Interest of the Regional Hegemon

Nigeria had a material, a geopolitical and an immaterial interest in bringing about a high-intensity intervention by ECOWAS. Material interests are more controversial to establish because the intervention was very costly. However, rumors persist that Nigerian army personnel were highly corrupt and even involved in the illegal diamond trade in the region (Salomon 2008: 242, Teh 2001). Furthermore, Nigeria had a strong geopolitical interest. The biggest military power in the region was able to project its capabilities in two regional conflicts and thereby substantiate its status as a regional power (Körner 1998: 169). The immaterial interest of Nigeria was determined by domestic and international considerations. Domestically, General Abacha was in the process of preparing the next attempt to democratize Nigeria. By pushing for an intervention, Abacha was able to present himself as a guardian of democracy. Internationally, Nigeria's commitment to democracy could be used to counterbalance critiques on the human rights situation in Nigeria (Körner 1998: 169).

In a nutshell, Nigeria had a very strong interest in a high-intensity intervention. But was it Nigeria who executed an ECOWAS decision or did it make ECOWAS decide? The following chronology details the process leading up to the adoption of the ECOMOGII mandate.

Table 10.3 From coup to ECOMOGII mandate

Date	Event
05/25/1997	Coup d'état takes place.
05/26/1997	Nigerian troops are reinforced in Freetown.*
05/27/1997	President Abacha says that "ECOWAS has pledged to restore democracy in Sierra Leone" although there was no decision by the ECOWAS Authority to adopt such a position (Sierra Leone Web News 1997).
06/02/1997	Talks between ECOMOG and the Armed Forces Revolutionary Council break down.
06/02/1997	Nigerian troops shell Freetown.
06/26/1997	ECOWAS-Foreign Ministers Council creates "Committee of four".
06/27/1997	Nigerian troops enforce blockade although it had not been decided by the C4.**
07/30/1997	Peace negotiations between C4 and president Koroma break down.
08/04/1997	Abacha declares that economic sanctions will be enforced although this had not been decided.
08/28/1997	ECOWAS-Authority adopts sanctions and enlarges ECOMOG mandate.

Source: Own compilation based on Sierra Leone Web News.

Notes: * Nigerian troops had been based in Sierra Leone since 1990 under the ECOMOGI mandate for Liberia. The troops' actions in Sierra Leone from May to August 1997 with the goal of reinstating Kabbah were not covered by the original ECOMOG mandate. ** In the resolution by the C4, three measures were proposed: "the use of dialogue; the application of sanctions, including an embargo; and the use of force" (ECOWAS 1997).

The process shows that Nigerian actions were legitimized *ex post* by ECOWAS decisions. Until the adoption of the official military mandate in August, President Abacha, who was also chairman of the Authority, framed unilateral Nigerian action as ECOMOG/ECOWAS activities.

Considering that democratic identity was weak and domestic and international pressures ambiguous, no intervention should have taken place. It was Nigeria that determined ECOWAS's reaction. It had significant interests in a high-intensity intervention and pushed for a decision that took account of these interests. International pressure obviously made it easier for ECOWAS to intervene—but it was not the decisive factor. In the last case study, the relevance of the democratic identity on the decision-making in ECOWAS will be established.

A Coup with a Medium-Intensity Intervention (Guinea 2008)

On December 22, 2008, Guinean president Conté died. According to the Guinean constitution, the president of the national assembly, Aboubacar Somparé, should have succeeded him. Yet, a group of young soldiers took power and suspended the constitution. In view of this blatant breach of constitutional order, ECOWAS was very quick to respond. On December 26, 2008, a first mission was sent to Guinea. This early presence on the ground showed that ECOWAS was determined to push for a rapid (re)turn to democracy. On January 10, 2009, ECOWAS suspended Guinea's membership while maintaining a "permanent and constructive dialogue" with the provisional government, imposed an election date that was one year before the one proposed by the junta (end of 2009), and made clear—via sanctions—that it would not accept the participation of any current members of government or of the military in these elections (ECOWAS 2009).

A Strong Democratic Identity

This medium-intensity intervention can mainly be attributed to the strong democratic identity of ECOWAS at the time. Over the last 11 years ECOWAS membership had changed significantly. With almost 90 percent of member states considered as "partly free" or "free," the membership of ECOWAS is more homogenously democratic. Only two countries remain "not free."

This development in member states is mirrored on the regional level. Member states have adopted several documents relating to democratic standards: the Protocol-Mechanism, (ECOWAS 1999), the Protocol on Democracy and Good Governance (ECOWAS 2001b), and the ECOWAS Conflict Prevention Framework (ECPF) defining standards of legitimate governance institutions (ECOWAS 2008).

For example, the Protocol-Mechanism creates a strong form of prohibition and sanctions: "In the event of an overthrow or attempted overthrow of a democratically elected government" (ECOWAS 1999: article 25e) the "mechanism" is started, leading to "all forms of intervention ... particularly ... the deployment of political and military missions" (ECOWAS 1999: article 10-2c) decided by the Mediation and Security Council (MSC) which comprises nine member states and takes decisions with "a two-thirds majority" (ECOWAS 1999: article 9-2). These moderately precise provisions provided for a high level of delegation. In 2001, the Protocol on Democracy and Good Governance was adopted and further increased precision regarding what constitutes a democracy. The protocol explicitly states: "Zero tolerance for power obtained or maintained by unconstitutional means" (ECOWAS 2001b: article 1c). It also determines how competitive elections should be conducted (ECOWAS 2001a: section 2). In 2008, the ECOWAS Conflict Prevention Framework further increased breadth and precision of democracy standards, making ECOWAS a regional organization with democracy standards that are highly legalized on all dimensions.

Table 10.4 Level of legalization of democracy standards, 1991–2008

Document	Degree of precision	Degree of obligation	Degree of delegation
Declaration of Political Principles (1991)	Low	Low	Low
Revised Treaty (1993)	Low	Low-Moderate	Low
Protocol-Mechanism (1999)	Low-Moderate	High	High
Protocol-Democracy (2001)	Moderate	High	High
ECPF (2008)	High	High	High

Source: Own compilation.

In 2008, standards of democracy are far developed on the regional level. They are very precise and some even apply directly in member states. This development is mirrored on the continental level. The African Union adopted four crucial documents regarding unconstitutional changes of power: the Constitutive Act of the African Union (AU 2000a), the Lomé Declaration and Decision of July 12, 2000 (AU 2000b, 2000c), and the African Charter on Democracy, Elections and Governance (AU 2007). The provisions are precise and their enforcement is delegated to the Peace and Security Council.

Considering the more democratic membership of ECOWAS, the high level of legalization of pro-intervention norms and the reinforcing effect of similar norms on the continental level, the democratic identity of ECOWAS was strong at the time of the coup, which contributes to explaining the intervention by ECOWAS.

A Moderate Degree of Domestic Non-State and International Political Pressure

The population welcomed the coup—not necessarily because they appreciated the junta, but because the constitutionally correct alternative was not a good one either. Available accounts speak of "moments of joy and feelings of relief [own translation]" (Souaré and Handy 2009: 1).

By contrast, the AU, United States and the EU unequivocally condemned the coup and urged ECOWAS to intervene, the AU even suspending Guinea's membership (Souaré and Handy 2009: 2).

Because of the stark contrast between international and domestic pressure, the value of this variable remains "moderate" and has, at best, a moderating effect on the outcome.

A Weak to Moderate Interest of the Regional Hegemon

Nigeria's interest in intervening in Guinea has to be considered weak to moderate. Some material and geopolitical interests were present, but there were no specific interests at stake. Guinea is the second largest producer of bauxite in the world and also has some important gold mines (Yabi 2010: 38). This material wealth undoubtedly explains "a special attention by the international community [own translation]" (Yabi 2010: 47). Bauxite, however, is a raw material for aluminum production that is usually processed in industrialized countries and therefore cannot explain a strong Nigerian economic interest. Exports from Guinea to any other ECOWAS member state were always very low: about one percent of total export value in 2001 (ECOWAS 2001a). The geopolitical dimension is more important because Guinea is located in the vicinity of Sierra Leone and Liberia where Nigeria has had a strong military presence. Also, it is close to Senegal, which competes with the Nigerian leadership role.

Considering, however, the internal instability of Nigeria manifesting itself in the contestation of election results, the unresolved situation in the Niger delta and economic difficulties, these rather indeterminate geopolitical and material interests did not constitute a strong hegemonic interest for intervention (Bergstresser 2009).

Considering the moderate degree of pressure from "below" and the limited interest of Nigeria to push for an intervention, it is the strong democratic identity in conjunction with high international pressure that explains the medium-intensity intervention in Guinea.

Conclusion

Coups d'état have been part of the political landscape in West Africa since independence. For a long time, neither regional organizations nor neighboring countries reacted to unconstitutional changes in or prolongations of power. Then, "pigs started to fly": ECOWAS intervened in member states after unconstitutional power accession or prolongation. But, why has ECOWAS intervened in some cases of military coups d'état against democratic governments and not in others? And, why has ECOWAS, when it intervened, used different means to do so?

Three alternative explanations have been explored in three case studies. The first explanation assumes that the strength of the democratic identity of the RO leads the RO to intervene. If a homogeneous democratic membership, a high level of legalization of democracy standards, and norm congruence between regional and continental pro-intervention norms are present, then the democratic identity is strong and the RO intervenes. The second explanation addresses domestic non-state and international state pressure. If domestic non-state actors and other countries or international organizations put high pressure on the RO to intervene, then the RO intervenes. The third explanation addresses the role of the regional hegemon. If it is in the material, geopolitical and immaterial interest of the hegemon, then the RO intervenes.

Table 10.5 Case study results

Case	Strength of democratic identity	Degree of domestic and international pressure	Interest of regional hegemon	Type of intervention
Nigeria 1993	Weak	High	Weak	I No intervention
Sierra Leone 1997	Weak	Moderate	Strong	IV High-intensity intervention (military)
Guinea 2008	Strong	Moderate	Low–moderate	III Medium-intensity intervention (sanctions)

Source: Own compilation.

In the first case study, we were able to see that domestic non-state and international pressure are not sufficient to cause an intervention. In the second case study, it became apparent that a high-intensity intervention occurred mainly because of the strong hegemonic interest. In the third case study, findings point out that a medium-intensity intervention occurred mainly because of a strong democratic identity combined with international pressure.

The varying intensity of the two interventions in Sierra Leone and in Guinea depends on the underlying causes for the intervention. If material and geopolitical interests of the hegemon are at stake, a high-intensity intervention is much more likely. In the absence of these interests an intervention is, however, not impossible. Whereas high degrees of pressure from "below" and "above" are not sufficient to cause an intervention, a strong democratic identity, in the absence of hegemonic interest, is a necessary condition for the RO to conduct a low- to medium-intensity intervention—indicating a possible actor quality of the RO itself.

While further research could address the remaining cases of unconstitutional access to or prolongation of power in West Africa, it would also be interesting to see if processes in other regional organizations work similar—or if it is only in West Africa that pigs fly.

References

Abbott, K., Keohane, R. O., Moravcsik, A., Slaughter, A.-M. and Snidal, D. 2000. The Concept of Legalization. *International Organization*, 54(3), 401–419.

Acharya, A. 2004. How Ideas Spread: Whose Norms Matter? Norm Localization and Institutional Change in Asian Regionalism. *International Organization*, 58(Spring), 239–275.

Akude, J. E. 2009. *Governance and Crisis of the State in Africa – The Context and Dynamics of the Conflicts in West Africa*. London: University of Cologne.

AU. 2000a. *Constitutive Act of the African Union*.

AU 2000b. Decision on Unconstitutional Changes of Government in Africa CM/2166 (LXXII). AHG/Dec.150 (XXXVI).

AU 2000c. Declaration on the Framework for an OAU Response to Unconstitutional Changes of Government. AHG/Decl.5 (XXXVI).

AU 2007. African Charter on Democracy, Elections and Governance.

Bergstresser, H. 2009. Nigeria 2008, in *Africa Yearbook 5. Politics, Economy and Society Souht of the Sahara in 2008*, edited by A. Mehler, H. Melber and K. v. Walraven. Leiden: Brill, 145–160.

Checkel, J. T. 1999. Norms, Institutions, and National Identity in Contemporary Europe. *International Studies Quarterly*, (43), 83–114.

Clapham, C. 1996. *Africa and the International System*. Cambridge: Cambridge University Press.

ECOWAS. 1991. *Declaration A/Dcl.1/7/91 of Political Principles of the Economic Community of West African States*.

ECOWAS. 1993. *Treaty of the Economic Community of West African States*.

ECOWAS. 1997. *Final Communiqué of a Special Meeting of Foreign Ministers on June 26*. [Online]. Available at: www.sierra-leone.org/Other-Conflict/ECOWAS-062697.html [accessed: March 15, 2011].

ECOWAS. 1999. *Protocol Relating to the Mechanism for Conflict Prevention, Management, Resolution, Peace-keeping and Security*.

ECOWAS. 2001a. *External Trade Statistics*. [Online]. Available at: www.ecostat.org [accessed: September 21, 2010].

ECOWAS. 2001b. *Protocol A/SP1/12/01 on Democracy and Good Governance Supplementary to the Protocol Relating to the Mechanism For Conflict Prevention, Management, Resolution, Peacekeeping and Security*.

ECOWAS. 2008. *The ECOWAS Conflict Prevention Framework (Regulation MSC/REG.1/01/08)*.
ECOWAS. 2009. *ECOWAS Leaders Reject Military Transition in Guinea*. Press Release 3/2009.
Edi, E. M. 2007. *Globalization and Politics in the Economic Community of West African States*. Durham, NC: Carolina Academic Press.
Evera, S. v. 1997. *Guide to Methods for Students of Political Science*. Ithaca and London: Cornell University Press.
Falola, T. and Heaton, M. M. 2008. *A History of Nigeria*. Cambridge: Cambridge University Press.
Finnemore, M. 2003. *The Purpose of Intervention*. Ithaca and London: Cornell University Press.
George, A. L. and Bennett, A. 2005. *Case Studies and Theory Development in the Social Sciences*. Cambridge, MA: Belfer Center for Science and International Affairs.
Jong Choi, Y. and Caporaso, J. A. 2002. Comparative Regional Integration, in *Handbook of International Relations*, edited by W. Carlsnaes, T. Risse and B. A. Simmons. London: SAGE Publications, 480–499.
Keck, M. E. and Sikkink, K. 1998. *Activists Beyond Borders: Advocacy Networks in International Politics*. Ithaca: Cornell University Press.
Körner, P. 1998. Sierra Leone 1997, in *Afrika Jahrbuch 1998*, edited by R. Hofmeier. Wiesbaden: Leske + Budrich, 167–170.
Marshall, M. G., Gurr, T. R. and Jaggers, K. 2010. Polity IV Project-Political Regime Characteristics and Transitions, 1800–2009. *Polity IV Project-Dataset Users' Manual*.
McGowan, P. 2003. African Military Coups d'État, 1956–2001: Frequency, Trends and Distribution. *Journal of Modern African Studies*, 41(3), 339–370.
Mearsheimer, J. J. 1994. The False Promise of International Institutions. *International Security*, 19(3), 5–49.
Nolte, D. 2006. *Macht und Machthierarchien in den internationalen Beziehungen: Ein Analysekonzept für die Forschung über regionale Führungsmächte*. German Institute of Global and Area Studies Working Paper No.29, October 2006. Hamburg.
OAU. 1990. *AHG/Decl.1 (XXVI)*. Addis Ababa.
OAU Council of Ministers. 1997. 66th ordinary session. Sierra Leone. CM/Dec.357 (LXVI).
Osaghae, E. E. 1998. *Crippled Giant: Nigeria since Independence*. London: Hurst & Company.
Pedersen, T. 2002. Cooperative Hegemony: Power, Ideas and Institutions in Regional Integration. *Review of International Studies*, 28(4), 677–696.
Pevehouse, J. C. 2005. *Democracy from Above. Regional Organizations and Democratization*. Cambridge: Cambridge University Press.

Salomon, K. 2008. *Konfliktmanagement durch ECOWAS und SADC – die Rolle Nigerias und Südafrikas in subregionalen Interventionen: Ein Beitrag zum Frieden?* Münster: Westfälische Wilhelms-Universität zu Münster (Westf.).
Sierra Leone Web News. 1997. *News May 1997*. [Online]. Available at: www.sierra-leone.org/Archives/slnews0597.html [accessed: March 15, 2011].
Souaré, I. K. and Handy, P.-S. 2009. Bon coups, mauvais coups? Les errements d'une transition qui peut encore réussir en Guinée. *Institut d'Etudes de Sécurité*, ISS Papier 195.
Suberu, R. T. 1997. Crisis and Collapse: June–November 1993, in *Transition Without End. Nigerian Politics and Civil Society Under Babangida*, edited by L. Diamond, A. Kirk-Greene and O. Oyediran. London: Lynne Rienner, 281–302.
Teh, T. 2001. *ECOMOG: Dirtier than a Lie*. [Online]. Available at: www.theperspective.org/dirtier.html [accessed: March 16, 2011].
UN Security Council. 1997a. *Security Council Resolution 1132*.
UN Security Council. 1997b. *Statement by the President of the Security Council. S/PRST/1997/29*.
Van der Vleuten, A. 2007. Contrasting Cases: Explaining Interventions by SADC and ASEAN, in *Closing or Widening the Gap? Legitimacy and Democracy in Regional integration Organizations*, edited by A. Ribeiro Hoffmann and A. v. d. Vleuten. Aldershot: Ashgate, 155–172.
Van der Vleuten, A. and Ribeiro Hoffmann, A. 2010. Explaining the Enforcement of Democracy by Regional Organizations: Comparing EU, Mercosur and SADC. *Journal of Common Market Studies*, 48(3), 737–758.
Williams, P. D. 2007. From Non-intervention to Non-indifference: The Origins and Development of the African Union's Security Culture. *African Affairs*, 106(423), 253–279.
Yabi, G. O. 2010. *Le Rôle de la CEDEAO dans la Gestion des Crises Politiques et des Conflits. Cas de la Guinée et de la Guinée Bissau*. Friedrich-Ebert-Stiftung, Bureau Régional, Abuja.
Zimmermann, E. 1981. *Krisen, Staatsstreiche und Revolutionen-Theorien, Daten und neuere Forschungsansätze*. Opladen: Westdeutscher Verlag.

PART 5
Effects on Member States

Chapter 11
MERCOSUR's Contribution to Democratic Consolidation

Christian Pirzer

Introduction

The European Coal and Steel Community (ECSC), precursor to the European Union (EU), was founded in 1951 with the intention to stabilize post-war Europe through economic development and the diffusion of democratic values. After 60 years of existence, its success regarding these principles can hardly be questioned. Nowadays democracy is consolidated in nearly all EU member states and the further enlargement of the union has contributed to the subsequent democratization of the new member states. Thus, it is fair to state that the European Union actively promotes democratic rule. But is this a uniquely European experience or is it possible that other democratic regional organizations can promote democratization processes within their member states as well?

The Southern Common Market (MERCOSUR) was founded on March 26, 1991. The most important motivations for regional integration were the growing economic pressure that resulted from globalization, a belief in the effectiveness of trade liberalization and regional cooperation, and the need for protecting new democratic systems (Manzetti 1993: 108–109). Particularly, the motivation of democracy-protection seems reasonable, since simultaneously to the integration process all four MERCOSUR member states were passing through a process of re-democratization. After periods of authoritarian political leadership, the first democratic elections were held in Argentina in 1983, in Brazil and Uruguay in 1985, and in Paraguay in 1989. Ever since these democratic elections, none of the states has fallen back to autocracy and the regimes of Argentina and Paraguay even managed to consolidate their democracies. Thus, since the early 1990s two parallel developments in the Southern Cone have taken place: the creation of a new integration project named MERCOSUR and the democratic persistence of the MERCOSUR member states. Keeping these processes in mind, the question arises whether the two developments took place independently of one another, or if there is a causal relationship between the two phenomena.

This chapter aims to answer this question by analyzing one particular enforcement mechanism of democratic consolidation provided by MERCOSUR. For the analysis, I use a widespread definition of democratic consolidation that incorporates three dimensions: the structural, the attitudinal, and the behavioral dimension. In the central section of this chapter, I illustrate how MERCOSUR can assist its member states in the consolidation process of the latter two dimensions. For the theoretical part, I use causal linkages between regional organizations and democratic consolidation from state of the art literature. After the illustration of the enforcement mechanism, I test the hypotheses with quantitative and qualitative data of the MERCOSUR member states.

Theoretical Backgound

The analysis in this chapter is based on a regional organization, since the small amount of literature that exists on the relation of democracy assistance and international organizations has a clear focus on this particular type of organization (Whitehead 1996: 395). In agreement with McCormick (1980) and Nye (1987), I argue that regional organizations have a high degree of causal processes such as socialization binding, monitoring and enforcement which makes processes of democratization more easily to emerge within these organizations. In line with this expectation, most literature dealing with the relation of regional organizations and democracy argues in favor of the assumption that regional organizations can contribute to the promotion of democratization processes in their member states (cf. Keohane et al. 2009; Mansfield and Pevehouse 2006, 2008; Pevehouse 2005). Mansfield and Pevehouse (2008: 269), for example, claim that especially new democratic regimes in the process of democratization have particular reasons to enter democratic regional organizations.[1] The coordination of policies in order to harmonize interactions and the creation of mechanisms to solve arising transnational problems leads to a major dependence of states on their counterparts – they become more vulnerable regarding the actions taking place in other member states. Thus, in order to influence political and economic stability of the member states, regional organizations are likely to create mechanisms to provide compliance of political and economic norms and values. For the case of MERCOSUR, Pevehouse (2005: 179–186) ascribes the consolidation of democracy in the member states primarily to the regional organization. By contrast, van der Vleuten and Ribeiro Hoffmann (2010) provide some alternative explanations for the democratic consolidation of MERCOSUR member states. They argue that the democratic regional power Brazil and international actors like the United States, the EU and the Organization of American States (OAS) played the key role in the resolution of democratic crises and the consolidation process.[2] Despite the importance of these alternative or more likely additional explanations, this chapter focuses primarily on the influence of MERCOSUR and discusses the imposition of credible democratic

---

1   On the relation between regime type and member state behavior on the regional level, see Chapter 8, this volume.

2   For an analysis of the importance of a regional hegemon and international actors in case of coup d'état in ECOWAS see Chapter 10, this volume.

commitments as an enforcement mechanism of democratic consolidation. I argue that this instrument, often imposed by regional organizations, can make democratic consolidation more likely. Credible democratic commitments can influence both the behavioral and the attitudinal dimension of democratic consolidation. To analyze the impacts this mechanism can have on democratic consolidation, I first illustrate the theoretical connection between the variables and the incentives regional organizations possess to implement this instrument. Afterwards, I define and operationalize the concept of democratic consolidation applied in this chapter. In a last step, I analyze qualitative and quantitative data of the MERCOSUR member states to control if the theoretical assumptions can be underpinned by empirical evidence.

Credible Democratic Commitments as an Enforcement Mechanism of Regional Organizations

According to Pevehouse (2005: 37–38), regional organizations can pursue two major ways to affect the democratic consolidation process of their member states. Due to the fact that in most cases membership and material assistance of a regional organization is made conditional upon democratic norms and political liberalization, regional organizations can both bind the ruling regime to democratic procedures and deter regime opponents from anti-democratic behavior. However, the imposition of such democratic commitments is obviously more likely if the regional organization mainly consists of democratic states. Comparisons of different regional organizations confirm that those with a high "democratic density" more often impose democratic commitments on their member states than organizations composed of authoritarian states (Pevehouse 2005: 46). Usually, credible democratic commitments are implemented in the form of a membership clause, which requires member states to stick to the democratic game and allows the organization or its institutions to interfere if democratic conditions are violated. In line with Pevehouse (2005), I argue that democratic regional organizations are more likely to place conditions on membership, since such demands require a high degree of shared interests.

In sum, credible democratic commitments in a regional organization can influence the democratic consolidation of member states in two ways: they can bind the ruling regime to democratic procedures and deter regime opponents from anti-system behavior. For the further analysis, I separate these two different impacts by developing two different hypotheses (hypothesis H1 and hypothesis H2).

> H1: Credible democratic commitments by a regional organization will positively influence the democratic legitimacy of the member states' democratic regimes.

Due to the imposition of credible democratic commitments by a regional organization, the democratic regimes of the member states are likely to gain political legitimacy. If this assumption were true, what would be the explanatory factors? Why and how are credible democratic commitments connected to political legitimacy?

Firstly, regional organizations can assist young democracies in their consolidation process by serving as a device of external commitment through which ruling parties can bind themselves to political liberalization and democratic norms (Mansfield and Pevehouse 2006: 138–139, Pevehouse 2005: 37). If provisions of the regional organization are violated, financial and reputational costs are imposed on the member states. In committing to a democratic regional organization, the ruling regime sends an important signal to both domestic elites and common citizens. This highly visible public and external validation of democratic norms can legitimize the political regime in the eyes of its citizens. Through this signal the consolidation process can move forward and both elites and masses will be more likely to invest in the new system and commit to the new democracy (Pevehouse 2005: 37). Even if there is no possibility of enforcement by the organization itself, membership in a democratic regional organization can assist in legitimizing the democratic reform process to citizens (Pevehouse 2005: 39). According to this argument it is easier for domestic political actors to implement consolidation policies[3] at the national level if decisions are backed by a democratic regional organization with high international reputation. Moreover, the participation in a democratic regional organization itself can be a form of "international recognition of a country's democratic credentials" (Klebes 1999: 3) and can lead to acceptance in the international society. This psychological benefit can be important to both elites and masses (Pridham 1995: 174). In addition, the association with a democratic organization can be seen as a chance to break with vestiges of any authoritarian past (Pridham 1994: 26–27). Thus, owing to the imposition of credible democratic commitments regional organizations can provide positive incentives for the adherence to democratic norms on part of the ruling regime in the process of democratic consolidation.

> H2: Credible democratic commitments by a regional organization will make anti-democratic behavior in member states less likely.

Due to the imposition of credible democratic commitments by a regional organization, domestic anti-democratic behavior in the form of military coups and executive auto-coups is less likely. If this assumption were true, what would be the explanatory factors? Why and how are credible democratic commitments connected with anti-democratic behavior?

According to Pevehouse (2005: 37–40), a democratic membership clause is connected with anti-democratic behavior in two ways: it influences the behavior of the ruling democratic regime actors as well as of system opponents. Concerning the former, the undermining of constitutional procedures is less likely because

---

3 Typical examples of such policies are political and economic liberalization.

violation of conditions made up by the organization bears heavy reputational and domestic audience costs for the ruling regime (Fearon 1994, Leeds 1999). These audience costs can be potentially high and flow from the fact that especially young democracies attempt to establish a reputation as upstanding members of the international community and the regional organization. Losing this membership means a risk of backlash from both elites and mass publics who would undoubtedly blame the regime leaders for ruining their chances at international acceptance (Pevehouse 2005: 40). Secondly, a democratic membership clause influences the behavior of system opponents as well. Actors who lose or think they might lose under a democratic regime are more likely to undermine or overthrow the regime. Regarding these actors, regional organizations can provide negative incentives and thus lead them to support democratic rules (Pevehouse 2005: 41). The argumentation runs in the same direction of impact explained above. By implementing conditions on democratic rules, regional organizations increase the costs of any actor who may operate against these conditions. These potential costs for anti-democratic behavior can serve as a deterrent against coups or attempts of transgression of authority, because actors must calculate whether the costs imposed by the regional organization will undermine their own attempts to consolidate their power after a coup (Mansfield and Pevehouse 2006: 163). Normally these costs can include a loss of interregional trade, economic aid, military assistance and protection and international status. Including these assumptions in their consideration, anti-democratic actors are more likely to remain loyal to existing democratic rules and institutions (Pevehouse 2005: 37). By focusing on coups as the most common type of a democratic breakdown in MERCOSUR member states, we have to take into account that "coups are an affair of civilian and military elites" (Barracca 2004: 1477; cf. Mainwaring 1992: 302–303). Thus, potential anti-democratic behavior in form of coups, in the majority of the cases, is promoted by domestic or foreign elites. However, according to Kahler (1997: 308), even "elites that are not imbued with democratic norms may choose to follow democratic rules of the game in order to win the economic benefits of membership."

Measuring Democratic Consolidation

The Concept of Democratic Consolidation

Before evaluating whether democracy is consolidated in a particular country, it is first necessary to prove that a regime is democratic. Without democracy there cannot be democratic consolidation. In literature about democracy we find many different definitions of this concept (Dahl 1971, 1989, Diamond et al. 1989, Mainwaring 1999). In accordance with the Polity IV Project (2010), I define a regime as democratic when it has completed the transition to democracy. After the process of democratic transition has been completed, however, there are still many tasks that need to be accomplished, many conditions that must be fulfilled, and attitudes and habits that must be cultivated in order to consider a democracy as consolidated (Linz and Stepan 1996: 5). In the research on democratic consolidation scholars have adopted definitions that incorporate a great diversity of consolidation tasks. In accordance with Schedler (2001), I use a minimalist notion of democratic consolidation that considers a democratic regime to be consolidated when it is "likely to endure" (O'Donnell 1996: 37) and when we may expect it to "last well into the future" (Valenzuela 1992: 70). This "classical and most widespread" (Schedler 2001: 67) concept of democratic consolidation benefits from advantages in measurability and verifiability. Although it is not without shortcomings, in it we find at least a great deal of consensus about minimum standards of a liberal democracy (Schedler 1998: 104).

The Operationalization of Democratic Consolidation

In the task of making democratic consolidation measurable, some of the most notable and widely used frameworks include behavioral, attitudinal and structural dimensions (Diamond 1999, Linz and Stepan 1996, Schedler 2001). I adopt this three-part division because it is commonly seen as the most adequate approach to measure the complex and comprehensive influences of independent variables on democratic consolidation (Mainwaring 2000: 60, Schedler 2001: 66). The behavioral dimension of democratic consolidation looks primarily at anti-system behavior of political and social key actors within the democratic system. Consolidation of the behavioral dimension requires that none of these actors are engaging in anti-system behavior, but instead are sticking to democratic rules (Schedler 2001: 70). For the analysis of MERCOSUR the focus on anti-system behavior in form of coups seems reasonable, since it is historically the most common way of authoritarian regression in the Southern Cone (Polity IV Project 2008). The attitudinal dimension of democratic consolidation relies on preferences and perceptions of political and social actors, including common citizens. In this dimension, one does not only look at the simple absence of overt rule violation, but rather intends to find out whether the actors' normative, strategic or cognitive rationalities conform to the stability requirements of democratic regimes (Schedler 2001: 75). For many scholars, democratic legitimacy – "the genuine, non-instrumental, intrinsic support for democracy" (Schedler 2001: 75) – constitutes the defining element in this area of democratic consolidation (Diamond 1999, Linz and Stepan 1996, Merkel 1998). The structural dimension of democratic consolidation is based on the expectation that democracies are more likely to survive if they rest upon solid structural foundations. In this dimension scholars mainly focus on the socioeconomic and the institutional performances of regimes (Schedler 2001: 80).

While it seems undisputable that behavioral, attitudinal and structural factors all have some bearing on the process of democratic consolidation, the present analysis deals primarily with the former two dimensions, since, in accordance with Schedler (2001: 82), these two variables seem to have more causal impact on democratic consolidation than the structural dimension. Following Schedler's (2001: 69, 82) assumption, structural variables represent a proximate source of actors' attitudes. Attitude in turn works as a prime mover of actors' behavior, and the behavior of actors contributes directly to either the maintenance or collapse of democratic regimes. Thus, when trying to get insights in the process of democratic consolidation it seems plausible to focus above all on the analysis of the behavioral and the attitudinal dimension. Especially if democracy is consolidated in the behavioral dimension, authoritarian reversal is almost impossible.

The Southern Common Market (MERCOSUR)

The particular regional organization analyzed in this chapter is the Southern Common Market. MERCOSUR is a regional organization mainly concerned with trade and economic issues.[4] Aside from the important economic motivations, we find two other factors of interest for the creation of MERCOSUR. The first is the effort to drive democratic stability in the region forward. Although this interest is not explicitly mentioned in the earlier official documents, we still find several statements and informal presidential agreements proving this intention.[5] With the adoption of the Ushuaia Protocol (UP) on July 24, 1998 this underlying preference structure of the member states became finally institutionalized through a democratic membership clause, which aimed at preventing military coups and other dangers for democracy.

Security is yet another relevant factor for the success of MERCOSUR. Some scholars even draw parallels between the relation between Argentina and Brazil since the 1980s and the German–French rapprochement after World War II (Mecham 2003: 369). Anyway, "[i]t is widely acknowledged that domestic and regional security motivations were behind the integration initiative that started in 1985 and resulted in Mercosur" (Oelsner 2009: 198).

MERCOSUR's Credible Democratic Commitments

"MERCOSUR, like the European Community itself, has placed consolidating democracy and preserving peace in the Southern Cone among its paramount objectives" (Smith 1993, quoted in Manzetti 1993: 109).

Surprisingly in this context, the original Treaty of Asunción did not include any direct reference to that. In fact, the words "democracy," "democratic" or "democratization" are not even mentioned in the document. Seemingly, rather

---

4   For information about the foundation, the structure and the decision-making process in MERCOSUR see Chapter 4, this volume.

5   See the presidential Declaration "Las Leñas" (MERCOSUR 1992) and Presidential Declaration of Potrero de Los Funes about the democratic commitment in MERCOSUR (MERCOSUR 1996).

technical reasons are to blame for that, which seems plausible looking at the following declarations. On June 27, 1992, the presidents of the MERCOSUR member states agreed at a summit in the Presidential Declaration of Las Leñas to "defend representative democracies" (Matsushita 2000: 42). Four years later this step was reaffirmed: "The full validity of the democratic institutions is an indispensable requirement for the existence and development of Mercosur" (MERCOSUR 1996: Preamble; author's translation). After the coup attempt in Paraguay in 1996, MERCOSUR state parties together with Bolivia and Chile expressed on July 24, 1998 their commitment to democracy once again. This led to the more precise Ushuaia Protocol on Democratic Commitment in the Southern Common Market. The protocol states that "fully functioning democratic institutions are an indispensable condition for the existence and development of Mercosur" (MERCOSUR 1998: Preamble). Due to the incorporation in the Treaty of Asunción, this democratic commitment is codified and binding for all state parties (MERCOSUR 1998: Article 8). The commitment allows measures that "may range from suspension of the right to participate in various bodies of the respective integration processes to suspension of the rights and obligations deriving from those processes" (MERCOSUR 1998: Article 5). Hence, membership can be suspended from the economic bloc in the case of a democratic breakdown (MERCOSUR 1998: Article 3). Additionally, the commitment to democracy must be adhered to by any prospective member of the organization (MERCOSUR 1998: Article 1; cf. Muñoz 1998: 16); so it is a necessary condition for the participation in MERCOSUR.

Since the implementation of the Ushuaia Protocol, MERCOSUR member states twice made reference to it. The first time was during the attempted military coup in Paraguay in 1999. Based on the agreements and obligations made in the protocol, member states interfered with diplomatic pressure to prevent a democratic breakdown in Paraguay. The second time was during the membership negotiations with Venezuela. In the decision 16/05 of the MERCOSUR council, the state parties decided that for membership in the organization, Venezuela had to associate itself with the Ushuaia Protocol (MERCOSUR 2005). Until today the Paraguayan Congress still impedes the membership negotiations with reference to the democratic requirements expressed in the Ushuaia Protocol (Infobae.com 2010).

Development of Democratic Legitimacy in the MERCOSUR Member States

As shown above, democratic commitments were strengthened at the regional level since the foundation of MERCOSUR. These commitments became credible since the implementation of the democratic membership clause in 1998. Thus, following hypothesis H1, an increase of democratic legitimacy on part of the citizens is to be expected.

To analyze the development of democratic legitimacy within MERCOSUR state parties, I use data from the Latinobarómetro survey. Since 1995, Latinobarómetro collects inter alia data regarding the attitude toward democratic support for countries in the region of Latin America. This particular data is commonly used for the analysis of democratic legitimacy (Barracca 2004, Latinobarómetro 2009, Schedler 2001).

At first glance, the results seem quite insignificant. From 1995 to 2009 democratic support in MERCOSUR state parties persisted constantly at an overall low average around 60 percent (Figure 11.1). Only in Uruguay, where democracy was already consolidated, did the democratic support remain continually at a high level of about 80 percent. During the economic crisis in 2001, support for democracy decreased significantly in all member states irrespective of the credible democratic commitments imposed by MERCOSUR in 1998. With the end of the economic crisis, however, the support for democracy increased again. This development indicates a strong relationship between economic performance and democratic legitimacy, particularly during periods of economic crisis (cf. Przeworski et al. 1996). With regard to the influence of credible democratic commitments on democratic legitimacy, the results are difficult to interpret. During the period in which an impact of the credible commitments was expected, the economic crisis broke out. Through this crisis, external parameters changed significantly, so that in this analysis no reliable conclusions can be drawn on the influence of this variable.

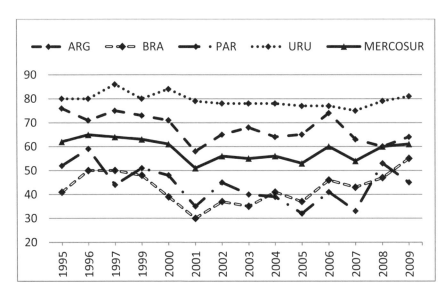

Figure 11.1 Democratic support in MERCOSUR member states and MERCOSUR average (in % of the population), 1995–2009

Development of Anti-Democratic Behavior in the MERCOSUR Member States

Following hypothesis H2, a decrease of anti-democratic behavior in the form of coups is to be expected in the MERCOSUR state parties. To get a comprehensive insight in the organization's ability to prevent coups, it is reasonable to first look at the pre-MERCOSUR regime development of the state parties. In accordance with Linz and Stepan (1996), I argue that the Southern Cone is historically receptive to authoritarian regression, especially through military coups. I further argue that MERCOSUR holds an important stake in breaking with this tradition through the prevention of democratic breakdowns.

Historically, all four MERCOSUR member states have experienced authoritarian political leadership, military coups and infrequent periods of democratically elected governments (Polity IV Project 2008). After the foundation of MERCOSUR, however, no state party returned to autocratic rule. Table 11.1 illustrates the total number of coups and coup attempts since 1946 in MERCOSUR state parties. During the pre-MERCOSUR period, 23 coups or coup attempts took place. Of these, 15 were successful. However, most of these coups happened under autocratic regimes without affecting the democratic character of the political regime. Out of the 15 successful coups, four caused a significant adverse regime change and two resulted in a democratic breakdown.

Table 11.1 Number of coups and coup attempts in MERCOSUR member states, 1946–2010

	ARG	BRA	PAR	URU	TOTAL
Pre-MERCOSUR (1946–1968)					
Coups and coup attempts	9	2	5	0	16
Coups resulting in ARC	1	1	0	0	2
Coups resulting in DB	1	0	0	0	1
Pre-MERCOSUR (1969–1991)					
Coups and coup attempts	5	0	1	1	7
Coups resulting in ARC	1	0	0	1	2
Coups resulting in DB	0	0	0	1	1
Post-MERCOSUR (1992–2010)					
Coups and coup attempts	0	0	2	0	2
Coups resulting in ARC	0	0	0	0	0
Coups resulting in DB	0	0	0	0	0

Source: Author's own calculation based on Polity IV (2008, 2010).
Note: ARC (adverse regime change) if coup event resulted in a negative change in POLITY score of six points or more; DB (democratic breakdown) if the coup event resulted in a negative change in POLITY score, and turned down a democratic elected government.

During the 20 years of MERCOSUR's existence only two coups attempts took place of which none has been successful. This decrease in the number of successful coups and coup attempts underpins hypothesis H2 with empirical evidence. It is, however, important to concede that the decrease in anti-system behavior did not start with the foundation of MERCOSUR. While most of the coups took place during the 1950s and 1960s, a decreasing trend already occurred during the following decades (see Table 11.1). Although MERCOSUR's democratic commitments still consolidated this development, a clear effect is not measurable with quantitative data. To ascribe the positive impact on coup prevention to MERCOSUR, it is therefore important to focus on the particular behavior of the organization during a democratic crisis. In the following, I illustrate the 1996 Paraguayan coup attempt in detail, focusing on MERCOSUR's contribution in avoiding authoritarian regression.[6]

The Paraguayan coup attempt on April 26, 1996, is seen by some scholars as a clear example of the influence that a regional organization can play in the context of democratic consolidation (Dominguez 1998, Guilhon Albuquerque 1999, Valenzuela 1997, 1999). For the first time since the foundation of MERCOSUR, a member state has been facing an attempted military coup, and for the first time MERCOSUR has been challenged not only as a trade community but also as a political body whose commitments to democracy were an inherent part of its charter (Guilhon Albuquerque 1999: 273). The crisis broke out on April 22, 1996, when General Lino Oviedo, commander of the army, rebelled against his dismissal by Paraguayan president Juan Carlos Wasmosy. Oviedo threatened to stage a military coup and demanded the resignation of the president. The crisis ended with Oviedo stepping down after massive support for Wasmosy and the democratic rule of law.[7] During this military crisis in Paraguay, the governments of the other MERCOSUR state parties acted promptly by exerting strong pressure against the coup perpetrators and immediately applying coercive diplomacy (Guilhon Albuquerque 1999: 273). Although MERCOSUR has not yet possessed a formal democratic clause, "the presidents of Brazil, Argentina and Uruguay reacted immediately, overtly referring to the regional organization" (van der Vleuten and Ribeiro Hoffmann 2010: 747–748). In two detailed analyses Arturo Valenzuela (1997, 1999) shows how diplomatic efforts at the presidential level have been pivotal in the resolution of the Paraguayan coup attempt. President Wasmosy received official supportive phone calls from all MERCOSUR member state representatives imploring him to remain in office and the foreign ministers of Argentina and Uruguay and the deputy foreign minister of Brazil announced that they would arrive the following day. At the same time General Oviedo himself was

---

6 A detailed illustration of the 1999 Paraguayan coup attempt will be excluded, because the line of action on the part of MERCOSUR was similar to the 1996 coup attempt.

7 For more comprehensive information about the Paraguayan coup attempt see: Valenzuela (1997, 1999), Guilhon Albuquerque (1999: 272–273), and Pevehouse (2005: 179–180).

contacted by foreign counterparts, including the minister of the army of Brazil, who urged him to desist in his actions (Valenzuela 1997: 50). In a private meeting kept secret from the press and foreign governments, Brazilian president Cardoso pledged his country's support for Wasmosy, noting that Brazil and MERCOSUR partners would not tolerate a disruption of the constitutional order in a member state. Although he did not pledge military support for Paraguay, he still assured Wasmosy that Brazilian high command, traditionally close to their Paraguayan counterparts, would not support Oviedo's rebellious stance (Valenzuela 1999). The "overwhelming response," particularly of Brazil, Uruguay and Argentina, provided the president with needed encouragement to stay in office (Valenzuela 1997: 53). Therefore many observers conclude that Paraguay's partners in MERCOSUR were key actors in stopping the coup attempt (Dominguez 1998: 131, Valenzuela 1997: 54).

Conclusion

Since the foundation of MERCOSUR in 1991, the Argentinean and especially the Paraguayan regime improved in their democratic performance, and, more significantly, none of the MERCOSUR member states suffered democratic setbacks. The overall assessment confirms that democratic regimes in the Southern Cone have never been as stable as they are today. However, the debate about the triggers that caused this development remains controversial. While some scholars argue that democracy in the region improved due to the specific interest of the regional power Brazil, or because of the pressure of international key actors (van der Vleuten and Ribeiro Hoffmann 2010), others claim that MERCOSUR is a key factor in the consolidation process (Mansfield and Pevehouse 2006, 2008, Pevehouse 2005). In any event, democratic consolidation appears to be a highly complex process with far too many variables influencing the consolidation process, making it impossible to extract the *one decisive variable*.

The intention of this chapter was to gain insight into the influence of MERCOSUR in the process of democratic consolidation. In order to analyze the hypotheses, a minimalist concept of democratic consolidation was employed and a three-part definition that focuses on the structural, the attitudinal and the behavioral dimension of democratic consolidation was adopted. To assess whether MERCOSUR indeed influenced the consolidation process of its member states, I used the mechanism of credible democratic commitments that links regional organizations to democratic consolidation. In the empirical part of this chapter, I applied the hypotheses to MERCOSUR and checked if the expected outcomes occurred.

However, the results of this analysis are somewhat ambiguous. While outcomes in the behavioral dimension can be explained by the influence of MERCOSUR, the expected contribution of MERCOSUR to the consolidation of the attitudinal dimension could not be confirmed with certainty. In the latter dimension, I expected an increase in democratic legitimacy due to MERCOSUR's credible democratic commitments in 1998. However, because of the strong intervening effect of the economic crisis in 2001, which affected citizens' attitude toward democracy significantly, no clear implication was observable that could be reduced to the influence of MERCOSUR. By contrast, in the behavioral dimension the empirical outcome confirmed the hypothesis. Due to democratic commitments of MERCOSUR since 1992 and the imposition of a democratic membership clause in 1998, a decrease in anti-democratic behavior was to be expected, and indeed occurred. MERCOSUR actively contributed to the solution of the only two democratic crises in Paraguay in 1996 and in 1999, without affecting the democratic stability of the region. This positive impact of MERCOSUR in the behavioral dimension of democratic consolidation is the most important result of this analysis. As mentioned above, behavior of political and social key actors contributes directly to either the preservation or collapse of a democratic regime. If democracy is consolidated in this dimension, authoritarian reversal is almost impossible. Thus, besides the European Union, MERCOSUR is another regional organization that actively deters authoritarian regression in its member states.

References

Barracca, S. 2004. Is Mexican Democracy Consolidated? *Third World Quarterly*, 25(8), 1469–1485.
Dahl, R. 1971. *Polyarchy*. New Haven: Yale University Press.
Dahl, R. 1989. *Democracy and its Critics*. New Haven: Yale University Press.
Diamond, L. 1999. *Developing Democracy: Toward Consolidation*. Baltimore: Johns Hopkins University Press.
Diamond, L., Linz, J. J. and Lipset, S. M. 1989. *Democracy in Developing Countries*. 4 vols. Boulder: Lynne Rienner.
Dominguez, J. I. 1998. The Americas: Found, and then Lost Again. *Foreign Policy*, 112, 125–137.
Fearon, J. D. 1994. Domestic Political Audiences and the Escalation of Interstate Disputes. *American Political Science Review*, 88(3), 577–592.
Guilhon Albuquerque, J. A. 1999. Mercosur: Democratic Stability and Economic Integration in South America, in *Regional Integration and Democracy. Expanding on the European Experience*, edited by J. J. Anderson. Lanham: Rowman & Littlefield, 261–283.
Infobae.com. 2010. *Paraguay replica: Venezuela no ingresará al Mercosur porque no es una democracia plena*. [Online]. Available at: http://america.infobae.com/notas/5195-Paraguay-replica-Venezuela-no-ingresara-al-Mercosur-porque-no-es-una-democracia-plena [accessed: April 12, 2011].
Kahler, M. 1997. *Liberalization and Foreign Policy*. New York: Columbia University Press.

Keohane, R., Macedo, S. and Moravcsik, A. 2009. Democracy-Enhancing Multilateralism. *International Organization*, 63, 1–31.

Klebes, H. 1999. *The Quest for Democratic Security: The Role of the Council of Europe and U.S. Foreign Policy*. Washington, DC: United States Institute of Peace.

Latinobarómetro. 2009. *Informe Latinobarómetro 2009*. [Online]. Santiago de Chile. Available at: www.latinobarometro.org [accessed: November 24, 2011].

Leeds, B. A. 1999. Domestic Political Institutions, Credible Commitments, and International Cooperation. *Amercian Journal of Political Science*, 43(4), 979–1002.

Linz, J. J. and Stepan, A. 1996. *Problems of Democratic Transition and Consolidation: Southern Europe, South America and Post-Communist Europe*. Baltimore: Johns Hopkins University Press.

Mainwaring, S. 1992. Transition to Democracy and Democratic Consolidation: Theoretical and Comparative Issues, in I*ssues in Democratic Consolidation: The New South American Democracies in Comparative Perspective*, edited by S. Mainwaring, G. O'Donnell and J. S. Valenzuela. Notre Dame: University of Notre Dame Press, 294–341.

Mainwaring, S. 1999. *Democratic Survivability In Latin America*. Working Paper No. 267 – May.

Mainwaring, S. 2000. Democratic Survivability in Latin America, in *Democracy and its Limits: Lessons from Asia, Latin America, and the Middle East*, edited by H. Handelman and M. A. Tessler. Notre Dame: University of Notre Dame Press, 11–68.

Mansfield, E. and Pevehouse, J. 2006. Democratization and International Organizations. *International Organization*, 60(1), 137–167.

Mansfield, E. and Pevehouse, J. 2008. Democratization and the Varieties of International Organizations. *Journal of Conflict Resolution*, 52(2), 269–294.

Manzetti, L. 1993. The Political Economy of Mercosur. *Journal of Interamerican Studies and World Affairs*, 35(4), 101–141.

Matsushita, H. 2000. The First Integrated Wave of Regionalism and Democratization in the Americas. A Comparison of NAFTA and MERCOSUR. *The Japanese Journal of American Studies*, 11, 25–48.

McCormick, J. 1980. Intergovernmental Organizations and Cooperation Among Nations. *International Studies Quarterly*, 24(1), 75–98.

Mecham, M. 2003. Mercosur. A Failing Development Project? *International Affairs*, 79(2), 369–387.

MERCOSUR. 1992. *Presidential Declaration "Las Leñas."* Las Leñas, Argentina.

MERCOSUR. 1996. Declaration of Potrero de los Funes. [Online]. Available at: www.mercosur.int/msweb/Documentos/Publicados/Declaraciones%20 Conjuntas/003670856_CMC_25-06-1996__DECL-DPR_S-N_ES_ CompromDemo.pdf [accessed: November 24, 2011].

MERCOSUR. 1998. *Ushuaia Protocol on Democratic Commitment in the Southern Common Market*. Ushuaia, Argentina.

MERCOSUR. 2005. *Consejo del Mercado Común, Decisión No. 16/05*. Ushuaia, Argentina.

Merkel, W. 1998. The Consolidation of Post-Autocratic Democracies: A Multi-level Model. *Democratization*, 5(3), 33–67.

Muñoz, H. 1998. The Right to Democracy in the Americas. *Journal of Interamerican Studies and World Affairs*, 40(1), 1–18.

Nye, J. S. 1987. *Peace in Parts: Integration and Conflict in Regional Organizations*. Reprint. Latham: University Press of America.

O'Donnell, G. 1996. Illusions about Consolidation. *Journal of Democracy*, 7(2), 34–51.

Oelsner, A. 2009. Consensus and Governance in Mercosur: The Evolution of the South American Security Agenda. *Security Agenda*, 40(191), 191–212.

Pevehouse, J. C. 2005. *Democracy from Above: Regional Organizations and Democratization*. Cambridge: Cambridge University Press.

Polity IV Project. 2008. Polity IV Country Reports 2008. [Online]. Available at: www.systemicpeace.org/polity [accessed: November 24, 2011].

Polity IV Project. 2010. Political Regime Characteristics and Transitions, 1800–2009. [Online]. Available at: www.systemicpeace.org/polity/polity4.htm [accessed: November 24, 2011].

Pridham, G. 1994. The International Dimension of Democratization: Theory, Practice, and Inter-regional Comparisons, in *Building Democracy? The International Dimension of Democratization in Eastern Europe*, edited by G. Pridham, E. Herring and G. Sanford. New York: St. Martin's Press, 7–31.

Pridham, G. 1995. The International Context of Democratic Consolidation: Southern Europe in Comparative Perspective, in *The Politics of Democratic Consolidation: Southern Europe in Comparative Perspective*, edited by R. Gunther, P. Diamandouros and P. H.-J. Baltimore: Johns Hopkins University Press, 166–203.

Przeworski, A., Alvarez, M., Cheibub, J. A. and Limongi, F. 1996. What Makes Democracies Endure? *Journal of Democracy*, 7(1), 39–55.

Schedler, A. 1998. What is Democratic Consolidation? *Journal of Democracy*, 9(2), 91–107.

Schedler, A. 2001. Measuring Democratic Consolidation. *Comparative International Development*, 36(1), 66–92.

Smith, P. 1993. The Politics of Integration: Concepts and Themes, in *The Challenge of Integration: Europe and the Americas*, edited by P. Smith. Coral Gables: University of Miami North-South Center.

Valenzuela, A. 1997. Paraguay: The Coup that Didn't Happen. *Journal of Democracy*, 8(1), 43–55.

Valenzuela, A. 1999. *The Collective Defense of Democracy: Lessons from the Paraguayan Crisis of 1996*. Carnegie Commission on Preventing Deadly Conflict. Washington, DC.

Valenzuela, J. S. 1992. Democratic Consolidation in Post-Transitional Settings: Notion, Process and Facilitating Conditions, in *Issues in Democratic*

Consolidation: The New South American Democracies in Comparative Perspective, edited by S. Mainwaring, G. O'Donnell and J. S. Valenzuela. Notre Dame: University of Notre Dame Press, 57–104.

van der Vleuten, A. and Ribeiro Hoffmann, A. 2010. Explaining the Enforcement of Democracy by Regional Organizations: Comparing EU, Mercosur and SADC. *Journal of Common Market Studies*, 48(3), 737–758.

Whitehead, L. 1996. Democratic Regions, Ostracism, and Pariahs, in *The International Aspects of Democratization: Europe and the Americas*, edited by L. Whitehead. Oxford: Oxford University Press, 395–412.

Chapter 12

ASEAN and Civil Society: An Incompatible Relationship?

Corinna Krome

Introduction

> It takes six months to create new political institutions, to write a constitution and electoral laws. It may take six years to create a half-way viable economy. It will probably take sixty years to create a civil society.
>
> (Dahrendorf 1990: 42).

Human rights, democracy and political participation are actively promoted concepts in regional organizations such as the European Union. The Association of Southeast Asian Nations (ASEAN) however, is not well known for promoting, let alone protecting, participative values in the region. Even today, ASEAN founds its cooperation on principles such as non-intervention and sovereignty.

With this in mind, one might think that an organization that grants autocratic regimes membership has no, or at least only a marginal, impact on civil society movements in its member states. Yet, as ASEAN has recently incorporated the aim to include civil society actors in its declarations, one might ask what mechanisms and institutional arrangements the association actually possesses to further engage with these non-state actors.

Drawing upon a general review of the literature, ASEAN's primary documents and a comparative analysis of the member states, the following question will be at the heart of this chapter: to what extent can and does ASEAN have an impact on civil society organizations (CSOs) in its member states?

Accordingly, this chapter seeks to explore the structural conditions of CSO empowerment, to examine the organization's mechanisms and to consider ASEAN's actual impact in the region over the preceding decades. I argue that, particularly since the end of the 1990s, ASEAN has sought to involve civil society actors and has therewith transformed into an increasingly people-oriented organization.

I will first provide an overview of ASEAN's historical evolution, as well as some definitions of key terms and a brief review of the most relevant literature. Furthermore, I will describe pertinent theoretical approaches and the methodology employed. Finally, the main section will analyze empirical findings related to ASEAN's empowerment of civil society.

Even though the organization remains elite-driven, this chapter shall illustrate that, to differing degrees, CSOs are encouraged to be active participants in the region. According to the aforementioned quotation, it takes 60 years for civil society to emerge—were 40 years enough for ASEAN?

Forty Years of ASEAN: A Historical Overview of ASEAN

The five founding nations—Indonesia, Singapore, Thailand, Malaysia and the Philippines—established ASEAN with the ratification of the Bangkok Declaration on August 8, 1967. With the admission of the Sultanate Brunei Darussalam in 1984, Vietnam in 1995, Myanmar in 1997 and Cambodia and Laos in 1999, the political systems of ASEAN's 10 member states diversified, ranging from Indonesia's proactive democratic approach to Myanmar's isolationist authoritarianism.[1]

Regarding the past 40 years, the association has been characterized by the oft-cited "ASEAN way": an informal structure with core principles such as the maintenance of sovereignty, non-interference and decision-making processes based on "*musyawarah* (consultation) and *mufakat* (consensus)" (Chachavalpongpun 2009: 16). With the 5th Meeting of the ASEAN Standing Committee (ASC) in Manila from June 16–18, 1986, one could, however, detect at least a slight broadening of intergovernmental cooperation as ASEAN drafted the first formal "Guidelines on ASEAN's Relations with Non-Governmental Organizations." In the same period, CSOs were regarded as "having a complementary role [to the state] in promoting development" (Tay 2002: 73)—a development that was characterized as the first of "three waves" of CSO emergence in the Southeast Asian region (Riker 1995). With the end of the Cold War, the focus was increasingly directed on economic cooperation (ASEAN 1992: Article 10 (5)). Simultaneously, during the second wave of the CSOs' emergence, non-state actors managed to foster their relations with ASEAN, as they were progressively characterized as "being an autonomous and countervailing power to the state" (Tay 2002: 73). Especially in the course of their enlargement at the end of the 1990s, ASEAN claimed to "envision a socially cohesive and caring ASEAN ... where the civil society is empowered" (ASEAN 1997: 5). Accordingly, Southeast Asian CSOs—traditionally "sceptical of ASEAN as a potential platform for pushing their organizational agenda" (Ramirez 2008: 2)—ceased to address and rely upon extra-regional bodies such as the UN exclusively, and began to view ASEAN as a "body that could influence domestic policy" (Collins 2008: 317). These changes, culminating in the minimal revision of the original guidelines on Civil Society on April 3, 2006 and the enactment of the comprehensive 2007 ASEAN Charter, established "a people-oriented ASEAN in which all sectors of society ... are encouraged to participate in, and benefit

---

1 For a more comprehensive overview of the historical evolution, see for example Cockerham (2009) or Smith and Jones (2006).

from, the process of ASEAN integration and community building" (ASEAN 2009: 2).[2] This impetus for democratization was accompanied by the third wave of civil society emergence in Asia, characterized by governmental attempts "to moderate the growing pressures from civil society groups and to incorporate them as an instrument of state" (Tay 2002: 74). I argue that this attempted control and cooptation of civil society actors by the state can however—in some cases and to some extent—be circumvented through ASEAN's new regional provisions.

According to ASEAN's Guidelines, a CSO is "a non-profit making association of ASEAN persons, natural or juridical, organized to promote, strengthen and help realize the aims and objectives of ASEAN cooperation" (ASEAN 2006: 1).[3] As these criteria implicitly include CSOs' compliance with ASEAN's goals, this definition is not a sufficient indicator for the seriousness of ASEAN's purported people-orientation and openness for pluralism. Obviously, ASEAN's potential influence on completely independent CSOs must also be examined. According to Dosch (2008: 82), "two sorts of civil society groups exist in the region: 'traditional' organizations such as academic think tanks and private-sector businesses on the one hand, and so-called 'alternative' groupings, such as NGOs and grassroots movements, on the other hand." Private businesses that aim at realizing their own interest-maximizing policy are excluded from the definition used in this chapter. However, initiatives by think tanks and academics, as well as alternative groupings (NGOs and grassroots movements), will be taken into account.[4] Thus, in this study, the term "civil society" refers to non-state actors that meet regularly on a voluntary basis, are banded together for a common non-profit-oriented purpose and have "institutionalize[d] problem-solving discourses on questions of general interest" (Habermas 1996: 367).

Reviewing Literature on ASEAN

The interrelation of ASEAN's engagement with CSOs has been interpreted in ambiguous ways in academic literature: whereas certain authors assume that ASEAN has no great influence on the structures of its member states, others credit ASEAN as having the ability to make domestic impacts.

The first assumption can be traced to the aforementioned "ASEAN way," in that scholars have argued that ASEAN's loose and informal institutional design and its reliance on "political persuasion rather than legal enforcement"

---

2   The ASEAN Charter entered into force on December 15, 2008.

3   Prior to these guidelines, the term non-governmental organization (NGO) was used instead of CSO. In the following, both terms will be used interchangeably. Likewise, the term "Track II Diplomacy" will be used, indicating the informal dialogue and interaction with actors from civil society organizations.

4   Academic institutions are also included. For example the ASEAN-ISIS is included because the association describes itself as an "association of non-governmental organizations registered with ... ASEAN" (ASEAN-ISIS 2010).

(Chachavalpongpun 2009: 16) have led to domestic implementation failures (Alagappa 2003: 23, Denoon and Colbert 1999: 506, Kahler 2010, Narine 2008, Schmidt 2007: 2, Solingen 2005). In line with more "realist" analyses, ASEAN's states are thus said to work toward the protection of their own diverse national interests, and do not aim at empowering CSOs on a regional level. Likewise, rationalist scholars such as Rother (2004), Rüland and Jetschke (2008) and Rüland (2009) stress the tendency of "political realism in Southeast Asia" (Rüland and Jetschke 2008: 406).

Yet, there are also scholars who accord the organization greater significance in reference to domestic impact and CSO involvement (see the "second image reversed" literature, for instance Gourevitch 1978, Pevehouse 2005).[5] Especially with the adoption of the new Charter, scholars argue that the core principles of sovereignty and non-interference are slightly weakened (Emmerson 2008: 25, Katsumata 2004: 238, Loewen 2006: 2). A sign of this is, for example, the emergence of criticisms against human rights violations in authoritarian regimes such as Myanmar (Katanyuu 2006: 825). Accordingly, scholars like Acharya (2003, 2009) or Caballero-Anthony (2005, 2008), who are more optimistic than Dosch (2008) or Sukma (2008), stress the association's increasing engagement with the issue of participative movements within the region—be it due to international pressure, the desire for more credibility or domestic motivations.

In sum, even though there are many scholars who cover ASEAN implementation failures and successes, several analyses fail to provide clear concepts, causal explanations or empirical evidence. Furthermore, many studies focus on the impact of civil society actors on the regional organization. However, the question of whether ASEAN actually has an impact on the development of CSOs has to this point not thoroughly been discussed.[6]

Accordingly, this chapter seeks to fill this gap in conceptualizing ASEAN as an independent variable and CSO empowerment in ASEAN member states as the dependent variable, focusing on the causal mechanisms that ASEAN provides and on the actual empirical evidence for domestic change in the field of democratization.

Theoretical Framework

First of all, Börzel's work (2010) on European causal mechanisms to empower CSOs in the new member states of Eastern Europe can be transferred to the Asian region. From Börzel's point of view, mechanisms such as technical assistance, material incentives, capacity-building and normative persuasion offer "new legal and political venues for … CSOs to push their interests" (Börzel 2010: 1, Magen

---

5 Most literature regarding the impact of ASEAN is devoted to environmental (Ramcharan 2003: 56) and economic issues (see Narine 2008, Ravenhill 2008).

6 Except the excellent review of ASEAN–CSO relations by Collins (2008).

et al. 2009: 13). Accordingly, the EU offers CSOs supplementary resources and platforms for interaction "with like-minded organizations" (Börzel 2010: 1), leading to an increase in dialogue. I argue that the same phenomenon can be observed in the ASEAN region.

Furthermore, the spiral model outlined by Risse et al. (1999) will be applied. Regarding the impact of international human rights norms on the behavior of nations, the authors argue that "norm-violating" states are "put... on the international agenda in terms of moral consciousness-raising" (Risse and Sikkink 1999: 5).[7] I argue that this concept can be transferred to the context of a regional organization. Accordingly, ASEAN could likewise "empower and legitimate the claims of domestic opposition groups against norm-violating governments" (Risse and Sikkink 1999: 5), and allow them to circumvent the autocratic regimes of their home countries.

Finally, Risse and Sikkink (1999) examine how principles stipulated in international declarations have an effect on domestic structures. This process of norm-internalization can be related to the three logics of action comprehensively outlined in Risse (2000): firstly, "processes of instrumental adaptation and the strategic bargaining" (Risse and Sikkink 1999: 5) adhering to the rationalist logic of consequentialism, are necessary for the internalization process. Furthermore, constructivists view "processes of moral consciousness-raising, argumentation, dialogue, and persuasion" (Risse and Sikkink 1999: 5) as essential, whereas from a sociological-institutionalist point of view, "processes of institutionalization and habitualization" (Risse and Sikkink 1999: 5) are more important for norm-internalization. Transferring these logics of behavior to the Asian context, I argue that ASEAN has promoted the internalization of the norm "participatory politics" in its member states.

Methodology

In order to answer the central questions outlined above, ASEAN's primary documents, blueprints, summit declarations and action plans since its inception are carefully screened.[8]

---

7 On norm diffusion, see for instance Finnemore and Sikkink (1998).

8 The analysis was based on the following documents: Political-Security Blueprint 1.3.2009, Economic Blueprint 1.3.2009, Socio-Cultural Blueprint 1.3.2009, Charter 20.11.2007, Vientiane Action Programme (VAP) 29.11.2004, Security Community Plan of Action, Bali Concord II 7.10.2003, Hanoi Declaration 23.7.2001, Initiative for ASEAN Integration 2000, Hanoi Plan of Action 1998, Second Protocol Amending Treaty of Amity and Cooperation (TAC) 1998, ASEAN Vision 2020 1997, Treaty on the Nuclear Weapon-Free Zone 15.12.1995, Protocol to Amend the Framework Agreement on Enhancing ASEAN Economic Cooperation 15.12.1995, Common Effective Preferential Tariff Scheme (CEPT), Scheme for the ASEAN Free Trade Area (AFTA) 28.1.1992, Protocol Amending the TAC 15.1.1987, (TAC) 24.2.1976, Bali Concord I 24.2.1976, ZOPFAN 27.11.1971 and Bangkok Declaration 8.8.1967.

As there is neither quantitative data nor comprehensive indicators to measure the significance of CSO development in ASEAN member states, a regional overview and a qualitative case study on human rights serve as a proximate illustration of ASEAN's impact.[9] To this end, the case selection is based on the assumption that progress observable in a highly sensitive field, such as human rights promotion, might also imply change in other, more innocuous sectors (Börzel and Risse 2003). To this end, Burma was additionally selected as a least-likely case as ASEAN would be least expected to have an impact on this autocratic regime. As human rights activist Ohn Mar puts it: "if there is democratic change in Burma, then there [will also be change] within ASEAN" (Ohn Mar 2009).

Even though many other internal or external factors are viewed as highly relevant determining factors that might explain a rise or fall in the significance of CSOs in the region, this chapter will limit its scope to ASEAN's influence on the regional development of CSOs.

An Organization between Rhetoric and Reality—Empirical Findings

To Empower or not to Empower Civil Society? ASEAN's Rhetorical Actions

Even though the organization is known for its elite-centered nature, ASEAN has, for example, good relations with academics from the ASEAN Institute for Strategic and International Studies (ASEAN-ISIS), a Track II Dialogue that has existed since 1988. Furthermore, from 1979 on, ASEAN conceded civil society organizations accreditation and acknowledged their increasing relevance. More precisely, one week after the formal "Guidelines for ASEAN Relations with NGOs" were adopted, the foreign ministers of the 19th Ministerial Meeting (June 23–28, 1986) edited a Joint Communiqué where they acknowledged the essential position NGOs hold in "promoting ASEAN cooperation and goodwill, particularly at the level of people-to-people contact" (ASEAN 1986).

In the following review, the historical development of the topic "civil society" in ASEAN's documents and the possible increase in precision of ASEAN's legal texts is illustrated. Table 12.1, classified by essential issue areas, does not include the two comprehensive guidelines on ASEAN–CSO relations from 1986 and 2006 as no substantial changes have been made. Simply, in the 2006 guidelines, CSOs should "help promote the development of a people-centered ASEAN Community" (ASEAN 2006: 1). In other respects, both documents are almost identical. Table 12.1 begins with the Vientiane Action Program (November 24, 2004) and ends with the ASEAN Socio-Cultural Community (ASCC) and ASEAN Political-Security Community (APSC) Blueprints (March 1, 2009), as codified in the Bali Concord II.

---

9   The only comprehensive index measuring CSO empowerment, the Civicus CSO Index, introduced in 2006, is only available for Vietnam and Indonesia and therefore not auxiliary for a comparative assessment.

Table 12.1 Development of civil society in ASEAN's documents

Source/Date/Issue	Vientiane Action Program November 29, 2004	ASEAN Charter November 20, 2007	ASEAN Community Blueprints (ASCC and APSC) March 1, 2009
Goal: **Empowerment of CSO**	"Increase the participation of organizations such as AIPO, APA, ABC, ASEAN ISIS and the academia."	—	"Expand the role of civil society and citizens groups in integrity efforts and governance;" "Engage ASEAN-affiliated non-governmental organisations in ASEAN Community building process."
Mechanism	"Participation of at least one representative each from those organisations in the track-two activities … Holding of regular consultations between AIPO Chair and ASEAN Standing Committee Chair."	—	"Develop modalities for interaction between … ASEAN-ISIS network, and ASEAN sectoral bodies;… Hold consultations between AIPA and appropriate ASEAN organs;" "Convene the ASEAN Social Forum and the ASEAN Civil Society Conference on an annual basis to explore the best means for effective dialogue, consultations and cooperation between ASEAN and ASEAN civil society."
Goal: **People-Orientation**	"Promote … participation in political systems, culture and history of ASEAN Member Countries through increasing people-to-people contacts and track-two activities."	"To promote a People-Oriented ASEAN;" "All sectors of society are encouraged to participate in, and benefit from, the process of ASEAN integration and community building"	To "promote a people-oriented ASEAN in which all sectors of society, regardless of gender, race, religion, language, or social and cultural background, are encouraged to participate in, and benefit from, the process of ASEAN integration and community building. … ASEAN should also strive towards promoting and supporting gender-mainstreaming, tolerance, respect for diversity, equality and mutual understanding."
Mechanism	"Two track-two events per year … Annual publication … for dissemination to universities, think tanks and similar institutions. Exchange of experience and training in order to enhance popular participation."	"The ASEAN Foundation shall support the … ASEAN community building by promoting … people-to-people interaction … among the business sector, civil society, academia and other stakeholders."	"Encourage the holding of at least two track-two events per year, including academic conferences, workshops and seminars; Release periodic publications on the dynamics of ASEAN Member States' political systems, culture and history for dissemination to the public; and Intensify exchange of experience and training courses in order to enhance popular and broader participation."

Source: Own compilation based on ASEAN documents.

This review shows that the number of references to civil society organizations increased in the past decade. Whereas the systematic engagement with non-state actors was almost of no concern whatsoever to the organization prior to 1997 (aside from the guidelines), the association now claims to use CSOs for the promotion of people-participation, human rights, democratic values and institutions as well as good governance in the region and in the member states.[10] Following and adhering to the same principles and norms stipulated in the European Union, it seems as if ASEAN follows a global governance script, mimicking the EU's policies (Jetschke 2009).

In line with the spiral model, one could claim that the member states now find themselves in "self-entrapment" (Risse 2000: 23) as they have voiced their goal to engage with civil society on a regional level. Whether this rhetorical action now leads to actual further engagement is yet to be seen. ASEAN itself sees its aspiration as already successfully implemented:

> Since the adoption of the ASC Plan of Action in 2004 ... there was increased participation by organisations, such as academic institutions, think-tanks, and civil society organisations in ASEAN meetings and activities. Such consultations and heightened interactions fostered good relations and resulted in positive outcomes for the region (ASEAN 2009: 3).

In the next section, this chapter will examine the instruments and mechanisms used by ASEAN to see whether the association actually has the means to fulfill its goals.

ASEAN's Mechanisms

ASEAN refers to accredited CSOs as being among the "entities associated with ASEAN" in the appendix of the ASEAN Charter. In an enumeration, the ASEAN Inter-Parliamentary Assembly (AIPA), 19 business organizations, think tanks and academic institutions (such as ISIS) and over 50 accredited civil society organizations from different issue areas are named with their date of affiliation (Charter Appendix). To forge a partnership with ASEAN, organization applications must be approved by the Secretariat as well as the Secretary-General and then "be submitted to the ASEAN Standing Committee for its consideration" (ASEAN 2006: Article 6). When certain criteria, such as the ASEAN nationality of members, the adherence to its aims and objectives and the compliance with the organization's policies are fulfilled, admission is granted and they can benefit from certain privileges (ASEAN 2006: Article 8 a–e, Collins 2008: 315). One can argue that ASEAN uses the accreditation process of these civil society actors as a mechanism for their own empowerment. However, it seems more likely that ASEAN wants to

---

10   CSOs are also used, for instance, to help enforce mechanisms against drug abuse and disaster management (ASEAN 2009: 47).

ensure their conformity with its own goals (Collins 2008: 316). Accordingly, either CSOs from innocuous issue areas such as sports (for example an ASEAN Chess Confederation) or music are affiliated, or ASEAN grants economic organizations, such as from the health and fishery sector, accreditation.[11] In general, one cannot be certain of the CSOs' independence once they are accredited. In the following, a distinction between accredited CSOs and not-accredited CSOs will thus be made.

Mechanism 1: rights and participation Accredited CSOs with ASEAN enjoy certain rights. Besides the permission to "use the name 'ASEAN' and display the official ASEAN logo" (ASEAN 2006: Article 9), these CSOs can attend meetings and participate in ASEAN actions as the association has formally ensured that there is an "interaction and fruitful relationships between the existing ASEAN bodies and the CSOs" (ASEAN 2006: Article 5 a–c). In line with the rationalist logic, this mechanism provides certain incentives and privileges for the actors: CSOs can submit recommendations, proposals and written statements on relevant topics to the ASEAN Secretariat (ASEAN 2006: Article 3). At least according to the documentary provisions, CSOs now seem to have a voice in ASEAN's policies.

In addition, ASEAN also promotes dialogue with "not-accredited" civil society actors in institutional drafting processes, such as the ASEAN Charter (ASEAN Dialogue with Civil Society Organisations 2009). Whereas in the EU involvement of non-state actors serves "as a means to increase effectiveness and democratic legitimacy" (Börzel 2010: 2), ASEAN's institutional arrangements do not in practice incorporate the CSOs' ideas and recommendations on issues such as democracy or human rights (Dosch 2008: 82).[12]

Mechanism 2: money, financial and technical assistance Affiliated CSOs are eligible to "submit [their] own project proposals for Third Party funding" (ASEAN 2006: Article 9), which has then to be approved by the ASEAN Secretariat and the ASEAN Standing Committee. Through these channels, the access to financial resources is facilitated. In general, CSOs should yet "be self-reliant in terms of its material requirements" (ASEAN 2006: Article 9). As an unaccredited CSO, one also has the opportunity to address the ASEAN Foundation for project support. These projects must be approved according to certain criteria, one being that "the project must directly benefit people at the grassroots level" (ASEAN Foundation 2010). However, as the ASEAN Foundation was founded by ASEAN members in 1997 and is closely linked to the ASEAN Secretariat, projects included in the ASEAN Foundation framework are—just as the accredited CSOs—mainly related

---

11 There are also engineering, law, construction and port associations. Apparently, only one organization is related to the topic of human rights (women's empowerment organization).

12 In the drafting process of the ASEAN Charter, above all, the Eminent Persons Group (EPG) was essential to represent CSOs from the region (for further information see Collins 2008: 316, Ramirez 2008: 6).

to "innocuous" fields such as fisheries and technology, and occasionally education and poverty reduction (ASEAN Foundation 2010).

In terms of capacity building and technical assistance, affiliated CSOs have access to "the facilities of the ASEAN Secretariat for ... official meetings and other official activities in Jakarta" (ASEAN 2006: Article 9). Furthermore, ASEAN provides CSOs with a database, research studies and yearly key publications. ASEAN claims to have set up training programs and workshops for CSOs which aim at strengthening democratic values and democratic institutions. For example, ASEAN claims to promote an "understanding of the principles of democracy among ASEAN youth at schools at an appropriate stage of education" (ASEAN 2009: 6). Whether these rhetorical actions were, however, actually implemented is yet to be seen.

In sum, there are certain material incentives, capacity building and facilitation processes by ASEAN (Magen et al. 2009: 13) that would—from a rationalist perspective—explain an increase of CSO significance in the region.

Mechanism 3: networks The establishment and provision of networks among CSOs can be considered as ASEAN's most important mechanism. First of all, several joint projects and workshops among CSOs are facilitated and organized by the association (see Table 2.1). Accordingly, CSOs gain at least theoretically the opportunity to harmonize their strategies, to interact on a regularly basis, to circumvent their respective governments and to gain visibility in the international context. However, despite these provisions, ASEAN ensures that their affiliated CSOs do not "take legal action against any ASEAN Member Country or the ASEAN Secretariat" (ASEAN 2006: Article 14). Moreover, the ASEAN Standing Committee can end the CSO membership when they "engage in acts inimical to ASEAN or any of the ASEAN Member Country" (ASEAN 2006: Article 13) upon request by member states or ASEAN bodies. Thus, "the nature of this engagement is ... one determined and directed by the state elite. It is a top-down process where ASEAN establishes the objectives that the CSOs pursue" (Collins 2008: 315).

Mechanisms: A Short Summary

One can conclude that ASEAN's mechanisms are not as comprehensive and precise as might be expected when one looks at the association's stipulated goals. Whereas, in the EU, the *Acquis Communitaire* and the democratic conditionality of the Copenhagen Criteria operate as adequate mechanisms to "legally prescribe ... public involvement in the policy process and [to] open ... new legal and political venues for civil society organizations" (Börzel 2010: 1), ASEAN has not yet been able to fully respect and include non-state actors' interests. In particular, ASEAN's CSO accreditation process, which at first glance appears to be a means to increase CSOs' influence, can be rated as a weak and disingenuous instrument of empowerment.

Operating from a rationalist point of view and bearing in mind the three logics of action, one can observe that the CSO–state relationship is based on incentives and strategic bargaining processes. Indeed, some states only include CSOs in order to bolster their claim to openness to pluralism, simultaneously monitoring the compliance of non-state actors to their own goals. In this regard, opportunities for deliberative argumentation and equal dialogue are not yet given in CSO–state interactions. However, following constructivist accounts, one can argue that ASEAN's provisions for CSO–CSO interaction seems to have initiated "processes of moral consciousness-raising, argumentation, dialogue, and persuasion" (Risse et al. 1999: 5).

Having evaluated ASEAN's mechanisms, one could argue that a gap remains between the "rhetorical goals of cooperation and the organization's substantial achievements" (Jetschke 2009: 408).

Civil Society in ASEAN's Member States—An Analysis

In order to illustrate the impact of ASEAN, the following section begins with an assessment of the status quo of CSO development in each ASEAN country. It is important to understand the historical extent of these countries' cooperation with ASEAN if one is to assess the impact of this organization. By showing the countries that cooperate with the association and the extent to which they do so, one is in a better position to evaluate the influence of ASEAN in the sphere of CSOs.

From Burma to Indonesia: A Regional Overview

The member states' approach to CSOs is heterogeneous: in Indonesia, the number of non-governmental organizations has exponentially increased since the abdication of President Suharto in 1998 (Collins 2008: 318). Since then, many non-state actors "have been vocal adherents of majority decisions, democracy, and human rights" (Rüland 2009: 378) and have worked on deepening and encouraging ASEAN cooperation. Likewise, the civil society sector in the Philippines is one of the most diverse and numerous in ASEAN (Hernandez 2008: 2). Thailand has also established good relations with its CSOs and has especially shown its dedication to the subject in preparing a discussion paper for an ASEAN state–CSO Forum in 2006 that aimed to reinforce networks and partnerships among the civil society movements (Raper 2006: 9).

In Malaysia, non-state actors were strengthened significantly under the rule of Abdullah Ahmad Badawi, who served as prime minister from 2003 to 2009 (Collins 2008: 320). During his time in office, Malaysia launched the first ASEAN Civil Society Conference (ACSC) in December 2005. With this event, a direct interaction between the ASEAN heads of states and CSOs from all 10 member states was facilitated through the Malaysian government (Collins 2008: 320).

In the other six states, however, the growth rate of CSOs remains rather low. For example, the Singaporean Home Affairs Minister, Wong Kan Seng, stated that several CSO initiatives may "attract severe punishment, including caning and imprisonment" (Wong Kan Seng, as quoted in Collins 2008: 320). In Cambodia, NGOs predominantly in the sector of "rehabilitation, reconstruction and development" (Raper 2006: 16) have been involved in national policies over the past decades. In Vietnam, even though numerous organizations exist, there is no comprehensive legal framework provided for their independent empowerment (Norlund 2006: 27). Subsequently, "many NGOs face insufficient financial resources for their operations, are weak and lack human personnel" (Raper 2006: 16). Given the weakness of their recent track record in the enablement of CSOs, one could expect a similar situation in Laos, Brunei and Myanmar. Surprisingly, all ASEAN member states except Myanmar do, however, possess Track II Diplomacy Networks that are affiliated with ASEAN-ISIS (Wahyuningrum 2009).[13]

In sum, the varying degrees of CSO inclusion show that the intensity of CSO empowerment remains highly dependent on the respective members' domestic politics and structures. Hence, a qualitative assessment of ASEAN's engagements is necessary to illustrate the causal relationship between ASEAN and the rise of CSO significance in the member states.

Participatory Actions: ASEAN's Provisions for Human Rights CSOs

With the establishment of the ASEAN human rights body in particular, ASEAN has stipulated the aim to "strengthen interaction between the network of existing human rights mechanisms as well as other civil society organizations" (ASEAN 2009: 6) in all 10 member states and all ASEAN bodies. Yet, the engagement of member states with human rights associations still remains dependent on their respective domestic structure.

In the four countries with the most vivid civil society participation, National Human Rights Institutions (NHRIs) such as the Commission of Human Rights in the Philippines, KOMNAS HAM in Indonesia, SUHAKAM in Malaysia and the NHRCT in Thailand were established and affiliated with ASEAN.

These actions have been supported and strengthened by ASEAN's human rights-related forums such as the roundtable discussion on Human Rights in ASEAN and the Regional Consultation on ASEAN and Human Rights (Wahyuningrum 2009).[14]

---

13 Brunei Institute of Policy and Strategic Studies (BDIPSS), Cambodian Institute for Co-operation and Peace (CICP), Indonesian Centre for Strategic and International Studies (CSIS), Laos Institute for Foreign Affairs (IFA), Malaysian Institute for Strategic and International Studies, Philippines' Institute for Strategic and Development Studies (ISDS), Singapore Institute of International Affairs (SIIA), Thailand's Institute for Security and International Studies (ISIS), Vietnam's Institute for International Relations (IIR).

14 For more information on human rights, see Chalermpalanupap (2009: 131).

However, even though the official task of these bodies is to further the "promotion and protection for human rights and [ensure] the fundamental freedoms in their countries" (ASEAN Human Rights Commission 2008: 1) their power remains advisory in nature, and they often lack the means to formulate their requests independently from the state.

Over the past decade in particular, ASEAN has launched CSO seminars and multi-stakeholder conferences, including the ASEAN Secretariat's "1st ASEAN Socio-Cultural Community Forum" in 2010 (FES 2010). Currently, the most significant forums in which human rights CSOs and ASEAN engage with one another are the ASEAN People's Assembly (APA), the ASEAN Civil Society Conference (ASCS), the ASEAN People's Forum (APF), the Solidarity for Asian People's Advocacy (SAPA) and the South East Asian Committee for Advocacy (SEACA).

Since the year 2000, APA has tried to connect Senior Officers of the ASEAN Secretariat with CSO representatives in the region. According to Collins (2008: 321), these meetings are increasingly respected by ASEAN member states. The first ASEAN Civil Society Conference and ASEAN People's Forum, launched in 2005, resulted for example in CSO statements that were directly forwarded to ASEAN leaders (Ramirez 2008: 6).

Presently, these meetings take place "in conjunction with the annual ASEAN Summit" (Ramirez 2008: 6) and are thus a great opportunity to directly exchange views with the ASEAN heads of state as they "provide a platform for CSOs to have their voices heard" (Ramirez 2008: 2). Even though this growing number of CSO networks and gatherings clearly illustrates a relatively significant inclusion of non-state actors in ASEAN's policy-making, it is important to highlight the constraints that are part and parcel of such meetings.

First of all, the importance of the CSO–state meetings is not always acknowledged by the member states: in 2009, for instance, more than 500 non-state representatives from all 10 member states met for three days in Chaam, Thailand, to discuss relevant topics, such as human rights violations in Singapore and Burma (FIDH 2009).

However, the heads of state from Cambodia, Burma, Laos, Singapore and the Philippines refused to discuss with their selected nationals and instead brought their own regime-friendly civil society partners. The failure of the meeting, which would only have been the second meeting between heads of state with CSOs in ASEAN history shows that not all "ASEAN states ... understand [the CSOs'] fundamental role in any democracy" (FIDH 2009: 1).

Secondly, the CSO conferences contain the risk of forum shopping and interest-overlap: the profusion of conferences and meetings by CSOs "create[s] the perception of confusion over what CSOs want and thus hinders the likelihood of them achieving an institutionalized relationship with ASEAN" (Collins 2008: 322).

One can nevertheless conclude that some of the rhetorical aspirations outlined above have—to a certain extent—been met. Even though the interaction with CSOs remains very low in certain states, ASEAN still provides a platform for

CSO–CSO dialogues, suggesting that there is a liberal exchange of information and discussion (Koh 2009). Thus, one can identify increasing interaction and dialogue between civil society actors—a fact that can be directly ascribed to ASEAN provisions.

Friend or Foe? ASEAN's Engagement in Myanmar

These CSO–CSO networks might even have an impact, however slight, on countries such as ASEAN's problem child, Myanmar (McCarthy 2008: 911). At the CSO gatherings, human rights violations in Burma could be for the first time actively discussed on a regional level. Accordingly, even Burmese CSOs have been eligible to participate in ASEAN's workshops for some years now. At the 15th Summit in Hua Hin, Thailand, for example, a Burmese woman, Khin Ohn Mar, was selected to represent Burmese CSOs. In her opinion the "summit is the place to reveal and openly discuss the situation in Burma in terms of democracy, human rights, politics, economics, social and cultural problems" (Burma News 2009). In the course of the discussions, she aimed at criticizing Burma for the imprisonment of Daw Aung San Suu Kyi, for neglecting dialogue between the regime and certain ethnic groups as well as for general human rights violations (Burma News 2009). However, pro-regime stakeholders disagreed with an external CSO representative and replaced her with government-friendly Sitt Aye and Win Myaing, "the latter also being a former high-ranking police officer" (Mizzima News 2009). Ohn Mar's presence, representing the voice of the Burmese people, could have been a signal and an opportunity to circumvent national restrictions through regional provisions. In interacting with other civil society actors and ASEAN senior officials, the Burmese issue could have been put on the table and the Burmese leaders could have been more or less openly criticized for their "systematic human rights violations" (Burma News 2009). However, with the ongoing refusal of independent CSO representatives, there are pressing doubts that ASEAN's initiatives and the increasing criticism will suffice to impact Burma's autocratic structure. Until today, Burma still upholds ASEAN's principle of non-interference and it is unlikely that we will observe positive change in the near future.

Conclusion—Summary and Prospects

This chapter has shown that ASEAN has increasingly worked on its relations with civil society actors in the past few decades. On the basis of relevant theories, it could be demonstrated that ASEAN has established certain mechanisms such as networks, workshops and research projects. Even though these seem to be rather weak instruments, ASEAN's provisions to empower civil society actors have increased and an actual impact on the CSO significance in the region might be observable in the near future. However, as most notably the accredited CSOs lack independence and as ASEAN's member states' regimes, norms, identities, ethics and economic situations still differ widely, an ambiguous attitude toward CSO involvement continues to exist: whereas members such as Indonesia, Malaysia and the Philippines actively promote the inclusion of non-state actors, other nations like Burma rather work on co-opting and instrumentalizing civil society actors for their own goals.

As ASEAN does not, however, hinder the non-state actors' empowerment, a tendency toward more people-oriented policies can be observed. I argue that even though ASEAN lacks legally binding agreements, the informal empowerment mechanisms might play a great role in terms of state compliance and the involvement of non-state actors. One can conclude that even though ASEAN's direct impact is difficult to measure, the organization plays an important role in setting the topic of CSO engagement on the regional agenda.

With regard to ASEAN's weak institutional design, it would therefore be interesting to conduct further research on the organization's reasons to involve non-state actors. Does ASEAN use its rhetorical action in order to gain reputation and legitimacy in the international system? Or does ASEAN have an intrinsic desire to follow its purported people-orientation? In this sense, there is also a need for studies that explore the reasons for civil society actors' engagement with an organization in which the nation-state still rules, and in which the core principles of the "ASEAN way" still dominate.

To this end, this chapter tried to illustrate the *zeitgeist* of an organization that has experienced a shift from being completely nation state-based to constituting a people-oriented forum that encourages the discussion of issues such as human rights in the region.

Returning to the initial quotation, I thus conclude that 40 years were indeed enough for ASEAN to realize how important the involvement and empowerment of non-state actors is—no longer merely on a rhetoric level.

References

Acharya, A. 2003. Democratisation and the Prospects for Participatory Regionalism in Southeast Asia. *Third World Quarterly*, 24 (2), 375–390.

Acharya, A. 2009. *Constructing a Security Community in Southeast Asia: ASEAN and the Problem of Regional Order*. London: Routledge.

Alagappa, M. 2003. Institutional Framework: Recommendations for Change, in *The 2nd ASEAN Reader*, edited by S. Siddique and S. Kumar. Singapore: Institute for Southeast Asian Studies, 22–27.

ASEAN. 1986. *Joint Communiqué of the 19th ASEAN Ministerial Meeting Manila*. Manila, the Philippines.

ASEAN. 1992. *Agreement on the Common Effective Preferential Tariff (CEPT) Scheme for the ASEAN Free Trade Area*. Singapore.

ASEAN. 1997. *ASEAN Vision 2020*. [Online]. Kuala Lumpur, Malaysia. Available at: www.aseansec.org/1814.htm [accessed: March 15, 2011].

ASEAN. 2006. *Guidelines On ASEAN's Relations with Civil Society Organisations.* Jakarta, Indonesia.

ASEAN. 2009. *ASEAN Political-Security Community Blueprint (APSC).* [Online]. Available at: www.aseansec.org/22337.pdf [accessed: April 3, 2011].

ASEAN Dialogue with Civil Society Organisations. 2009. Drafting of the TOR for the ASEAN Commission on the Promotion and Protection of the Rights of Women and Children. *Dialogue with Civil Society Organisations (CSOs).* Bangkok.

ASEAN Foundation. 2010. *Criteria of Project Approval.* [Online]. Available at: www.aseanfoundation.org/index2.php?main=criteria_approval.htm [accessed: September 27, 2010].

ASEAN Human Rights Commission. 2008. *Terms of Reference of the ASEAN Human Rights Commission.* Technical Working Group (TWG) Meeting of ASEAN NHRI Forum. Cebu, Philippines.

ASEAN-ISIS. 2010. *Institute of Strategic and International Studies.* [Online]. Available at: www.siiaonline.org/?q=node/2040 [accessed: March 3, 2011].

Börzel, T. A. 2010. Why You Don't Always Get What You Want: EU Enlargement and Civil Society in Central and Eastern Europe. *Acta Politica*, 45(1–2), 1–10.

Börzel, T. A. and Risse, T. 2003. Conceptualizing the Domestic Impact of Europe, in *The Politics of Europeanisation*, edited by K. Featherstone and C. Radaelli. Oxford: Oxford University Press, 57–80.

Burma News. 2009. *Burmese Woman in Exile to Represent CSO at ASEAN Summit.* [Online]. Available at: www.bnionline.net/news/mizzima/7254-burmese-woman-in-exile-to-represent-cso-at-asean-summit.html [accessed: September 26, 2010].

Caballero-Anthony, M. 2005. *Regional Security in Southeast Asia: Beyond the ASEAN Way.* Singapore: ISEAS.

Caballero-Anthony, M. 2008. Challenging Change: Nontraditional Security, Democracy, and Regonalism, in *Hard Choices: Security, Democracy, and Regionalism in Southeast Asia*, edited by D. Emmerson. Singapore: Institute of Southeast Asian Studies, 191–219.

Chachavalpongpun, P. 2009. *Road to Ratification and Implementation of the ASEAN Charter.* Singapore: Institute of Southeast Asian Studies.

Chalermpalanupap, T. 2009. *10 Facts about ASEAN Human Rights Cooperation.* ASEAN Secretariat.

Cockerham, G. 2009. Regional Integration in ASEAN: Institutional Design and the ASEAN Way. *East Asia*, 27(2), 165–185.

Collins, A. 2008. A People-Oriented ASEAN: A Door Ajar or Closed for Civil Society Organizations? *Contemporary Southeast Asia*, 30(2), 313–331.

Dahrendorf, R. 1990. Has the East joined the West? *New Perspective Quarterly*, 7(2), 41–43.

Denoon, D. B. H. and Colbert, E. 1999. Challenges for the Association of Southeast Asian Nations (ASEAN). *Pacific Affairs*, 71(4), 505–523.

Dosch, J. 2008. Sovereignty Rules: Human Security, Civil Society, and the Limits of Liberal Reform, in *Hard Choices: Security, Democracy, and Regionalism in Southeast Asia*, edited by D. Emmerson. Singapore: Institute of Southeast Asian Studies, 59–91.

Emmerson, D. K. (ed.). 2008. *Hard Choices. Security, Democracy, and Regionalism in Southeast Asia*. Singapore: ISEAS Publications.

FES. 2010. *ASEAN Secretariat Symposium on Methods of Stakeholder Involvement in Regional Organisations. Friedrich-Ebert-Stiftung*. [Online]. Available at: www.fes-asia.org/pages/posts/asean-secretariat-symposium-on-methods-of-stakeholder-involvement-in-regional-organisations-14.php [accessed: September 30, 2010].

FIDH. 2009. *Member States of the ASEAN to Undermine Independent Civil Society Participation. International Federation for Human Rights*. [Online]. Available at: www.fidh.org/Member-states-of-the-ASEAN-to-undermine [accessed: Sptember 20, 2010].

Finnemore, M. and Sikkink, K. 1998. International Norm Dynamics and Political Change. *International Organization*, 52(4), 887–917.

Gourevitch, P. 1978. The Second Image Reversed: The International Sources of Domestic Politics. *International Organization*, 32(4), 881–912.

Habermas, J. 1996. *Between Facts and Norms. Contributions to a Discourse Theory of Law and Democracy*. Cambridge: MIT Press.

Hernandez, C. G. 2008. The Role of Civil Society in Philippine Democratization. *KAS-VASS Conference*. Hanoi.

Jetschke, A. 2009. Institutionalizing ASEAN: Celebrating Europe though Network Governance. *Cambridge Review of International Affairs*, 22(3), 407–426.

Kahler, M. 2010. Regional Institutions in an Era of Globalization and Crisis: Asia in Comparative Context. *2010 Annual Meeting of the American Political Science Association*.

Katanyuu, R. 2006. Beyond Non-Interference in ASEAN. The Association's Role in Myanmar's National Reconciliation and Democratization. *Asian Survey*, 46(6), 825–845.

Katsumata, H. 2004. Why is Asean Diplomacy Changing? From "Non-Interference" to "Open and Frank Discussions." *Asian Survey*, 44(2), 237–254.

Koh, T. 2009. *ASEAN Charter at One: A Thriving Tiger Pup*. Singapore: Singapore Research Institutions.

Loewen, H. 2006. *Die ASEAN als Impulsgeber ostasiatischer Integration*. GIGA Focus 2 / 2006, February 2006. Hamburg, Institut für Asienkunde.

Magen, A., Risse, T. and McFaul, M. (eds). 2009. *Promoting Democracy and the Rule of Law. American and European Strategies*. Basingstoke: Palgrave Macmillan.

McCarthy, S. 2008. Burma and ASEAN. Estranged Bedfellows. *Asian Survey*, 48(6), 911–935.

Mizzima News. 2009. *Civil Society Representatives Barred from ASEAN Summit*. [Online]. Available at: www.mizzima.com/news/regional/2954-civil-society-representatives-barred-from-asean-summit.html [accessed: May 23, 2011].

Narine, S. 2008. Forty Years of ASEAN: A historical Review. *The Pacific Review*, 21(4), 411–429.

Norlund, I. 2006. *The Emerging Civil Society. An Initial Assessment of Civil Society in Vietnam*. Hanoi: CIVICUS Civil Society Index.

Ohn Mar, K. 2009. *A Headache for ASEAN*. [Online]. Available at: http://democracyforburma.wordpress.com/2009/09/15/khin-ohn-mar-a-headache-for-asean [accessed: September 20, 2010].

Pevehouse, J. C. 2005. *Democracy from Above. Regional Organizations and Democratization*. Cambidge: Cambridge University Press.

Ramcharan, R. 2003. ASEAN and Non-Interference, in *The 2nd ASEAN Reader*, edited by S. Siddique and S. Kumar. Singapore: Institute of Southeast Asian Studies, 52–56.

Ramirez, M. 2008. Asia DHRRA and ASEAN: A Case Study on the Process of Civil Society Engagement with a Regional Intergovernmental Organization. Montreal: FIM Forum.

Raper, M. 2006. ASEAN at 40: Realising the People's Expectations? Summary Record of the ASEAN GO-NGO Forum on Social Welfare and Development. *ASEAN GO-NGO Forum on Social Welfare and Development*. Hanoi: International Council on Social Welfare (ICSW).

Ravenhill, J. 2008. *Global Political Economy*. Oxford: Oxford University Press.

Riker, J. V. 1995. Reflections on Government-NGO Relations in Asia: Prospects and Challenges for People-Centred Development, in *Government-NGO Relations in Asia: Prospects and Challenges for People-Centered Development*, edited by N. Heyzer. Hampshire: Palgrave Macmillan, 194–196.

Risse, T. 2000. Let's Argue! Communicative Action in World Politics. *International Organization*, 54(1), 1–39.

Risse, T. and Sikkink, K. 1999. The Socialization of International Human Rights Norms into Domestic Practices: Introduction, in *The Power of Human Rights. International Norms and Domestic Change*, edited by T. Risse, S. C. Ropp and K. Sikkink. Cambridge: Cambridge University Press, 1–39.

Risse, T., Ropp, S. C. and Sikkink, K. (eds). 1999. *The Power of Human Rights. International Norms and Domestic Change*. Cambridge: Cambridge University Press.

Rother, S. 2004. *Normen, Identitäten und die Logik der Anarchie: Die ASEAN aus konstruktivistischer Perspektive*. Freiburg: Arnold-Bergstraesser-Institut.

Rüland, J. 2009. Deepening ASEAN Cooperation through Democratization? The Indonesian Legislature and Foreign Policymaking. *International Relations of the Asia-Pacific*, 9(3), 373–402.

Rüland, J. and Jetschke, A. 2008. 40 years of ASEAN: Perspectives, Performance and Lessens for Change. *The Pacific Review*, 21(4), 397–409.

Schmidt, A. 2007. *Die ASEAN-Charta: Viel Lärm um Nichts?* Kurzberichte aus der Internationalen Entwicklungszusammenarbeit. Asien und Pazifik. Singapore: Friedrich-Ebert-Stiftung.

Smith, M. L. R. and Jones, D. M. 2006. Making Process, Not Progress. ASEAN and the Evolving East Asian Regional Order. *International Security*, 32(1), 148–184.

Solingen, E. 2005 East Asian Regional Institutions: Characteristics, Sources, Distinctiveness, in *Remapping East Asia: The Construction of a Region*, edited by T. J. Pempel. Ithaca: Cornell University Press, 31–53.

Sukma, R. 2008. Political Development: A Democracy Agenda for ASEAN?, in *Hard Choices: Security, Democracy, and Regionalism in Southeast Asia*, edited by D. Emmerson. Singapore: Institute of Southeast Asian Studies, 135–151.

Tay, S. S. C. 2002. The Future of Civil Society: What Next?, in *Singapore in the New Millennium. Challenges facing the City-State*, edited by D. da Cunha. Singapore: Institute of Southeast Asian Studies, 69–107.

Wahyuningrum, Y. 2009. *Understanding ASEAN: its Systems & Structures*. Oxfam International.

Chapter 13
Monetary Integration Through the Backdoor: Does NAFTA Promote Monetary Policy Harmonization in North America?

Alexander Spielau

Introduction

It is generally argued that the set of underlying forces behind North America's economic integration will evolve over time. The North American Free Trade Agreement (NAFTA) clearly sped up two key interactions: trade and investment (Reyes-Heroles 2004: 395). One of the effects of such greater involvement of market actors (especially the financial and banking sectors) in each other's countries is that NAFTA has led to a broader range of cross-border activities and transactions than before it was adopted (Lucio 1999: 194). The resulting macroeconomic and price convergence in North America provides a favorable context for prudent fiscal and monetary policies, making further, especially monetary and fiscal, integration necessary (Reyes-Heroles 2004: 398). The discussions on monetary integration in NAFTA and corresponding empirical observations during the 1994 Mexican currency crisis, as well as the adaptation of US monetary policy standards by Mexico, led to a debate about political harmonization in an evolving North American economic integration. As there is no agenda for leading NAFTA toward a currency union or implementing an exchange rate mechanism to cope with spillovers,[1] the question of unintended effects of NAFTA matters.

The question that this chapter addresses is, thus, what factors promote monetary policy harmonization on domestic level; and can the observed changes be explained by the membership in a regional organization? This chapter argues that NAFTA produces spillovers in the monetary realm and enforces adjustment pressures on the United States' neighbors through trade integration and business cycle synchronization. Hence, it produces an incentive for harmonization efforts in the field of monetary policy. Due to the relative size of the US market compared with those of Mexico and Canada, it will be assumed in this chapter that

---

1 Spillovers are understood in a neo-functionalist sense as externalities of (economic) activity within an integration process, which has effects on other actors or processes not directly involved in it. It creates, thus, strong incentives for further integration.

coordination does not have to be tripartite but is rather likely to be an adjustment process of Mexico and Canada to US policies and developments.

To show the suspected interrelation of the NAFTA induced domestic effects and the changes in monetary policy, a most similar system design comparison is conducted between Portugal and Spain after joining the European Community (EC) in 1986 and Mexico after joining NAFTA in 1994. The Canada–US relationship is excluded, as it was already relatively integrated and coordinated due to long-standing cooperation before NAFTA had been implemented. To prepare the comparison, the chapter outlines the state of NAFTA and its effects on the member countries. Afterwards, more generally, the chapter turns to the interrelation of regional organizations and changes in the realm of monetary policy. Then, the research design is presented, followed by the analysis of the independent variables.

NAFTA and the State of Integration in North America

NAFTA succeeded the Canada–United States Free Trade Agreement (CUFTA) of 1988. Together with its supplementary agreements on labor and environmental cooperation,[2] it came into force on January 1, 1994. The parties agreed on having a 15-year transition period in which the phasing out of existing duties and quantitative restrictions as well as the removal of barriers to trade should be pursued, and the treaty being fully implemented. Due to the fact that security matters changed after the 9/11 terrorist attacks and that several crises hit the North American economies, an enlargement of the existing cooperation schemes was necessary. One of those cooperative arrangements is the Security and Prosperity Partnership signed in March 2005.

Considering the logic of rational institutionalism, states cooperate on the basis of a certain common interest respectively on the basis of a certain negotiation objective (Shepsle 2006). NAFTA's primary objective is to strengthen cooperation between the partners via market liberalization and harmonization of their trilateral economic relations. In this context, one should specifically note the role of neoliberal philosophy, which has played a vital role in the formation of this free trade area (Duina 2006: 22). Practically, the primary objective of NAFTA is the elimination of all tariffs and many of the non-tariff barriers to trade of goods and services, as well as the promotion of conditions of fair competition in the free trade area (NAFTA 1993: Chapter 1, Article 102).

Although NAFTA is regarded as the most comprehensive trade agreement ever conducted and implemented (see, amongst others, Zamora 1997: 13), the expected shift of competencies to the regional level, and thus, the transfer of sovereignty, is

---

2   These are the North American Agreement on Labour Cooperation (NAALC) and Environmental Cooperation (NAAEC).

limited.[3] This is mainly explained by US preference for unilateralism, as well as Canadian and Mexican preferences for dealing bilaterally with the United States; therefore, no institution with a "legislative" role has been established. This has neutralized efforts to create a North American Community (Zamora 1997: 16–17). Moreover, NAFTA can be seen, and was explicitly set, as a counterpart to the European Union as there was no mechanism for further political integration planned and included. In sum, NAFTA does neither allocate legislative power to a supranational authority nor does it de jure affect the allocation of legislative power to subdivisions within the NAFTA parties (Zamora 1997: 14). Decisions have to be made and implemented on the domestic level, thus making NAFTA an intergovernmental agreement.

Yet, NAFTA does have some significant internal effects on its members. It is supposed to have a trade creating as well as diverting effect, when one differentiates between different industries (Bayoume and Eichengreen 1994, Hillberry and McDaniel 2002, Scheerer 2004). Overall, NAFTA is perceived to be responsible for positive developments. In particular, interregional trade has developed relatively well, to the disadvantage of trade with Europe and Latin America (Coughlin and Wall 2003).

Focusing on the domain of economic affairs, however, the treaty provides regulations in the domain of competition and industry (rules of origin, customs, standards, etc.), economic freedoms (capital liberalization, trade in goods and services), energy and transport, and agriculture (including subsidies). Otherwise, NAFTA does not interfere in macroeconomic policy and employment, regional, economic and social cohesion policy, monetary policy, or in tax policy, which altogether remain solely in the national sphere. No provisions were made to have an institutionalized macroeconomic or monetary coordination on a regional level; nor has NAFTA created a regional development fund for Mexico comparable to the EU Structural Funds. Furthermore, existing institutions like the North American Development Bank remain chronically underfunded and do not get the attention needed to pursue their duties.

Effects on Monetary Policy Integration through Regional Organizations

Generally, Mundell (1961) argued that the nation-state has always been the wrong unit around which to organize economic and political life. Only by coincidence would the optimum size of the currency area match the national territory. As a consequence, he outlined conditions for the assessment of optimal organization of economic action. In his opinion, a region should implement a common currency if it is an Optimum Currency Area (OCA), i.e. that in the absence of national monetary policies the currency area has to rely on factor mobility (capital and

---

3 For a more comprehensive analysis of the state of integration in NAFTA, see Chapter 5, this volume.

labor) if asymmetric shocks hit several regions or states within this currency union (Mundell 1961: 658–661). However, necessary for a functioning OCA according to Mundell is also the existence of a fiscal transfer mechanism equalizing constant intraregional factor-imbalances. Member countries should also have or reach similar business cycles, which allow the common central bank to promote growth in downturns and to contain inflation in booms. This is generally reached by a high level of macroeconomic convergence through deeper trade integration by means of trade liberalization among the members of a prospective monetary area (Rose and Stanley 2005). Also, according to Donelly, it is most important for OCA theory whether economic activity is widely diversified (Donelly 2004: 12).

Yet, as pointed out before, monetary integration does not have to be a currency union, and there are several stages prior to this. One can differentiate five types of monetary cooperation, ranging from ad hoc exchange rate policy agreements to projects of a common supranational currency (Fritz and Metzger 2006: 11–12). The stage of non-cooperation is characterized by a lack of commitment and in some cases non-fulfillment of (binding) agreements by the neighboring countries. This might result in beggar-thy-neighbor policies in case of a shock caused outside the region. This stage can, however, be overcome by monetary cooperation. In doing so, the respective countries coordinate their monetary policy closer to common goals. This can happen in three forms at different degrees of coordination. Firstly, it might be a regional liquidity fund or a binding commitment for mutual provision of liquidity in the event of external shocks. The latter includes intraregional swap arrangements, credit lines, or intraregional reserve pooling (Fritz and Metzger 2006: 11). Secondly, there can be an intraregional exchange rate ban, or target zones, which can be either based on a regional currency basket, a lead currency or at bilateral exchange rates. Lastly, fixed but adjustable rates among regional currencies is the strongest form of cooperation before reaching the status of a currency union. This step also constitutes the final point in monetary integration by either the creation of a single currency or the adoption of a regional currency (Fritz and Metzger 2006: 12).

However, to outline the political side of cooperation, this also means that the respective cooperating countries mutually apply their monetary policy instruments in the narrow and broad sense[4] under at least consideration or direct participation of other (foreign) policy interests (Floyd 2010).

---

4 Monetary policy has specific monetary aims (narrow sense) such as the maintenance of the internal and external value of the monetary unit (stability of the price-level and stability of the exchange rate). However, in mixed economies monetary policy aims also at the realization of economic objectives outside the monetary sphere (broad sense), such as the overall economic equilibrium, i.e. inflation or deflation control, employment, and the regulation of the balance of payments. Thus, monetary policy is also an instrument aiming at the establishment and maintenance of conditions necessary to achieve those goals (see Blanchard and Illing 2006, Floyd 2010).

Monetary Integration in the NAFTA Case

Against the original intention of its drafters, NAFTA is heading toward common-market schemes in some areas. However, there are currently no such initiatives for institutionally coordinated monetary or exchange rate policies (Fritz 2006: 127–128). According to Fritz, the only exception is the swap line, which is an agreement between the states' central banks to dedicate a limited sum of money to supporting transnational payments (Courchene and Harris 2000, Fritz 2006). Moreover, in spite of the dominance of the US dollar, there seem to be no signs of the United States being actively willing to "dollarize" the region by promoting the partners' central banks to become members of the Federal Reserve System of the United States (Fritz 2006: 127–128).[5]

Yet, even if NAFTA fails to include any formal agreement for monetary coordination, the experience of the past 10 years has shown that there is good reason to interpret it as a case of implicit monetary coordination. This particular assumption can be evidenced by two significant changes. On the one hand, the United States acted in the wake of the 1994/1995 currency crisis in Mexico as a lender of last resort, providing significant resources (USD 20bn) for the consolidation and reactivation of the Mexican economy. Thus, some analysts interpreted the strong US commitment[6] as a signal that the Mexican peso could rely on backing from US monetary and fiscal authorities (Weintraub 2004: 139). The United States did not help Mexico in its 1982 currency crisis. That is to say, within the NAFTA framework, the United States and Mexico were moving toward an implicit monetary coordination arrangement (Fritz 2006: 129–130). Different from other Latin American countries, Mexico experienced a soft landing after its crisis as it recovered from the economic contraction (-6.2 percent in 1995). Until the beginning of the recession in the US economy in 2001, the Mexican economy experienced an annual growth of 5.4 percent (Banco de Mexico 2010). Fritz explains this partly by the privileged access to US markets, which allowed for an increase of almost 50 percent in exports in only two years, despite occurring on the basis of significantly reduced real wages due to the crisis.

On the other hand, Mexican monetary policies changed after the crisis. They started to give priority to countering inflation quickly, even at potentially high macroeconomic costs (Fritz 2006: 128). Moreover, Mexico does not seek to continue to peg its currency to the dollar, but is rather focusing on inflation

---

5   For Fritz the project of bilateral, coordinated dollarization seems unrealistic in the short and medium term. On the other hand, the Mexican government rules out the option of unilaterally dollarizing the Mexican economy.

6   Along with the US credit line of USD 20bn, the Clinton administration convinced the IMF to provide USD 17.8bn to Mexico as well as encouraged the European central banks to support Mexico via the Bank of International Settlements.

targeting to achieve monetary convergence.⁷ This might seem counterintuitive at first. However, this move is explained by Mexico's willingness to follow US monetary policy guidelines. The rigid pro-cyclical policy of the Mexican central bank and the strict adherence to orthodox recipes (Fritz 2006) acted as a signal to the US government and central bank to provide supporting resources in case of a new currency crisis. However, the US acceptance of a role as lender of last resort is not certain as financial market actors could run speculative attacks to test the interventionist commitment of the Federal Reserve Bank in such an implicit regime of monetary coordination. Thus, the implicit arrangement could at a certain point be replaced by a formal arrangement within NAFTA (Fritz 2006).⁸

A Comparative Research Design

As this chapter tries to address whether the spillovers resulting from NAFTA promote monetary policy harmonization efforts in the member countries, the dependent variable of this research design is the monetary policies changes on the domestic level. The underlying hypothesis is that NAFTA produces spillovers into the monetary realm and enforces macroeconomic convergence of the neighbor countries, but especially Mexico, to the United States through trade integration and business cycle synchronization. Thus, it produces an incentive for harmonization efforts in the field of monetary and fiscal policy. Yet, it has to be considered that due to the relative size of the US market compared to those of Mexico and Canada, coordination does not have to be tripartite but is rather likely to be an adjustment process of Mexico and Canada to US policies and developments.

As this research design is aware of the problem of multiple causation of monetary policy harmonization, it does not claim to have found a general explanation for monetary integration as being the result of regional organizations. It rather argues that within a regional organization that facilitates economic and trade integration, it is most likely that member countries will reasonably achieve, or must find a way to adapt, to each other to cope with spillover consequences. Other factors, which do not explain integration along the reasoning of this chapter can, however, function as enhancers of underlying processes of growing interdependence, when countries agree to join a regional organization.⁹

---

7   In 2001, the Mexican central bank established inflation targets of 6.5 percent for 2001, 4.5 percent for 2002 and 3 percent for 2003, allowing a margin of 1 percent in each direction—so far being moderately successful (Schmidt-Hebbel and Werner 2002: 4).

8   In fact the United States accepts such a role, including the willingness to repeat a similarly comprehensive intervention as in the 1994–1995 crises, thus putting Mexico in a unique and highly privileged position. The consequence is an increasing confidence in the peso stability, permitting lower interest rates and higher domestic investment, and resulting in higher growth rates.

9   Yet a probabilistic analysis is not feasible due to the low number of applicable cases.

Causal Factors for Monetary Integration

The chapter identifies four factors, which shall serve as independent variables. These factors are able to cause further monetary integration via monetary policy harmonization in the member countries. First, the existence of physical institutions, such as exchange-rate or currency regimes, constitutes the foundation of political adjustment (Vernengo 2006b: 1). However, these kinds of regimes do not necessarily exist or connect to regional organizations. Thus, it is possible to argue that they are sufficient to explain cooperation, as they are the result of explicit integration or cooperation processes, although they are not necessary for it.

Second, the state–market relationship, being either neoliberal or coordinating, can have an effect on monetary policy harmonization efforts. This approach—coming from the Varieties of Capitalism (VoC) debate—differentiates between two groups of countries: the Liberal Market Economies (LME) and the Coordinated Market Economies (CMEs) (Becker 2007, Hall and Soskice 2001).[10] In regard to monetary policies, this approach translates into different levels of acceptance toward intervention and (politically induced) distortion of markets by introducing currency regimes. In theory, CMEs should be more willing to accept institutionalized, politically organized arrangements for macroeconomic coordination, whereas LMEs should be willing to let the markets find solutions to changes in the degree of interdependence. Yet, standard VoC models were not designed for Latin American economies as those differ significantly to advanced capitalist economies in regard to the shape of their institutions and the interactions between them. Hence, Schneider (2009) developed the preliminary concept of a Hierarchical Market Economy (HME). Additionally, they added the characteristic of "tendency towards the standard types" into their model as Latin American economies vary in their particular institutional shape due to underdevelopment of market institutions, corruption, informality and strong presidential systems. Yet, this new model was criticized as essentially being heuristic and not fully theoretically developed (Schrank 2009). Thus, this chapter will treat Mexico as an HME but qualify its value by its tendency toward either neoliberal or coordinating.

Third, the existence of large and dominating actors in a region can facilitate adjustment from smaller neighbors in case of an open relationship in regard to trade.[11] Thus, without having a regional organization or a currency regime, political harmonization could be a result of market pressure in the smaller country due to growing dependence. However, in most of the cases such a situation goes hand-in-hand with the introduction, sooner or later, of certain exchange rate mechanisms.

---

10 The VoC approach argues that firm behavior and their strategies are based on distinctive national institutional structures which act in a complementary way. The relationship of complementarity produces two ideal-types of capitalist configurations: LMEs which are present in the Anglo-Saxon world, and CMEs which are located mostly in Central and Northwest Europe as well as in Japan (Hall and Soskice 2001).

11 Hence, this variable serves as a proxy for the existence of a hegemon.

Finally, having an OCA theoretical background, one can argue that joining a regional organization with an economic focus results in domestic effects, which constitutes an environment where the OCA criteria for further monetary integration are satisfied. Those are business cycle synchronization as well as trade and financial market integration, which are enforced by regional organizations. The logic behind this is that both processes enhance macroeconomic convergence due to mutually growing connectedness of firms and markets, and, thus, growing interdependence of the economies. This does not mean that nominal parameters within the member countries (such as inflation rates, budget deficits or debt levels) have to become exactly the same or follow each other synchronically.[12] It rather makes sense to understand macroeconomic convergence as budget discipline and price-level stability (Fritz and Metzger 2006: 12). In any case, macroeconomic convergence seems to be an indispensable requirement for the transition to further monetary integration schemes (Fritz and Metzger 2006: 12).

Design Outline and Case Selection

To operationalize the hypothesis, this chapter uses the four outlined independent variables, which are able to influence monetary policies toward harmonization and integration (see Table 13.1). Within the framework of a most different system design, those independent variables which do not explain the empirical phenomenon are supposed to vary among each other. However, to corroborate the suspected causality there needs to be at least one independent variable, which shows the same outcome (explanatory variable), and therefore, causes the outcome of the dependent variable.

What is problematic, however, is finding adequate cases for comparison. As this chapter seeks to compare Mexico's case of joining NAFTA and being subject to an integration process causing monetary policy harmonization, one needs to find cases which qualify for this comparison by serving certain conditions:

1. Respective countries have to be open and mixed economies, to be able to reach trade integration with other countries.
2. Respective countries need to have joined a regional organization at a time close to that of Mexico joining NAFTA (1994) to have similar world-economic conditions, such as increasing trade relations, globalization and the dominance of similar economic ideologies (like monetarism and neoliberalism).
3. Respective countries, however, also need to have been in a different (lower) stage of development as the leading partner countries in the regional organization. This is reasonable because Mexico was perceived to be on the level of an emerging economy, whereas the United States and Canada were already industrialized economies at the stage of post-industrialism.

---

12   Therefore, considerable divergence in inflation rates, budget deficits and debt levels should not be very surprising.

Table 13.1 Operationalization of the research design

	Variable	Coding
IV I	Exchange rate regime in the RO	Fixed or floated exchange rate
IV II	State–market relationship	Neoliberal, regulatory/coordinating
IV III	Existence of a dominating economy in the region	Yes/no
EV	Domestic, economic effects of RO	Trade integration: low, medium or high; business cycle synchronization: low, medium or high
DV	Monetary policy changes on domestic level	Policy changes regarding inflation targeting, price stability, adjustment and stabilization of the exchange rate and money supply: yes or no

Source: Author.

Note: The abbreviations used in this table are IV—independent variable, EV—explanatory variable (also independent), DV—dependent variable, and RO—regional organization. Moreover, one should consider a few points regarding the operationalization. IV I is binary coded as either taking the state of being fixed to another currency (or a basket of currencies) or being floated, and, thus, dependent on everyday market evaluation. To indicate "yes" as value for IV III, an economy needs a market size significantly higher than its neighbors in combination with having an important, cross-border used currency. Yet, as this coding is vague in quantitative terms, the chapter shows the importance by using those qualitative characteristics.

Although there is no spatial limit for cases, the time frame and the requisite properties and characteristics leave just two cases for comparison: the enlargement of the European Community in 1986 with Spain and Portugal. In their economic development both countries were significantly behind the EC average and the leading economies. However, they showed impressive transformation after their democratizations in the 1970s, and progress to open and mixed economies with mostly liberalized markets.[13] The underlying problem is that NAFTA was the first free trade area of Northern industrialized economies with a Southern emerging economy. Thus, even the case of Portugal and Spain has to be qualified.

However, there are some critical comments to be made. First, one has to admit that the very small number of cases increases the risk of a selection bias

---

13 Other enlargement rounds are either too far away to account for (Greece 1982), because significant economic distortions happened in the early 1980s, or the joining countries were not (significantly) different to account for a lower stage of economic development (Sweden, Finland and Austria 1995). Also, in spite of having dominating actors, other regional organizations such as MERCOSUR do not suffice for the properties needed to compare to the Mexican case.

(King et al. 1994: 128–129), and thus, a loss of explanatory power. Second, the mostly dichotomous nature of variables means a loss of information. And last, the European Community was and is explicitly about political integration. Thus, policy harmonization is a necessary step. However, this chapter argues that integration and harmonization appears regardless of a political will to integrate or not.

Empirical Analysis

The chapter now turns to the empirical analysis of the aforementioned variables, starting with an investigation on domestic monetary policy changes in the Spanish and Portuguese case. After six years of negotiating for entry, Spain joined the EC in 1986. It gained entry partly through a series of reforms in the private sector and banking. To support that, in 1984 and 1986 the Spanish central bank (Banco de España) implemented a new monetary strategy. Most importantly, the bank changed its nominal effective position[14] from an index of developed countries to an index of EC countries excluding Greece and Portugal. In 1988, this was again replaced by a bilateral nominal exchange rate against the German mark (Ayuso and Escrivá 1998: 135–138). Thus, the focus of its monetary policy was redirected toward Europe. Moreover, since 1986, exchange rate stability was achieved via controlling monetary supply and interest rates. Those policy changes were later formalized in the convergence criteria of 1993, especially in its commitments to stability in the European Monetary System (EMS) (Ayuso and Escrivá 1998: 141–145). According to Galy (1993: 9), both the connection between the opening up of the Spanish economy toward EC competition, and the progressive implementation of antitrust EC directives, led to the stabilization of the peseta. Its subsequent anchoring in the European Exchange Rate Mechanism (ERM) provided the conditions for price convergence between Spanish and EC goods. Overall, there is no doubt that EC membership played a significant role in reaching those achievements. Portugal's efforts were similarly impressive as the Spanish commitments to reform. The Portuguese central bank (Banco de Portugal) received important responsibilities in the area of monetary and credit control and the regulation of the money market in the year 1986 (Banco de Portugal 2010). Prior to that, its duties had been money supply and the supervision of the banking system, after it was nationalized in 1974 (Banco de Portugal 2010). Portugal managed to control fiscal deficit before and after it joined the EC (12 percent of GDP in 1984, decreasing afterwards to about 5.4 percent of GDP in 1990). Moreover, it also changed its exchange rate policy—as Spain did—toward stabilization via interest rates and the issuance of bonds.

However, by signing the European Single Act in 1986 and the Treaty of Maastricht in 1992 Spain and Portugal also became members of the single market

---

14 This nominal effective position is important for the determination of the exchange rate value.

and the ERM, which was directed to prepare the ground for a monetary union with a single euro-currency. By integrating on monetary terms both countries made themselves subject to convergence criteria: most importantly to achieve a certain level of economic convergence and convergence of national legislation and the regulations governing their central banks and monetary issues (Banco de Espana 2010b). These criteria are of extraordinary importance as they make monetary policy changes toward a harmonization mandatory. To conclude, both countries showed a change in monetary policy prior to and after joining the EC.

Assessing the Reason for Monetary Integration

In the following, the chapter will turn to the four outlined independent variables and try to assess their outcomes for each of the selected cases.

Exchange rate regime in the RO In respect of the exchange rate regime in the regional organization, the analysis shows that Mexico introduced a floated exchange rate regime after it experienced a currency crisis in 1984. Since then, however, it has tried to keep its exchange rate relatively constant to the US dollar by market interventions, yet, without having this connection institutionalized in any way. Thus, there were no changes in Mexico's exchange rate regime since 1984, which would account for significant monetary policy changes. In regard to Spain and Portugal, by joining the EC they became part of the second attempt of monetary integration leading to a common currency, the EMS of 1979, which was a successor of the "currency snake." The currency snake was a system for the progressive narrowing of the margins of fluctuation between the currencies of the member states of the EC. Thus, both Portugal and Spain introduced a fixed exchange rate regime when they entered the EC. The process of integration led to both countries becoming members of the third stage of the European Economic and Monetary Union (EMU) in 2001, introducing the euro. As such, the euro represents a fixed exchange rate regime with no chance of an adjustment to the underlying (former) national currency (Scheller 2006).

State–market relationship Concerning the state–market relationship, this chapter follows the line of critics and focuses on the tendency of the Mexican economy in regard to financial markets, banking and international business. There, due to the NAFTA influence, the Mexican state–market relationship has developed since the late 1980s in a neoliberal direction, putting as much responsibility as possible into market forces to consolidate the banking sector, and (at least tries) to make it competitive to the North American market. This also translates into the monetary realm (Schneider 2009: 5). In contrast to Mexico, both Portugal and Spain are considered by the standard VoC literature as being CMEs. As such, both have an institutional configuration, which favors strategic coordination over market coordination of economic action. Although aspects of both kinds of coordination appear in all capitalist economies, the balance between these two types of coordination varies across political economies (Hall and Gingerich 2001: 4). Consequently, they approach economic coordination not in the first place by competitive markets but through processes of strategic interaction of different actors on an economy-wide level. This, however, impacts on the structure and the degree of market efficiency of the respective economies.

Existence of a dominant economy in the region   Coming to the third independent variable, the NAFTA region shows the existence of a hugely dominant economy, the United States. It accounts for almost 90 percent of North American GDP, and is by far the biggest trading partner of its neighbors (Pastor 2002: 96). Another feature of this dominance is that the dollar has gained importance within the respective national economies. There is even evidence of dollarization in the region (Vernengo 2006a). Yet, although its neighbors are becoming more dependent on the dollar, the United States is calling the shots on monetary policy (Hufbauer and Schott 2005: 484–485). In Europe, on the other hand, no dominating economy existed in 1986 or even today. At the time when Spain and Portugal joined the EC, the largest economy, Germany, accounted for roughly 23 percent of EC-GDP. Yet, Germany was followed by France and the UK with each of them accounting for 13 percent (Eurostat 2010). Moreover, the biggest trading partner for Spain at that time was France and not Germany (Banco de Espana 2010a). Thus, one can conclude that Mexico and the two European cases did and still do indeed vary on the existence of a dominating economy.

Internal effects of the regional organization   In regard to the domestic economic effects, NAFTA clearly sped up two key interactions: trade and investment (Reyes-Heroles 2004: 395), and produces multiple opportunities for increased trade. Thus, the degree of openness of the three economies continues to rise (Reyes-Heroles 2004: 401–402). One of the effects of such greater involvement of market actors (especially the financial and banking sector) in each other's countries is that NAFTA produced a functional amalgam of US, Mexican and other foreign banks, which participate in a broader range of cross-border activities and transactions than before NAFTA was adopted (Lucio 1999: 194). And this dynamic could in the medium term lead to the borderless regional financial market as it was envisioned by NAFTA drafters (Lucio 1999, Makler 1999). Referring to Reyes-Heroles, this (and the production of goods for the NAFTA market) leads to two other aspects, on the one hand, macroeconomic convergence, and the other, the locking of prices for domestic goods to international prices. This provides a favorable context for prudent fiscal and monetary policies, making further, especially monetary and fiscal, integration necessary (2004: 398).

Moreover, according to Pastor, the three countries have reached a level of interdependence in which a shock in one country leads to consequences in at least one of the other two (2002: 91). Gruben and Koo (2006) argue that between Mexico and the United States some convergence among their business cycles has occurred, and that a similar, but less pronounced, change to synchronicity might have occurred between Canada and Mexico at least in comparison with previous periods. According to them, this suggests that a positive move toward currency union has occurred. Overall, most of the scholars see at least a medium degree of business synchrony reached between Mexico and its NAFTA partners (Blecker 2009, Kose et al. 2004, Pacheco-Lopez 2005).

Spain and Portugal were both part of the European Free Trade Area before they joined the EC, which meant that their trade relations were already more highly integrated with their EC neighbors compared to those of Mexico and the United States. However, the empirical analysis by Böwer and Guillemineau (2006: 3–6) shows that joining the EC and implementing the single market intensified not just bilateral trade across the euro area countries, but also contributed to higher business cycle synchrony from the mid 1980s until 2005. Moreover, the introduction of the euro led to an intensification of intra-industry trade which has become the main driving force ensuring the coherence of business cycles (Afonso and Furceri 2007).[15] This finding is confirmed by other scholars such as Montoya and de Haan (2007). In conclusion, due to the aim of high economic integration in the EC and later in the EU, trade is extraordinarily integrated and business cycles are becoming more and more synchronized to a euro-area average.

Evaluation and Concluding Remarks

This chapter started its analysis from the empirical observation that Mexico changed its monetary policy after joining NAFTA, although there was no political commitment or agenda to do so. Succinctly, it was asked whether the spillovers resulting from NAFTA promote fiscal and monetary harmonization efforts in the member countries. It was argued that NAFTA produces spillovers due to trade integration and business cycle synchronization. Consequently, monetary policies of the member countries were affected. Yet, it was assumed that the relative size of the US market causes an adjustment process of Mexico and Canada to US policies and developments. The chapter tried to show the suspected interrelation of the NAFTA-induced domestic effects and the changes in monetary policy by a most different system design, comparing Mexico to Portugal and Spain after joining the EC in 1986.

---

15 For Spain, business cycle synchronization vis-à-vis the EMU countries expanded from 0.51 for the period of 1980–1992 to 0.87 for the succeeding period until 2005. Portugal increased its business cycle synchronization also from 0.34 to 0.73 (Afonso and Furceri 2007: 17).

Table 13.2 Outcomes by variable

	Variable	Mexico	Spain and Portugal
IV I	Exchange rate regime in the RO	Floated exchange rate	Fixed exchange rate—currency band (now: common currency)
IV II	State–market relationship	Neoliberal	Regulatory/coordinating
IV III	Existence of a dominating economy in the region	Yes	No
EV	Domestic, economic effects of RO	Trade integration: high; business cycle synchronization: medium	Trade integration: high; business cycle synchronization: high
DV	Monetary policies changes on domestic level	Yes	Yes

Source: Author.

Table 13.2 summarizes the outcomes of this comparison. It shows that, as previously assumed, Mexico and its European counterparts vary on the three independent variables (exchange rate regime in the regional organization, state–market relationship, and existence of a dominating economy in the region). However, there was similarity in regard to the domestic effects. All countries showed increased trade integration and subsequently increased business cycle synchronization.

As the outcome was also similar, the chapter concludes that a relation between joining a regional organization and having the need to harmonize monetary policy afterwards is validated for the investigated cases. Generally, the difference seems to be that changes in the European cases have been intended and were driven by political and institutional spillovers, whereas in the NAFTA case, the monetary policy harmonization in Mexico seems to be an unintended product of functional spillovers. Although the results were gained by qualitative analysis, and are thus subject to a certain extent of subjectivity and fuzziness, the overall tendency suggests a relation between joining a regional organization, and having the need to harmonize monetary policy ex post.

Furthermore, the hypothesis can be accepted for further comparisons in other regions and other time frames. It can be expected that other regions will also show tendencies of monetary harmonization if they participate and integrate economically in regional organizations. In particular, the ASEAN (+3) cases will be interesting in that regard when they start to seriously integrate economically with their neighbors. Nevertheless, Lorca-Susino (2010) suggested that the potential negative integration effects of the current economic crisis and financial turmoil in the euro-zone should be reconsidered when focusing on monetary regionalism. High adjustment costs due to persisting macroeconomic imbalances between the lead economies (such as Germany, Finland and France) and the so-called PIIGS countries (Portugal, Italy, Ireland, Greece and Spain) could result in a rebound of economic (and political) nationalism. Thus, financial crises might serve both as triggers for more integration and cooperation (see Chapter 4, this volume) as well as disintegration and less cooperation.

References

Afonso, A. and Furceri, D. 2007. *Sectoral Business Cycle Synchronization in the European Union*. ISEG Department of Economics Working Paper WP 02/2007/DE/UECE.
Ayuso, J. and Escrivá, J. L. 1998. Trends in the Monetary Policy Strategy in Spain, in *Monetary Policy and Inflation in Spain*, edited by J. L. M. de Molina, J. Vinals and F. Gutiérres. Madrid: Banco de Espana, 131–158.
Banco de Espana. 2010a. *Economic Indicators*. [Online]. Available at: www.bde.es/infoest/indecoe.htm [accessed: September 20, 2010].
Banco de Espana. 2010b. *The Eurosystem*. [Online]. Available at: www.bde.es/webbde/en/secciones/eurosist/eurosist.html [accessed: September 20, 2010].
Banco de Mexico. 2010. *Monetary Policy and Inflation*. [Online]. Available at: www.banxico.org.mx/politica-monetaria-e-inflacion/monetary-policy-and-inflation.html [accessed: September 16, 2010].
Banco de Portugal. 2010. *Brief History of the Banco de Portugal*. [Online]. Available at: www.bportugal.pt/en-US/OBancoeoEurosistema/Historia/Pages/default.aspx [accessed: March 4, 2011].
Bayoume, T. and Eichengreen, B. 1994. *One Money or Many: Analyzing the Prospects for Monetary Unification in Various Parts of the World*. Princeton Studies in International Finance No. 76, September. Princeton, NJ, Princeton University.
Becker, U. 2007. Open Systemness and Contested Reference Frames and Change: A Reformulation of the Varieties of Capitalism Theory. *Socio-Economic Review*, 5(2), 261–286.
Blanchard, O. and Illing, G. 2006. *Makroökonomie*. München: Pearson Studium.
Blecker, R. A. 2009. External Shocks, Structural Change, and Economic Growth in Mexico, 1979–2007. *World Development*, 37(7), 1274–1284.
Böwer, U. and Guillemineau, C. 2006. *Determinants of Business Cycle Synchronization Across Euro Area Countries*. ECB Working Papers No. 587. Frankfurt a.M., European Central Bank.
Coughlin, C. C. and Wall, H. J. 2003. NAFTA and the Changing Pattern of State Exports. *Papers in Regional Science*, 82(4), 427–450.

Courchene, T. J. and Harris, R. G. 2000. North American Monetary Union: Analytical Principles and Operational Guidelines. *North American Journal of Economics and Finance*, 11(1), 3–18.

Donelly, S. 2004. *Reshaping Economic and Monetary Union: Membership Rules and Budget Policies in Germany, France and Spain*. Manchester: Manchester University Press.

Duina, F. 2006. *The Social Construction of Free Trade: The European Union, NAFTA and Mercosur.* Oxford and Princeton: Princeton University Press.

Eurostat. 2010. *Long GDP Series for Historic EU Totals*. [Online]. Available at: http://epp.eurostat.ec.europa.eu/portal/page/portal/eurostat/home [accessed: September 16, 2010].

Floyd, J. E. 2010. *Interest Rates, Exchange Rates and World Monetary Policy*. Berlin and Heidelberg: Springer.

Fritz, B. 2006. So Far from God and So Close to the US Dollar: Contrasting Approaches of Monetary Coordination in Latin America, in *New Issues in Regional Monetary Coordination: Understanding North-South and South-South Arrangements*, edited by B. Fritz and M. Metzger. London: Palgrave Macmillan, 126–146.

Fritz, B. and Metzger, M. 2006. Monetary Coordination Involving Developing Countries: The Need for a New Conceptual Framework, in *New Issues in Regional Monetary Coordination: Understanding North-South and South-South Arrangements*, edited by B. Fritz and M. Metzger. London: Palgrave Macmillan, 3–25.

Galy, M. 1993. Opening Up of the Spanish Economy in the Context of EC Integration, in *Spain: Converging with the European Community*, edited by M. Galy, G. Pastor and T. Pujol. Washington, DC: IMF, 2–12.

Gruben, W. C. and Koo, J. 2006. Does NAFTA Move North America towards a Common Currency Area?, in *Monetary Integration and Dollarization: No Panacea*, edited by M. Vernengo. Cheltenham: Edward Elgar, 79–92.

Hall, P. A. and Gingerich, D. W. 2001. Varieties of Capitalism and Institutional Complementarities in the Political Economy: An Empirical Analysis, in *Debating Varieties of Capitalism: A Reader*, edited by B. Hancké. Oxford: Oxford University Press, 135–179.

Hall, P. A. and Soskice, D. 2001. An Introduction to Varieties of Capitalism, in *Varieties of Capitalism: The Institutional Foundations of Comparative Advantage*, edited by P. Hall and D. Soskice. Oxford: Oxford University Press, 1–68.

Hillberry, R. H. and McDaniel, C. A. 2002. *A Decomposition of North American Trade Growth since NAFTA*. US International Trade Commission Working Paper 2002-12-A. Washington, DC.

Hufbauer, G. C. and Schott, J. J. 2005. *NAFTA Revisited: Achievements and Challenges*. Washington, DC: Institute for International Economics.

King, G., Keohane, R. O. and Verba, S. 1994. *Designing Social Inquiry: Scientific Inference in Qualitative Research*. Princeton: Princeton University Press.

Kose, M. A., Meredith, G. M. and Towe, C. M. 2004. *How Has NAFTA Affected the Mexican Economy?* IMF Working Paper WP/04/59. Washington, DC, IMF.

Lorca-Susino, M. 2010. *The Euro in the 21st Century: Economic Crisis and Financial Uproar*. Farnham: Ashgate.

Lucio, S. E. I. 1999. The Effect of NAFTA on the Entry of Foreign Banks in Mexico and in the United States, in *Banking in North America: NAFTA and Beyond*, edited by J. Haar and K. Dandapani. Oxford: Elsevier Science, 183–195.

Makler, H. M. 1999. Regional Integration and Trends in Financial Services, in *Banking in North America. NAFTA and Beyond*, edited by J. Haar and K. Dandapani. Oxford: Elsevier Science, 12–31.

Montoya, L. A. and de Haan, J. 2007. *Regional Busines Cycle Synchronization in Europe*. Bruges European Economic Research Papers No. 11, June 2007. Bruges.

Mundell, R. A. 1961. A Theory of Optimum Currency Areas. *The American Economic Review*, 51(4), 657–665.

NAFTA. 1993. *North American Free Trade Agreement*. Mexico City, Ottawa and Washington, DC.

Pacheco-Lopez, P. 2005. The Impact of Trade Liberalisation on Exports, Imports, the Balance of Payments and Growth: The Case of Mexico. *Journal of Post Keynesian Economics*, 27(4), 595–619.

Pastor, R. A. 2002. NAFTA Is Not Enough: Steps toward a North American Community, in *The Future of North American Integration: Beyond NAFTA*, edited by P. Hakim and R. E. Litan. Washington DC: Brookings Institution Press, 87–117.

Reyes-Heroles, J. F. 2004. North American Integration: A Spontaneous Process or a Driven Enterprise?, in *NAFTA's Impact on North America*, edited by S. Weintraub. Washington, DC: Center for Strategic and International Studies, 391–410.

Rose, A. K. and Stanley, S. D. 2005. A Meta-Analysis of the Effect of Common Currencies on International Trade. *Journal of Economic Surveys*, 19(3), 347–365.

Scheerer, G. 2004. *Zehn Jahre NAFTA*. SWP Diskussionspapier der FG 4, October 2004. Berlin, SWP.

Scheller, H. K. 2006. *The European Central Bank: History, Role and Functions*. Frankfurt/Main: European Central Bank.

Schmidt-Hebbel, K. and Werner, A. 2002. *Inflation Targeting in Brazil, Chile,and Mexico: Performance, Credibility, and the Exchange Rate*. Central Bank of Chile Working Papers Working Paper No. 171. Santiago de Chile, Central Bank of Chile.

Schneider, B. R. 2009. Hierarchical Market Economies and Varieties of Capitalism in Latin America. *Journal of Latin American Studies*, 41(3), 533–575.

Schrank, A. 2009. American Political Economy: Varieties of Capitalism or Fiscal Sociology? *Economy and Society*, 38(1), 53–61.

Shepsle, K. A. 2006. Rational Choice Institutionalism, in *Oxford Handbook of Political Institutions*, edited by R. A. W. Rhodes, S. A. Binder and B. A. Rockman. Cambridge, MA: Harvard University Press, 23–38.

Vernengo, M. 2006a. From Capital Controls to Dollarization: American Hegemony and the US Dollar, in *Monetary Integration and Dollarization: No Panacea*, edited by M. Vernengo. Cheltenham: Edward Elgar, 245–258.

Vernengo, M. 2006b. Monetary Arrangements in a Globalizing World: An Introduction, in *Monetary Integration and Dollarization: No Panacea*, edited by M. Vernengo. Cheltenham: Edward Elgar, 1–9.

Weintraub, S. 2004. Trade, Investment, and Economic Growth, in *NAFTA's Impact on North America*, edited by S. Weintraub. Washington, DC: Center for Strategic and International Studies.

Zamora, S. 1997. Allocating Legislative Competence in the Americas: The Early Experience under NAFTA and the Challenge of Hemispheric Integration. *Houston Journal of International Law*, 19, 53–71.

PART 6
Conclusion

Chapter 14
Do All Roads Lead to Regionalism?

Tanja A. Börzel

Introduction

After the end of the Cold War, students of International Relations observed an expansion of inter-state activities at the regional level. Regional and sub-regional groupings appeared to gain momentum as the way in which countries cooperate and should cooperate to pursue peace, stability, wealth and social justice. The surge and resurgence of regionalism has triggered the proliferation of concepts and approaches. There is new and old regionalism, regionalism in its first, second and third generation; economic, monetary, security and cultural regionalism, state regionalism, shadow regionalism; cross-, inter-, trans- and multi-regionalism; pure and hybrid regionalism; offensive, extroverted, open or neoliberal as opposed to defensive, introverted, closed, resistance, regulatory and developmental regionalism; lower level and higher level regionalism; North, South and North–South regionalism; informal and institutional regionalism – just to name a few of the labels the literature has come up with to account for the new trend in International Relations.

The concept of regionalism is as diverse as its object of study. There is no commonly accepted definition of what a *region* is (see Sbragia 2008). Most would agree that a region implies some "geographical proximity and contiguity" (Hurrell 1995: 353), and mutual interdependence (Nye 1965: vii). Some would add a certain degree of cultural homogeneity (Russett 1967), sense of community (Deutsch et al. 1957) or "regionness" (Hettne and Soderbaum 2000). *Regionalism*, then, refers to processes and structures of region-building in terms of closer economic, political, security and socio-cultural linkages between states and societies that are geographically proximate.

This volume adopts a rather narrow understanding of regionalism as processes and structures of state-led regionalism with a focus on the delegation of policies and political authority to regional institutions. The focus on what some would perceive as "old regionalism" allows the volume to extend existing roads into hardly explored territory as well as to build some new roads in already charted land.

Exploring *Terra Incognita*

New and Old Regionalism

Research on regionalism used to concentrate on the European Community/European Union as a long-standing pathfinder in regional integration. The *New Regionalism* literature, which criticizes the Euro-centrism of integration research and questions its usefulness in studying regionalism, which takes many different forms, is less state-driven and results from a more spontaneous and endogenous process, which involves a variety of non-state actors organized in formal and informal networks (Farrell et al. 2005, Hettne et al. 1999, Söderbaum and Shaw 2003). However, contributions to this volume show that we do find state-led regionalism in all parts of the world, including those that have been neglected by both the "old" and "new" regionalism literature. The area of the former Soviet Union alone features more than three dozen regional initiatives based on intergovernmental negotiations and treaties (Chapter 2, this volume). The "alphabet soup" of post-Soviet regionalism shows great similarities with the "Spaghetti Bowl" regionalism in Africa.

New regional initiatives have proliferated after the end of the Cold War. Yet, many of them remain shallow. The chapters in this volume remind us that the "new urge to merge" (Schulz et al. 2001: 1) is not only a matter of increasing numbers as the literature on International Political Economy likes to argue (see Choi and Caporaso 2002, Hancock 2009: 17–25). The large bulk of new regional initiatives are regional trade agreements, many of which are still not in force, do not have more than two members, which are in the majority of cases not contiguous either, and are Preferential Trade Agreements (PTA) or Free Trade Agreements (FTA) (see Börzel 2012). The number of regional organizations has not surged (Chapter 1, this volume). Whether the (quantitative) increase in PTA and FTA indicates a (qualitative) shift away from "introverted, defensive regional blocs" toward innovative and open forms of regionalism that are more compatible with the global trade regime remains an open question (Bhagwati 2008, Milner 1992).

While shallow regionalism has been spreading, we also see a deepening and widening of existing forms that started in some cases well before the 1990s. Long-standing regional organizations have experienced the delegation of more authority and new policy competencies as well as the admission of new members. With the creation of the Asian Free Trade Area, the Association of Southeast Asian Nations (ASEAN) established for the first time a dispute-settlement procedure breaking with the ASEAN way of informal and consensus-based institutions (Chapters 5 and 6, this volume). The ASEAN Charter provides another major step toward both more political and more legalized integration (Chapters 9 and 12, this volume). The League of Arab States (LAS), which has shared the reluctance of ASEAN to delegate political authority to regional institutions, has become more forthcoming and is planning institutional changes that bear some striking similarities with some changes the Economic Community of West African States (ECOWAS) introduced (Chapter 7, this volume). Similar to MERCOSUR (Chapter 11, this volume) and ASEAN (Chapter 12, this volume), ECOWAS committed its members to democracy and seems to have outpaced the EU with its power to use military coercion in order to safeguard democracy (Chapter 10, this volume).

Persisting Diversity or Emerging Similarity?

Next to a trend toward the delegation of new policy competencies and more political authority, regional organizations have developed some interesting similarities despite the differences in their original goals and institutional set-up. Not only do LAS, ASEAN, ECOWAS and MERCOSUR aspire to deeper forms of trade and monetary integration, for instance by seeking to turn their free trade area into a customs union or a common market and to harmonize their monetary policies (Chapter 13, this volume). They have also taken on new tasks in the realm of external and internal security, dealing with issues, such as nuclear non-proliferation, disarmament, territorial disputes, domestic political stability, migration, terrorism or human trafficking. Even the North American Free Trade Area (NAFTA) has developed some, albeit rudimentary, forms of security cooperation (terrorism, drugs and migration) in the aftermath of September 11, 2001.

States are still reluctant to delegate political authority to regional organizations. But they have agreed to formalize decision-making procedures, opening them for majority decisions, and to set up enhanced dispute-settlement procedures, which may take the form of courts or tribunals. While legislative authority firmly remains in the hands of national governments, the powers of executive bodies have been strengthened, and in some cases, parliamentary assemblies with consultative status have been created (Chapters 4, 6, 7 and 12, this volume).

While regional institutions do not converge toward a particular model, contributions to this volume show that they have developed increasing similarities, with regard to the delegation of new policy competencies as well as of executive and adjudicative authority. At the same time, important differences remain. The member states of MERCOSUR, ASEAN and the LAS have not been willing to match the delegation of political authority witnessed in the EU or ECOWAS (Chapters 4, 5, 7 and 9, this volume). And the judicial authority of the North American Free Trade Area (NAFTA) with regard to dispute settlement is not matched by any legislative and or executive authority (Chapters 5 and 6, this volume).

Overall, the volume finds both increasing similarities and persisting differences among regional organizations. They only become visible through the comparison of regional initiatives across time and space. The contributions testify to the fruitfulness of comparing such different cases as the LAS and ECOWAS (Chapter 7, this volume) or NAFTA and ASEAN (Chapters 5 and 6, this volume). Such cross-regional comparisons reveal new and important insights on the growth, evolution and changes of regional organizations. As long as they focus on specific aspects rather than regional organizations as a whole, they steer clear of comparing apples and oranges.

Re-charting *Terra Cognita*

Analyzing and comparing regional organizations across the globe does not only break new empirical ground. It also sheds new light on old questions. The volume focuses on state-driven forms of regionalism rather than more spontaneous and endogenous processes, which involve a variety of non-state actors organized in formal and informal networks (for an approach including the latter see Shaw et al. 2011). How relevant these "new" forms of regionalism are and to what extent existing theories are adequate to capture them is first of all an empirical question (see Hettne 2005: 543, Hettne and Soderbaum 2000, 2008, Schulz et al. 2001: 2).[1] However, the comparative analysis of regional organizations outside Europe confirms as well as challenges theories of "old" regionalism. The contributions to this volume systematically probe the extent to which prominent theories travel from Europe to other regions of the world that do not share the same level of economic development and interdependence and are more heterogeneous with regard to their political regimes than the states in the Northern hemisphere.

Old Theories and New Puzzles

It is not only the economy, stupid! The International Political Economy and the European Integration literature offer convincing arguments why states in Europe and North America set up regional institutions in the first place. A key driver of state-led regionalism is economic interdependence. Regional institutions allow to realize welfare-enhancing effects, such as reduced transaction costs, economies of scale, technological innovation due to greater competition, more foreign direct investments, and greater economic and political weight in international markets and institutions (see Hancock 2009: 25–29, Mattli 1999b: 46–47). Since global markets entail increased trans-border mobility and economic linkages, trade issues are less cumbersome to deal with at the regional than at the multilateral level (Schirm 2002). Coping with negative externalities (for example diversions of trade and investment) provides another rationale to pursue economic regionalism. States may either seek membership in regional institutions generating the external effects as many European countries have done in the case of the EU and some of the South American countries do with NAFTA. Or they create their own regional group. NAFTA can be interpreted as the US reaction to the fortification of the Single European Market and the emerging economic regionalism in Asia (Chapter 13, this volume). In a similar vein, the decision in 1992 to complement the ASEAN security community with an ASEAN free trade area is partly explained by concerns over the global positioning of regional markets vis-à-vis NAFTA and the Single European Market (Chapters 5 and 6, this volume). The attraction of foreign direct investment and gains in international bargaining power rather than

---

1   For a suggestion on how to overcome the "false divide" see Warleigh-Lack (2006, Warleigh-Lack et al. 2011).

increasing intra-regional trade also explain why Cambodia, Laos, Myanmar and Vietnam sought to join ASEAN (Chapter 3, this volume).

Yet, there is more to regionalism than economic factors. The contributions to this volume show that power is crucial in explaining the commitment of states to regional organizations. Setting up regional institutions to overcome market failures and collective action problems involves costs, too, and may create a(nother) collective action problem. A rationalist solution is hegemonic leadership. Powerful states often act as "regional paymaster, easing distributional tensions and thus smoothing the path of integration" (Mattli 1999a: 56, see Gilpin 1987: 87–90, Yarbrough and Yarbrough 1992). Yet, they do so for different reasons. Brazil has championed MERCOSUR to establish itself as a regional power and to contain US influence in Latin America (Chapter 4, this volume). Likewise, the United States has acted as a regional hegemon for NAFTA to counterbalance the Single European Market (Clarkson 2008). And Russia seeks to consolidate its influence in its "near abroad" by forming and re-forming regional organizations (Chapter 2, this volume). While using regionalism to establish and affirm their regional hegemony, powerful states are reluctant to bind themselves by regional institutions. The intergovernmental nature of MERCOSUR and NAFTA and their limited scope of regional integration are largely explained by the unwillingness of Brazil and the United States to delegate authority to regional institutions (Chapters 4 and 5, this volume). At the same time, the United States has agreed to a highly legalized and inflexible agreement that does not leave much levy to the member states. This degree of self-binding goes far beyond what other regional powers have committed to and poses a puzzle to power-based approaches. Powerful states do not always get what they want as the case of Nigeria in ECOWAS seems to suggest (Chapter 10, this volume). Brazil has to compromise with Argentina since the United States provides an exit option for the latter. Interpresidentialism plays a key role in the functioning of MERCOSUR (Chapter 4, this volume). Leadership by government diplomacy provides a functional equivalent for regional institutions, not only in MERCOSUR but also in ASEAN through the so-called ASEAN way (Chapter 5, this volume). Finally, power-based theories of regionalism have little on offer to explain the differential commitment of small states. Paraguay, Uruguay, Mexico and Canada may seek to bind their regional hegemon (Chapters 4, 5 and 13, this volume). However, by joining MERCOSUR and NAFTA, respectively, they also become (even) more vulnerable to its dominance. Moreover, why is it that some former Soviet republics decided to bandwagon with Russia and Uzbekistan while others engaged in attempts to counterbalance their regional dominance (Chapter 2, this volume)?

Opening the black box of the state and taking into account differences in domestic structures might be one way of filling the gap interest- and power-based approaches face in explaining why states form, develop, join and leave regional organizations. Democracy and market economy provide important context conditions many theories of regionalism take for granted because of their focus on the Northern hemisphere where there is not much variation. The contributions to this volume on Latin America and Africa confirm that democratic regimes are more likely to commit to regional institutions (Chapters 8 and 11, this volume), particularly if they allow to lock-in domestic reforms consolidating and promoting democracy (Pevehouse 2005, Ribeiro Hoffmann and van der Vleuten 2007). Like their European counterparts, African, Latin American, Arab and Asian leaders have supported regionalism as a source of domestic power, not only with regard to safeguarding democratic reforms (Barnett and Solingen 2007, Herbst 2007, Morales 2002, Nesadurai 2008, Okolo 1985).

Weak states are particularly inclined to engage in "regime-boosting regionalism" (Söderbaum 2004) because they are more dependent on economic growth to forge domestic stability, tackle societal problems, and strengthen their international standing in terms of bargaining power and legitimacy (Chapter 3, this volume). Moreover, non-state actors can more easily circumvent their governments in seeking transnational exchange (Bach 2005). Yet, states must not be too weak either – political instability can be a major obstacle to regionalism (Edi 2007). Furthermore the lack of state capacity creates serious issues for the effectiveness of regional organizations when it comes to compliance with regional norms and rules (Chapter 9, this volume). Neo-patrimonialism is equally ambivalent. While regional organizations provide governments with additional perks for buying-off the loyalty of their clients (Chapter 8, this volume), regionalism can also curb resources, for instance by decreasing tariff revenues (Allison 2008, Collins 2009).

From why to how: explaining institutional design Theories of regionalism provide a whole range of explanatory factors for the genesis and growth of regional organizations. They are less equipped to account for the differential outcomes and (changes in) institutional designs we find across different regions. Why have the member states of ASEAN opted for a low level of precision and obligation that leaves them high flexibility to further develop their regional project, while the United States, Canada and Mexico concluded a "complete contract" (Cooley and Spruyt 2009), which does not preview any further delegation of policies and political authority to NAFTA (Chapter 5, this volume)? Different types of uncertainties might provide part of the explanation but have difficulties in accounting for the different degrees of legalization and flexibility found in MERCOSUR and ECOWAS where smaller countries also have an interest in binding the regional hegemon (Chapters 4, 7 and 10, this volume). Nor do uncertainties explain why the members of ECOWAS delegated more political authority to regional institutions than the EU member states.

The choice of regional institutions may be rational but it is not necessarily driven by economic and power considerations only. Market or problem pressures increase the demand for (more) regional institutions. But even if certain institutions effectively serve specific functions and help solve similar problems, states always have choices. Increases in intra-regional trade account for the creation of dispute settlement mechanisms (DSM) in NAFTA but fail to explain why ASEAN established DSM in the absence of substantial intra-regional trade when AFTA was established and the infrequent use of the (enhanced) DSM when intra-regional trade increased (Chapter 6, this volume). While functional demand and power-driven supply factors already have difficulties in accounting for institutional variation across time and space, they have even less to say about why such diverse regional organizations as LAS and ECOWAS appear to develop similar institutions (Chapter 7, this volume).

The chapters dealing with questions of institutional design show that the supply of regional institutions can stem from other factors than regional hegemons. Regions or international actors actively promote or passively provide blueprints for region-building. "Pax Americana" and "Pax Europaea" are two "global scripts" (Meyer et al. 1992) on regionalism. The first one is based on regional trade cooperation promoted by the United States and international organizations, including the World Trade Organization, the World Bank and the International Monetary Fund (Grugel 2004). The second is advocated by the EU, striving for regional integration, which is broader in scope and infringes more strongly on the sovereignty of states (Börzel and Risse 2009). Regional organizations that struggle to become more effective may look to other organizations that are considered as success cases for policies and rules that effectively solved similar problems and are transferable into their context (Dolowitz and Marsh 2000, Meyer and Rowan 1977). Next to lesson-drawing, regions may also emulate others for normative reasons, to increase their legitimization (symbolic imitation; see Polillo and Guillén 2005) or to simply imitate their behavior because its appropriateness is taken for granted (mimicry; see Haveman 1993, Meyer and Rowan 1977). Seeking international legitimacy and signaling commitment to trade liberalization motivated ASEAN to set up a DSM that has been hardly used so far (Chapter 6, this volume). Emulation also might be driving the recent deepening and broadening of ASEAN, whose new charter bears some striking resemblances to EU institutions (Jetschke 2010, Katsumata 2009). Likewise, ECOWAS and LAS might be following a global script that entails the establishment of certain regional institutions and for which, at least in the case of ECOWAS, the EU provides a reference model (Chapter 7, this volume). With the establishment of the euro, the EU has become an example to follow for countries in Latin America, Africa and Asia, which may defy supranationalism but see a common currency as an anchor of regional stability (Chapter 13, this volume, Lorca-Susino 2010). Whether the EU will continue to inspire other regions to seek economic and monetary integration will depend on how well the EU handles the current financial crisis. Will the EU deepen integration and develop common economic and fiscal policies or will its member states relapse in defensive nationalism as they did during the oil crisis in the early 1970s?

New Questions and New Puzzles

When regionalism hits home: from policy harmonization ... Questions about the genesis and growth of regional organizations, and, more recently, their institutional design have dominated research on (comparative) regionalism. The domestic impact of regionalism is far less explored. Second image reversed approaches in IR, which study the impact of the international system upon domestic politics (Gourevitch 1978), have made little headway in comparative regionalism. Economists have analyzed the economic effects of regional free trade agreements on trade and investment flows, economic growth, poverty and social inequality (Musila 2005, Preusse 2004, Weintraub 2004). Their impact on domestic policies, institutions and political processes has remained largely ignored. Rather, studies have looked for policy harmonization in different sectors for individual countries, particularly in the case of NAFTA. These can also entail spillover effects on policies that are not subject to the free trade agreement (Chapter 13, this volume).

Similar to international institutions, such as the World Bank or the International Monetary Fund, regional organizations can use conditionality to promote domestic structural change by promising or granting additional benefits, such as financial and technical assistance, a loan, debt relief, or conditional membership in an organization. Or they incur costs through economic and diplomatic sanctions. "Reinforcement through reward" (Schimmelfennig and Sedelmeier 2006) or "correction through punishment" offer the opportunity for a redistribution of resources among domestic actors, empowering those who push for domestic change. Alternatively, regional organizations can resort to political dialogue and other instruments of socialization, which seek to change actors' behaviour through persuasion and learning, often with the help of change agents or entrepreneurs (Checkel 2005, Finnemore 1993, Finnemore and Sikkink 1998, Kelley 2004).

... to structural change The workings of the causal pathways through which regional organizations may impact upon the domestic structures of their members have so far only been systematically explored for the case of the EU (Börzel and Risse 2003, Cowles et al. 2001, Schimmelfennig and Sedelmeier 2005). The European Union certainly is a most likely case in this regard. Not only are EU institutions strong and its policies comprehensive. Yet, MERCOSUR, ECOWAS, the African Union or ASEAN have increasingly defined institutional requirements for "good governance" which their members have to respect. Next to human rights, the rule of law, democracy and the fight against corruption form part of the governance package many regional organizations seek to promote.

Contributions to this volume show that even regional organizations, whose members are not all consolidated democracies, commit their members to democratic norms and are at times even equipped with coercive powers to safeguard democracy (Chapter 10, this volume). Governments of young democracies can bind themselves and their successors to political liberalization and democratic norms by external commitment (Mansfield and Pevehouse 2006, Moravcsik and Vachudova 2003, Pevehouse 2005: 37). Democracies do not only show greater commitment to regional organizations (Chapter 8, this volume). Joining a democratic regional organization significantly decreases the probability of democratic breakdown (Chapter 11, this volume), even though it may require a regional hegemon and/or international and domestic pressure to make the regional organization actively intervene (Chapter 10, this volume).

The active engagement of ECOWAS and, to a lesser extent, MERCOSUR, still appears to be the exception rather than the rule. Yet, the case of ASEAN demonstrates that regional organizations can also have a less direct and probably more long-term effect, establishing a political opportunity structure that provides civil society actors with rights, money and networks and entrapping their member states in their commitment to human rights and democracy (Chapter 12, this volume). These findings show that processes of "differential empowerment" found in the EU and NAFTA (Aspinwall 2009) also work in other regions.

Conclusion

This volume clearly demonstrates that regionalism has gained prominence in the twenty-first century, not only as an "emerging regional architecture of world politics" (Acharya and Johnston 2007), but also as a field of study. The debate on the rise of regionalism shows that we need to have a clear understanding of what we mean by regionalism and how we measure it. More than 40 years ago, Joseph Nye complained that "integration theorists have talked past each other" using different concepts and measurements (Nye 1968: 855). His criticism still holds today – there is a Babylonian variety of definitions and analytical frameworks and only a few students of regionalism have engaged in a systematic comparison of different forms around the globe. In some ways, research on old regionalism was more comparative than many studies of new regionalism (see for instance Etzioni 1965, Haas and Schmitter 1964, Nye 1970, 1971).

The contributions to this volume underscore the necessity for and fruitfulness of comparing regions across time and space. Systematically exploring the genesis, growth, institutional design and effectiveness of regional organizations puts mainstream approaches to a serious test and the debate about new regionalism into perspective. There are many roads to regionalism and not all of them lead to new forms of regionalism. Regions outside Europe leave much to be explored with regard to why states build, develop, join and leave regional organizations. Little do we know about their effects both on member states and the architecture of world politics. While there is not one dominant form, regionalism has become part of a global governance script, in which regional organizations do not only feature as an effective and legitimate way to foster peace and prosperity but which sees "regions as the fundamental, even driving force of world politics" (Fawn 2009).

References

Acharya, A. and Johnston, A. I. (eds). 2007. *Crafting Cooperation. Regional International Institutions in Comparative Perspective.* Cambridge: Cambridge University Press.

Allison, R. 2008. Virtual Regionalism, Regional Structures and Regime Security in Central Asia. *Central Asian Survey*, 27(2), 185–202.

Aspinwall, M. 2009. NAFTA-Ization: Regionalization and Domestic Political Adjustment in the North American Economic Area. *Journal of Common Market Studies*, 47(1), 1–24.

Bach, D. C. 2005. The Global Politics of Regionalism: Africa, in *Global Politics of Regionalism. Theory and Practice*, edited by M. Farrel, B. Hettne and L. Van Langenhove. London and Ann Arbor: Pluto Press, 171–186.

Barnett, M. N. and Solingen, E. 2007. Designed to Fail or Failure to Design? The Origins and Legacy of the Arab League, in *Crafting Cooperation. Regional International Institutions in Comparative Perspective*, edited by A. Acharya and A. I. Johnston. Cambridge: Cambridge University Press, 180–220.

Bhagwati, J. 2008. *Termites in the Trading System. How Preferential Agreements Undermine Free Trade.* New York: Oxford University Press.

Börzel, T. A. 2012. Comparative Regionalism: European Integration and Beyond, in *Handbook of International Relations*, edited by W. Carlsnaes, T. Risse and B. A. Simmons. London: Sage.

Börzel, T. A. and Risse, T. 2003. Conceptualising the Domestic Impact of Europe, in *The Politics of Europeanisation*, edited by K. Featherstone and C. Radaelli. Oxford: Oxford University Press, 55–78.

Börzel, T. A. and Risse, T. 2009. *The Diffusion of (Inter-)Regionalism. The EU as a Model of Regional Integration.* KFG Working Papers. Research College "The Transformative Power of Europe." Freie Universität Berlin, (7).

Checkel, J. T. 2005. International Institutions and Socialization in Europe: Introduction and Framework. *International Organization*, 59(4), 801–826.

Choi, Y. J. and Caporaso, J. A. 2002. Comparative Regional Integration, in *Handbook of International Relations*, edited by W. Carlsnaes, T. Risse and B. A. Simmons. London: Sage, 480–499.

Clarkson, S. 2008. *Does North America Exist? Governing the Continent After NAFTA and 9/11.* Toronto: University of Toronto Press.

Collins, K. 2009. Economic and Security Regionalism among Patrimonial Authoritarian Regimes. *Europe Asia Studies*, 61(2), 249–281.

Cooley, A. and Spruyt, H. (eds). 2009. *Contracting States. Sovereign Transfer in International Relations.* Princeton: Princeton University Press.

Cowles, M. G., Caporaso, J. A. and Risse, T. (eds). 2001. *Transforming Europe. Europeanization and Domestic Change.* Ithaca: Cornell University Press.

Deutsch, K. W., Burrell, S. A. and Kann, R. A. 1957. *Political Community and the North Atlantic Area: International Organization in the Light of Historical Experience.* Princeton: Princeton University Press.

Dolowitz, D. P. and Marsh, D. 2000. Learning from Abroad: The Role of Policy Transfer in Contemporary Policy-Making. *Governance*, 13(1), 5–24.

Edi, E. M. 2007. *Globalization and Politics in the ECOWAS Countries*. Durham, NC: Carolina Academic Press.

Etzioni, A. 1965. *Political Unification: A Comparative Study of Leaders and Forces*. New York: Holt, Rinehart & Winston.

Farrell, M., Hettne, B. and Van Langenhove, L. (eds). 2005. *Global Politics of Regionalism: Theory and Practice*. London and Ann Arbor: Pluto Press.

Fawn, R. 2009. "Regions" and Their Study: Wherefrom, What For and Whereto? *Review of International Studies*, 35(S1), 5–34.

Finnemore, M. 1993. International Organization as Teachers of Norms: The United Nations Educational, Scientific, and Cultural Organization and Science Policy. *International Organization*, 47(4), 565–597.

Finnemore, M. and Sikkink, K. 1998. International Norm Dynamics and Political Change. *International Organization*, 52(4), 887–917.

Gilpin, R. 1987. *The Political Economy of International Relations*. Princeton: Princeton University Press.

Gourevitch, P. 1978. The Second Image Reversed: The International Sources of Domestic Politics. *International Organization*, 32(4), 881–912.

Grugel, J. B. 2004. New Regionalism and Modes of Governance. Comparing US and EU Strategies in Latin America. *European Journal of International Relations*, 10(4), 602–626.

Haas, E. B. and Schmitter, P. C. 1964. Economics and Differential Patterns of Political Integration: Projections about Unity in Latin America. *International Organization*, 18(4), 705–737.

Hancock, K. J. 2009. *Regional Integration. Choosing Plutocracy*. Houndmills: Palgrave Macmillan.

Haveman, H. A. 1993. Follow the Leader: Mimetic Isomorphism and Entry Into New Markets. *Administrative Science Quaterly*, 38(4), 593–627.

Herbst, J. 2007. Crafting Regional Cooperation in Africa, in *Crafting Cooperation. Regional International Institutions in Comparative Perspective*, edited by A. Acharya and A. I. Johnston. Cambridge: Cambridge University Press, 129–144.

Hettne, B. 2005. Beyond the "New" Regionalism. *New Political Economy*, 10(4), 543–571.

Hettne, B. and Söderbaum, F. 2000. Theorising the Rise of Regionness. *New Political Economy*, 5(3), 457–473.

Hettne, B. and Söderbaum, F. 2008. The Future of Regionalism, in *Regionalisation and Global Governance: The Taming of Globalization*, edited by A. F. Cooper, C. W. Hughes and P. De Lombaerde. London: Routledge, 61–79.

Hettne, B., Inotai, A. and Sunkel, O. 1999. *Globalism and the New Regionalism*. Basingstoke: Macmillan.

Hurrell, A. 1995. Explaining the Resurgence of Regionalism in World Politics. *Review of International Studies*, 21(4), 545–566.

Jetschke, A. 2010. *Is Regional Integration Contagious? European Integration and Regional Organization in Asia*. KFG Working Papers.

Katsumata, H. 2009. ASEAN and Human Rights: Resisting Western Pressure or Emulating the West? *The Pacific Review*, 22(5), 619–637.

Kelley, J. 2004. International Actors on the Domestic Scene: Membership Conditionality and Socialization by International Institutions. *International Organization*, 58(3), 425–457.

Lorca-Susino, M. 2010. *The Euro in the 21st Century: Economic Crisis and Financial Uproar*. Aldershot: Ashgate.

Mansfield, E. D. and Pevehouse, J. C. 2006. Democratization and International Organizations. *International Organization*, 60(1), 137–167.

Mattli, W. 1999a. Explaining Regional Integration Outcomes. *Journal of European Public Policy*, 6(1), 1–27.

Mattli, W. 1999b. *The Logic of Regional Integration*. Cambridge: Cambridge University Press.

Meyer, J. W. and Rowan, B. 1977. Institutionalized Organizations: Formal Structures as Myth and Ceremony. *American Journal of Sociology*, 83(2), 340–363.

Meyer, J. W., Kamens, D. H., Benavot, A., Cha, Y.-K. and Wong, S.-Y. 1992. *School Knowledge for the Masses: World Models and National Primary Curricular Categories*. Bristol, PA: Falmer Press.

Milner, H. V. 1992. International Theories of Cooperation among Nations: Strengths and Weaknesses. *World Politics*, 44(3), 466–496.

Morales, I. 2002. The Governance of Global Issues through Regionalism: NAFTA as an Interface between Multilateral and North-South Policies. *Journal of Social Science*, 55(1), 27–55.

Moravcsik, A. and Vachudova, M. A. 2003. National Interests, State Power, and EU Enlargement. *East European Politics and Societies*, 17(1), 42–57.

Musila, J. 2005. The Intensity of Trade Creation and Trade Diversion in COMESA, ECCAS and ECOWAS: A Comparative Analysis. *Journal of African Economies*, 14(1), 117–141.

Nesadurai, H. E. S. 2008. The Association of Southeast Asian Nations (ASEAN). *New Political Economy*, 13(2), 225–239.

Nye, J. S. 1965. Patterns and Catalysts in Regional Integration. *International Organization*, 19(4), 870–884.

Nye, J. S. 1968. Comparative Regional Integration: Concept and Measurement. *International Organization*, 22(4), 855–880.

Nye, J. S. 1970. Comparing Common Markets: A Revised Neo-Functionalist Model. *International Organization*, 24(4), 796–835.

Nye, J. S. 1971. *Peace in Parts: Integration and Conflict in Regional Organizations*. Boston: Little, Brown.

Okolo, J. E. 1985. Integrative and Cooperative Regionalism: The Economic Community of West African States. *International Organization*, 39(1), 121–153.

Pevehouse, J. C. 2005. *Democracy from Above: Regional Organizations and Democratization*. Cambridge: Cambridge University Press.

Polillo, S. and Guillén, M. F. 2005. Globalization Pressures and the State: The Worldwide Spread of Central Bank Independence. *American Journal of Sociology*, 110(6), 1764–1802.

Preusse, H. G. 2004. *The New American Regionalism*. Cheltenham: Edward Elgar.

Ribeiro Hoffmann, A. and van der Vleuten, A. (eds). 2007. *Closing or Widening the Gap? Legitimacy and Democracy in Regional Integration Organizations*. Aldershot: Ashgate.

Russett, B. 1967. *International Regions and the International System. A Study in Political Ecology*. Chicago, Rand-MacNally.

Sbragia, A. 2008. Comparative Regionalism: What Might It Be? *Journal of Common Market Studies*, 46(Annual Review), 29–49.

Schimmelfennig, F. and Sedelmeier, U. 2005. *The Europeanization of Central and Eastern Europe*. Ithaca, NY: Cornell University Press.

Schimmelfennig, F. and Sedelmeier, U. 2006. Candidate Countries and Conditionality, in *Europeanization. New Research Agendas*, edited by P. Graziano and M. P. Vink. Houndmills: Palgrave Macmillan, 88–101.

Schirm, S. A. 2002. *Globalization and the New Regionalism. Global Markets, Domestic Politics and Regional Co-operation*. Cambridge: Polity Press.

Schulz, M., Söderbaum, F. and Öjendal, J. 2001. Introduction. A Framework for Understanding Regionalization, in *Regionalization in a Globalizing World. A Comparative Perspective on Forms, Actors and Processes*, edited by M. Schulz, F. Söderbaum and J. Öjendal. London and New York: Zed Books, 1–21.

Shaw, T. M., Grant, J. A. and Cornelisson, S. (eds). 2011. *The Ashgate Research Companion to Regionalisms*. Aldershot: Ashgate.

Söderbaum, F. 2004. *The Political Economy of Regionalism. The Case of Southern Africa*. Basingstoke: Palgrave Macmillan.

Söderbaum, F. and Shaw, T. M. 2003. *Theories of New Regionalism: A Palgrave Reader*. Houndmills: Palgrave Macmillan.

Warleigh-Lack, A. 2006. Towards a Conceptual Framework for Regionalisation: Bridging "New Regionalism" and "Integration Theory." *Review of International Political Economy*, 13(5), 750–771.

Warleigh-Lack, A., Robinson, N. and Rosamond, B. (eds). 2011. *New Regionalism and the European Union: Dialogues, Comparisons and New Research Directions*. London: Routledge.

Weintraub, S. (ed.) 2004. *NAFTA's Impact on North America*. Washington, DC: Center for Strategic and International Studies.

Yarbrough, B. V. and Yarbrough, R. M. 1992. *Cooperation and Governance in International Trade: The Strategic Organizational Approach*. Princeton: Princeton University Press.

Index

accession 5-6
   CLMV 48-56
   Eastern European countries 45-48
   Post-Soviet space 36
   Spain and Portugal 243
   Venezuela 74, 206
anocracy 163-164
      Arab League *see* League of Arab States
ASEAN 48-49, 82, 84-86, 94, 107-112, 160-162, 166, 173, 216-218, 220-229
   Bali Concord II (2003) 82
   Bangkok Declaration (1967) 84
   Charter (2007) 82, 85, 111, 160-162, 216-217, 256
   Cosmetics Directive 170-171
   Dispute Settlement Procedure (DSP) of 108-113, 163, 256, 260
   Economic Community 159-161
   Economic Ministers Meeting (ASEM) 109
   Free Trade Area (AFTA) 52-53, 82, 84-86, 94, 108-110
   Human Rights Body 226-227
   Secretariat 160-162, 223-224
   Senior Economic Officials Meeting (SEOM) 109-110
   Singapore Declaration (1992) 107
   Single Window Initiative 167-169
   Summit 107
   Way 82, 108, 216
autocracy 163-164
Argentina 61, 67-74, 199, 205, 209-210, 259

Brunei 90-93, 95, 168-169, 216, 226
Burma *see* Myanmar

Cambodia 49-56, 161, 165, 216, 226-227
Canada 89, 91, 93, 95-97, 105, 107, 236
Canada-United States Trade Agreement (CUFTA) 82, 236
Central Asian Cooperation Organization (CACO) 27, 29, 32, 34
Central Asian Economic Community (CAEC) 27, 29, 34
Central Asian Economic Union (CAEU) 27, 29, 34
Central Asian Union (CAU) 27, 29
central banks 65, 238-240, 244, 245
China 35, 49-51, 54, 92, 160
civil society (organizations) 142-143, 215-229
CLMV 48-55, 166
   Collective Security Treaty Organization (CSTO) 27, 29, 32, 35
commitment 7-8, 142, 146-155
   democratic 199-211
   implementation of regional 161-166, 172-173
   institutions 60, 67-68, 74
Common Economic Space (CES) 27, 29, 31, 35-36
Commonwealth of Independent States (CIS) 26-37
Côte d'Ivoire 124, 126, 185, 187
compliance 7-8, 84-85, 159-173
   theory 162-164
coup d'état
   definition of 180
   deterrent against 203, 205
   Guinea (1998) 185, 190-192
   in ECOWAS 184
   in MERCOSUR 208-209
   Nigeria (1993) 185-187
   Paraguay (1996, 1999) 206, 209-210

Sierra Leone (1997) 185, 187-190
crisis 141-142
    currency 235, 239-240, 245, 248-249
    democratic 180, 209
    economic 59, 70-73, 207

demand for dispute settlement procedures 101-113
demand for regional integration 6, 47, 51-53, 60, 66, 74
democracy 143-147
    consolidation of 203-205
    crises of 186-194, 208-211
    stability of 190-191
diffusion 7, 111, 125-131
diplomacy 69-74, 226, 259
dispute settlement
    ASEAN 84, 101, 108-111, 113
    ECOWAS 101, 119-120
    LAS 119-120
    mechanism/ procedure 85, 102-103, 260-261
    MERCOSUR 63-64, 68, 101
    NAFTA 85, 105-107, 113
    WTO 101, 109-112

ECOWAS 118-121, 141-143, 179-180
    Conflict Prevention Framework (2008) 190-191
    Declaration of Political Principles (1991) 186
    ECOMOG 189-190
    institutional design 118-121
    Mediation and Security Council 190-191
    Protocol Relating to the Mechanism for Conflict Prevention, Management, Resolution, Peace-Keeping and Security (1999) 190-191
    Protocol on Democracy and Good Governance (2001) 190-191
    Treaty of Cotonou (1993) 122-124, 188
    Treaty of Lagos (1975) 118-121, 146-147
emulation 128-131; *see also* diffusion
enlargement *see* accession
Eurasian Economic Community (EurAsEc) 30, 32-34, 36, 38

European Communities 244-247
European Exchange Rate Mechanism 244-245
European Monetary System 244-245
European Union 46-48, 111-112, 130, 261-263
Europeanization 8-9, 145

flexibility (of institutional design) 6-7, 85-87, 96-97
Foreign Direct Investment 51-55, 111-113
Free Trade Area of the Americas 62-63
Freedom House Index 126-127, 181-182

global script 129-130, 261
government effectiveness (World Bank) 165-166
GUAM 33-35
Guinea 190-192

hegemon
    Brazil as 69
    definition 183
    leadership by 68
    Nigeria as 123-124, 188-190, 192-194
    Russia as 34-35
    US as 259

implementation 148-149, 162-164
Indonesia 169, 172, 225
institutional design 6-7, 63-65, 83-87, 105, 108-109, 260-261
    convergence of 118-121, 129, 130
interdependence (economic) 6, 61-62, 73-74, 102-103, 106-107, 246-247
intergovernmentalism 5, 69-70, 121
interpresidentialism 69-70, 259
intervention 180
    military 187

Laos 49-50, 52-53
leadership *see* hegemon, leadership by
League of Arab States 118-121
    Pact of Arab States (1945) 118-121
    Reform Plan (2004) 124-125
legalization 6-7, 83-84, 181-182, 191
legitimacy 54, 111-112, 129, 202, 206-207

Malamud, Andrés 59, 70; *see also* interpresidentialism
Malaysia 94-95, 225
Mansfield, Edward D. 145-146, 200-201
Mattli, Walter 27, 59-61
member states, heterogeneity of 6-7, 69, 46-47, 143-145, 183-184
MERCOSUR 63-65, 199, 205-206
    Declaration of Las Leñas (1992) 206
    Parliament 64, 68
    Protocol of Brasilia (1991) 63-64, 101
    Protocol of Olivos (2002) 63-64
    Protocol of OuroPreto (1994) 63, 65
    Protocol of Ushuaia (1998) 63, 205-206
    Regional Fund (FOCEM) 69
    Treaty of Asunción (1991) 62-64
Mexico 95-96, 239, 245-248
monetary policy 72-73, 235
    coordination/ integration 235, 238-239
Myanmar 49-55, 228

NAFTA 82-83, 85-86, 103-107, 236-237
    NAAEC 82
    NAALC 82
    Treaty (1994) 105
neofunctionalism 5-6, 38, 235
neo-liberal institutionalism 6, 46, 121, 125
neopatrimonialism 8, 37, 141, 144, 147-148, 155, 260
neo-realism 6, 38, 46
new regionalism *see* regionalism
Nigeria 124, 183, 186-190, 192
non-tariff barriers *see* tariffs

Optimum Currency Area 237

Pevehouse, Jon C. 145, 182-183, 201-203
Philippines 111, 166, 169, 225-227
policy harmonization 240-242, 248, 261-261
Polity IV 143-145, 203-204
Portugal 243-249

ratification 66, 148-154, 162
Rational Design of International Institutions 6, 88, 122
regime type 7, 141-155

region (definition of) 3-4, 81
regional integration 5, 10
    causes/drivers 6, 15, 30-33, 39, 46-47, 59-60, 70, 111, 122, 199
    effects on member states 16, 200-204, 235-240
    effects on outsiders 35, 60
    failure/success of 26-27, 73, 259
regionalism (definition of) 4-5, 81-82, 255
    new 5, 38, 47, 63, 256
    shadow 147
    virtual 37-40
regional security 8, 124, 205
regional organization (RO)
    accession to ROs *see* accession
    definition of 3, 4, 11
    democratic identity of 181-182, 184, 186, 187-188, 190-193
    design of *see* institutional design
    enlargement 6, 46, 55, 216, 243
regulatory quality (World Bank) 165-166
Russia 25-39, 48, 259

Senegal 124, 183, 187, 192
Sierra Leone 3, 187-189, 192-193
Singapore 94, 110, 166, 168-169, 227
Spain 243-247
state capacity 159, 162, 164-166, 169, 172-173, 260
Stone Sweet, Alec 101-103
supply of regional integration 6, 59-60, 67-70, 261

tariff
    automatic reduction of 65
    common external 62, 65, 72
    non-tariff barriers 82, 84, 162, 236
    reduction 73, 84, 86
Thailand 94, 163, 166, 169, 225-228
trade
    ASEAN 51-53, 90-95, 107-108, 110-111, 113, 168-170
    EC 247
    ECOWAS 123, 256
    intra-regional trade 31, 53, 55, 61, 65, 95, 101, 103-104, 106-108, 110-111, 113, 121, 163, 169, 259, 260-261

introversion index 103-104, 106-108
LAS 124
MERCOSUR 61-62, 65-67, 205, 209, 256
NAFTA 90-93, 95-96, 103-104, 106-107, 113, 235-238, 243, 246-247

uncertainty 16, 60, 66, 83, 87-88, 97
United Nations 129-130, 188
United States (of America) 31-32, 62, 95-96, 105, 107, 187, 192, 235-237, 239, 246-247, 259-260

varieties of capitalism 241
Vietnam 49-54, 94, 163, 169-170, 226
vulnerability 88, 95-96

World Trade Organization 32, 68, 73, 84, 101, 109-112, 261

THE INTERNATIONAL POLITICAL ECONOMY OF NEW REGIONALISMS SERIES

Other titles in the series

Global and Regional Problems
Towards an Interdisciplinary Study
*Edited by Pami Aalto, Vilho Harle
and Sami Moisio*

The Ashgate Research Companion to
Regionalisms
*Edited by Timothy M. Shaw, J. Andrew Grant
and Scarlett Cornelissen*

Asymmetric Trade Negotiations
*Sanoussi Bilal, Philippe De Lombaerde
and Diana Tussie*

The Rise of the Networking Region
The Challenges of Regional Collaboration
in a Globalized World
*Edited by Harald Baldersheim, Are Vegard
Haug and Morten Øgård*

Shifting Geo-Economic Power of the Gulf
Oil, Finance and Institutions
*Edited by Matteo Legrenzi
and Bessma Momani*

Building Regions
The Regionalization of the World Order
Luk Van Langenhove

National Solutions to Trans-Border
Problems?
The Governance of Security and Risk
in a Post-NAFTA North America
Edited by Isidro Morales

The Euro in the 21st Century
Economic Crisis and Financial Uproar
María Lorca-Susino

Crafting an African Security Architecture
Addressing Regional Peace and Conflict
in the 21st Century
Edited by Hany Besada

Comparative Regional Integration
Europe and Beyond
Edited by Finn Laursen

The Rise of China
and the Capitalist World Order
Edited by Li Xing

The EU and World Regionalism
The Makability of Regions in the 21st
Century
*Edited by Philippe De Lombaerde
and Michael Schultz*

The Role of the European Union in Asia
China and India as Strategic Partners
*Edited by Bart Gaens, Juha Jokela
and Eija Limnell*

China and the Global Politics
of Regionalization
Edited by Emilian Kavalski

Clash or Cooperation of Civilizations?
Overlapping Integration and Identities
Edited by Wolfgang Zank

New Perspectives on Globalization and
Antiglobalization: Prospects for a New
World Order?
Edited by Henry Veltmeyer

Governing Regional Integration for
Development: Monitoring Experiences,
Methods and Prospects
*Edited by Philippe De Lombaerde,
Antoni Estevadeordal and Kati Suominen*

Europe-Asia Interregional Relations
A Decade of ASEM
Edited by Bart Gaens

Cruising in the Global Economy
Profits, Pleasure and Work at Sea
Christine B.N. Chin

Beyond Regionalism?
Regional Cooperation, Regionalism and
Regionalization in the Middle East
*Edited by Cilja Harders
and Matteo Legrenzi*

The EU-Russian Energy Dialogue
Europe's Future Energy Security
Edited by Pami Aalto

Regionalism, Globalisation
and International Order
Europe and Southeast Asia
Jens-Uwe Wunderlich

EU Development Policy
and Poverty Reduction
Enhancing Effectiveness
Edited by Wil Hout

An East Asian Model for Latin
American Success
The New Path
Anil Hira

European Union and New Regionalism
Regional Actors and Global Governance
in a Post-Hegemonic Era.
Second Edition
Edited by Mario Telò

Regional Integration and Poverty
*Edited by Dirk Willem te Velde
and the Overseas Development Institute*

Redefining the Pacific?
Regionalism Past, Present and Future
*Edited by Jenny Bryant-Tokalau
and Ian Frazer*

The Limits of Regionalism
NAFTA's Labour Accord
Robert G. Finbow

Latin America's Quest for Globalization
The Role of Spanish Firms
*Edited by Félix E. Martín
and Pablo Toral*

Exchange Rate Crises
in Developing Countries
The Political Role of the Banking Sector
Michael G. Hall

Globalization and Antiglobalization
Dynamics of Change in the New
World Order
Edited by Henry Veltmeyer

Twisting Arms and Flexing Muscles
Humanitarian Intervention and
Peacebuilding in Perspective
*Edited by Natalie Mychajlyszyn
and Timothy M. Shaw*

Asia Pacific and Human Rights
A Global Political Economy Perspective
Paul Close and David Askew

Demilitarisation and Peace-Building
in Southern Africa
Volume II – National and
Regional Experiences
*Edited by Peter Batchelor
and Kees Kingma*

Demilitarisation and Peace-Building
in Southern Africa
Volume I – Concepts and Processes
*Edited by Peter Batchelor
and Kees Kingma*

Reforging the Weakest Link
Global Political Economy and Post-Soviet
Change in Russia, Ukraine and Belarus
Edited by Neil Robinson

Persistent Permeability?
Regionalism, Localism, and Globalization
in the Middle East
*Edited by Bassel F. Salloukh
and Rex Brynen*

The New Political Economy of United
States-Caribbean Relations
The Apparel Industry and the Politics
of NAFTA Parity
Tony Heron

The Nordic Regions and the European Union
*Edited by Søren Dosenrode
and Henrik Halkier*